THE PLAYS OF MAHESH DATTANI

A STUDY IN THEMATIC DIVERSITY AND DRAMATIC TECHNIQUE

THE PLAYS OF MAHESH DATTANI

A STUDY IN THEMATIC DIVERSITY AND DRAMATIC TECHNIQUE

By

Dr. Dipti Agrawal

Deptt. of English
Banaras Hindu University
Varanasi – 221 005 (U.P.)
(India)

DISCOVERY PUBLISHING HOUSE PVT. LTD.
NEW DELHI-110 002

Published by:
Tilak Wasan

DISCOVERY PUBLISHING HOUSE PVT. LTD.
4383/4B, Ansari Road, Darya Ganj
New Delhi-110 002 (India)
Phone : +91-11-23279245, 43596064-65
Fax : +91-11-23253475
E-mail : parul.wasan@gmail.com
discoverypublishinghouse@gmail.com
web : www.discoverypublishinggroup.com

***First Edition:* 2013**

ISBN: 978-93-5056-311-3

THE PLAYS OF MAHESH DATTANI
A STUDY IN THEMATIC DIVERSITY AND DRAMATIC TECHNIQUE

Printed at:
Dynamic Printers
Delhi

Preface

Drama in India has its own universality and identity through specific aesthetics, artistic objective and creative methods. The arena of Indian theatre is vast and intrinsic and can be classified into four categories- the classical, the ritual, the folk and the modern. Its excellence lies where even in a single performance different elements are combined such as dance, drama, mime, song, instrumentation, puppetry etc. the 1960s and 1970s were witness to a surge of theatrical activity in the metropolitan cities of India. There was widespread conviction that the spate of new plays being written and performed in these first post-independence decades in many parts of the subcontinent, from Calcutta to Bombay, from Bangalore to Delhi, with a birth of new realism which emerges from the problems and issues of a rapidly industrializing India.

This work analyses that, with Mahesh Dattani, English drama in India acquired a new maturity. Dattani sought thereby to establish an explicitly Indian point of view in dramatic creations that could do justice to what he saw as the Indian system of values, feeling free to bend Western and Eastern notions blithely all the while. His plays dealt with domestic interiors, presenting psychological studies of man-woman relationships, often coupled with a desire for social reform. He attempted to present the ordinary individual, rather than the exalted, and to trace the course of events as they emerged from a mundane existence, caught up in the vicissitudes of everyday, without theoretically, attempting to impose a pattern on the course of conduct motivated by character. This trend coincided with and was supported by translations from the plays of John Galsworthy, Bernard Shaw and Henrik Ibsen. Dattani makes effective use of stage lights, isolating, blending and fading the parts of the reality he wishes to expose or withhold. More attention is paid to stage set and lighting so that the internal conflict could be better brought out than the text alone is able to mediate. Dattani's early experience with film scripts and radio plays made him aware of the use of lights, composition of scenes, and economy of dialogue. The domestic world presented seems self-contained, each scene being linked to the other by the forces of psychological motivation. Towards the end, the emotions of the characters bursts forth in a virtual paroxysm of words, long speeches in which they lay bare their inner conflicts and seek understanding.

The content and form is embedded so naturally which lend Mahesh Dattani an acclaimed writer of the world stature. Psychological states of mind are expressed as naturally as in real life, wordiness being the chief fault of bad plays. The dialogues are composed without inflated figures of speech and with such economy, that it becomes possible to gauge the character of the persons concerned on the basis of their utterances. The plot is so constructed as to seem self-generating, and it is possible to read all action as the expression of internal states of mind. It is for this reason that Kalidasa, Bhavbhuti and Shakespeare, that *Shakuntala, Hamlet* and *Macbeth* were the objects of such veneration and such world fame. In playwriting, intellect alone is of no avail. It is the study of characters from the most diverse walks of life, the exchange of dialogue with the lowest and the meanest, and knowledge of the most diverse disciplines- politics, ethics, and jurisprudence and so on- that form the essential preconditions for the successful composition of the plays of Mahesh Dattani.

The present collection of chapters is a comprehensive effort for an in depth analysis of major themes integrated in his plays and to appreciate the synthesis of the innovative stage techniques to enhance the theatrical depth of his writings as well as to stick an everlasting effect on the audience. In the first chapter, these is a detailed account of the development of Indian drama in English and Dattani's significant contribution in the advancement of Indian drama in English through the intermingling of innovative techniques into his bold themes. Dattani's unconventional approach in gender issues has been examined in the five plays named: *Bravely Fought the Queen, Tara, Thirty Days in September, Where There's a Will* and *Dance Like a Man,* in the second chapter, where he focuses on the psychoanalytical aspects of gender discrimination. The idea of taboo relationship and deniable position of homosexuals and eunuchs is the central motive of the third chapter, which include plays, *On a Muggy Night in Mumbai* and *Bravely Fought the Queen.* In the fourth chapter, the play *Final Solutions,* deals with the rising trend of communalism and the accompanying violence which has created a feeling of insecurity among the religious minorities and ethnic groups such as Muslims. Fifth chapter analyzes some of the techniques used by Mahesh Dattani in his plays performed on the stage more for the live audience than for the readers.

To conclude, Dattani's plays are primarily realistic entertainment, and that is what brings the audiences in. his plays can be done again and again because they are fine pieces of drama, absorbing, entertaining and containing within them elements that leave an audience with a feeling of taking something precious away after the play is over. To provide a creative work that is powerful and tightly written,

Dattani produces his plays with a craftsman's care, one that evokes feelings that are both funny and sad, but ultimately human and moving. What makes Mahesh Dattani one of India's finest playwrights is in the manner that he speaks to the audience straight from the heart, with the beautiful intermingling of his mind through using brilliant and innovative techniques.

I would like to thank Discovery Publishing House Pvt. Ltd., for bringing out this book. No words of gratitude can suffice to thank my family; my mother, my husband and my brothers for their continuous help and cooperation.

I don't know how to convey what I owe to Prof. Meena Sodhi, Professor of English and the Principal of Women's College, Banaras Hindu University. Without her intellectual and emotional support, I could not have formalized this work.

Dipti Agrawal

Contents

Contents

1

Theatrical Spaces and Contemporary Indian English Theatre

(i)

Drama, as a dynamic art form, is present in almost every society through the ages; it is the most wide-ranging, the most polyphonic of all the arts; representing life as well as a way of seeing it. The drama of India has a universal history, originality, identity, longevity and a universal presence. It has a very distinct identity of its own specific aesthetics, artistic objective and creative methods, which are relevant even today. Indian drama is basically a plurality of aesthetic forms; its history being older than two thousand years; this unique phenomenon of the literary world is older than the Greek tragedy and Chinese ancient drama. From the time of composition of *Natyashastra* (450 B.C.) in India, it was the performance, which was of prominent importance rather than the written text. This 'theatre' as understood in India, from time immemorial is a 'total art' form that includes poetry, prose and drama. Indian theatre evokes the texture of everyday life through dialogue, balances art with nature, draws on history and religion and represents the manners and feelings of people. It is to 'create another universe' to represent 'this real (or illusory) universe'.

In a country like India, where fifteen national languages and more than eight hundred dialogues prevail, it is really difficult to enter in a vast and intrinsic arena of 'Indian theatre', which is both idiomatically heterogeneous and polyglot in character. It encompasses the classical (Kathakali, Bharatnatyam etc.), the Ritual (Raas, Raamlila, Theyyam etc.), the folk (Chhau, Therukuttu etc.), and the modern ("living newspaper" productions, theatre for educational purposes and large scale commercial plays and musicals) and even in a single performance different elements combined such as dance, drama, mime, song, instrumentation, puppetry too. The reasons for this obscurity lie in the linguistic plurality of Indian theatrical practice, the difficulties that attend any rigorous historicization of "Indian theatre", and the intensely problematic relation of such concepts as modernity, contemporaneity, and postcoloniality to drama, theatre and performance in present-day India. Thus we have access to a theatrical inheritance that includes diverse acting traditions and genres that have no parallel in any other country, history or civilization. Kanhailal says:

> Traditionally theatre is a form of communication, expression and Inter-human shaped by a people within their own culture and sensibility and aesthetic in learning an idiom from their own eco-system, where they have been breathing a free flow of life among themselves (40).

The main motive of ancient Indian drama was first and foremost arousing one or another '*rasa*' by the production of drama, which is also called the 'juice', 'sap' or 'flavour'. Bharata, the originator of *NatyaSastra*, emphasizes that when all the components of the drama, beginning with *vibhava* and *anubhava* are presented, the realization of *rasa* manifests itself in the spectator. Conversely, when any element required for the manifestation of *rasa* is missing, the realization is rendered difficult, indirect, or incomplete. Thus theatre is viewed experimentally as *rasa*. The *rasa* recognized in Sanskrit poetics are *sringara* (erotic), *hasya* (comic), *karuna* (pathetic), *raudra* (furious), *vira* (heroic), *bhayanaka* (terrible), *bibhatsa* (odious), and *adbhuta* (marvellous), and *santa* (peaceful). Therefore, Sanskrit theatre became a means of realizing this intense, immediate, and direct *rasa*, or aesthetic experience. But the '*rasas*' have also changed with the span of time and so as Vasudha Dalmia asserts, these can be categorized differently:

> Traditional categories need re-interpretation and expansion if they are to remain comprehensive and serve new needs. The chief goals/ designs, *uddeshya*, of theatre demonstrate the heterogeneity- the mixture of aesthetic with socially oriented goals- which is an indication of the categories that are replacing and supplementing the older classifications; rasa, for example, is still a consideration, but has a much reduced significance. The goals of theatre are five-fold: (1) comic, (2) erotic, (3) spectacular, (4) social reform, and finally (5) patriotism. The first three are barely discussed. It is the last two which call for remark: these are to be created by the reinterpretation of old tales, by the creation of a public forum where social issues can be discussed, and where the love of the country is to be generated (37).

In modern India, a new kind of artistry is being assigned to drama and theatre which is giving some major plays new visibility beyond national borders. The term contemporary theatre is used in the present context in a broad sense to include not only classical art forms like Kathakali and Kuttiyattam, but even modern experimental theatre. This intermingling of ancient Indian theatrical elements with that of Western theatre is for two centuries in the all important areas of theory, aesthetic form, institutional organization and translation. It borrowed its organizational structures, textual features, and performance conventions from Europe (especially England), superseded traditional and popular indigenous performance genres, and found its core audience among the growing English-educated Indian middle class. But in practice the new form was absorbed quickly into the material, social and ideological structures of a complex and literate culture with long-standing theatrical traditions in many Indian languages. Therefore, the influence of the Western textual models produced a body of new "literary" drama and dramatic theory in several Indian languages and the theatre of the past fifty years is not a seamless extension of either colonial or pre-colonial traditions but a product of new theoretical, textual, material, institutional, and cultural conditions created by the experience of political independence, cultural autonomy and new nationhood. Although presently it is confined to the urban audience, it has developed as a multi-lingual, multi-cultural Indian theatre. The forms and institutions of performance were therefore borrowed, but the content of colonial theatre became deeply embedded in Indian myth, history, literature, society and politics. Through translation, adaptation, and intercultural appropriation, contemporary Indian theatre also maintains an extensive intertexuality with classical and modern European and Anglo-American drama. That is why western theatre workers in the last fifty years have been drawn to Indian theatre for the unprecedented physical and mental capacity which art in the west has tried to track down since modernism. Anand Lal claims that:

> No analysis of contemporary Indian theatre can afford to ignore the profound Indian influence on world theatre (35).

Today most of the modern theatre critics debate over Western alien qualities and Indian native qualities of theatre and insist to return to the 'roots' or to pure indigenous dramatic forms again. One group of critics maintained that Indian theatre was a singular entity and the recourse of roots simply meant turning to this singular entity once again; the various regional streams had always fed into it. The other group asserted that there was no such seamless continuum from the ancient to the modern and that there was multiple and heterogeneous streams that criss-crossed through the ages. And in this perspective, Sanskrit literature too is an outsider to India as it came with the successive invasions of Aryans from the Middle East into the Indian subcontinent during the second century B.C., mixed with the original inhabitants, forming what is now a vast majority of India's culture and civilization. This history of foreign influence of India shatters all present debates of 'intrinsic' and 'extrinsic' theatrical qualities. As India has always assimilated and accommodated other foreign forms and techniques and was always enriched and endowed rather than eclipsed. According to Vasudha Dalmia some critics regard the western theatre as the 'arch foe'.

The problem clearly lay in insisting that all roots were buried in the past and Indian modernity had a history. When the use of traditional and folk forms is argued, the stock phrase used is "discovery of roots" or "going to the soil". True, but are all our roots ancient? There can be modern roots too, which one has to discover to deal with contemporary reality and experience. Tradition was not so faint- hearted. It would survive in some meaningful way into the present. And if a given traditional form failed to do so and to remain relevant in our fast-changing world, it is better to let it die and go ahead in the quest of expression with the belief that new traditions will grow and continue to enrich humanity and its culture. Eugenio Barba argues that there are those who think in terms of ethnic, national, group or even individual identity in theatre must also think of one's own theatre in a transcultural dimension, in the flow of a 'tradition of traditions'. It is through exchange, rather than isolation, that a culture can develop, that is, transforms itself organically. (Barba *42*)

Since theatre constituted an important part of cultural life in India from pre-colonial times – whether performed in enclosed theatre houses or in the street, in the form of puppet theatre, folk drama or mythological drama- examining theatre as a locus of sociopolitical struggles take on special significance. The emergence of different Western dramatic forms and the succession of the production of new experimental modern dramatic forms has been an intense process. As Chaman Ahuja says:

> Our contemporary theatre has been neither all western kind of theatre nor has it all been derived from the ancient classical tradition. A lot of interactive variety has inhered the productions of the last forty years-dramatization of myths, reinterpretation of old myths for contemporary relevance; old plays in old forms, old plays in new styles; classical plays in classical forms, classical plays in folk forms, classical plays adapted to realistic stage; western plays in western style, western plays adapted to folk forms; eastern plays for classical stage; new plays in folk forms, new plays in the classical tradition, new themes for western stage- plus non-conventional theatre like street plays, solo performances, poetry-on-stage etc. Here is, indeed, God's plenty which even Polonius would have found difficult to club into categories (72-73).

Modern drama in India, which is pre-dominantly urban, emerged in the nineteenth century when the British colonizers built the earliest proscenium-arch auditoria in India and introduced a new kind of dramatic writing which was completely alien to the traditional Indian dramaturgy. According to the Indian view of life, the purpose of drama and theatre was to create pleasure or bliss (Rasa) by representing different situations, mental states and feelings of human beings. But the purpose of Western drama on the other hand, was to reveal struggles of life in their various forms; thus the imitation of reality, proved alien in the country of so deep moral and aesthetic values. It is created by and primarily for people who may be regarded as middle and upper middle class.

However, drama is still evolving and searching for its own distinctive identity and not flourishing in the modern times like poetry and novel in India. One reason is the plurality of Indian languages, and this linguistic fragmentation, according to Aijaz Ahmad, prevents monopoly of any one language over another. (Ahmad, *In Theory,* 245) Drama is complete or live only when it is staged and in the comparison of other arts of writing, painting, singing etc, doing theatre is far more expensive. It needs patronage for supporting and funding for its theatrical performance. As Samuel Johnson has put it:

> The drama's laws, the drama's patrons give. For we that live to please, must please to live. (A prologue spoken by Mr. Garrick on opening Drury Lane Theatre)

In ancient India, Sanskrit drama flourished under the patronages of Guptas. So that it became 'golden period' for Indian drama. Not only in India, in all other countries of the world, drama only flourished under the patronage of someone or some institution as the Elizabethan patronage of the British drama from ancient times is well known to everyone. As Manohar Malgonkar says:

> Under Guptas Sanskrit attained prominence. It virtually became the state language with Gupta kings patronizing it. Prominent dramatists like Kalidasa, Shudraka, Vishakhadatta belonged to Gupta age. Humorous and erotic Bhana plays were written during this period.

Since ancient times Sanskrit theatre enjoyed royal patronage. Bhasa mentions one Rajsimha as his patron king. Ashvaghosh flourished under Kanishka's patronage. Chandragupta Vikramaditya was the king in whose court Kalidasa found patronage. Shudraka himself was a king. Vishakhadatta's patron king was Parthivaschandragupta who is identified with Chandragupta 2. and Shudraka who wrote three plays: Ratnavali, Priyadarshika and Nagananda-was himself a king (Varadpande 237).

By the eleventh century, after the invasions of Muslim kings, what has come down to us as classical Sanskrit drama had in all probability ceased to be performed, both through lack of patronage and through the emergence of modern languages, as they were interested more in poetry and painting. Although popular drama and lyric were likely to have flourished in small regions as some ritual or only for entertainment. But until the arrival of British, no original and significant drama was written or performed.

When Bengal came under the rule of the East India Company from the Nawab Sirajuddaulah of Bengal, British theatre formed part of cultural life in India as early as 1757. The prominent playhouses included the Calcutta Theatre, the Sans Souci Theatre, and the Chowringhee Theatre. Built in 1775, the Calcutta theatre was patronized by leading members of Calcutta society, based on western model, encouraged by the governor-general, and consisted of actors who "were all respectable people." (Das Gupta. *The Indian Stage*, 1938, 187) To give the natives a taste of "authentic" British culture, English officials henceforth encouraged "proper" productions of the plays in schools. In 1837, students at Hindu College and Sanskrit College presented plays of Shakespeare on special occasions such as prize ceremonies. The reason behind their successful establishment is that no significant theatre activity prevailed in India after the downfall of Sanskrit theatre around A.D.1000. The Muslim conquests of north India brought about complete decline of this theatre by the twelfth century and therefore there remained little for Colonialism to displace. This urban theatre succeeded not by colonialist fiat but because it was a new form of representation with seemingly endless potential and because it became, in certain locations, a viable commercial institution.

Patronage in colonial India was inevitably linked with the British and the critique of the ruling power could only be articulated with certain reservations. At most, the urban intelligentsia of the times could be described as a 'dependent sub-elite' as they were always dependent for career advantage on the British, and had no control of the economy or government. Although the feelings and sentiments could not flourish under colonial rule because of the fear that the theatre could arouse the Indian people against British. Thus we note that the colonial period both discouraged and encouraged Indian people to involve in more and more theatrical activities.

In 1765, one Russian drama lover Horasin Lebedef and Bengali drama lover Gulokhnath had staged two English comedies *Disgaij* and *Love is the Best Doctor*, which were held as the first modern drama. But the real beginning and development was in translations from Sanskrit and English dramas. Through translation, adaptation and intercultural appropriation, Indian theatre of the colonial era maintains an extensive intertextuality with classical and modern European and Anglo American drama.

Jones's 1789 English translation of Kalidasa's Sanskrit play *Abhijana Sakuntalam* (1789, commonly known in the west as *Sakuntala*), and H.H.Wilson's *Select Specimens of the Theatre of the Hindus* (2 vols., 1827), marks the first significant translation of old Indian texts- Wilson translated six major Sanskrit plays, summarized of twenty-three others and gave a brief discussion of the dramatic texts available; the task of translations was taken over mainly by Indians who wanted to share in the revival of their own national theatre and perform the plays in the modern languages of the subcontinent. The translations have therefore twofold importance as the ancient Indian dramatic works which were eclipsed for a long time after the decline of Sanskrit theatre began to revive again and thus it helped in popularizing and rejuvenating the precious Indian dramaturgy again. Consequently, the large–scale translations and adaptations of European as well as Indian canonical play in Indian and western languages began on a large scale. In English, mostly the plays of Shakespeare were adopted for regional translations as *Comedy of Errors, The Merchant of Venice, Hamlet, Othello, Cymbeline, All's Well that Ends Well, A Midsummer's Night Dream*, etc. besides Goldsmith's *She Stoops to Conquer* was again a favorite play among Indian translators. In Sanskrit *Shakuntala* (by Kalidasa). *Mrichchakatika* (by Sudraka), *Ratnavali* etc. were translated into English vernacular and different regional languages.

As a result, modern Indian dramatists began to assimilate these foreign methods and techniques into their original dramatic works which may be called a perfect synthesis of Sanskrit, folk and western culture and hence a real Indian drama. Indian Drama, written both in English and translated into English from other languages, has registered a remarkable growth in recent years. The translations have forged a link between the East and the West, North and South and contributed to the growing richness of contemporary creative consciousness. Urban theatre may have been an 'alien' form at its inception, but it went through the same rigorous process of indigenization and assimilation as the print genres of poetry, fiction and non-fictional prose. Nineteenth century performances ranged over plays in English, European plays in English translation, Indian-language versions of English and European plays, translations of Sanskrit plays into modern Indian languages, and original Indian-language plays that were western in form but not in content.

The politics of colonial censorship following the official banning of *Nil Darpan* and the rise of nationalist drama; local hybrid reconstructions of Shakespearean plays, grassroots performances organized by the Indian People's Theatre Association (IPTA); a theatrical reassessment of the 1857 mutiny; and women's street theatre in post independence India. According to Nandi Bhatia:

> ...theatre in colonial and postcolonial India has consistently participated in providing possibilities for resistance to and reassessment of ruling ideologies through multiple methods of engagement ranging from mythology, folk forms, reenactment of oppressed histories, revival of historical stories, and hybrid Anglo-European productions (2).

Since the first translation and circulation of *Nil Darpan*, political plays that attempted to expose colonial power structures had begun to draw the attention of British officials. These included Upendra Nath Das's *Surendra-Binodini* (1875), *Gaekwar Durpan (The Mirror of Baroda*, 1875), *Gajadananda Prahasan (Gajadananda and the Prince*, 1875), and Dakshina Charan Chattopadhyay's *Chakar Durpan (The Tea Planter's Mirror*, 1875). Running through all these plays was a nationalistic impulse that constituted attacks on the British government in one form or another.

Nil Darpan is invoked as the seminal text that initiated a powerful tradition of political drama as it situated the theatre's possibilities of establishing direct and verbal links of communication, and the immediacy with which it brings alive social realities, in order to show the centrality of this historical moment both for the development of theatre as a powerful medium of protest and as a target for the repressive politics of the British government. But the colonial machinery, which manifested in the indictment and imprisonment of Reverend James Long of the Church Missionary Society for translating and circulating *Nil Darpan* in India and in Britain, and ultimately responded to increasing dramatic threats through heavy censorship and control, was, on the other hand, critically responsible for strengthening perceptions about drama as a political weapon. The Censorship Act of 1876 empowered local government authorities to "prohibit dramatic performances which [were] seditious or obscene, or otherwise prejudicial to the public interests." (Home Department Proceedings, 1876)

The restriction of the development of Indian drama was not only by the colonizers but also by indigenous social reform organizations such as the Brahma Samaj in Bengal and Arya Samaj in North India. Aimed at reforming Hindu society and perceiving theatrical activity as detrimental to it, these organizations uncompromisingly condemned theatre along with other activities such as gambling, going to prostitutes, smoking and drinking. They also prohibited women from performing. One result of these restrictions was the containment of upper-caste women in the stranglehold of patriarchy.

Ultimately, in the pre-Independence period, as a result of European contact, a cultural stream of urban drama developed that was, to a large extent, influenced by Anglo-European traditions, performed selections from European plays or classical Indian drama, and was patronized by men of wealth and respectability, who performed plays in their homes or in theater that operated on astronomical financial budgets and presented to the public through a policy of tickets. The style of drama also became Western, adopting the conventions of the proscenium and footlights, the drop curtain, and prompting from behind. Interactions with colonial drama and censorship of indigenous theatre resulted in new and innovative theatrical forms that both departed from existing indigenous dramatic conventions of classical theatre and appropriated traditions suitable for the historically specific audiences.

The disapproval for popular theatre forms, rural or urban, and the elite attempt to marginalize them, did not mean that they disappeared. On the contrary, they flourished through the nineteenth till well into the twentieth century, and the commercial urban Parsi or Company theatre, continued to borrow heavily from them, though without express acknowledgement. But however vital their mode of expression and whatever their entertainment value, in the early decades of the twentieth century, it would have been difficult to convince the wider public that these rural and urban popular forms could ever come to be regarded as repositories of tradition. But each coin has two facets; likewise the influence of western drama has two contrary but significant effects on Indian drama. It is true that it took shape in a completely different way in comparison to Sanskrit and folk theatre but also with this, the crippled Indian drama received new lease of life and witnessed a revival as both cultures influenced each other. Before the emergence of western dramaturgy, the drama in India was confined in small regions of India in different forms and there was not any significant dramatic genre or drama as such. Foreign troupes came to India and performed many English plays and also did significant translations of ancient Indian plays. Mahesh Elkunchwar also mentions the importance of western influence on Indian theatre and says:

> The liberalism, the catholicity of taste, the spirit of frank enquiry into human life, a stress on individuality rather than on a system of accepted social and moral values: all these are gifts to us given by the west (22).

Theatre, both in preparation and performance, needs a collection of materials, skills and human beings. In an article in *Rasa: The Indian Performing Arts in the Last Twenty Five Years*, Anand Lal has given an estimate of average cost expended before first performance of a drama is more than one lakh, including rehearsal expenses, transport, music, make up, printing, publicity and other properties. And in India very few organizations invest money in this because of the fact that this source of entertainment was no profit in comparison to cinema. Though recently the corporate sector has come forward with some funds and the Tatas have established the massive National centre for the performing arts in Bombay; the Shri Ram centre is another such endeavor in Delhi, and various companies' present annual cash awards. Thus theatre deserves greater financial support and more comprehensive care and nourishment from society and its patrons to survive.

The development of new theatre in different Indian languages began mostly in those cities which were founded by the English merchants and the British rulers as their commercial, industrial or administrative centers, like Calcutta, Bombay, and Madras etc. In Bengali and Marathi, it became most active, prosperous and popular. A modern urban theatre has existed in these languages since the mid nineteenth century and they have a complex history of anti-colonial resistance, especially between 1872 and 1910. Then, there came the drama of such languages as Hindi, Kannada, Gujarati, Tamil and Malayalam, which began their development as modern dramatic media a little later than Bengali and Marathi during the colonial period. Original theatre in these languages appears in such metropolitan and urban centers as Delhi, Jaipur, Lukhnow, Bangalore, Mysore, Bombay, Ahmedabad, Madras and Trivendrum. The theatre of such languages as English, Punjabi, Urdu, Manipuri and Telugu comes in performance, which has some playwrights of worldwide importance; but in such languages as Kashmiri, Sindhi, Oriya and Assamese, there is no significant modern urban theatre tradition at all. Therefore, theatre of Bengali,

Marathi, Kannad etc. coupled with the innovativeness of English theatre, added a whole fresh dimension to the artistry of Indian Natya. All these theatres have their roots associated with the British rule as the seed of the contemporary drama in India was sown during that era. Drama was no longer only the narrative form of the heroes and celestial beings, as they were in classical period, but it became a true representation of the 'unedited realisms' of Indian social life. Revealing new understandings about the contradictions and conflicts, and multiple layers of protest and power struggles among colonizers and colonized; shaped by notions of class, class, gender and religious differences, some drama retained patriarchal positions and replicated the social and communal patterns within Indian society. The use of the term subaltern, which denotes a people defined by their subordination in terms of caste, class, gender, race, religion etc, is related to such differentiation, which enables a class-aware society. This theatre started with an intention of private entertainment; however gradually it became the weapon of protest against the British raj.

As far as English drama in India is concerned, it arrived in the later part of the 17th century with the arrival of the 'East India Company' and gained a dimension with the establishment of the three Presidency towns by the British-Calcutta, Mumbai and madras. Around the same time, three major universities were founded in these three cities, and English education was firmly underway. An entire class of intelligentsia was thus initiated and exposed to western literature and drama. These cities then had the typical urban middle class audiences which again helped in the thriving prosperity of the English theatre. English drama in India represented a portrayal of the realisms of daily life and culture of the British people. On the other hand, it also depicted the British exploitations, social injustices, corruption and regular instances of the poverty, sufferings and agony of the common people and thus became the weapon of the protest against the British raj.

In 1831, Krishna Mohan Benerji wrote the first Indian English play, *The Persecuted or Dramatic Scenes of the Present State of Hindoo Society in Calcutta.* It is the earliest social play on the historic theme of East-West encounter which presents the conflict between Indian orthodoxy and the new ideas which came from the west. After 1870, however, urban theatre assumed a vital political role and mediated the dominating colonial themes, in which colonial contests of power was discarded. Therefore, when drama started being written in Indian languages and began to be performed on the stage by Indian actors, it emerged as a forum for social and political ideas designed to influence opinion and raise social consciousness and theatre quickly became a powerful weapon to promote social and political reforms against the colonial rule and power. The example is the production of *The Mirror of Indigo Planters*, or *The Blue Mirror (Nildarpana)* is Lucknow, in which a white planter was depicted as raping an Indian peasant woman. Being aware of theatre's potential to contribute to social unrest, the British colonial government led to the dramatic performances act in 1879 and thus wide-spread censorship in the following five decades. Nandi Bhatia points out:

> ...in reproducing and acting out the histories of colonial exploitation and domination, much Indian drama became an invigorating arena for the interplay of anti-colonial struggles and change (Staging 3).

Therefore, the emergence of the pre-independence Indo-English drama out of its early romantic phase into social realism runs parallel to the gradual intensification of the national movement for freedom. Drama is the reification of human action or performance and universalization of the hidden truths of the human situations. Drama enacts man's relationship with man, which is fundamental to every social science. The performance of a drama is theatre. Panini has used the word 'Natya' for performance on a stage. The success of drama is completely outward. It is social literature. The social consciousness and the sociality of the playwright, actor and spectator together create the theatrical experience.

Theatre has, in all its history and its greatest moments, brought to man hope, courage, an uplifting of heart, an awareness and understanding of what he is up against, a vision towards better times to come and a determination to battle for them. In India too, theatre began to take up issues of social abuses, religious bigotry, political oppression and economic exploitation and even under the oppressive conditions of foreign rule, theatre dared to question the basis of imperialism and colonialism. The socio-political situation existing in the country is faithfully mirrored right from the early phase of reformist exuberance to the growth of the revolutionary consciousness among the common masses of India. The dramatists had to wage a two-pronged battle-one for their emancipation from the politico-economic exploitation by the foreign rulers, and the other against the colonial weight of outdated traditions, hide-bound casteism, blind conformism to religious dogma, and other social ills.

By 1920, a new drama in almost all the Indian languages came to the fore, it was a drama largely influenced by prevailing movements like Marxism, Psychoanalysis, symbolism and surrealism. The dramatic works of most of the Indian English playwrights of this time reveal this, such as Michael Madhusudan Dutt, Rabindranath Tagore, T.P. Kailasam, Sri Aurobindo, Harindranath Chattopadhaya, Bharati Sarabhai etc. Although Michael Madhusudan Dutt and Rabindranath Tagore wrote in Bengali, they translated several of their plays into English. M.C.dutt translated his plays *Ratnavali* (1859) and *Sharmishtha* (1859) in English and wrote a play in English, *Is This Called Civilization*? (1871).

These dramatists attempted to present the conflict of an individual with his environment, social conditions, with other individuals or within his own mind, drawing their stories from Indian mythological episodes, folk tales, historical events as well as contemporary situations; but the whole are conceived and developed as in the western play. Except for a few, the dramatic qualities in their works are negligible and the plays seem more like melodramas. The playwrights of this period now began to be more and more realistic and the main themes are critique of class ideology, problem of landlordism, exploitation of mill workers, Bengal famine and the problem of refugees after Partition, received large outdoor performances etc with urgent political messages.

An exception is mainly Rabindra Nath Tagore, who has done bold experiment to synthesize the techniques and dramatic usages of the Sanskrit and traditional theatres like the Jatra with the methods of western theatre as he admired Shakespeare, Ibsen and Maeterlink. He produced some popular and original dramatic plays in which he attempted the basic contradictions of life in contemporary society. He wrote more than sixty plays between 1881 and 1938, staged most of them at his family estate in Jorasanko (Calcutta) or the school he founded at Shantiniketan, and acted or recited various roles in them himself until well into the 1930s.

His most famous symbolic poetic plays *Chitra* (1892), *Raja (King of the Dark Chamber,*1910), *Dakghar* (*The Post Office,*1912), *Muktadhara*(1922), *Rakta Karabi* (*Red Oleanders,*1925), *Sacrifice* in Bengali are quite familiar to us in English. But before independence, his dramatic works were considered as mere dramatic poems or poetic drama like Sanskrit theatre by many Indians. It is only in the sixth decade of the 20th century, when Sombhu Mitra produced his play *Raktakarabi*, the significance of his works was recognized as valid drama.

While Tagore's plays have the synthesis of Sanskrit, folk and western drama, the plays of Sri Aurobindo and Harindranath Chattopadhyaya left a large dramatic corpus chiefly on mythical or religious subjects. Aurobindo was greatly influenced by western dramatists of Elizabethan period such as Marlowe, Shakespeare and of the Victorian period, Robert Bridges, Stephen Phillips etc. in all his five complete plays based on these western models- *Persues, Vasvadutta, Rodogune, The Viziers of Bassora* and *Eric,* he reveals that all works are steeped in rich poetry and romance recalling the spirit and flavour of the distinctive dramatic type as we have seen in a different way in Bhasa, Kalidasa, and Bhavabhuti. But as like others, his dramas are also labeled as 'close drama' as being indifferent for performance. But above all his works reveal that he was the robust optimist about the future of mankind.

Harindranath Chattopadhyaya added a new dimension to Indian English drama with his leftiest learnings and revolutionary and realism which he revealed in both his devotional plays- *Raidas*, *Chokhamela*, *Pundalik*, *Saku Bai*, *Jayadeva* and *Tukaram* (deals with the lives of Maharashtrian Saints etc.) and his social plays- *The Window*, *The Parrot*, *The Coffin*, *The Evening Lamp* and *The Sentry's Lantern* (depict social problems and sympathies for suffering masses). Having symbolic and didactic in style, the theme of his plays are sympathy for the exploited, revolt against a stultifying code of morality, insurgence against the brute forces of imperialism etc. Iyenger describes them as manifestoes of 'the new Dawn of Realism'.

Another bilingual author, T.P.Kailasam gets inspiration to contribute to the field of Indian English drama through his long stay in England. The themes of all his plays such as, *The Burden* (1933), *Fulfillment* (1933), *The Purpose* (1944), *Karna: the Brahmin's Curse* (1946), and *Keechaka* (1949) are taken from the Puranic themes of the Ramayana and Mahabharata but he represents them in Shakespearean style. Though he blends the best of both the Indian and western traditions, he illustrate them from his own point of view of judging their significance in the context of their story and in the fitness of contemporary era. Like Shaw, Kailasam has a tendency to indulge himself in elaborate stage directions, a fact that highlights his strong theatrical sense. But sometimes his plays are difficult to stage because of the lengthy dialogues of the plays. His dramatic style cannot be considered as great but because of his 'quest for greatness' and his bold, original approach to characters in the epics brought him a great success on the stage. On a question as to why he wrote in English, he confessed "the delineation of ideal characters requires a language which should not be very near to us" (Bhatta 87).

Then, the first distinct woman dramatist, Bharati Sarabhai came into prominence through her works like *The Well of the People* (1949) and *Two Women* (1952). These works were the direct outcome of her association with Gandhiji and Nehru and thus depicts the Gandhiyan theme of 'Daridra Narayana". Her plays also render the conflicts between tradition and modernity and the material and spiritual.

After Harindranath, playwrights became more and more realistic, reformist, and satiric and turned against the superstitious beliefs of the society. Some of them are V.V.Srinivasa Iyengar's Dramatic Divertissements in two volumes; A.S.P.Ayyar's *IN the clutches of the Devil* (1921), *Sita's Choice* (1935), *The Slave of Ideas* (1941), *The Trial of Science for the murder of Humanity* (1942), Lobo Prabhu's *Collected Plays* (fourteen plays), in which *Apes in the Parlour, The Family Cage, Flags of the Heart* etc. are significant.

The First World War also had its impact on the writers. It brought them face to face with the actual creativity. This impact on the Indo-English writers was two-fold: firstly, they now sought to portray more realistic, less idealized and a more earthly presentation of life in their works; and secondly the writers, inspired with a nationalistic fervor, found in literature a convenient medium to dramatize and popularize their cause. They felt that nationalism and liberty were prizes worth fighting for. The struggle for independence in India was not merely a political struggle, but an all pervasive experience that became a part of the life of almost all the sensitive and enlightened Indians. It is this coincidence which is responsible for a flowering the maturity of the Indo-English drama in the thirties during which period the freedom movement percolated to the very grass-roots of Indian society.

Parallel to this struggle for political freedom was another one on the social plane. It was a fight against superstition, caste system, poverty, illiteracy and many other social ills. No Indian writer, writing in that decade, could avoid reflecting this upsurge in his work. The socio-political movement, which had caught the imagination of the entire nation, also inspired the Indo-English writers. They had the added advantage of western literal education. Though, this pre-independence crop of dramatists, despite the poetic excellence, thematic variety, technical competence and symbolic and moral significance of their works, did not give enough weight to the actability and stage worthiness of their plays.

With the intensification of the struggle for national independence, the Indo-English writers rightly realized that drama too had a vital role to play in it. The constructive programmes launched by Mahatma Gandhi and other national leaders deepened the political and social consciousness of the writers. Along with the nationalistic fervor the other movements like socialism, communalism, fascism etc, also became an obsession with the angry young intelligentsia of the times. These political ideologies, already popular in Europe and China, emerged in the country in the thirties as a reaction to the prevailing conditions: oppression and tyranny of British imperialism, gross futility and waste brought by the World War 1, economic exploitation of the poor and under-privileged class, illiteracy and evils of the caste system. Besides, the visit of Tagore and Nehru to the Soviet land and the formation of the All India's Progressive Writers' Association in the thirties made the writers portray the Indian peasantry in the hope that social transformation of society could be feasible only through mobilizing the opinion of the under-privileged classes- the economically exploited, politically subjugated and socially oppressed Indian performance.

The Second World War, the independence and the partition of the country were other historical forces that gave further impetus to the Indo-English dramatists. There was enough material in the society torn by communal frenzy, political maneuverings, social disparities and corruption in bureaucracy for the thematic treatment by the dramatists to stir the imagination of the countrymen to a new awakening. And this could best be done through the medium of drama. Though the dramatic style and language of the Indo-English dramatists discussed above was westernized in the colonial era, but the spirit behind them was Indian, 'through the Indian, for the Indian'. Besides the contribution of these dramatists, the period during and after independence brought a new development in Indian drama and theatre through the establishment of several major and numerous smaller theatrical institutions. These recognizably modern institutions, conventions and practices have continued from the colonial period (the 1850s to the 1940s) into postcolonial times (the late 1940s onward) and aided in developing both Indian regional theatre and western oriented theatre in India. The IPTA (Indian Peoples' Theatre Association) was established in 1943 and continued till 1964; in the post-independence period, performing arts were employed as an effective means of public enlightment during the First Five Year Plan (1951-54). Rustam Bharucha has rightly maintained that 'the I.P.T.A. was responsible for changing the very structure and conception of theatre in various parts of India' (*Rehearsals*, 42).

IPTA was not only concerned in a given context to traditional forms alone, either 'classical' or 'folk'; but tried to assimilate freely with a little self-consciousness, borrowing formal elements from one or the other tradition, be it rural or urban. Rustam Bharucha has put the reason of its success in India in the world as IPTA has become:

> ...an indispensable point of reference for almost any discussion on cultural politics in India. But when it is being named in cultural discourse, we should qualify that what is being referred to is the movement of the early 1940s- those short-lived, euphoric years before the disintegration of the movement. The IPTA, I would suggest, is better read as a utopic movement in our

> cultural history, rather than as a disintegrating movement- though the lessons of its disintegration need to be absorbed in the formulation of an ongoing cultural praxis (*In the Name,* 50).

The Sangeet Natak Akademi as the National Music and Drama Academy was established in Delhi in January 1953 as the national academy for the performing arts. In the last All-India Conference of IPTA was held in Delhi in 1957-8. It was recognized that the Sangeet Natak Akademi was supposed to play in the future and offered cooperation and help so that 'the aid that is being given by the Akademi can thus be utilized most efficiently and effectively'. (Pradhan, *Marxist*, 279)

The primary object of the Akademi, as seen initially, was to provide patronage and converse tradition:

> The idea of establishing an organization to coordinate all the activities in the sphere of dance, drama and music came to the forefront and assumed a new urgency and importance in independent India… the necessity of such an organization was all the more compelling in view of the fact that all of a sudden the erstwhile princely patronage of the arts had ceased to function or was fast ceasing. In the void thus created, the art traditions were faced with the grave risk of breaking down in an atmosphere of general decline in our cultural and artistic values (Sangeet 2).

The Sangeet Natak Akademi established the National School of Drama (NSD) in Delhi in 1959, as the national institute for theatre training in methods of acting, directing and stagecraft under the directorship of Ebrahim Alkazi. According to Vasudha Dalmia:

> The NSD was an attempt at centralization of theatre with all its advantages and drawbacks. The advantages in these early years of Independence were clear: the School provided and sustained a forum for mediation of the many regional forms and plays and if offered an institutional base for visiting directors (172).

Other units and institutions like Anamika in Calcutta; Safdar Hashmi's Janam (People's Theatre Front)(1973-89) in Delhi; Badal Sircar's Satabdi (Calcutta); Theatre Unit (Bombay); R.P.Prasanna's Samudaya (Karnataka,1975-mid 1980's), KSSP (Kerala), ARP (Association of Rural Poor) in Tamil Nadu and K.V.Subbana's Ninasam (Heggodu, Karnataka from 1949). Other theatre workers lead groups which use a mixture of traditional form and contemporary focus: Kavalam Pannikar's Sopanam in Trivendrum, Mallika Mrilani Sarabhai's Darpana in Ahemdabad (1948), Rangayana, Founded by B.V.Karanth in Mysore in 1991; the Calicut university school of drama in Trichur and so on. These institutions brought new exuberance in the development of theatre in different languages and regional theatres, which eclipsed Western influences.

While under the influence of British, multi-lingual theatre in India had developed, the theatre in English could not flourish on expected lines. Unlike the novel and poetry, drama is not a form only to read as a text. The word 'drama' comes from the Greek word *dran*- to do. That is to say, drama is a performing art, a living art in a way that no other genre of literature is. It is an art that involves the playwright, the actor and the audience in a single creative effort. Drama, being a performative art, has an immediacy of appeal which poem and fiction may not need. Drama can be fully realized and live only when it is staged. And except Tagore, no indo-English dramatists of colonial period had this theatrical quality in them. They were hardly 'stage worthy', indeed, such attempts can be seen as mere literary exercises; not real theatre that would draw audiences. Its tradition consists of obscure texts for reading not performance. Moreover, drama is a composite art form including the playwright, the actor and the audience to share the dramatic experience, and a language, like English, not the mother tongue proved alien for such interaction with the audience. Thus drama only touched the mind and could not touch the heart of Indian. This deficiency prevailed even after the independence. The institutions too, mentioned above like

IPTA, Sangeet Natak, NSD etc. focused on developing Indian vernacular drama and paid little or no attention to the expansion of English drama. M.K.Naik tells this 'Cindrella' and Anand Lal points out:

> English language theatre in India has traditionally been regarded by critics as a cul-de-sac. Barring some interesting amateur experiments by a handful of groups in our four or five megapolises, nearly fifty years of using English as the essential link language in an independent nation has not produced significant results on the stage (*Rasa,* 18).
>
> Though both English and Hindi continue to share the honor of being the two most important target languages of translation-English being the more important when it comes to print, making as it does for national visibility-Indian vernacular languages outpaces English when it comes to performance and the issue of audience appeal.
>
> This dual paradox suggests that in Indian writing, the naturalization of English has been effective when the radical of presentation is the printed word, but not when the radical of presentation is the acted or spoken word. In this respect, Indian drama and theatre are very similar to Indian film, television, video, and music. India has the largest film industry in the world, but virtually no English-language cinema; one of the largest television audiences in the world, but little original English-language programming besides news, news programmes, and documentaries; and a gigantic popular music industry, but little original English-language music....
>
> The reason for this preference is the idea that a language corresponds to a structure of experience in the world: theatre has the quality of lived experience when the language is the natural language of the characters it represents (Dharwadkar, *Theatre India*, 23).

After Independence in 1947, theatre spread throughout India as one of the means of entertainment and one of the means of protest. Not only India did stand apart as a socially and politically sovereign state but also Indian culture, art, music, literature all witnessed a colossal change. Drama and theatre in India in different Indian languages and regions gradually became an art form to illustrate the social and political ailments of independent India. Right after independence in India, the leftist movement in West Bengal used Bengali theatre as a typical means of advertisement or propaganda. Quite ideally therefore a new trend in multi-lingual and regional theatre gradually developed and the emergence of the group theatres is one of them. All these theatre groups carried somewhat an ideologic at the same time a distinct cultural inspiration to differentiate themselves from the typical artistry of the ancient Indian theatre.

Indians have published as many as 200-plus plays in English, though most remain unperformed; many are not even performable. The unsung socio-political work of Asif Currimbhoy appeared on Indian stage in the 1960 and it brought power, passion, and complexity to original Indian-English drama. He is rightly held as “India’s first authentic voice in Indian theatre” (Bowers, *Asif*, xii). Among the very few Indian dramatists writing plays in English, he made his debut as a dramatist for the stage. His twenty-nine plays are first and foremost meant for the stage and he brilliantly succeeded in producing “actable” plays. These plays featured a powerful engagement with life, a compelling quest for truth and equally strong compassion for the humanity. The most popular of them are: *The Doldrummers* (1961), *The Dumb Dancer* (1962), *Goa* (1966), *Inquilab* (1971), *Sonar Bangla* (1972) etc. Currimbhoy achieved his social purpose without moralizing or compromising his art. Rich in theatrical devices, his work-incorporated monologues, choruses, chants, songs, mime, slide projections, and filmed footage. His plays were ignored by Indian directors, but had successful runs in the USA: *The Dumb Dancer* at Café La Mama, off-off Broadway (1965), and Goa on Broadway (1968). Afterwards, *Goa* was selected to inaugurate the Shri Ram Centre, Delhi (1970), and Tarun Roy produced I*nquilab* in Bengali translation in Calcutta (1973). Currimbhoy also wrote movie scenarios and television scripts.

Presently, major threats to Indian theatre come from the spread of television industry and cinema produced in the Mumbai film industry. Lack of finance for staging plays is another major reason. However in the last three decades, Indian English playwrights can boast of "the first group of modern dramatic authors in India whose work is 'serious' as well as 'successful' in both modes" (Dharwadkar, *Theatre of*, 58).

Therefore, since the 1960s, new generations of playwrights, directors, actors and actresses have appeared on the scene who has given a new shape to the stage by a pluralistic experimentation with the various prevailing trends in the various parts of the country- classical and folk, traditional and western, commercial and amateur. Not only this, these individual playwrights and directors have given birth to distinctive styles of their own, while sharing certain common contemporary social concerns that make them Indian at the core. As a result, their plays get translated into different Indian languages which are staged in far-flung corners of the country, as well as rendered into English and other languages of the west for presentation at international drama festivals where they have won acclaim. Thus, the successful assimilation of western form and techniques to improve the quality of dramatic Indian text and acting skills with traditional forms by Indian playwrights led them to the world stage. According to Vasudha Dalmia:

> The 1960s and 1970s were witness to a surge of theatrical activity in the metropolitan cities of India. There was widespread conviction that the spate of new plays being written and performed in these first post-independence decades in many parts of the subcontinent, from Calcutta to Bombay, from Bangalore to Delhi, at long last brought to fruition the promise of the long overdue Indian national theatre. Not only was there a birth of new realism, emerging from the problems and issues of a rapidly industrializing India, urban theatre seemed to be on the verge of being able to successfully turn to new use the myriad folk forms which were being 'discovered' (5).

Kumud Mehta confined this new artistry in four major dramatists of the period 'the four pillars' or 'the big four' who wrote in different languages as Mohan Rakesh in Hindi, Badal Sircar in Bengali, Girish Karnad in Kannada, and Vijay Tendulkar in Marathi; but later on all were translated into English to be famous world wide. All the four dramatists used different style of writing and presenting their plays from one another and they are successful in attracting Indian and other country's people by their new innovative experiments in theatre. Kumud Mehta rightly described their immense contribution in giving an identity to the Indian theatre:

> By the sixties this realization assumed concrete shape in the works of four playwrights writing in four different languages. Their experience was shared to such a degree by theatre practitioners all over the country that productions of their plays came to be considered a national theatre movements (89).

Apart from officially sponsored activity, the theatre workshops and festivals generated by the National School of Drama, other institutional frames, part professional, part amateur, also emerged: new auditoria, theatre groups, and at least two Delhi based journals devoted entirely to theatre, which, though privately funded, manage to sustain themselves over several decades; they accompanied, critiqued, and helped to consolidate the burgeoning theatre activity. The Hindi Journal *Natrang,* edited by Nemichandra Jain, published essays on the major themes of the day, interviews, reviews, and play scripts in Hindi, as well as translations of scripts from other Indian languages into Hindi. Rajinder Paul edited the English-language journal *Enact(*Delhi (1967-82)*)* bimonthly, which published English translations of plays, as also interviews, reviews of plays, and reports from various regional centers. As Paul noted in the May 1971 *Enact* editorial:

> By all available accounts, Indian theatre is passing through a very significant phase. A phase which is continually providing it with maturity.... Their plays

[the reference is once again to the Big Four: Rakesh, Sircar, Tendulkar, Karnad] have become nationally known, crossing the rigid regional barriers. Obviously, this couldn's have happened but for the enthusiastic, almost altruisitic, efforts of the translators. A new Sircar's play is available in Hindi the moment it is scripted. So is the case with Tendulkar's and Girish's plays. Through Hindi, their plays are translated into other regional languages.

English language has as far as proved to be more important as the *lingua franka* for the translation of other Indian language plays as well as the language of original composition. English took over the role that had been performed unto that classical time by Sanskrit and Persian. The most surprising aspect of this issue is that it is after India's Independence that the most visible effects of this stamping of England can be seen in the increasing westernization of its literate classes and the prolific growth of Indian writing in English. With the resilience and power to absorb Indian cultures that had marked India's political and cultural history through countless invasions and infiltrations, English language and literature were appropriated to a large extant by India. However what is very visible is that the two have had some kind of relationship with each other-have not been immune to each other. This is evident in the persistence of the theme of east-west encounter in Indian as well as British writing in English. Not only did the introduction of English as the medium of higher education result in the consciousness of western modes of political philosophy and government, it made the wide world accessible to the educated Indian through the English language. For most educated Indians cultural conflict/ synthesis became an important part of their mental constitution. For the Indian writer in English this becomes vitally significant. Although controversy still rages in India over the use/teaching of English, writing in English by Indians has by now a history of over a century and a half. Meenakshi Mukherjee points out how:

> "the unabating interest... in the inter-action of the two sets of values that exist side by side, and often coalesce, in twentieth century India" has resulted in the constant recurrence of the east-west motif for over half a century (66).

English has become an international language and has also served in India as a common language for about two centuries. Even for the English writers, English is no more a colonial language. They are using it without suggesting a self-conscious distancing from the Indian situation and without showing lack of commitment to Indianness. Those writers who are aware of their inheritance, complexity and uniqueness their works express without any conscious efforts both the tradition and the actual. In fact, if the Indian sensibility is indissolubly wedded both to the exterior landscape and the interior vision, we shall be able to understand and enjoy it in its fullness in a work of art. The well known writer and journalist, Khuswant Singh, considers the English language to be "England's greatest bequest to India and India's greatest national asset." This spring he wrote: "the surest way of arresting progress and putting the clock back is to ban the use of English." (*International Herald Tribune*, 2)

Presently, the works of most of the dramatists are either written originally in English or translated in English by their own or others to win recognition both in India and outside. It has no longer any colonial baggage which blocks any rational arguments about it. Bhaskar Ghosh in an article in *Theatre India* says:

> English is a language known to over 200 million Indians, to many of them it is their mother tongue. It is the state language in three states, and the medium of higher education and research. The work of the government of India is conducted in English and it has been formally declared in the constitution to be one of the two official languages of India. It has truly become an Indian language and it is hardly surprising that it should be used by a number of theatre groups in the country (62).

Modern Indian theatre is more complete and significant than ever before as it is closely related to modern Indian life of the people and society and is playing a leading role in keeping different regions, classes and castes, united and related. As Sumanta Banerjee points out:

> While India as a nation is increasingly getting fractured by religious, regional, linguistic, ethnic and other kinds of fissures, is the midst of all this it is the modern theatre in India which has emerged as an art form that appears to hold us together, cutting across these divisive lines. Although still primarily confined to the urban audience, it has developed as a multi-lingual, multi-cultural Indian theatre (5).

Angry protests were raised against the political and social powers, institutions, establishments and rejection of the constraining conventions became inevitable. For the first time after Independence, India fought two major wars within three years - with China in 1962, with Pakistan in 1965-with disastrous consequences on our economic growth. Again in 1966, large parts of rural India were gripped by food scarcity, and thousands died. The compelling situation drove the young dramatists to hostility and revolt to frustration and extremity. Now it is more ironical, artistic and aesthetical. In contemporary Indian drama, along with a sense of urbanity, an attitude of irony, frequent use of mythological sequences as structural images, a continuous involvement with the problems of expediency and eternity are very much visible. In short, there are some specific social phenomena shared by all Indians like the breakdown of the joint family system, the breakdown of the rural middle class, exploitation by the politicians and the business community, the communal problem, the problems of rural poverty, and urban unemployment, the frustration of the educated unemployed, the general middle class taboo on sex and endless religious superstitions. All these provide a common bond and make the Indian protagonist the familiar frustrated young urban male who, on one side, lives with his racial unconscious and talks of idealism and spirituality and on the other side, he feels trapped between the inner lack of freedom and of progress, and the eternal imposition of a free and progressive existence. But one can feel that the slant is more towards a re-search of all that is embedded in this racial unconscious.

There was not only political changes, but also intellectual ferment, a period of experiments with new ideas and formalist styles influenced both by contemporary trends in the West as well as reinterpretation of indigenous traditions. The Theatre of the Absurd, the plays of Beckett, Ionesco, Adamov and Genet, the Philosophy of Existentialism of Sartre and Camus and Brecht's theories were replacing in the thinking of Indian playwrights and producers. The rediscovery of old Indian mythology, past history and folk cultural forms and intermingling them to these western influences developed a creative alliance that has enriched the pan-Indian modern theatre. Nandi Bhatia has pointed out that:

> In post-Independence India, the role of theatre in attacking social problems such as dowry, female infanticide, and sati and in demanding the rights of workers, students and other subordinated groups further attests to its function as a central cultural force where political, social and ideological struggles engage one another. Despite censorship, social activists, doctors, university students, teachers, workers and women's groups have sought the critical attention of the state and the public, through dramatization of prevailing injustices and processes of disempowerment (*Acts of Authority*, 10).

Mahesh Dattani has divided modern Indian theatre in three categories: The Classical, The Continual, and The Radical. In the 1960-70, the theatre of roots movement began in the modern theatre and writers began to revisit the past, and borrow ideas from epics and history, mythology and folklore. Dharamvir Bharati and Mohan Rakesh, primarily as Hindi authors, are mainly closest to nineteenth and earlier twentieth century precursors as Michael Madhusudan Dutt,

Rabindra Nath Tagore, Jaishankar Prasad and Premchand etc. Bharati wrote only one full-length play, *Andha Yug* (Blind Age, 1954), an epic drama in blank verse. Based on *Mahabharata,* it deals with the eternal values of life that are damaged or broken and reestablished again and again. He took epic material, linked it to the contemporary political scene, and thus bridged the gap between the past and the present interlacing the play with a strong moral debate: the wrongs and rights of violence, the importance of the human will and the responsibility of the decision makers. Therefore, he laid down the pattern to be followed by several others.

Mohan Rakesh, 'Who defines writing as a natural expression of his responses to life' [Dharwadkar, *Theatre,* 60], bring a completely new sensibility to the realistic genre through his dramatic words :*Ashadh ka ek Din* (*One Day in Ashadha,*), *Lahron ke Rajhans* (*Swan of the Waves*), *Adhe-Adhure* (also translated as *Halfway House*) and the unfinished *Pair Tale ki Zamin (Ground Beneath the Feet).* Rakesh narrated the life and romance of the famous Sanskrit poet Kalidas in his play *Ashadh ka ek din.* His other plays deal with middle class urban life, examine human relationships and question societical norms and ethical codes. Although both these playwrights of modern Indian theatre began to write before independence but only after independence their works came to be widely known and recognized as powerful plays.

Like the above dramatists, Girish Karnad, a Kannad playwright, depicts the middle class society in the same synthesis of classical, folk and western. When he began to write, British troupes offering performances of western plays were welcomed by Indians. He thought of presenting truly Indian themes in a modernist style, by borrowing relevant aspects from Western theatre as well as Sanskrit and Folk theatre. But this reconstruction of an ancient Indian mythological story was heavily influenced by the ideas and dramatic forms of Camus, Sartre and other western writers. That's why he intermingles myths and legends with a view to make them a vehicle of a new vision and to show the absurdity of modern life with all its elemental passion and conflicts and man's eternal struggle to achieve perfection. In all his plays *Yayati, Tughlaq, Hayavadana, Anjumallige (Fearing Jasmine), Hittina Hunja (Dough-Cock), Naga-Mandala, Tale Danda, Agni Mattu Male (The Fire and The Rain),* he tried to depict a symbolic synthesis of old and new and thus bringing out the significance of past in comparison of present. His works also gain identity in foreign lands and became very popular. He works through abstractions and philosophical ideas, through questioning of tradition and traditional moral constructs and generates the conflictual element from this questioning. The binary oppositions which is the basis of the caste-class hierarchic society can be seen in his plays, for example in *Hayavadna*, the existentialist questions of Padmini in the context of society which operates on assumptions of binaries: head/body, knowledge/skill, fair/dark, soft/hard, high/low, Devadatta/Kapila. Padmini wanted both Devadutta's clever head and Kapila's strong body. Thus the fusion of folk/traditional/mythological and ritual material and forms with contemporary language in a conscious attempt to draw on traditional dynamics in a contemporary context. The issues they address are highly relevant in the present India, but the narrative derives from traditional tales and epics and the performance includes folk modes of e.g. song, dance and comic repartee.

Badal Sircar who is known as 'barefoot playwright' has created a genuine people's theatre, which he called 'Third', 'New', 'Free', 'Synthetic' 'Angan Mancha' etc. and which later on know as 'experimental theatre' is "a composite of a four way flow of influences, actor to actor, audience to actor, actor to audience and audience to audience." (Sircar, *India Today*, 157). Badal Sircar himself described his own motive:

> Now, I have to work for urban audiences and all I know is the problem of these people, it's a very narrow theatre, I admit. And I have no intention of carrying this theatre to the rural areas at all, because it is not about the problems of rural people, so I have no right to carry it to

> them. So I want to take it from my point; now how folk art lives, or should be preserved or recreated. I am interested in propagating my type of problems. I use theatre as I learnt it and probably everybody would agree that the concept of theatre came from the West... but now with the complexity of the middle-class increasing, we are searching for new forms because we are finding the 'naturalistic form' and the proscenium arch inadequate to voice our problems. So we want to break this tradition inherited from the West. So while I do not want to borrow the folk form to serve my own purpose (Awasthi, 38).

This theatre is an exclusive replacement of the imported proscenium simply in order to establish its non-Englishness and it is his conviction that theatre had to break the barriers between performer and spectator, spectator and spectator. The experimental theatre marks a definite break with the previous tradition of theatre. It is characterized with realism in the theme, structure, dialogues, setting and performance of the play. The presentation of the contemporary daily life is its main purpose. Aparna Dhawadkar says:

> The avant-garde (rather than traditionalist) variation that Badal Sircar has named the 'Third theatre' also draws on Grotowski and Schechner, providing an alternative to both bourgeois urban realism and feudalistic rural forms (*Theatre of,* 70).

Older than both Karnad and Tendulkar, Sircar's major contribution has been in the collaborative assimilation of folk forms, the theatre of the absurd, and the 'happenings' of the sixties, into a common dramatic mode. Sircar has depicted the world of everyday reality in his plays like *Evam Indrajit* (1963), his first and most successful existentialist play including themes of absurdist meaninglessness, *Baki Itihas* (*Remaining History,* 1965), *Pralap (Delirium,* 1966), *Tringsha Shatabdi (Thirtieth Century,* 1966) and *Pagla Ghora (Mad Horse,* 1967), *Shesh Nei (There's No End,* 1969). According to Ralph Yarrow:

Sircar's work, both scripted and co-devised, represents a significant strand in the spectrum from folk to urban, from improvised to scripted, from indoor to open air, from 'Indian' to 'Western' (155).

Where Rakesh and Karnad deconstruct the invention of heroes and villains in cultural and political history, Sircar deconstructs history itself. Indeed, *Baki itihas* effaces the question of institutionalized history altogether by selecting private rather than public experience as its subject, and then by arguing that the life of the individual is inseparable from collective human experience. It is this collectivity, which Sircar calls "history" that the postcolonial subject must confront fully, because he or she is first and foremost a citizen of the world.

Vijay Tendulkar, the Marathi playwright, is considered the pioneer of avant-garde movement in Indian context. He has not only won many prestigious awards like Kamladevi Chattopadhyaya award, Sangeet Natak Akademi award and Kalidas Samman award; but also as assistant editor of Marathi dairies like Navbharat, Maratha and loksatta. He has experimented not only with subject matter but also with the form and structure of the play by demolishing the three act play and creating new models back of the page. All the three traditions, i.e. The Classical, The Folk (like 'tamasha'), and The Modern are used by him and effectively presented in all his plays, *Shrimant (The Wealthy,* 1955), *Manus Navache Bet (An Island Called Man,* 1956), *Shantata!Court Chalu ahe (Silence! The Court is in Session* 1967, translated into many Indian languages), *Gidhade (The Vultures,* 1970) *Sakharam Binder* (1972), *Ghashiram Kotwal* (1972), *Kanyadan (Giving Away the Daughter,* 1983).His other important plays include *Chimnyancha Ghar Hota Menacha (The Sparrows' Nest Was of Wax,* 1959), *Mi Jinkalo Mi Haralo (I Won, I Lost,* 1963), *Kawlyanchi Shala (School For Crows,* 1963), *Dambadwipcha Mukabla (Face-off on Hypocrisy Island,* 1969) *Ashi Pakhare Yeti ('That 's How Birds Arrive'* 1970), *Pahije Jatiche (Wanted From the Right Caste,* 1976), *Mitrachi Gostha (A Friend's Story,* 1981), and *Kamala* (1981).

He depicts the isolation of individuals, agonies, suffocations, sufferings and cries of man, focusing on the middle class society. The theme of violence (influenced by Artaud) is prominent in his plays as he used to think it is the inseparable quality in human nature and he presents violence raw and natural, without mingling of fancy, as he says:

> Unlike the communists I don't think violence can be eliminated in a classless society, or for that matter, in any society. The spirit of aggression is something that human being is born with. Not that it is bad. Without violence man might have turned into a vegetable (George 512-13).

With all the tactics of irony, satire, pathos and mock element, Tendulkar raises several questions about love, sex, marriage and moral values prevalent in Indian society and specially the hollow mindset of the middle class society. He is a fighter for cultural freedom; the freedom which is stifled at present by various forces. Mahesh Elkunchwar defines Tendulkar's plays, as one

> "who really confronts the problems of his time and accepts the challenges of his subject material", expressing a "new voice", and "disturbing new insights into the human problems..." (22).

However, these [the Big Four] were not the only playwrights who were translated into English and various Indian languages. Others are also significant in writing in other Indian languages as well as initially in English. Having the dramatists of the same genre, the realistic Drama, Mahesh Elkunchwar wrote in Marathi, while Asif Currimbhoy, Gurcharan Das, Nissim Ezekiel, Lakhan Deb, Gieve Patel, Pratap Sharma, Poile Sengupta and Mahesh Dattani are writing originally in English. Their English plays of these playwrights based on realistic models are following: Nissim Ezekiel's *Three Plays* (1969), consisting of *Nalini, A Marriage poem* and *The Sleep Walkers*; Lakhan Deb's *Tiger Claw* (1947) and *Murder at the Prayer Meeting* (1976); Gurcharan Das's *Larins Sahib* (1970), *Meera* and *9 Jakhoo*

Hill; Gieve Patel's *Princes* (1970); Pratap Sharma,'s *The Professor Has a Warcry* (1970) and *A Touch of Brightness* (1970); Poile Sengupta's *Mangalam, Alipha, Thus Spake Shoorpanakha,* and *So Said Shakuni* etc.

Marathi playwright Mahesh Elkunchwar is said to have been different from others as being autobiographical and self reflective. He became interested in writing for theatre after he chanced to see Vijay Tendulkar's *Mi Jinkalo Mi Haralo (I Won, I Lost,* 1965). He directly dealt with the issues of gender relations and family. His important plays includes: *Rudravarsha (Angry Rain,* 1968), *Garbo* (1973), *Vasanakand* (*Period of Desire,* 1974), *Pratibimb (Reflection,* 1987), *Wada Chirebandi* (*Old Stone Mansion,* 1985), *Magna Talyakathi (Pensive by the Pond,* 1994), *Yuganta (End of an age,* 1994), *Atmakatha (Autobiography,* 1988), *Vasansi Jirnani* (*As Discarded Clother,* 1996), *Dharmaputra (Godson,* 1997) and *Sonata* (premiered in English translation, 2001).

Elkunchwar deals with the disintegration of traditional joint family and traditional village life under the onslaught of modern forces of urbanization and industrialization. All his plays has marriage as one of the nodal points in its structure and present women as victims of the caste biases and patriarchal thinking in the family but on the other hand, also present them as agents of change. His plays also dare to dream of a system of family based on the foundation of mutual respects, love and understanding. This theme has always been neglected as he said the family is not static. It presents itself as a developing from inequality to equality, injustice to mutual understanding and suppression to human understanding. This is the contribution of Elkunchwar to Marathi theatre and gender issue.

Manjula Padmanabhan was the first Indian to earn international acclaim with her play *Harvest*, a futuristic play that deals with the exploitation of the human body in the 21st century. It won the highest Greek honour. Alienation and marginalization play a large role in her books. Her other works include *Lights Out* and *Getting There.*

One distinct feature of the contemporary theatre has been the emergence of the director on the scene. Now a day most of authors are also the directors. While Utpal Dutt and K.N.Panikkar directed and staged many classical, Sanskrit and historical dramas, Padamsee etc. contributed a lot in popularizing and producing many contemporary realistic plays. Among the groups and directors who are engaged in the present time can be described thus by Anand Lal:

> Among English language troupes, the Theatre Group (Bombay), led first by Ebrahim Alkazi and later by Padamsee, is the most long-lived and accomplished. It staged original plays by Gieve Patel (1940-); Gurcharan Das (1943-), whose dance-drama *Mira* had premiered at La Mama, off-off-Broadway, in 1970; and the freshest and most promising Indian-English dramatist, Mahesh Dattani. The Madras Players, who produced Girish Karnad's self-translated plays and held a competition for new scripts jointly with the daily The Hindu, and Delhi's Yatrik also encouraged original playwriting. The annual Deccan Herald theatre festival in Bangalore gave a boost to English drama by such local authors as Dattani and Poile Sengupta (*The Oxford*, 122-123).

Thus, in the textual and performative fields of post-independence theatre, ancient, pre modern, and modern, Indian and Western, dramatic and narrative works coexist, interpenetrate, and speak through each other. Although Shakespeare and Brecht have been the dominant foreign influences, given the prevalence of translation, adaptation and transcultural appropriation the Indian and Western canons in their entirety are, in effect, the intertexts of contemporary dramatic production.

(ii)

A good and complete theatre will always enrich the audience, will make them familiar with those aspects of life that they may not have been acquainted with very clearly and the audience go away not only satisfied but with some new sensibilities, some new awareness, some ideas which they would have got from a truly fine play, well presented. None of the great international playwrights wrote plays as political tracts, stridently dwelling on injustice, exploitation, oppression and so on. These may have been aspects of a particular play but only aspects, never the only ingredient. Great playwrights have been more concerned with people, with human beings, their frailties and their courage or strength in adversity. According to Mahesh Dattani:

> In drama, one explores the distortions of everyday speech, the weight and flow of everyday movement, and endeavours to bring to them a sense of music (Maheshwari 2).

Contrary to traditional theatre, realistic plays, in their presentational style, focus more on contemporary life. Their action is invented, not derived from preexisting narratives; their settings are urban or semi-urban, and their primary level of signification is literal rather than analogical or allegorical. Domestic settings, love, marriage, parent-child conflicts, generational shifts, and the quotidian pressures of urban life appear as the common subjects of plays. Social realism and proscenium performance defined modernity in India in the colonial period, though no significant urban-realist plays appeared by Indian playwrights that time. Although, after independence such playwrights as Mohan Rakesh, Badal Sircar, G.P.Deshpande, Mahasweta Devi, and Satish Alekar offered stylized variations on realism in their plays of different languages with the assimilations of historical, environmental, political, and absurdist theatre. But the major contemporary practitioners who have given the realistic mode an Indian identity, far from the shackles of colonialist, are Vijay Tendulkar, Mahesh Elkunchwar, and Mahesh Dattani. The social realism of Tendulkar, Elkunchwar, Rakesh and Dattani has created radically modern perspectives on caste, class, sexuality, gender, family relationships, home and nation. In its totality, the contemporary tradition of urban, realist, predominantly domestic drama is large and varied and includes some of the most influential plays of the last five decades. The full impact of realistic urban drama as a distinct kind of theatre emerges only when all three of levels- visual, psychological, and emotional levels of communication are taken concurrently into account. Shanta Gokhale notes:

> the preferred mode of writing and presentation was realism, for it was felt that it was through this mode that the 'modern' sensibility could best express itself (102).

As it is already illustrated in the previous section, in the post-independence period, despite the output of such authors as Nissim Ezekiel, Gieve Patel, Gurcharan Das, Pratap Sharma, Asif Currimbhoy, Drama in English has not acquired a strong theatrical base or textual currency. The result was that a major play in a language other than English soon acquired a national, and sometimes an international, audience through translation, especially into English; plays written originally in English, however, remained on the periphery of contemporary Indian theatre and were rarely translated into the indigenous languages of the subcontinent.

The reason for this preference is the idea that a language corresponds to a structure of experience in the world: theatre has the quality of lived experience when its language is the 'natural' language of the characters it represents. To actually translate the text into a living performance that a given Indian audience is to watch and relate to is quite another thing. This is the crux of the problem that posed and still poses the major obstacle for Indian dramatic performances in English. As Girish Karnad comments ironically in a 1993 interview:

> "writing in English about characters who are presumably speaking in an Indian language for audiences for whom English is a second language is not a situation conducive to great drama" (*NTQ*, 365).

Theatre has been variously called the 'poor cousin' of Indian English writing. English language drama in India continues to be described as "one of the twin Cinderellas of Indian writing in English", and, more unsparingly, as a lost cause and a form of writing that ought to be dead if it is not already so. (Naik., *Perspectives*, 1997. 180) The perceived lacuna of Indian English drama has often been blamed on the limited scope of English as a language of everyday conversations in India. The plays of Mahesh Dattani are perhaps the first to challenge effectively the assumption that Indian drama written in English represents a disjunction between language and sensibility, material and medium. He denies English drama's inferiority to English novel:

I think this is the wrong perception prevailing among the academics, especially the view that writing for the stage is inferior to writing a novel or writing poetry. I think it is important to keep in mind that the playwright is actually a craftsman. He is a "wright" and not "write".... It's more to do really with dramatic structure and less with literary skills. I think the skill of the playwright is listening to day-to-day speech and not making it sound flowery.... It has more to do with understanding human relationships and how conflict can be presented on stage (Mohanty 170).

That is what is so exciting about the plays of Mahesh Dattani, the harbinger of new aesthetics, new themes, new theatre and new dramaturgy in the modern Indian drama. His dialogues are generally quite crisp and natural while at the same time successfully weaving in culture- specific markers- gender constitutes an important preoccupation of Dattani's oeuvre. Dattani, the young Bangalorean and the first English playwright to receive the prestigious Sahitya Akademi award in 1998 since its inception in 1955 for his book *Final Solutions and Other Plays* (1994), has shaped and reshaped contemporary Indian theatre.

> [Dattani's work] probes tangled attitudes in contemporary India towards communal differences, consumerism and gender... a brilliant contribution to Indian drama in English. – *Sahitya Akademi award citation (1998)* (*CP1*, Cover Page)

Mahesh Dattani is a successful playwright, an occasional director, an acclaimed scriptwriter (especially for BBC-4 radio plays) and now an award-winning film-maker (with *Mango Soufflé* at Barcelona Film Festival 2003). Dattani does not see his choice of English as arbitrary, as a 'postcolonial' gesture, or as an example of 'the empire writing back'- a phrase that he incidentally describes as 'politically incorrect'. (*CP*1, ii) English is simply the language in which 'he can best express what he wants to say". (Katyal, *STQ*, 9). He describes the significance of theatre in an interview to Ranu Uniyal when asked what according to him 'theatre' is:

> I think, of all the arts and of all the writing genres, theatre perhaps is the most dynamic because no other art form is as vibrant.... Because the kind of chemistry that can be created between audience and performer on a very immediate, on a gut level, I don't think any other genre offers that and I think that is what makes it very valuable tool, as an agent of social change maybe without being didactic or... without being preachy and at the same time as a very raw form of communication, and it need not have a very special language, the way classical dance does or opera or classical music does where it is the privilege of a few who understand the language of that genre. Whereas theatre can be appreciated by anyone, the most uneducated person by any standard of our society could relate to it as much as the most educated (180).

Like other subaltern theories of literature, post-colonialism stands for those who have been sentenced by history of subjugation, diaspora and displacement, empowering the marginalized by retrieving the voices, spaces and identities silenced by colonial power, and the plays of Girish Karnad, Vijay Tendulkar, Mahesh Elkunchwar and others display these complexities of post-colonialism being inherited from the colonial and pre-colonial times. Mahesh Dattani emerges as a compelling playwright who rearranges the social fabrication and projects the postcolonial dichotomy operating at different levels. Dattani's work may signal a new phrase in the naturalization of English as a theatre medium in India. Dattani chooses realist representations of contemporary urban social experience as the appropriate subject of drama and theatre. As a theorist, he invokes the dominant legacy of realism and naturalism in modern western theatre and the strong traditions of social realism in India from the nineteenth century to the present. He has a definite point of view for drama; he says:

> It is a craft of communicating through the language of action (Dasgupta, maheshdattani.com).

His inter-disciplinary approach uses music, dance and theatre in theatrical productions and films, that are primarily adaptations of his own plays. Dattani used to write social-domestic drama, credible portraits of urban family, domestic interiors, and presenting psychological studies of man-woman relationships, often coupled with a desire for social reform. Human relationships and the family unit have indeed been at the heart of Dattani's representation. This trend coincided with and was supported by translations from the plays of John Galsworthy, Bernard Shaw, and most importantly, Henric Ibsen. He presents the ordinary individual, rather than the exalted, and to trace the course of events as they emerged from a mundane existence, caught up in the vicissitudes of everyday, without, theoretically, attempting to impose a pattern on the course of conduct motivates the character. He says:

> In drama, one explores the distortions of everyday speech, the weight and flow of everyday movement, and endeavors to bring to them a sense of music (Maheshwari 4).

Born in Bangalore on 7 August 1958, Dattani studied in Baldwin's High School and St. Joseph's college of Arts and Science, Bangalore. Graduated in history, economics and political science and post-graduated in marketing and advertising management, he has worked as a copywriter in an advertising film and subsequently with his father in the family business. Though fascinated by Gujarati plays (their dazzling costumes, gaudy sets, the surreal world of theatre), often performed in Bangalore in his childhood which his parents brought him to see. Though he never imagined himself to be a literary personality and a part of it and always expected to spend a normal life like others. Dattani himself asserts that Film and Theatre are not his formal education. He studied history, economics and political science and then he did a post-grad in marketing management. He learnt on the job and started by assisting theatre groups, by writing back stage and then moved on to direction, acting and writing as well.

Still in college in the early 1980s, Dattani joined Bangalore Little Theatre and participated in workshops, acting and directing plays. He also underwent Western ballet training under Molly Andre at Alliance Franchise de Bangalore (1984-87) and Bharatanatyam training under Chandrabhaga Devi and Krishna Rao, Bangalore (1986-90). Therefore with the span of time, he began on getting involved in theatrical activities side by side of his studies. He asserts:

> I didn't know the world at my doorstep. I got involved in theatre and for a long time continued to do European plays in translation. [... Seeing] Gujarati theatre in Mumbai, I realized I had to unlearn a lot that I learnt in school. That is when my true education really began (Ayyar 24).

Dattani is the founder of a performing arts group called 'Playpen' (or 'Mahesh's Studio' as he himself calls it), established in 1984, which is dedicated to promoting scripts written both in English and translations of contemporary plays from regional languages. It is a mini 'amphitheatre' with three rows of semi-circular seating spotlights and high mud walls covered with bougainvillea and jasmine. Here he also conducts his workshops on acting, playwriting and directing and even hosts art exhibitions related with the various phases of performance dynamics. Here he writes his plays using a computer and also gives them final touches by the rehearsals in Playpen. Playpen is among the few privileged groups in the country to have its own rehearsal and performing space. No institution in India provides such a strong emphasis on promoting new voices in theatre. Mahesh Dattani has also conducted several theatre workshops and regular courses in India as well as in the USA, the UK and Malaysia. In spite of the meager achievement of the Indian drama in English, it is heartening to know that just as English plays from England were produced in India, now English plays written by Indians are gaining ground in England and the United States, namely because of the brilliant efforts of Dattani in its development. The author of more than fifteen plays, he made his directorial debut with *Mango Soufflé*.

As he was well versed in English language and he began his dramatic career by producing English plays, made it his language of expression. Later, when he began to feel those foreign plays inappropriate for Indian audience, he began to write original plays. When challenged in a seminar at the University of Bangalore as to why did he not write in his own language, he gently replied that he did, as he used the language in which he could best express what he wanted to say. He began to depict Indian sensibility in English which is no more a colonial baggage but a lingua franca of contemporary modern Indian society. Dattani's use of English is so spontaneous in his plays that one very often forgets the language, he categorically states:

> I really feel that people have to come to terms with the fact that English is an Indian language! Just as it is American or Canadian or Australian. We should celebrate the fact that India has this enormous capacity to absorb from all sources. This is exactly how we have survived colonization, unlike the poor Native Americans. We may claim to be rigid and pure, but we are the most flexible and impure of all races! The sooner we come to terms with that; we can get on with the rest (Ayyar 24).

Like his friend Vikram Seth, Mahesh Dattani is proud to be an Indian, writing in English. Like him he is a citizen of the modern world; he lives in Karnataka but writes about the whole nation of India, about the world he lives in. It is this ability of Dattani's to write in neither an 'Indian' idiom which is neither strained nor self-conscious most of the time that is his basic strength. Theatre is an important medium for cultural and political expression, and theatre in English, in our urban centres particularly, attracts both an audience and corporate sponsorship.

Influenced by such dynamic principles, Dattani acknowledges the significance of established literary tradition and simultaneously makes a praiseworthy attempt to create a tradition of his own to promote the spirit of Indian English drama at the global level. Mahesh Dattani defends his writing in English by saying that his characters are essentially Indian and that the language is the one developed in India and is a 'hybrid language that is spoken in a unique, uninhibited manner'. Dattani asserts that from one's childhood; one attains English education in the metropolitan cities. And therefore the very first education begins with the Indian English, the knowledge of our tradition and all that comes rather later on. The same happened with him too. So it became his personal language where he can express himself comfortably:

> English as a language is very cosmopolitan. It has become our personal language. That's the reason why I started reading English plays. Moreover, at that time I was not well aware of the Indian art form. It was only when I started to learn Bharatnatyam, that I got to know about our culture (Chatterjee 9).

Dattani feels that English theatre scene is a product of the English-educated urban milieu, reflecting certain rootlessness, unconnected from the richness of folk and classical arts of the country. This is in contrast to its regional counterparts, like, say Marathi theatre, where audiences and practitioners have retained an unbroken culture of aesthetics. This anxious, tense, urban milieu is indeed the milieu he has explored in many of his plays and screenplays, receiving critical and audience approbation. He says in an interview:

> Like many urban people in India, you're in this situation where the language you speak at home is not the

> language of your environment, especially if you move from your hometown. And you use English to communicate, so you find that you're more and more comfortable expressing yourself in English [...but] I wanted to do more Indian plays [and that] became a challenge, because there weren't many good translations, but they didn't do anything for me (Mee, *Drama Contemporary*, 14).

We cannot think about writing a play without referring to the process of play making and Dattani, as a multi-dimensional playwright, actor, dancer and filmmaker, is a perfectionist in this area. O'Neil enumerates, the director's craft gradually appropriated the functions of "critic, analyst, interpreter, historian, designer, actor, coach, manager, audience and administrator." The most complex expression of the new 'balance of power' is perhaps the relationship between literary playwrights who do not direct their own work and directors of literary drama who do not create their own texts for performance- that is between non-directing authors and non-writing directors. But Dattani is both so can be called 'directing author' and 'writing director'. His plays consists both dramatical lines and theatrical lines, which make them appropriate to be staged.

The plays of Dattani act as the Shakespearean mirror reflecting a society and characters which audiences can believe in, can see themselves in. For a moment the audience or reader can identify with the crises and consciousness of others there on the stage, in that vast space of the universe that the dramatist creates. Dattani's passion for theatre gives us those flashes of lightning, those moments, scenes and dramas of illumination in his own personal and individual way.

Dattani's realism give expression to marginal voices in India at this time, which carries not only voices from the neglected margins of society, but from the mainstream, the educated middle-class, the upholders of norms, and also those who carefully defied them, in whom was invested the responsibility for creating a modern society in their newly independent country. The theme and setting in his plays co-mingle to produce visual, psychological and emotional experience of spectatorship. The full impact of realistic urban drama as a distinct kind of theatre emerges only when all three of these levels of communication are taken concurrently into account. Dattani is primarily influenced by the plays of Shaw, Ibsen, Tennessee Williams and Arthur Miller. In India Girish Karnad is his role model:

> I think Girish Karnad was a kind of role model. He once told me that he enjoys theatre, and he acts in commercial films for the money. He is the most important living playwright we have in our country. Other models are Mahesh Elkunchwar, Vijay Tendulkar and of course, Madhu Rye. I also admire Badal Sircar for doing what he believed in. he stopped doing proscenium theatre when he did not believe in it anymore (Banerjee 9).

The upper-class urban tragicomedy of Mahesh Dattani has reenergized the drama of poisoned relationships in the challenging medium of English, although the playwright's penchant for plot-driven coups de theatre inserts a measure of superficiality and sensationalism into an otherwise accomplished oeuvre. In this inventive dramaturgy, the stage either represents several domestic spaces simultaneously, or several spaces among which home is central. The plays of Dattani like those of the dramatists mentioned above, home is again a place of resentment, neurosis, confrontation, and barely suppressed violence, until a last minute reversal exposes some guilty secret from the past that has fueled the mundane family antagonisms.

Dattani is also indebted to Alyque Padamsee and Lillette Dubey, the two outstanding contemporary directors associated with the development of Indian English theatre, for producing and popularizing his plays all over the world. As Mahesh Dattani points out in his Preface:

> Alyque believed in my work even before I believed in it myself. He gave me the courage to call myself a professional playwright and director (*CP1*, xiii).

Realism seems to dominate the settings and dialogues of most of his plays, even though scenes may be strung together in a theatrical manner. His realism is one of urban interiors, domestic and professional. He depicts the conflict of individuals both within themselves and in their relationship with their partners, other family members, credible portraits of urban family life and, often their relationships only indirectly, with society. Domestic interiors, presenting psychological studies of man-woman relationships, often coupled with a desire for social reform. The emotions of the characters cumulate gradually. Towards the end, they burst forth in a virtual paroxysm of words, long speeches in which they lay bare their inner conflicts and seek understanding. This trend coincided with and was supported by translations from the plays of John Galsworthy, Bernard Shaw, and most importantly, Henrik Ibsen. Unlike Ibsen's plays, Dattani's plays also produce healing effect, rather than a destructive one. He also has the Ibsenite talent for revealing the secrets of a family, but goes beyond this by making his characters turn towards the future in exorcising the past: "Will the scars our parents lay on us remain forever?" cries Kiran in *Where There's a Will.* Although Dattani used to take western realistic mode and pattern in his writings, yet there's something very 'Indian' about all the activities of him when he loves the traditional art forms, especially Bharatanatyam which is integral to *Dance Like a Man.* His plays:

> fuse the physical and special awareness of the Indian theatre with the texual rigour of western models like Ibsen and Tennessee Williams. It is a potent combination, which shocks and disturbs, through its accuracy, and its ability to approach a subject from multiple perspectives. Postcolonial Indian and multi-cultural Britain both have an urgent need for a cultural expression of the contemporary; they require public spaces in which the mingling of eastern and western influences can take place. Through his fusion of forms and influences, Mahesh creates such a space (*CP*1, 229).

Like George Bernard Shaw, in another age and in a different country, Dattani too is aware of the possibility that theatre is a strong source of reforming society as well as expressing oneself totally. There are, it seems to Dattani, senses in which theatre can be both a means of liberation from confining systems and structures and a positive engagement with them. For him, the spectrum in the play involves differing dimensions of confrontation with self and other, as well as different categories of performance and their effects on audiences. This makes his work actually breathing and energetic, as he says:

> ... the sheer fact that I'm projecting a milieu that is close to the audience- I think that may itself be an achievement. That's what makes my theatre alive (Mohanty 171).

Therefore, Dattani's plays are primarily realistic entertainment, and that is what brings the audiences to the theatre. His plays can be done again and again because they are fine pieces of drama, absorbing, entertaining and containing within them elements that leave an audience with a feeling of taking something precious away after the play is over. What makes Mahesh Dattani one of India's finest playwrights is in the manner that he speaks to the audience straight from the heart. Anita Nair summarizes his motive:

> He aims not at changing society but only seeks to offer some scope for reflection in the hope that his plays will give the audience some kind of insight into their lives (*The Gentleman*, 2).

For this, he does not provide ready made solutions or fully resolved endings and let the audience itself speculate over this. Dattani asserts in an interview to Anita Nair:

> I see myself as a craftsman and not a writer. To me being a playwright is about seeing myself as a part of the process of production. I write for the sheer pleasure of communicating through this dynamic medium (*The Gentleman*, 2).

The distinction between a playwright and a 'writer' using any other mode is clear in these lines. Playwriting is only one part of the many necessary ingredients of a play and for its completion; this written text has to be inter-related with the performance. Dattani explains that the playwright has to realize that it is not writing to be read and that the actors are going to take away the script and do other things with it:

> If you look at my plays, you would find that each character, every character has, you know, his or her space in the play, which an actor can develop (Katyal 24).

The success of every play depends upon a general agreement by all participants- author, actors and audience. And Dattani, while co-mingling these, expects his audience to share the pleasure of that communication for the complete effect of the play:

> Theatre is a collective experience and the audience have to finish in their own heads what the playwright began (Nair, *The Gentleman*, 2).

His plays come with all the emotions we all have experienced- on our way up or down. No black, no white, just grays here. Just the way it is in life. It has to do with the role of the 'self' in the environment of human possibility, and the role of theatre in the environment of social organization; with kinds of awareness engendered by theatre and performance and with ways in which they translate into action. Dattani has a definite worldview too:

> I believe that the world is what make of it. Just as our actions create our karma, each of us can contribute to the preservation and betterment of our world by creative action. We are all different. But if we create an atmosphere that is conductive to growth and learning, different worlds can retain their uniqueness and yet find common grounds (Banerjee, *The Pioneer*, 4).

Therefore, Dattani breathed new values into the empty shell of theatre. He believes in distilling new meanings from that social rapport, which is theatre and such productions that can shatter the ways of seeing and doing theatre. When one approaches the plays of Dattani, one feels that the huge door, normally closed for everyone, has swung noiselessly open and one is confronted with that are normally lost to everyone. Ralph Yarrow says:

> The arguments suggest that although theatre may not, as Bharucha says, have changed the world so far, 'it is possible to change our own lives through theatre'. Among the motivations to change which its activity on the fringes offers are: redrawing of the boundaries of understanding and possible action; focus in many forms on issues which would otherwise be overlooked; expression by voices which would otherwise be silent (26-27).

Dattani belongs to the category of radical theatre artist and does not follow the history as Karnad and Bharati did. But he is also of the view that without a great history, no further developments happen in any country or place and to explore and develop new forms, we need the strong base of a precious history. The problem clearly lay in insisting that all roots were buried in the past. Indian modernity also had a history in the meantime. Similarly, the director Rajinder Nath expresses his views:

> When the use of traditional and folk forms is argued, the stock phrase used is 'discovery of roots" or "going to the soil". True, but are all our roots ancient? There can be modern roots too, which one has to discover to deal with contemporary reality and experience (28).

Assessing the same claims with reference to the issue of "indigenousness", Elkunchwar asks why "theatre in the villages alone [is to] be considered indigenous, and not theatre in the cities? An Indian who gets a Western education is also part of the Indian reality; an Indian theatre that is influenced by Western theatre- especially after such a long history of exchange- is part of our Indian experience." (Karnad., *Contemporary*, 175)

Therefore, approaching the issues from various aesthetic and ideological positions, theatre practitioners of different persuasions have collectively mounted a substantial theoretical defense of urban life as an appropriate and desirable subject of contemporary theatrical representation. Dattani himself asserts about traditional theatre forms:

> Yes, they're wonderful, they're very sophisticated, they're impressive, but are they really India? That's something I would like to question and challenge. Are they really reflecting life as it is now, that is the question I would like to ask. They're fine, but there is the danger that if you look at them as if they're quintessential India you're doing those forms a great disservice, because you're not allowing them to change. What we need to do now is look at those forms and say we're approaching the twenty-first century, this is who we are and this is our legacy, so where do we take that. That's not happening, and that's a matter of serious concern (Mee, *Mahesh Dattani's Plays*, 162).

Furthermore, he asserts that contemporary urban experience, with its emphasis on city, home, and family, is no less 'rooted', 'authentic' and 'Indian' than the pre-modern material of indigenous performance. He himself says:

> I have tried to expose the underbelly of society through my own feelings and sensitivity, and explored the portrayal of a subaltern culture (Banerjee, *The Pioneer*, 4).

Dattani wants a national identity of this new theatre of our country and "to form our cultural identities we need all three: traditions, continuity and change. It is when we accept the need for all three in our theatre that we can truly have a theatre movement that is inextricably linked to the development of cultural, social and individual identities" (*JIWE*, 1).

Therefore, his apparently westernized Indian modernity, neo-traditionalism and realism lead alike to invention – both theoretical positions in effect produce syncretic forms of theatre that had not existed before him. He says:

> Our culture is so rich with tradition, and that's an advantage and a disadvantage as well, because... we're living in the present and there are so many challenges facing us- you just have to cross the road and you have an issue, and I think it is very important for our country to spawn new playwrights and new voices who reflect honestly and purely our lives, because I think that is our contribution to the world, and to our future as well(*CP*1, 319).

Dattani, being the radical and dynamic dramatist, locates himself as the changer of the prevailing norms and traditions, but without regressing into his past, it was a venture to carve a new hope and new tradition. He asserts:

> ... I do feel myself as the change element of that thread. I'm not so sure even that I want to go back to my roots. I don't need to resist it. I'm more interested in pushing it forward... I am pushing, and I'm pushing the audience (Vardhan 1).

According to Dattani, People generally come to see themselves or any part of their awareness reflected in the theatre and may be disillusioned and stop believing in theatre if they could not see themselves. He again says:

> If traditional and continual theatre is linked to our roots, radical theatre is linked to our spirit. It soars like a bird exploring new horizons and offering us vantage points that we didn't know existed. Both form and content have been enriched by radical thinkers in our theatre (*JIWE*, 3).

Mostly situations are subject to change, they are not fixed for once and for all. Therefore, we do need change and the dramatists need to develop new forms and languages according to the needs of contemporary society. Only than a drama can be appreciated and popularized by the audience. Dattani is a playwright, director and actor at the same time and never make compromise torn between the three roles and as he says:

> The actor, the playwright and the director are all complimentary to each other in a production. It is like gardening; where whole is made of many parts. So many conditions determine a garden's lushness, its beauty (Nair, *The Gentleman*, 2).

Mahesh Dattani has benefited from the experience of the language writers, has moved ahead of Asif Currimbhoy and Nissin Ezekiel and have learnt to use both language (with all its varied range of nuances and pinches) and structure (with its disruptive possibilities built in) and are now increasingly working with social concerns even if, at times, they used to choose fantasy or dystopia. Writing from the late 1980s, Dattani's plays, like Tendulkar's question some of the norms and conventions of society. One can only talk about one's own predicament and one's choices. The minute we make universal and general rules and insist that everybody follows them, there will be problem. And that is what is present in every society in which individuals are bound to live in the 'forced harmony'. This is in the centre of all the plays of Dattani and he achieves this through the language of theatre as he comments in his talk on 11Feb.2001 at Rabindra Kalakshetra as part of the Krishi Festival Plays to celebrate the 50th Anniversary of Bengali Theatre in Bangalore.

> Man has created a very complex language called theatre. A language that has the ability to redefine the natural concepts of time, space and movement. A language that goes beyond the verbal, a movement that goes beyond the physical. Through this language of theatre he has been able to see himself for who he is, what he has made of himself and what he aspires to be (Dattani, *JIWE*, 1).

Dattani brought up an extremely localized theatre committed to identity, nationalism, difference, of finding an original outlet to channel the silent feelings and instincts of the oppressed. With his wide range of themes, his focus is mainly on the Indian middle class life, morality and its conflicts with emphasis/stress on modern and hitherto taboo subjects like homosexuality, gender identity, human relationships, communalism etc. He has called a spade, a spade. Dattani makes himself conspicuous by picking up such sensational issues of the society which we know and read now and then but refuse to acknowledge their existence amidst us. Dattani's daredevil attitude towards society and its loopholes is surely commendable and impresses everyone a lot. His plays can be rightly termed as *deus ex machine*, in which an unexpected event suddenly appears to resolve a situation that seems hopeless usually appears at the end. His plays are meant to be enacted in order to be enjoyed. He effectively achieves an objective distancing by experimenting and juggling with theatrical devices. He maneuvers dramatic structures in order to create an objective and panoramic reality on the stage. However, he never makes theatre a propagandist soapbox but shows the dramatic form to hint at possibilities that are contextually alive.

In his career of twenty five years, he has also written for BBC Radio and is involved in an international project commemorating the 600th anniversary of Chaucer's Canterbury Tales. His *Collected Play* ha been published by Penguin, and some years ago, two of his plays, *Dance Like a Man* and *On a Muggy Night in Mumbai*, were produced in New York at the Tribeca Arts Centre. For Dattani, radio is more challenging than writing plays for screen on stage:

> I'd say radio is the most challenging as one needs to engage listeners without the support of visual aids. Besides, radio might not even have a captive audience and one has to capture attention through soundscapes. In radio, one has to focus on content rather than relying on melodrama, like one does on the stage (Kumar, *Times of India*, 9).

Although, Dattani has written many screen plays and radio plays besides stage plays, in this thesis, we are going to deal with dominant themes of homosexuality, gender discrimination, women exploitation, communalism, identity problem and child sexual abuse by his seven stage plays in this thesis, these are: *Where There's a Will (1988), Dance*

Like a Man (1989), Tara (1990), Bravely Fought the Queen (1991), Final Solutions (1993), On a Muggy Night in Mumbai (1993), Thirty Days in September. All these plays are different from one another in substance. Each of them deals with different hurdles in the path of a progressive society. His plays are primarily written to be staged – not to be read as stories in the drawing rooms or classrooms. The comic scenes which appear in the text of the first play are reduced in the second, to disappear entirely in the final play. Likewise, his plays moves more and more towards the more taboo subjects starting from the more general issues from the very first one. Moreover, his plays can be appreciated as a voyage from self awareness to self realization and from self realization to self defense.

In modern theatre, it has been acknowledged that drama cannot and should not survive in isolation. To seek a harmony of theatre and thought, drama must take into consideration the emerging issues related with socio-cultural practices. Dattani depicts a kind of social satire which attempted realist portraiture at the same time. Just as in his drama, if on the one hand Dattani fought for an individuation which inevitably thrust his characters into conflict-riddled situations that provoked rage at the barriers set up by so called tradition, on the other hand, he ended by finding resolutions that covered up the very roots of the issues and problems he had raised. He looked forward to effect change, not backward. Though he raises some prominent issues concerning the various maltreatments of the society, he ceased to be didactic in his attitude he asserts, theatre "is a reflection of what you observe. To do anything more would be to become didactic and then it ceases to be theatre" (Nair, *The Gentleman*, 2).

Dattani has sensitive insights into domestic psychology as well as the mindset of Indian teenagers in the cosmopolitan cities which are almost based on the Freudian understanding of the human self. It primarily treated a human being as an individual and not as a social being. Individuals are always in confrontation with the other or the self and also with the society and its morality. Men and women never became social beings but isolated individuals. Therefore, much of the oppositional energy in his theatre, in any case, is not directed against the colonial experience but against the oppressive structures of nation, patriarchy, caste, class and tradition. Prejudice, guilt, dishonesty, compromise-this is what Dattani's plays comprise of, the stuff of life itself.

The plays of Dattani follow the familial focus and conflictional structure of Western realist drama, but he is radically different. Firstly, in his plays not only one single protagonist struggle with home and society in individualistic terms. Rather, the struggles of the whole family, within the relations of every person are shown, who are trapped by cultural constraints and economic circumstances. In *Bravely Fought the Queen*, the emotionally stunted upper-class couples repeatedly draw attention to their own entrapment, but not even one character possesses the ability to arrest the collective descent into the state of hopelessness. Secondly, the conflicting structure of contemporary families in failure of ideal relationship between family members is compared with the idealistic relations of the past- of perfect love, duty, obedience and respect between husband and wife, father and son, older and younger, which are not been in Indian families now. Thirdly the plays stress the condition of victimization but do not allow the liberation or departure, adhering instead to a pattern of continued entrapment. Therefore, pervasive discontent, continued entrapment, self hatred etc create notable variations on the thematic structures popularized by Western realist drama, and he seems to be saying 'I might use the same torch, but I point it differently.'

One of Dattani's major themes is his fiery feminism. His women seem to say 'there is red blood in my veins; there is fire in my heart.' Therefore, his women are aware of their power to fight with the society. They have the right to feel, the space to live these feelings; the denial of this space to women, the sacrifices they are expected to make for their men, the boundaries placed on marital bonds as applying to women alone, women's internalization of their feelings and their willing compliance; later revealing to their revolt. The works of Mahesh Dattani appeared at a time when the family was reorganizing itself in accordance with the exigencies of professional life. The efforts of women to work outside the home are prevailing everywhere, yet they are facing much hostility and suffering from much self-doubt and self-condemnation. Dattani's major plays are largely concerned with these changes and ensuing shift in gender relations. As his other contemporaries, Dattani sets out to emancipate women, themselves as troubled and confused as their men, only to find himself, mediated through the constraints of the characters and plots he devises, driving them back into entrenched positions again. His work thus contains a number of strong women characters, who fight their way to the centre of the stage, only to suffer one or other kind of setback, disappointment, of humiliation.

Besides a culture which entraps not only women but men too under patriarchy in Indian family, childhood sexual abuse, comment on today's generation gap and an elegant satire on the role of money in our lives, the deniable position of gays, eunuchs, aids addicted persons etc. are some of the main themes of Dattani's plays. The main protagonists in a Dattani play might be eunuchs, gay or handicapped, or women who dare to think differently from their husbands/ fathers, but Dattani himself cannot be called either a 'women's writer' or a 'gay writer'- he is simply a writer. He cannot be slotted as a writer of the marginalized, because the margins, after all, depend on where you place the centre. But the characters of all his plays suffer likely under the suppressive pressure of society and struggling for their own freedom. While writing plays he explores both the masculine and the feminine self within him. His plays are a kind of social satire which attempts a realistic portraiture at the same time. He says:

> I think my own recurring theme is the individual's struggle over societal demands of inflictions. Whether it is *Dance Like a Man* or *30Days in September* or *Tara*,

> my protagonists are striving for their own space or freedom from an invisible, self-inflicted form of oppression (Banerjee, *The Pioneer*, 4).

His plays open up other ways of seeing and experiencing the world and his plays force us to look at things we might otherwise overlook. As he points out, however, the journey needs not to be in India: it can be a journey into one's self from a stance outside one's own cultural viewpoint. Like the feminism movement in west he also believes in the fluidity which the eunuchs and homosexuals have as they have no identity problem of having wife, son or father of someone. So they are more liberated than us. Just because Dattani does talk about gay issues, some people dismiss his writing, as being "not Indian". To this his reply is:

> I am Indian: this is my time and this is my place, and I'm reflecting that in my work, and that makes it Indian (Mee, *PAJ*, 24).

Thus, Mahesh Dattani through his plays focuses on many contemporary social issues.

> I write for my milieu, for my time and place- middle class and urban Indian... My dramatic tensions arise from people who aspire to freedom from society... I am not looking for something sensational, which audiences have never seen before... some subjects, which are under-explored, deserve their space. It's no use brushing them under the carpet. We have to understand the marginalized, including the gays. Each of us has a sense of isolation within given contexts. That's what makes us individual. (*The Hindu*, 3).

Dattani advise to anyone directing his play is to "relate the play to their audience first, not to try and find the "authentic Indianness" in the play,... because that's when you get very clichéd and boring, and you're not really translating to an audience" (Mee, *PAJ*, 22).

The sense of identity dominates all his plays as he chooses to deal with themes relating to the complex workings of the modern/urban Indian family, his protagonists search for their identities within the often oppressive structures of custom, tradition, gender and sexuality within this location. The main reason behind this may be connected to his own personal life, where he was himself rooted in the Gujarati milieu but his family was displaced and had to resettle in Bangalore; as a result he was constantly in search of his identity in a place where the linguistic community was alien to his own. English education and the constant need to use this third language as the vehicle of communication then somehow made itself an integral part of his identity. His plays reinforce the experiences and narratives of the marginalized in a society where stereotypes always hold center stage; ridden with prejudice, guilt, and dishonesty and where survival is not easy for the 'misfits'. Therefore, he not only presents a truthful picture of contemporary Indian society but also creates characters from his own life. Thus sometimes he becomes autobiographical in his approach:

> My family, my friends, acquaintances- they have, all in some way or another, figured in my plays (Banerjee, *The Pioneer*, 4).

Though Dattani knows that television has taken place of theatre as a cheaper and greater entertainment source, but he is still hopeful: "I am sure that theatre is here to stay." (Chatterjee, *The Statesman*, 5). Dattani has edited a collection titled *City Plays* (2004), which brings together works of Elkunchwar, Shanta Gokhale, and Manjula Padmanabhan in what city oriented playwrights consider a theoretically significant genre.

Mahesh Dattani can be rightly held as the 'Sutradhara' in the modern theatre. The *NatyaSastra* outlines the various duties of the stage manager (Sutradhara), who had to serve as manager of the theatre company as well as one of its principal actors. Today directors play multiple roles: they write plays, plus design scenery, lighting and costumes, and Mahesh Dattani is one of them. It may be more proper to describe Dattani in the modern Indian theatre as an individual capable of performing a multitude of functions and doing most of them as well, better than most of the other theatre personnel with whom he associates. John McRae writes in his introduction to Dattani's plays:

> They are plays of today, sometimes as actual as to cause controversy, but at the same time they are plays which embody many of the classic concerns of the world drama (*The Plays*, 55).

Occasionally, the playwright introduces a novel twist, such as a narrator or dialogue spoken by groups of characters. Occasionally also songs (Carnatic song of *Morning Raaga*) or traditional dance (Kathakali in *Dance Like a Man*) are introduced, which provide variety of proceedings. He also used 'stop action' technique over which the recorded thoughts of a character are played. The acts are divided into many scenes to accommodate the technique of flashback which is so common in films but not in theatre. In most of Dattani's plays, scenes are written as though they were composed for a film; multiple scenes, each having a limited purpose with regard to the overall dramatic action. His plot moves in too many directions at once. Not a single situation is really developed, and it is certainly not developed from within. About the stage settings of Dattani, Susan Oommen says:

> His plays provide the spatial and temporal parameters within which problematizations may be reviewed. On stage he uses memory, provides physical spaces for both past and present, locates separate actions at multiple levels, transforms faces into masks, frenzy into voices, within contexts that are only too familiar (348).

For example, in *Dance Like a Man*, firstly the scene opens with the conversation of Lata and Vishwas about their plan to marry. In the course of conversation, we learn that the parents of Lata, Jairaj and Ratna, are dancers and that they are away because of the illness of one of their musicians. When they return, they are still preoccupied with the same problem and hardly pay any attention to Vishwas. The parents give approval to Vishwas's marriage but are still worried about the musician because Lata has to give an important performance the next day. Then we find Ratna talking on phone in rather 'matlabi' behaviour and then there is a scene in which it is discovered that she has a drinking problem. In another scene in which the family read the 'rave' reviews that Lata's performance has received and which seems to be her mother's efforts more than those of Lata's performance. Cut to the past where Jairaj's father disapproved of his career as a dancer and with his wife manage to suppress her husband's career and in developing her own career in this same field. In this carelessness, her son died in infancy. Finally, we see Ratna and Jairaj in old age, and infer that they have achieved what they set out to but are dead from within.

However, the audience though interested in the multiple issues in the scene are confused about their preference for concentration: in the future of the young couple, or in the father's patriarchal dominance over son, or husband-wife relationship, or the death of the son, or Jairaj's grieve ness. It is Dattani's technique to not let the audience move by any certain scene but instead we see these flat scenes from distance.

Besides through 'flashback' technique, he shows the multi-leveled stage where interior and exterior become one, geographical locations are collapsed and different places at the same time without creating disturbance in the continuity of plays. This style also helps him to present past and present at the same time through the stream of consciousness or impressionistic or interior monologue technique. Dattani makes effective use of stage lights, isolating, blending, and fading the parts of the reality he wishes to expose or withhold. As John McRae notes:

> Mahesh Dattani takes the family unit and the family setting- again and again he uses the family home as his locale- and fragments them. As relationships fall apart, so, in a way, does the visual setting. Not for him the single room set. Rather, he experiments, with great technical daring, using split sets, 'hidden' rooms, interior

> and exterior: he stretches the space and fills it in every available direction, even out front, playing with the audience and its expectations (55).

In short, his settings are as fragmented as the families who inhabit them. More attention is paid to stage set and lighting so that the internal conflict could be better brought out than the text alone was able to mediate. His early experience with film scripts and radio plays gave him an awareness of the use of lights, composition of scenes, and economy of dialogue. For using this method, he starts the plays 'in medias res' and develops the plot through conscious or unconscious images of the past of the characters.

New modes are applied to represent the new awareness of its fragmentary nature. In between the dramatic lines, Dattani uses short and long silences, sometimes in between the lines, sometimes in the incomplete lines which are completed through silence. This silence itself occurs in such an intense dramatic time that the deep touching meaning of it is self-evident to the audience. The dramatic silence is not a neutral or negative state. It is not the same as stillness on stage before the play opens; nor is it the absence of sound as in an empty hall. The dramatic silence is a time duration that carries the charge of words spoken before and the anticipation of the words to be spoken afterwards.

An important feature of Mahesh Dattnai's plays is his unique characterization. He is an impartial observer of the characters of his play. He knows the world he is talking about and shows it just the way it is the hypocrisy, the prejudices, the dilemmas, nothing is spared. And yet, if there is a point where Mahesh stumbles, it is when unconsciously the characters who have his sympathies end up much more resolved and developed even if they are not the principle ones, Sharad, from *On a Muggy Night in Mumbai*, Anarkali from *Seven Steps Around the Fire* etc. His plays are flexible enough to give its characters opportunity to make their own spaces, as he observes:

> I also know that I have a lot to say and am probably not saying it well enough. But my characters have a lot to

> say too, and they seem to be doing rather well at having their say ... I am completely aware that it is my character that has done the work for me (*CP*1, xi).

But his aim is not to focus on one person at a time, this will not direct the audience to the whole play and to the real theme and motive of the play, but with the introduction of other characters as important ones. That's why he is so successful in delineating his women, gay, eunuchs and other characters as they are portrayed with such psychological details that the audience can correlate with them. He himself says:

> I can forget my own gender. So those scenes between women didn't come from an 'outside' view point at all. In fact, I am not even sure about the politics of gender since the times I don't even think about the gender of my characters. Its only when other characters in the play react to their own gender, or the gender of those around, that the issue comes alive (Subramanyam 130).

We cannot move with the characters because the playwright does not do so himself. We don't see the relationships being created or growing or ending; we only get flat explanations about them from the characters.

Dattani seems to have created them not because he cares about them but because each one is useful in illustrating something dreadful about Indian society. And while a writer had every right to show how dreadful Indian society is, these cardboard portrayals do not show it any more than they show anything else. To show the grossness of Ratna's behaviour, the playwright would need to show a great deal more than the grossness itself; he would need to demonstrate her pain, her attempts to silence her real self, her guilt, and her memories.

Natural, Svabhavik, is also the key term as regards play composition. Psychological states of mind should be expressed as naturally as in real life, wordiness being the chief fault of bad plays. The dialogues should be composed without inflated figures of speech and with such economy, that it becomes possible to gauge the character of the persons concerned on the basis of their utterances. The plot should be so constructed as to seem self-generating, and it be possible to read all action as the expression of internal states of mind. It is for this reason that Kalidasa, Bhavabhuti, and Shakespeare, that Shakuntala, Hamlet and Macbeth were the objects of such veneration and such world frame. In playwrighting, intellect alone is of no avail. It is the study of characters from the most diverse walks of life, the exchange of dialogue with the lowest and the meanest, and knowledge of the most diverse disciplines - politics, ethics, jurisprudence, and so on that from the essential preconditions for successful composition of plays.

As in reader oriented movement, the psychological relation between the reader and a work of art is established through detachment and distance, and it is writer's duty to decide the distance for the effects on reader into attending, then his reader may be repelled; if he undertakes too many then his reader may not get the point. Dattani did this as he says:

> Where am I focusing? Where do I want the attention to be placed? If I were to present it to the audience the way I see it, they wouldn't be able to connect. So they have to be taken through a journey of the familiar before they are presented with something that is totally alien (Nair, *The Gentleman*, 2).

The work of Dattani appeared at a time when the family was recognizing itself in accordance with the exigencies of urban life and middle-class women were beginning to participate in professional life. The efforts of women to work outside the home were sporadic, tentative, few and far between, yet they faced much hostility and suffered from self-doubt and self-condemnation. Dattani's major plays are largely concerned with these changes and the ensuing shifts in gender relations. As many other contemporaries, Dattani sets out to emancipate women, themselves as troubled and confused as their men, only to find himself, mediated through the exigencies of the characters and plots he devices, driving them back into entrenched positions again. His work thus contains a number of strong women characters, who fight their way to the centre of the stage, only to suffer one or other kind of setback, disappointment or humiliation.

Then if we look at his women characters, young and old women are presented in different ways like the traditional women as the mother is portrayed with some contempt, be it Sonal of *Where There's a Will*, Prema Gowda in *Do the Needful*, Baa in *Bravely Fought the Queen*, Aruna in *Final Solutions*; while the younger women are depicted as a scheming problem solver, Lata in *Do the Needful*, Ratna in *Dance Like a Man*, Bharati in *Tara* and so on. In contrast men are not treated with such disdain and are often shown to be as victims suffering from a woman's mechanisms- Jairaj and Ratna, Patel and Bharati, Hasmukh and Preeti etc. but he does not want to say that this is a definite view of life are simply a personification of his perceptions.

At the same time while in some plays, women and men both suffer in familial ideology like *Dance Like a Man* and *Where There's a Will*, in most of his plays women suffer more and even by men as we can see this horrible scene of suffering in *Thirty Days in September* in which child sexual abusing in the life of Mala changes her perspective of thinking for life and love. This is really horrible and dangerous thing in the life of women not only suffers but at the end revolt such kind of sufferings and demand for her individuality as in *Bravely Fought the Queen*.

The socio-domestic world presented in the plays of Dattani seems self-contained, each scene being linked to the other by the forces of psychological motivation. The emotions of the characters cumulate gradually. The alienation of the self from the self as well as the environment is clear in his plays. Towards the end, they burst forth in a virtual paroxysm of words, long speeches in which they lay bare their inner conflicts and seek understanding. The audience is never addressed directly, except in *Where There's a Will*, where there is a narrator like prologue speaker, the ghost of Hasmukh Mehta. In this kind of character close-up, stage directions, sometimes extending over the length, become an important part of the dramatic text. He details every movement and change of expression of the character, seeking subtle psychological depiction of these by the player, in fact positing the total identification of the player with the played.

Dattani never provides ready-made solutions or fully resolved endings. All the plays end with a question in the audience's mind. What is going to happen next? Even after reading and watching the play again and again the audience has nothing to drive back home. But it is his trick to make audience ponder over it and just not see its ending, go back home and forget but at least contemplate over the situation, can match their own situation with those that he has seen and think whether ending should be better for such an evil at home or in the society. He aims not at changing society but only seeks to offer some scope for reflection in the hope that his plays will give the audience some kind of insight into their own lives. John McRae rightly praises the universality of the plays of Dattani:

> His plays speak across linguistic and cultural divides- they will work equally effectively in England or Italy, India or Brazil. Yet they need never be transposed out of their clearly Indian settings. As Chekhov remains resolutely Russian while his plays speak universally, so Dattani has created images, characters, and plots which reverberate with the reality of India today. They use Indian mythology, Indian traditions, Indian dance, Indian English, and Indian social problems- yet speak of themes which touch any audience: the search for individual identity inside and outside the family, the need for happiness, love, sexual fulfillment, security; the loneliness and emptiness of superficially successful lives; belonging and not belonging, the pain and pathos of keeping up appearances (56).

Mahesh Dattani, as a playwright will never be a brand. His plays have varied content and varied appeal. His characters seldom mouth lines which will be quoted by just about everyone, nor does his thematic content rise to extraordinary heights. But what makes him one of India's finest playwrights is the manner in which he speaks to the audience, straight from the heart. Whether it is in a stage play like *On a Muggy Night in Mumbai* or in the radio play like *Do the Needful*, the characters speak his words. However he maintains the position of an outsider and never allows himself room in the plays he writes. In many ways it is a non-judgmental and hence the stance of an observer- there is little attempt to advocate change or even convey a message. The plays of Dattani are not and never have been merely entertainment, although first and foremost he knows a play has to keep an audience engrossed, caring about the characters, following the twists and turns of the plot, until that final cathartic, uplifting, and moving resolution. Angelie Multani lavishes praise on Dattani for giving English Theatre a remarkable place in the Indian context:

> Indian theatre in English is speaking to us in its own distinctive voice, of traditions, of problems and situations which we encounter in our daily lives, and it is speaking in our own accents, not borrowed or cultivated ones. There is still a long way to go and much more needs to be done, but Mahesh Dattani is emerging as one of the foremost Indian contemporary playwrights, taking English theatre in this country in a completely new direction (60).

Dattani's plays deal with real scenarios that are tough to turn away from. They are couched in Indian urban speak. They shy away from myth and make-believe to tackle reality head-on, no matter what the impact of the collision. They have worked onstage when directed sensitively, or read over BBC, or somewhat less powerfully- when rendered as cinema. Some talented young playwrights like Vijjay Nair and Gautam Raja also acknowledges him as their influence or inspiration. They prove indisputably that Dattani is in sync with millions of urbanities, to whom English is an Indian language. We are his audience, his characters, and his source of sustained feedback. Alyque Padamsee, a director, to whom Mahesh Dattani is heartily indebted, says:

> At last, we have a playwright who gives sixty million English-speaking Indians an identity. Thank you, Mahesh Dattani! (*CP*1, Cover Page)

Mahesh Dattani, from his years of being a 'reluctant' playwright to a highly successful (and celebrated) one, has carried on the business, as he says, "of holding a mirror up to society" (*CP*1: xv) through an art that is both entertaining as well as issue-based; self-aware and rooted in its milieu.

REFERENCES

Ahuja, Chaman, *Theatre India.* No. 11, 2005.

Awasthi, Suresh, "Proceeding of the Round Table on the Contemporary Relevance of Traditional Theatre", in *Sangeet Natak,* July-September, 1971.

Ayyar, Raj. "Mahesh Dattani: India's Gay Cinema Comes of Age", *Gay Today,* 8.48.2004. http://gay-today.com.

Banerjee, Sumanta. *Theatre India.* No. 6, Nov. 2002.

Banerjee, Utpal K. "Interactive Theatre", *The Pioneer,* 11 June, 2004.

Banerjee, Utpal K. "World of Marginalised Gender", *The Pioneer.* July 9, 2004.

Barba, Euginio. "The steps on the River Bank", in *Rasa: The Indian Performing Arts in the Lost Twenty-Five Years,* Vol. 2, Theatre and Cinema. ed. Ananda Lal. Calcutta: Anamika Kala Sangam, 1995.

Bharucha, Rustam. *In the Name of the Secular: Contemporary Cultural Activism in India.* Delhi: OUP, 1998.

Bharucha, Rustam. *Rehearsals of Revolution: The Political Theatre of Bengal.* Calcutta: Seagull Books, 1983.

Bhatia, Nandi. "Staging a Change: Modern Indian Drama and the colonial Encounter", Ph.D. diss., University of Texas Austin, 1996.

Bhatia, Nandi. *Acts of Authority, Acts of Resistance.* New Delhi: OUP, 2004.

Bhatta, S. Krishna. "Kailasam's English Plays", in *Perspectives on Indian Drama in English,* ed. M.K. Naik and Mkashi S. Punekar. Madras: OUP, 1977.

Bowers, Faubion, "Introduction", in *Asif Currimbhoy's Plays.* New Delhi: Oxford & IBH.

Chatterjee, Sumita. "Theatre is here to stay", *The Statesman.* 5 July, 2005.

Dalmia, Vasudha. *Poetics, Plays and Performances: The Politics of Modern Indian Theatre.* Delhi: OUP, 2006.

Dasgupta; Uma Mahadevan; eds. "The Minute I Write a Play, I want to direct it", 2001. http://www.maheshdattani.com.

Dattani, Mahesh. "Contemporary Indian Theatre and Ist Relevance", *JIWE* (The Journal of Indian Writing in English). Vol. 30, No. 1, Jan. 2002.

Dattani, Mahesh. *Collected Plays.* New Delhi: Penguin India, 2000.

Dattani, Mahesh. *Final Solutions and other Plays.* Manas, 1994.

Dattani, Mahesh. *The Hindu,* Sunday, March 9, 2003.

Desouza, Eunice, "Some Recent Plays in English", *Perspectives on Indian Drama in English.*

Dharwadkar, Aparna Bhargava. "Translation and Translators", *Theatre India,* Nov. 15-19, 2002.

Dharwadkar, Aparna Bhargava. Theatre of Independence, Drama, *Theory and Urban Performance in India Since 1947.* New Delhi: OUP, 2006.

Elkunchwar, Mahesh. "Experimentation in Marathi Theatre", in *Marathi Theatre.* New Delhi: Maharashtra Information centre, 1995.

George, K.M. *Hindi Drama, Comparative Indian Literature.* Madras: Macmillan India, 1984.

Ghosh, Bhaskar. *Theatre India,* No. 11, 2005.

Gokhale, Shanta. *Playwright at the Centre: Marathi Drama from 1843 to the Present.* Calcutta: Seagull, 2000.

Gupta, Das. *The Indian Stage,* Vol. I. Calcutta: Metropolitan Printing and Publishing House, 1938.

Home Department Proceedings, "Draft Bill to Empower Certain Dramatic Performances", March 1876, National Archives of India, Delhi.

International Herald Tribune, 25 September, 1990.

Kanhailal, Haisnam. *Theatre India.* No. 11, 2005.

Karnad, Girish. "Introduction", *Three Plays.* New Delhi: OUP, 1994.

Karnad, Girish. "Performance, Meaning and the Materials of Modern Indian Theatre", Interview with Aparna Dharwadkar, *New Theatre Quaterly.* 44, 1995.

Karnad, Girish; Paul, Rajinder; eds. *Contemporary Indian Theatre: Interviews with Playwrights and Directors.* New Delhi: Sangeet Natak Akademi, 1989.

Katyal, Anjum, "Of Page and Stage: An Interview with Mahesh Dattani", *Seagall Theatre Quaterly* - 24, Jan 2000. http://www.seagullindia.com.

Kumar, Meenakshi. "All the World's a Stage for Dattani". *HT City,* Wednesday, 17 December, 2003.

Kumar, Sunaina. "Theatre Producers don't Back Original Work", *Times of India.* 25 July, 2005.

Lal, Anand, ed. *The Oxford Companion to Indian Theatre.* New Delhi: OUP, 2004.

Lal, Ananda, ed. *Rasa: The Indian Performing Arts in the Last Twenty - Five Years,* Vol. 2, Theatre and Cinema. Calcutta: Anamika Kala Sangam, 1995.

Maheshwari, Belu. "Avante Garde Playwright", *Spectrum - The Sunday Tribune.* 14 Jan 2001. http://www.tribuneindia.com.

Mc Rae, John. "We Live in the Flicker: Reflections in Time on the Plays of Mahesh Dattani", in *The Plays of Mahesh Dattani: Critical Perspectives,* ed. Angelie Multani. New Delhi: Pencraft International, 2007.

Mee, Erin B. "Invisible Issues: An Interview with Mahesh Dattani", in *The Plays of Mahesh Dattani: Critical Perspectives,* ed. Angelie Multani. New Delhi: Pencraft International, 2007.

Mee, Erin B. "Mahesh Dattani: Invisible Issues", *Performing Arts Journal* 55, 1997.

Mee, Erin B. *Drama Contemporary: India.* New Delhi: OUP, 2002.

Mehta, Kumud. "Indian Theatre Today - Grappling with New Realities", Marg, Special Issue on Aspects of the Performing Arts of India. 34.3, 1981.

Mohanty, Sachidananda. "Theatre: Reaching out to People: An Interview with Mahesh Dattani", in *The Plays of Mahesh Dattani: A Critical Response,* ed. R.K. Dhawan and Tanu Pant. New Delhi: Prestige Publications, 2005.

Mukherjee, Meenakshi. *The Twice Born Fiction: Themes and Techniques of the Indian Novel in English.* New Delhi: Heinemann, 1971.

Multani, Angelie. "On Mahesh Dattani's *Dance like a Man*: The Politics of Production and Performance", in *STQ*, Issue 11, Sep 1996.

Naik, M.K.; Shankar Mokashi - Punekar. *Perspectives on Indian Drama in English,* Madras: OUP, 1997.

Nair, Anita. "An Unveiling of a Playwright in Three Acts", *The Gentleman,* May 2001. http://www.anitanair.net/pages/profiles-md.htm.

Nair, Anita. "Mahesh Dattani: A Profile". http://www.anitanair.htm.

Nath, Rajinder. "A Very Creative Idea Can Also Degenerate", *Sangeet Natak,* 77-78, 1985.

Oommen, Susan. "Inventing Narratives, Arousing Audiences: The Plays of Mahesh Dattani", *New Theatre Quarterly* 68, Cambridge University Press, Vol. XVII, Part 4, Nov. 2001.

Paul, Rajinder. *Enact,* editorial, May, 1971.

Pradhan, Sudhi, ed. *Marxist Cultural Movement in India,* Vol. 2, 1947-1958. Calcutta: Mrs. Santi Pradhan, 1983.

Sangeet Natak Akademi Report, 1953-1958.

Sircar, Badal, "Interview", *India Today.* December 16-31, 1985.

Subramanyam, Lakshmi. "A Dialogue with Mahesh Dattani", in *Muffled Voice: Women in Modern Indian Theatre,* New Delhi: Shakti Books, 2002.

Uniyal, Ranu. "Convering with Mahesh Dattani", in *The Plays of Mahesh Dattani: A Critical Response,* ed., R.K. Dhawan and Tanu Pant. New Delhi: Prestige Publications, 2005.

Varadpande, Manohar Laxman. *History of Indian Theatre.* New Delhi: Abhinav Publication, 1987.

Vardhan, Manisha. "I'm No Crusader; I'm a Theatre Person: Mahesh Dattani", June, 2004. http://www.3 to 6.com.

Walling, Michael. "A Note on the Play: *Bravely Fought the Queen*", in *Collected Plays of Mahesh Dattani,* New Delhi: Penguin, 2000.

Yarnow, Ralph. *Indian Theatre: Theatre of Origin, Theatre of Freedom.* Richmond, U.K.: Curzon Press, 2001.

2

Demolishing Stereotypes 'Men/Women'

Identity politics is not a new phenomenon within the feminist movement and has long been the centre of debates separating philosophical strands and chronological waves of feminist thought. It should also be noted that identity politics surrounding feminism and feminist solidarity is not limited to a particular geographical location, despite the Western media obsession with the 'Backlash' and specific references to a new 'Third Wave' in which women return to a reassertion of their femininity and partake in a bargain with patriarchy. Instead, identity politics is a factor shaping women's realities across the world from the post-communist states of Eastern Europe to the provinces of India and Pakistan too, as it has been seen, the heartland of the United States.

Valentine Moghadam, a prominent scholar of identity politics, notes that identities, in a post-structural cultural analysis, are products of historical and discursive practices, primarily influenced by culture, the state, mass media, religious bodies and educational institutions. She asserts that identities are neither fixed nor primordial, but instead fluid inter-sectionalities that are shaped by social and cultural surroundings and 'reflect the symbiosis of the economic, the cultural, and the political', in both the national and international context. (*Identity*, 9) Therefore, any analysis that undertakes a study of identities and intersectionalities must also be concurrently analyzing the surrounding climate and addressing the various powerful forces that vie for attention and reflection in women's chosen identities. Thus we are able to see that far from being outside the sphere of influence, women's identities are but a part of the complex web of characteristics that define the New Global Order.

Dualism and binary opposition are political tactics fostered by those in power in order to maintain hegemonic control and support. Diane Bell provides a helpful conceptualization in warning: 'Beware of binaries ... The juxtapositions are not a matter of simple opposites but rather mask the power of one side of the binary to control the other. (*Hawthrone*, 433) It comes as no surprise, then, that in the construction of simplistic, dualistic politics that states 'you are either with us or against us', feminist voices, with their celebration and embrace of plurality and multi-perspectivalism, are often left powerless in the face of rigid dichotomies.

Valentine Moghadam has explained the difficulties of feminist multi-perspectivalism in saying:

> Women have been exposed to contradictory, dissonant messages and practices, filled with false expectations and aspirations. This has rendered them vulnerable and receptive to an ideology that simplifies reality and promises escape from role conflict and ambiguity. (*Identity*, 9)

The separation is not only between women and the rest of the world, or feminism and women's issues, but just as strongly, and more fundamentally, between what is perceived as cultural/artistic, what is seen as theoretical and what is considered political. Identity politics has its roots in a very important tenet of equal but different, not same; it resists the power structures of caste, class and gender within progressive politics. In fact, it often seems to have become a peculiar form of wielding power: as if, now that your box has been recognized, you dare not leave it. A sense that we must forever work along the lines of what has been codified and ordained; blurring these lines is not permitted. What is individual and human in us with the universal, the socio-economic common identity we each embody?

Religious fundamentalism has been an equal threat to feminist identity and women's solidarity. Valentine Moghadam has noted that 'a central manifestation of fundamentalism-be it Islamic, Christian, Jewish, or Hinduism- is an attempt to circumscribe women's freedom and identity', and increases in fundamentalist practices have resulted in further divisions between women of conservative and liberal political and social values. (*Identity*, 9)

> Mother: Why should a boy not do housework?
>
> Son: Because the boy has to earn money when he grows up, therefore he must study well.
>
> Mother: You are wrong, my son. Women also make an earning for the family. And, there is a lot to learn in housework- house cleaning, cooking, laundry. By doing housework you will develop various skills of the body and will feel self reliant. In good housework you need to use your eyes, hands and brain. Therefore these activities are educative and they build your character. Men and women both need to be educated equally in housework because the home belongs to both. (Joshi, *Gandhi*, vii-viii)

The text is in the form of the mother teaching the child, taken from the primer written by Mahatma Gandhi for the children of primary schools. Because of his self-feminization and his feminization of politics, Gandhi was initiated as the parent of 'Indian Women Movement' and his depiction of women's innate qualities are enthusiastically and eagerly received by many feminists as it enlarged and affirmed their self-definitions.

This concept of 'otherness' stuck to women from the ancient times, continued to the present times, where women, in spite of their career growth in public life, always had been 'the last to be hired and the first to be fired' in the all spheres of her life, 'private' or 'public'. This differentiation is very well described by Simone De Beauvoir in *The Second Sex:*

> She is simply what man decrees; thus she is called "the sex", by which is meant that she appears essentially to the male as a sexual being. For him she is sex – absolute sex, no less. She is defined and differentiated with reference to man and not he with reference to her; she is the incidental, the inessential as opposed to the essential. He is the Subject, he is the Absolute – she is the Other. (xxii)

While fully recognizing that a woman's position is subjected to external influence, the fundamental identities like 'feminine-passive' and 'masculine-active' assert themselves in all known cultures and races, in various forms and various quantative proportions. Traditionally, the inferior words connoted to women are 'conjugal, slavery, annihilation, servant, devaluation, tyranny, passive, forbidden, doomed, abused, trapped, prey, domineer, helpless, imprisoned'. This immediately suggests a masochistic view of life, reinforced by the fact that for the male quite an opposite vocabulary has dug into like a tick: 'free, busy, active, proud, arrogant, master, existent, liberty, adventure, daring, strength, courage'.

A glimpse of the past status is essential for understanding the contemporary status of woman in India for several reasons, the product of the past socio-cultural configuration in which Indian womanhood was defined. The social system and the culture of any given time of any given society bear the mark of the social system and the culture preceding it. In India, the position of woman is not different from any other civilization and Simone De Beauvoir cogently defines it:

> The laws of Manu define woman as a vile being who should be held in slavery. Leviticus likens her to the beasts of burden owned by the patriarch. The law of Solon give her no rights. The Roman code puts her under

> guardianship and asserts her 'imbecility'. Canon law regards her as "the devil's doorway". The Koran treats woman with utter scorn. (*The Second*, 80)

The representation of women in literature, even in ancient Indian and western scriptures like *ManuSmriti, Ramayana, Mahabharata*, etc. is felt to be one of the most important forms of 'socialization', since it provided the role models which indicated to women, and men, what constituted acceptable versions of the 'feminine' and legitimate feminine goals and aspirations. Aristotle asserts:

> The female is a female by virtue of a certain lack of qualities; we should regard the female nature as afflicted with a natural defectiveness. (Beauvoir, *The Second*, xxii)

These lines expose what might be called the mechanisms of patriarchy, that is, the cultural 'mind-set' in men and women which perpetuated sexual inequality. Critical attention was given to books by male writers in which influential as typical images of women were constructed. Therefore, we cannot rely on exciting ideologies as they are all products of a male supremacist culture.

Indian women are credited with having resisted patriarchal oppression for more than 2000 years. The coalescence of isolated resistance into a movement in India in the nineteenth century emerged at about the same time as in the United States and Europe. Since the time of the first settlers in India, women were assigned a sub-ordinate role within the family, irrespective of wealth or condition, and were denied the political and civil rights enjoyed by men. The history of Indian civilization has been a history of alienation of the feminine world from the masculine world. Before the advent of the Vedic Aryan, there was pre Aryan Dravidian civilization in India which has come to light from the excavations at Mohenjodaro and Harappa, now famous as 'Indus Valley Civilization'. It transpires from a close look at the figurines that the divine form of that time was more prominently represented by Mother Goddess and not by the male God. This implies that there was matriarchy at that time and the status of women were higher. The advent of the Vedic Aryan (C. 4000-1000 B.C.) seems to have overturned the feminine ideal of pre-Aryan, Dravidian Indus Valley Civilization; the matriarchy came to be replaced by patriarchy. After the victory, Aryans introduced slavery in northern India. The seeds of inferiority of daughters and the worth of sons were sown, during the Vedic period, by according them certain duties by the 'four Vedas' brought by Aryan. The conquered women, taken as wives by Aryans, had no knowledge of the Vedic rituals which further degraded them. Consequently, women's role in Vedic rites and sacrifices turned out to be a mere formality and it gradually diminished as the days passed on. The Vedic Aryans were invaders, nomadic tribes who did not know writing, whose economy was a pastoral one, whose dominant gods were all male, considered the original inhabitants as their enemies and tried to make them inferiors and slaves.

Although, the Vedic period is said to be the most honored days of women where they distinguished themselves in learning, possessed and inherited property, participated in assemblies and occupied central place in the domestic domain, but it is not sure whether all women enjoyed the same rights and privileges. In post-Vedic period, near about 300 B.C., the position of the women began to be more and more degraded and continued to be demeaned. In the following epic period, Buddhist days and Muslim period, the women saw their worst days. The Hindu women were frightened from the Muslim invaders. All sorts of vices such as child marriage, purdah system, illiteracy and others became rampant. Therefore, the expanding frontier and the conquest of Muslims made Indian civilization essentially male. According to Altekar:

> Thus, for nearly 2000 years from 20B.C. to 1800 A.D., the position of women steadily deteriorated though she was fondled by the parents, loved by her husband and revered by her children. The revival of *sati*, the prohibition of remarriage, the spread of *purdah* and the greater prevalence of polygamy made her position very bad. (*The Position*, 34)

Bhakti movement did try to improve the condition of the women and the downtrodden, but it was lost with the rise of asceticism. The Renaissance of Indian women began with Raja Ram Mohan Roy (1774) in West Bengal in British period. He opposed the custom of *sati* and polygamy and encouraged widow-remarriage. It is the effort of him and others like Devendra Nath Tagore (1817), Ishwar Chandra Vidyasagar (1820), Rabindra Nath Tagore (1861), Swami Vivekanand (1863), Swami Dayanand Saraswati (1824) etc. that enlightened Indian public opinion. Significant legal reforms were the abolition of *sati* in 1827, the suppression of infanticide in 1725 and 1804, and the removal of restriction on remarriage of widow in 1856. This led to questioning of age-old social system. Reform movement of the renaissance period brought to the fore the plight of women. But, women's status remained at its nadir.

In the national movement, Gandhiji and Nehru drew women in the struggle for freedom which, in turn, created awareness among them towards their rights and status. But this was the independence movement and not the women's movement, and, hence, relatively less fortunate for women. Ideologically, the woman is considered a completely inferior species, inferior to the male and steadily deteriorating. Individually she has no personality; socially she is kept in utter subjection; morally, she is considered lacking the ethical fiber; economically, she is treated not worthy to have right to property; politically, she is excluded from the power positions. The portraits of woman in the Hindu India are paradoxical and sometimes contradictory. She is a 'Devi' (Goddess) as well as 'pramada' (seducer). She is sincere and truth-loving as well as weak in character and poor in judgment. She is the queen of the house as well as not worthy for freedom in her own house. The hypocrisy of Indian civilization and social practices is rightly exposed as there were two things on which all these books, the Dharma Shastras, the sacred epics, epics, the puranas and the modern poets (the popular preaches of the present day and orthodox high-caste man) were agreed, that women of high and low caste, as a class, were bad, rather very bad, worse than demons, as unholy as untruth and that they could not get moksha as men. The only hope of their getting this much desired liberation from karma and its results that is countless millions of birth and deaths and untold suffering was the worship of their husbands.

In post-Independence India the contemporary feminist movement began by basing itself firmly on principles of equality and asserting that gender-based structures, such as the sexual division of labour, oppressed and subordinated women. The difference between men and women was held largely to be a biological one, which should not affect women's right to equality with men in both public and private spheres. The symbol of the mother was now only rarely used as a rallying or entitling device: instead, two self-images replaced it, the woman as daughter and the working woman. Both in a way turned attention away from the woman as mother or wife: the former focused on the formation of a woman rather than her role; the latter looked at her productive rather than reproductive capacities. This marked a sharp turn from the pre-independence period, which was almost exclusively concerned with women in relation to men. But these reforms could not flourish because the leaders of the nation in the present times selfishly thought it fit to readjust the ancient laws with the new prevailing conditions so that they could deal adequately with the growing problems of the time. And, for that matter, every Hindu rule wished to govern according to the primeval law without least deviation in the beaten track marked out by Manu. The religious practices, rituals, scriptures and percepts which themselves are made by men, therefore, form the core of religious teachings which have been the part of historical forces that have created for women their existing secondary status in society. broken homes, conflicts and unhappy interfamilial relations, widening of spheres of occupational and social activities, radio, movies, television-each has inadvertently contributed to the evil surroundings in which both men and women have been growing over the last four decades.

The reason behind this continual deterioration of women from ancient times can be recounted by Marxist view of feminism, following the work of Karl Marx. According to him, hierarchical class relations (build on unequally distributed or owned sources of wealth, including monetary and other resources) are seen as the source of coercive power and operation, of all inequalities ultimately. Sexual operation is seen as a dimension of class power. In this model, the earliest forms of class division historically gave rise to male dominance; class oppression predates sex oppression and therefore of/ class hierarchy, led to the treatment of women as property. Power is not associated with sex but with the imperatives of class, private wealth, property and profit- for example, unequal power relations within capitalism- as derived from patriarchy (social systems of male domination, the rule of men).

Karl Marx and Fredrick Engels (Marxist theoretician) in the German Ideology had noted the sexual division was the first division of labour. Engels, saw the family as the first product of totalitarian and capitalistic impulses in men, "Within the family the husband is the bourgeois and the wife represents the proletariat" (Engels, *The Origin*, 65-66), with women held as property, and maintained that the myths of domesticity must be shattered in order for all people to enjoy equality and freedom. He says:

> The social institutions under which men [and women] of a definite historical epoch and of a definite country live are conditioned by ... the stage of development of labour, on the one hand, and of the family, on the other.... The less the development of labour and the more limited its volume of production ... the more preponderatingly does the social order appear to be dominated by ties of sex. (*The Origin*, Introduction)

In her phenomenal study *Sexual Politics* (1970), Kate Millet says that the essence of politics is power, and therefore all the cultures are saturated by a male supremacy that affects all aspects of our lives from war to literature. Kate

Millet argues that patriarchy as a universal mode of power relationships and domination for it penetrates class divisions, different societies and different historical epochs. It is the primary oppression simply because of its longevity; and specific variations within patriarchy are less significant than its general truth. This dominance which Millet defines as 'patriarchy' constitutes perhaps the most pervasive ideology of our culture and provides its most fundamental concept of power.

Simone De Beauvoir summed up the hierarchal relationships between men and women assumed in the concept of 'different but complementary', in these terms: 'He is the subject, he is the absolute- she is the *Other.* woman is not so much second-rate man in this context as that which is 'not man'.

In this Marxist perspective, the history of the devaluating of Indian women can be summarized in three stages: historical, materialist and psychological. Firstly, there was the historical emergence and development of systems of male domination through the creation of religious scriptures in ancient times. Secondly, the sexual division of labor based on these books (that is, to explore the 'material' – or concrete structural, bodily, physical-aspects of social organization which divide up and differentially value tasks and activities on the basis of sex). And finally, recognition of the deep-rooted nature of male dominance is in the very formation and organization of our selves (the psychological or unconscious internalizing of social patterns of sexual hierarchy). It is this psychological politics of the 'private sphere', which entrapped both male and female in the present times, is represented by Dattani in his plays. If one takes patriarchal government to be the institution whereby that half which is male, the principles of patriarchy appear to be two fold: male shall dominate female, elder male shall dominate younger.

Jacques Derrida understands Saussure, in his construction of structuralism, to have privileged the oral over the written, and notes that this primacy is located at the heart of the western philosophical tradition. In his deconstruction of Saussure, Derrida expands his argument; dichotomous oppositions similar to the pair writing/speech underline much of Western logic, and inherent to the logic of this opposition is the subtle privileging of one and the repression and subordination of the 'other'. This then assures the unique valorization of the 'positive' pole... and, consequently, the repressive subordination of all 'negativity'. Although Derrida limits his interest to 'western' logic, similar prioritized dichotomies can be identified in traditional Indian value system.

Gayatri Spivak in *Can the Subaltern Speak?* analyzes the question of female subaltern, when she describes women as doubly marginalized subjects in colonial/ postcolonial discourses: "within the effaced itinerary of the subaltern subject the track of sexual difference is doubly affected. It is rather, that, both as object of colonialist historiography and as subject of insurgency, the ideological construction of gender keeps the male dominate, if, in the context of colonial production, the subaltern has no history and cannot speak, the female as female is more deeply in shadow". Spivak quotes female subaltern as "doubly effected", the "otherness" of postcolonial literature.

Patriarchal society is a pre-capitalist social formation that has historically existed in varying forms in Europe and Asia in which property, residence, and descent proceed through the male line. In classic patriarchy, the senior man has authority over everyone else in the family, including younger men, and women are subject to distinct forms of control and subordination.

Just as in capitalism what a worker produces is not considered the property of the worker, so in a patriarchal context a woman's products - whether their children or rugs- are not considered her property but those of the patriarchal family. In a patriarchal context, women are considered a form of property. Their honour- and, by extension, the honor of their family-depends in great measure on their virginity and good conduct.

The real society, then, is one in which individuals are integrated into a moral community, bound together by faith, by common moral values, and by obeying the dictates of the family and religion....

While male and female roles are each respected and essential and complementary components of God's plan, men are the spiritual leaders and decision-makers in the family. It is women's role to support men in their position of higher authority through altruism and self-sacrifice. (Klatch, *SIFNS*, 675-676)

According to Mann the patriarchal society is one in which power is held by male heads of households. There is also clear separation between the public and private spheres of life. In the private sphere of the household, the patriarch enjoys arbitrary power over all junior males, all females and all children. In the public sphere, power is shared between male patriarchs according to whatever other principles of stratification operate. Whereas many, perhaps most, men expect to be patriarchs at some point in their life cycle, no female holds any formal public position of economic, ideological, military, or political power. Indeed, females are not allowed into this public realm of power. Within the household they may influence their male patriarch informally, but this is their only access to power. Contained within patriarchy are two fundamental nuclei of stratification: the household/family/lineage nexus and the dominance of the male gender.

The patriarchal belt is characterized by extremely restrictive codes of behaviour for women, rigid gender segregation, and a powerful ideology linking family honor to female virtue, as Kabeer notes:

> Men are entrusted with safeguarding family honor through their control over female members; they are backed by complex social arrangements that ensue the protection- and dependence- of women. (*New Left Review*, 95)

Nevertheless, the patriarchal family and patriarchal ideology persist in India and all over the world, because the law is always out of step with society; there is always a gap between the legal rules and existing social realities. Patriarchy's chief institution is the family. It is both a mirror of and a connection with the larger society; a patriarchal unit within a patriarchal whole. Mediating between the individual and the social structure, the family does affect control and conformity.

The family not only encourages its own members to adjust and confirm, but acts as a unit in the government of the patriarchal state which rules its citizens through its family heads. The eldest male parent is absolutely supreme in the household. His domination extends to life and death and is an unqualified over his children and their houses as over his slaves. All children thus become 'subjects' (develop a self) through the operation of a masculine regulatory principle.

According to Lacan, 'civilization' itself is the 'Law of the Father'. The self and sexuality are socially constructed in that there can be no (sexed) self- no masculine or feminine person- prior to the formation of the subject in language. For Lacan, each person becomes a person, enters human culture, by internalizing society's communicative rules or Symbolic order. This occurs through the formation of a separate and sexually specific (unconscious) self in the process of learning language. Individuals can only speak in the tongue of the Symbolic order but that order is viewed in psychoanalytic terms as the 'Law of the Father.'

Derrida proposes that meaning in the Symbolic order is not inevitable or intrinsic but is constantly being culturally and linguistically produced through a process of hierarchal differentiation. Therefore, these critics are concerned with the deconstruction or unpacking of the cultural/linguistic assumptions regarding the fixity and inevitability of forms of power- categories like sex, class and race/ethnicity with the aim of opening up alternative possibilities. Therefore postmodern/ poststructuralist feminists are critical of universalizing/ normalizing procedures, they question any assumption of a shared singular identity among women, an identity typically conceived as based in a universalized experience of oppression.

The identity politics that is being played in a new global order in the present times are largely about a struggle for power which is relevant in all the plays of Dattani. Within these powerful discourses, the battle for identity and women's allegiance rages on. These binary oppositions continue to tear us apart: personally and politically, which also poses a threatening challenge to women, who are lost in the sea of identity politics.

One must remember that it is not only men who play the fundamentalist role, but that 'women are also fundamentalist policy-leading characters, acting as spokes persons in the defense of family, morality, and decency.' (Correa, *DAWN*, 2). There was yet another aspect of the control over female sexuality. Since patriarchal society is not only about the domination of men over all women but also domination of some men over others, one way in which this domination is ensured by denying access to women or withholding women from junior men by their superiors. Men too suffer under the repressive burden of fixed gender identity and roles subscribed to them. The chapter unravels this sophistication in every modern family in India by every member in the family whether male or female through the plays of Dattani and their strife and struggles to come out from them.

Like Gandhi, Dattani too completely displaced the fixed gender identities and stereotypical ideologies in our society belonging to 'male' and 'female' as it prevails in the civilization of the whole world. Dattani uses his pen as a weapon to demolish male authority and hierarchical power structure and represents a point of view to recognize the world realities, a positivist holistic approach to life, a step towards sanity in human relationship, and perhaps the only mode for preservation of human existence on this planet.

There is no gendered 'reality', that the concepts 'man' and 'woman' are as some would put it, 'always already' fictive since human identity is itself a tenuous, textually produced epiphenomenon. The words 'woman' and 'man', 'female' and 'male', 'feminine' and 'masculine' are socially determined signifiers. 'Female' and 'male are inexorably enmeshed in the materiality and mythology of history which have almost always been experienced as gendered. Dattani lead to the deconstruction of the opposition between traditionally 'masculine' and traditionally 'feminine' values confronting the full political force and reality of such categories. He says in an interview to Lakshmi Subramanyam:

> Men and women are the biggest stereotypes in the whole world. (*Muffled*, 131)

Dattani, therefore, aims at rising of the consciousnesses of an entire culture. Right from childhood, beliefs and attitudes held in perpetuating an inferior position for the woman. Some of these are defined in stereotypical roles in text/religious books, unequal pay for equal work, and the traditional division of labour within the family. He envisages profound changes in traditional social structures, such as the family, in the economic role and power of women, and finally in the fundamental attitudes and personal relationships, leading to a just social order.

Mahesh Dattani resembles postmodernist in the rejection of the notion of foundational truth or essence in favour of a recognition that meaning/truth is not eternal or impartial but constructed, through exclusion and repression. Dattani insists that resistance to male privilege does not involve taking as given what has been supposedly associated with women and men and thus he refuse to sanctify a persecuted feminine and masculine identity supposedly shared by all women and men. Because of the concern to destabilize or deconstruct unitary conceptions of identity/self and their related skepticism regarding the emancipatory potential of such conceptions, Dattani urges the abandonment of any notion of identity, including sexual/ gender identity. Therefore, his plays can not be said to represent 'identity crises.' Rather they exhibit a complete deconstruction of identity and this freedom raises his characters to be 'alive', an elevation from deadly old customs and beliefs.

Gagnon and Simon have argued that sexuality is subject to socio-cultural moulding to a degree surpassed by few other forms of human behaviour. Foucault too rejects sex as an autonomous realm, a natural force. Rather, sexuality was seen as a historical apparatus. In other words, this approach recognizes the social and historical sources of sexual definitions. Foucault also rejects the 'very idea of a stable, centered identity as a repressive fiction' and construes resistance to power as resistance to (or even liberation from) identity. Foucault is of the view which regards the sexual self, indeed all that the self is, as 'a series of performances.' (Fraser, *Revaluing*, 7) The same is developed by Judith Butler, 'there is no gender identity behind the expressions of gender; that identity is performatively constituted by the very 'expressions' that are said to be its results.' (Benhabib, *The Polity*, 80)

Butler opposed the notion that the feminist movement requires the concept of a feminine identity: it means that there exist essential factors that define a woman as a woman. Instead, she elaborates the view that the fundamental features which define gender are social and cultural productions that produce the illusory effect of being natural. Butler proposes instead that we consider gender as a 'performative'- that to be masculine or feminine or homosexual is not something that one is, but a pre-established condition that one repeatedly enacts.

In all the plays of Dattani, the characters are always behind some visible or invisible mask on to play the gender roles, provided by the fixed traditional mindset, as it really happens to everyone in society consciously or unconsciously. All the activities in our life are a kind of performance to hide the real inner self behind the hypocritical faces, which is necessary to live in harmony in the hypocritical society. Therefore 'the stage is the world, and the world is the stage' for Dattani. As he puts it:

> I am so used to creating imaginary circumstances for imaginary people to act upon, putting it all behind an

> illusive mask of reality. Now the mask is elusive. It's all got to be real. I don't have my characters to hide behind; prodding them to say things I would not say and do things that I dare not do. (*The Week*, 5)

Dattani here echoes the words of Shakespeare who compared stage to the real life in his play *As You Like It*:

> All the world's a stage,
> And all the men and women merely players;
> They have their exists and their entrances;
> And one man in his time plays many parts. (Act 2, Scene 7)

In the five plays, discussed in this chapter, *Bravely fought the Queen*, *Tara*, *Thirty Days in September*, *Where There's a Will* and *Dance Like a Man*, the accent is not only the conflict of women with men but women with women and men with men themselves under the repressive culture, and a generational encounter to dismantle traditional conventions inflicted on them. We encounter characters that struggle for some kind of freedom and happiness under the weight of conventions, cultural construction of gendered identities and repressed desires. Together the plays interrogate all these and many more assumptions, and also testify to the spirit of rebellion, continue to motivate women and men even in situations of extreme opprations. Thus the plays of Dattani redefine gender issues in theatre as not only the problems of suppression and marginalization but also the effort to employ theatre as an instrument of change the Indian concept of the gender issues. To evaluate this theme, the chapter is divided in two parts: first part shows the construction and perpetuation of stereotypical roles by older generations to younger, whether to men or women (or accepting the mask), while Second part deconstruct these roles by new generation and for this the strong 'women' and 'weak' men is created by Dattani in his plays (or refuting the mask).

(a) Construction of gendered identity

Society is a masked ball, where everyone hides his real character, and reveals it by hiding. — Ralph Waldo Emerson "Worship" (Kimmel, *The Gendered*, 93)

Dattani's presentation of women in a fractured social space that constantly shifts them to a patriarchal space of control is interesting. His keen and astute insight into the position of women in a middle class domestic household as 'marginal' is worthy of appreciation. *Bravely Fought the Queen* presents the ways in which exploitation is now couched in terms of culture and refinement. Act one begins as a comedy of manners, in a hypocritical illusory surface of the mask, on a fashionable but ill-maintained living room of Jiten and Dolly Trivedi (locked in a loveless marriage with an uncaring husband). The audience is ushered into the women's world, with the mellifluous thumri by Naina Devi in the background and the focus is on Dolly who sits filing her nails abstractedly and having a mud mask (symbol of pretence and falsity) on the face. Alka, her sister, enters with full make-up and sari- a preparation for going out for the evening with her husband Nitin, for which Dolly is also getting ready. This is a projection of image of housewives in a stereotypical manner.

The action starts with the arrival of an unexpected visitor - Lalitha - who says that she had been asked by Jiten Trivedi, the boss of her husband Sridhar, to meet Dolly that very evening to discuss the masked ball where "everyone will be in costumes! And will have masks on!" (*CP*1, 237), to be held as an event-launch for ReVaTee "a new range of colour coordinated nightwear and underwear for women". This again is a symbolic representation of society, where everyone will be in costumes and masks to live in the forced harmony of stereotypical societical ideologies. And with this revelation, the unusual change of plan is introduced that the dinner is called off is announced by Lalitha. So later on when Dolly and Lalitha discuss the masked ball, the connotations of the mask are impossible to miss- the introduction of the world of make-believe of untruths, of paste-on realities and of the need to hide behind a façade to survive in the hypocritical world by their false performances. As Michael Walling puts it:

> This is a play about performance; and uses the theatre to demonstrate how, in a world of hypocrisy, acting becomes a way of life. Paradoxically, it is only by the overt performance of the theatre that such acting can be exposed for what it is. (*CP*1, 230)

With this revelation, the whole act of becoming suitable for the role of a wife is ridiculed by Dattani, and the dark secrets under the surface level begin to be unfolded, even after the continual negation of revealing her personal tragedy by Dolly as she wants to fit in the social identity given to her which keeps her to be always masked.

> LALITHA. Afraid?
>
> DOLLY. Afraid I would crack my mask. (*CP*1, 234)

But Dolly could not prevent the cracking of mask of happiness and harmony that social order ensures for patriarchy to continue for a long time as like other women she also used to be afraid of her husband, afraid of being tortured by him. We can recall Germaine Greers comments and co relate them with the women of Indian families:

> Women are afraid of man. Women can be routinely insulted and humiliated for years on end, repeatedly raped and sexually abused and yet keep silence, made to endure a life of kicks and blows from a husband, because they are afraid. They endure unending agonies because they have been made to believe that if they run away, they will be followed and much worse will be done to them and to their children. The beaten woman does not call the police because she knows that sooner or later, once the police have finished with the man who is oppressing her, he will return and do something unimaginably worse than any of the abominable things he has already done. The woman paralyzed by terror exists in her own mind as well as that of her abuses to be abused. She can see no way out, no possible rescue, because fear has blinded her. (*The Whole*, 272)

Being neglected by her husband Jiten, Dolly tries to fulfill her desire for love and care by a secret lover in Kanhaiya. Kanhaiya (who may be illusory or real) is a nineteen year old grandson of a friend of the vacationing cook who stays in the servant's quarters outside the house and who comes for clandestine trysts in the kitchen. She is taught to bear up every humiliation, beating, and molestation; thus she does not speak and stays as a slave in the family. And thus she becomes very vulnerable to violence and a victim of humiliation, torture and exploitation within the four walls of her house away from public gaze. The most tragic thing in her life is her own daughter Daksha, who delivers prematurely, beaten by Jiten while she is pregnant, and consequently the child is mentally retarded.

The play explores the psychological damage caused to women in the Trivedi household, by the prejudiced men who signify patriarchy. This is a play about sinners and their secret guilt; it is about violence against women, about exploitation of the weaker, about the mean, squalid corporate world. The play dramatizes the emptiness and sham in their lives of its enclosed women in rich families and self-indulgent, unscrupulous men, blurring the lines between fantasy and reality, standing on the brink of terrible secrets, deception and hypocrisies. Jiten, who had a very bad childhood, has turned into a demon of a man. He exercises control over the family both as an elder son and brother. All the relations are maintained strictly under the dictates of patriarchy. Jiten dominates the scene with his overbearing, egotistical and corrosive presence. He is a violent, alcoholic, lecherous wife-beater inclined to kill at the slightest provocation. Jiten is shown to be a cruel, imposing and most discourteous man who does not have the courtesy to talk politely to a lady. His rudeness to Lalitha, Sridhar's wife is an example to support this:

JITEN. Screw your wife!

——

SRIDHAR. Just don't talk to my wife, okay?

JITEN. I wouldn't lay her even if she got me the ReVaTee account. (*CP*1, 306)

Jiten maintains a simultaneous life with prostitutes, whom he entertains in his office. Any opposition from his accounts officer Sridhar is met with threat to the latter's his job. Jiten, has a violent lecher's approach to business is a combination of brainless obstinacy and clumsy scans. His savagery, brutality and unfaithfulness is similar to Osborne's character of Jimmy in *Look Back in Anger*, who inflicts pain on his wife Alison and has an affair with Helena to fulfill his sexual libido. Jiten epitomizes male chauvinism when he says:

> Men would want their women dressed up like that. And they have the buying power. Yes! So there's no point asking a group of screwed up women what they think of it. (*CP*1, 276)

The suffrage of women is twofold here: The first is that, women experience a considerable number of 'hidden crimes' in the 'safety' of the home or in intimate relationships with men like their husbands. Violence is an essential component of the relations between men and women and it is used by men in a power relationship to control and humiliate the victim. Secondly, here is a link between the actions of the lust-crazed psychopath and those of 'normal' man that is Jiten here. The first is the idea, put forward by Liz Kelly (1988), that there is a sexual violence continuum. The continuum links panoply of abusive acts (rape, sexual harassment, domestic battery, homicide etc.) with the everyday abuses and safety precautions in women's lives. Male control and domination of women's bodies expresses itself as aggressive male sexuality (and its converse, passive, masochistic female sexuality). Thus it is argued that acts such as violent rape, forced and consensual sex share common rituals of conquest and submission which make it difficult to distinguish the 'normal' from the 'aberrant'.

Women, for him are no more than sex objects; he does not even respect his old Baa and gets angry with Alka, Nitin's wife when he hears from Nitin that Baa's ancestral house has been willed by Baa to Daksha, his own daughter, and pressurizes Nitin to throw out his wife permanently, so that Baa will be pleased and sign the property away to her sons. Baa, while describing Jiten says:

> Jitu is just like his father. Just like him.(*CP*1, 284)

The husband of the old mother was a cruel and a dark man who harassed her. The kind of cruelty perpetuated on Baa by her husband is brought to light every now and then in the play when she feels jittery even after so many years of her husband's death. In a series of flashbacks, Baa's tragic past is revealed and shows how she suffered being married to a dominating and violent man who had not only prevented her from singing (her favourite hobby) in public, but also used to beat her up regularly and ill-treat her sons.

> I have married such a villager! Aah! You slapped me? Never, never slap me. Nobody has hit me. The men in our family are decent... Wait! Wait! (*CP*1, 288)

In her case the use of violence is wavering and dithering as she says:

> You hit me. I only speak the truth and you hit me? Go on. Hit me again. The children should see what a demon you are. Aah! Jitu! Nitin! Are you watching? See your father! (Jerks her face as if she's been slapped). No! No! Not on the face! What will the neighbours say? Not on the face! I beg You! Hit me but not on ... aaaah! (*CP*1, 278)

So, here we have two generations sharing the same experiences at the hands of their chauvinistic husbands and a yet to come third generation, Daksha who also experiences the maltreatment of her father even before her birth and is born as a disabled child. Dolly exposes Jiten's cruelty when she says:

> And you hit me! Jitu, you beat me up! I was carrying Daksha and you beat me up! (*CP*1, 311)

The result of the violence on the wife is the premature delivery of Daksha, the disabled daughter of Dolly and Jiten. Baa and Dolly's abuse and mistreatment are somewhat similar but it is Alka whose anguish and frustration is due to her husband's homosexual libido and her brother Praful's deceit of not revealing the reality of Nitin to her. The choices available to the sisters are either of resorting to subjection or suffering alienation. While Dolly had decided to remain within patriarchy all along, Alka tried to escape by finding solace in alcohol and always remain drunk to be in an illusory world. Violence is the norm with which the actions of the women are controlled. Alka is dominated first by her brother, Praful, on the name of living in a civilized society of a globalize world and then by her husband Nitin, a homosexual, who could not fulfill her desire of love. She infuriated both of them, and sarcastically says about Praful to Dolly:

> ...he is the descendent of a saint! A saint! (laugher hard) Like my husband. Such close friends! Friends from college. (Dolly gives her a look of warning). I didn't tell you. That time when you came home to... (pours herself a drink). Nitin and Praful were home, talking. I came home from school with the neighbour's son on his scooter instead of walking with you. I told him to drop me before our street came. He didn't understand and dropped me right at our doorstep. Praful saw. He didn't say a word to me. He just dragged me into the kitchen. He lit the stove and pushed my face in front of it! I thought he was going to burn my face! He burnt my hair. I can still smell my hair in fire- Nitin was right behind us. Watching! Just... Praful said, "Don't you ever look at any man. Ever. (*CP*1, 257)

Alka is passed from the guardianship of Praful to that of Nitin, a trusted friend, as if she is an animal or property to be controlled or watched over. Alka's oppression is so acute that she does not even have the right to express herself. The Trivedi household considers Alka an amoral drunkard. They mull over her to be a corrupting force, unable to be a mother and completely lacking in the values of a civilized family. She bears this humiliation, which is her husband's fault. Nitin's secret that he is a homosexual lies Alka's brother Praful and thereby prevents him from exercising full control on

Alka. Nowhere does he sympathize with her. When Alka dances in the rain, she is regarded as a drunkard and an immoral and uncivilized woman:

> JITEN. Ask her what she was doing outside in the rain.
>
> ALKA. I don't know! I don't know what I was doing outside. Aren't there times when you don't know what you are doing? (To Nitin) What's the harm in that? Huh? (Nitin doesn't respond) Tell me what's the harm?
>
> NITIN. None. There's no harm in that. (*CP*1, 299-300)

It is really ironic, that a man like Jiten who just passed his time with a prostitute in his office, tries to control Alka by the sweeping statements on morality. Therefore, both Dolly (who accepts domination and control) and Alka (who negates power and authority) suffer at the hands of their male counterparts. As Germaine Greer puts it:

> A woman's body is the battlefield where she fights for liberation. It is through her body that operation works, reifying her, sexualizing her, victimizing her, disabling her. Her physicality is a medium for others to work on; her job is to act as their viceroy, presenting her body for their ministrations and applying to her body the treatments that have been ordained. If she fails to present herself, if she refuses to accept the treatments, she is behaving badly. (*The Whole*, 106)

Hence, Dattani ridicules a society, which imparts rules which are fair to one sex and are unfair to the 'other'. Alka faces the burnt of domestic violence as she is thrown out of the house and her sister has to plead to the decision makers in the house to take her back. This sheds light on the various aspects related to the position of women in an urban, bourgeois set up. In the so-called liberated atmosphere women are still judged according to parameters that are age-old but have now taken new form. As Dattani reveals, even in a fast developing society, a woman taking alcohol is a taboo, though it may be a social requirement. The two conflicting attitudes are reflected in a conversation between Alka and Lalitha:

ALKA. Oh. In that case...let me just add some in mine.(*Picks up the bottle of rum and brings it to where her glass is.*) I have an occasional one. It's good for digestion. (*Pours a stiff one.*)

LALITHA. I have not-so-occasional ones at parties. It's nice to get high once in a while.

ALKA(*guardedly*). Your husband doesn't mind?

LALITHA. No. I don't think so. (*Drinks.*) As long as he is around when it happens, he doesn't mind. You must do a bit of social drinking too. (*CP*1, 244)

This exchange makes it clear the hypocritical stance of a patriarchal society in the world of capitalism and also the illusion about the liberation of women. In this conversation, it is obvious that like all other women, Lalitha too belongs to her man and she too has no freedom to do anything of her own free will.

It is made clear that Jiten has taken after his father, while Nitin is like Baa, in appearance at least. Nitin may be so cruel like Jiten, but he is the most deceitful character of all not only swindles his wife by hiding his homosexuality, but also tricks Baa by showering love and affection on her to be her inheritor. He is so hounded by money that he can even leave his wife for it, without any regret. This obsession is clear by a sequence of dialogue exchanged between Baa and Nitin in her room on the upper level. We hear Nitin asking his mother:

> Baa, this is important. Will you give me the house if I send her back-for good this time? (*CP*1, 302)

Afterwards, we learn that Baa has nominated Praful to serve as the trustee to the property she has willed to Daksha. The revelation makes Nitin burst out in anger and indignation:

> What have I done to deserve this? Oh God! All my life I have listened to you and obeyed you. Only once have I gone against your wishes, and you punish me for that? But he is to blame. Praful tricked me into marrying her! If you want to hate anyone, hate him. I hate him now!

> Do what you want with the property but don't let him run my life! He is out to get us! Alka can stay here, or go away, or drink herself to death, I don't care. It doesn't make a difference to me! But get him out of my life! (*CP*1, 305)

This is one level of patriarchal dominance over women by men, but the other issues are also raised to show another face of aristocratic set up in the bourgeois Indian society that is divided both at the level of class and gender. And in this sense, man also suffers with the hands of another man or institution to perpetuate these traditional settings. Jiten and Nitin, being the upper class males, have the prerogative of ownership in an advertising company. On the other hand is Sridhar, struggling to come into their position, as employer. In this case Dattani presents different layers of bourgeois society, a social system that gives power to those who have property and capital, derogates the ones that are located in a position subservient to the ones in power.

For this, Dattani uses the ad-world as the private point of a capitalist system and facilitates its profit-making motive. Consumer interest is important to maximize sales and enhance profits and not for salvaging the conscience of either the ad agency or the seller. The Trivedi brothers continuously preside over Sridhar on working for an ad-campaign for the sale of 'undies', named ReVaTee, ladies undergarments and night wear for women. They transform women into brand slogans that will titillate the viewers and in turn promote sale. However, Sridhar who relies on consumer surveys, does not like that idea as it is offensive for women. He says:

> They said we-haven't understood women... I told you about the market survey. About a dozen women. A cross-section of upper-middle class, upper class, and the stinking rich. We had given them a questionnaire each to fill up after seeing the AV... I can tell you what the bottom line was. They all said - in different words of course - but most of them used one word to describe it - offensive. They all found it highly offensive. (*CP*1, 274-275)

But all Sridhar's idea and surveys are continuously condemned by Trivedi Brothers. He is probably torn between the two and is unable to gauge the nuances of the situation in which, like Dolly and Alka, he too is a puppet. So after a lot of discussions Sridhar dismisses his efforts of looking at this ad campaign differently and finally submits to the requirements of the employers just to survive in the world of buying and selling. But his heart bleeds and becomes furious when ordered to bring a prostitute for Jiten, or else he will lose his job:

> JITEN. You call yourself an advertising professional and you don't want to pimp?
>
> SRIDHAR. This is insane…a man has his tolerance limit you know! And this is something-me pick up a woman for you!
>
> *(Jiten doesn't move his extended arm. Sridhar is fighting tears of humiliation. He snatches the keys and rushes out).* (*CP*1, 287)

Bravely Fought the Queen focuses, therefore, on the advertising sector and its impact on class and gender relations as a patriarchal institution. Firstly, employees like Sridhar have to bow to it; secondly, its dominance overlooks the sensitivity of women, when it is decided that this campaign has to suit the requirements of the male customers, even when it is a product for women. But her views, her responses are neglected and negated. In the metropolitan pockets of our existence and the consumer in a commercial transaction, and advertising plays a vital role in facilitating this connection. The play might be riddled with problems of its own kind, but the playwright is able to bring out the contradictory and multifarious nuances of the relationship between the refined 'social' lives and the world of buying and selling. And for Trivedi brothers, women are also like some product or thing, which they are buying and selling to the men. The ReVaTee 'undies' made for women, a product meant to enhance the comfort level of the women's basic requirements or the product that would suit her perception of her own sexuality, is viewed as having nothing to do with women, is rather ironical. According to Jiten (an embodiment of the view of the dominant male-centric power structure), there is nothing wrong with his approach as the consumer is not a woman but a man. It is men who will buy this product for their women and so the ad-campaign should been from the perspectives of men and not that of women's. As Jiten says:

> Yes! Men would want to buy it for their women! That's our market. Men would want their women dressed up like that. And they have the buying power. Yes! So there's no point asking a group of screwed up women what they think of it. They'll pretend to feel offended and say- 'oh, we are always being treated like sex objects'. (*CP*1, 276)

Therefore, in Jiten's view, the ad-campaigns have to suit the desire and the fantasy quotient of the male so as to enhance the desires of the male partner. Dattani's choice of the advertising agency as a patriarchal construction, the sale of products for women, and most of all, women as targets for the male gaze is apt. Ad-campaigns satiate the perversities of the male gaze as women are expected to dress themselves and throw themselves at their male partners. They determine the way we think, our behavioural patterns and ideological inclinations.

Almost all aspects of the media are normative, that is, they have to do with the ways in which beautiful people, or just folks, or ordinary Indians or extraordinary Indians should live their lives. They define the possible; and the possibilities are usually in terms of what is male and what is female. The media portrayal of 'the masculine citizen-soldier, the patriotic wife and mother, the bread-winning father who is head of household, and the properly reproductive family' has further assaulted feminist solidarity and identity. They think that the definition of a woman in terms of the man is the way it should be; and they back it up with psychosexual incantation and biological ritual curses. A woman has an identity if she is attractive enough to obtain a man, and thus, a home; for this will allow her to set about his life's task of 'joyful altruism and nurturance.' But just because it is good for business does not mean it is not wrong. It aids in prevailing wrong notions to mislead both 'men' and 'women' and entrap them into traditionally, a mindset devoid of all the individual feeling, identity and expression. Dattani professes:

> I think one has to come to terms with the fact that audiences are unpredictable and you have no control over their feelings unless you want to tell them that all is well with their world and they are perfect people. That they will accept as we can see in Bollywood and Ekta soaps where the 'heroine' is a paragon of virtue whose strength lies in sacrifice and always thinking of others. If that is the self perception of the bulk of our audience, I would rather have then laugh at an inappropriate moment either by way of contempt or just plain embarrassment. Even by rejecting the true feeling of these characters they are acknowledging their presence and their own attitude towards them. (Multani, *Mahesh Dattani's*, 170)

The ad world is the pivotal point of a capitalist system. The play also presents the fictious world of media and advertising to mislead persons and by presenting the women as 'looking glass' or having some great qualities; they make people believe and follow these things as the truth and way of life just for the benefit of some money, they sell these humanity.

The process of the sisters Dolly's and Alka's dressing and making-up for an evening out is questioned by the very fact that we are adopting a feminized gaze at it; we see how far these actions are in fact conventional social performances, aimed at the male gaze; as a result we question these convention. This is why, when we talk about this play as metatheatrical: the characters are men and women because they are playing roles.

In *A Room of One's Own* (1929), Virginia Woolf advances the notion that while women are indeed the victims of men, they collude in their own domestic and professional victimization by acting as a 'looking glass' for the reflecting back to men of their desired image. Germaine Greer too endorses these views:

> Women are illusionists. They fake light-heartedness, girlishness and orgasm; they also fake the roses in their cheeks, the thickness, colour and curliness of their hair, the tininess of their waists, the longness of their legs and the size and shape of their breasts. Men do not seem to have demanded this to them; rather women seem to have bedizened themselves in an all-out last-ditch attempt to grab the attention of otherwise uninterested males. (*The Whole*, 27)

Dolly and Alka, in the beginning of the play subdue themselves by imprisoning in the ideology of womanhood: the ideal of 'the Angel in the House'. Thus we are now leading to a third face of patriarchal dominance, where not only male perpetrators in the name of upholding the 'honour' code from ancient times have committed this plight on Indian women, but also women equally internalize and continue this code, which manifests itself not only through assaults on women by men but also through torments of women egged on by other women or by themselves in order to live in harmony in traditional stereotypical roles.

Baa is a representative of the tyrannical Trivedi brothers in the play and even without coming out of her bed in the uppermost level of the stage, is able to condition and control the other women in the house. Dattani presents the insecure Baa exercising patriarchal control over the affairs of the family as being the legal inheritor of the family property after the death of her husband. Baa is not merely a woman; she is the patriarch in the guise of a woman. She too has been subjected to violence in the domestic life. A frustrated wife in such a family often seeks her emotional fulfillment in her sons. Baa sees the picture of her husband in her elder son, Jiten and thus automatically develops an affection and inclination towards her own self younger son, Nitin who resembles her a lot. The mother-son intimacy comes out in the following lines:

BAA. Nitin! You don't like your father, no? he's not nice!... tell me you hate him! He hits me! Nitin tell me you hate him! Say it!

NITIN.Yes! I hate him! (*CP*1, 302)

Such a mother figure would obviously begin to feel insecure when the son gets married and the mother would certainly begin to feel that her domination over her son will soon get over. This feeling of insecurity will lead the mother to torture her daughters-in-law and poison the minds of both her sons against their wives. Freud considers this mother-son relationship very important for conjugal bliss as he writes in "Feminity":

> A mother is only brought unlimited satisfaction by her relation to a son; this altogether the most perfect, the most free from ambivalence of all human relationships. (*Women*, 187]

Baa provokes Nitin to get his wife Alka out of the house as she is good-for-nothing and even instigates Jiten to beat the pregnant Dolly as a result of which her child Daksha is born spastic. Baa's intervention is negative and destructive. In making Jiten beat up Dolly she vents her frustration of earlier times. But the future generation (Daksha) has to suffer because of the conflicts and frustrations of the elders. The injustice to Daksha is revealed at the moment Dolly's challenges Jiten in utter frustration:

DOLLY.You were angry with Praful and you hit me?

JITEN. (almost in tears). That was fifteen years ago! (310)

DOLLY. ... Your mother loved her more than was natural! Praful loved her. More than was natural...

JITEN. ... You know I didn't. It was Baa! Blame her but not me! She is my daughter! (Crying) Get her back! Get her from wherever she is. I want her home.

She (Dolly) demonstrates a spastic uncoordinated arm and neck movement with her eyes dilated. Laughs and turns around.

JITEN (sobbing). No! No. (points to Baa's room) She made me do it. She did it!

DOLLY. No! oh no! I will not let you get away so easily! They were your hands hitting me! Your feet kicking me! It's in your blood! It's in your blood to do bad! (*CP*1, 312)

The pathetic stipulation of Baa in the family has only replicated itself in her daughter-in-law in a different form, whereas the sons have inherited the power to perpetuate violence by associating with the figure of the father. It is indeed one of the contradictions in the patriarchal set-up that having been associated with the father figure, Jiten beats up Dolly at the behest of Baa. Consequently, the three generations share the same experience but the maltreatment of Daksha is even more malicious and atrocious as she gets the blot of her father even before her birth. The climax arises with its 'deep theatrical purity' as in the words of Michael Walling:

> When Dolly reveals the fact that her child was seriously disabled at birth by Jiten's violence, she begins to dance as Daksha would dance- disjointedly, wildly, with ever-increasing frenzy, until at last she breaks down in a gut-wrenching grief.
>
> ---
>
> 'Isn't that the way she dances?' it seems an innocuous line on the page. But this writing is writing beyond words: this is theatre. (*CP*1, 230)

Mahesh Dattani's next play *Tara* focuses on another contentious and highly relevant contemporary issue- the relative status of girl and boy children- but also extends it to engage with an interrogation of the feminine, as external or internal. *Tara* is enthralling in that it comments on a society that treats the children of the same womb differently and by making use of rather unlikely 'freak' case to lay bare the injustices in the conventional Indian family meted out to the girl child. And as always, like all other plays of Dattani, this stereotype comes too in a friendly garb, covering the ugly truths as Patels, parents of Chandan and Tara, look like the ideal parents but there are more things under this hypocrisy which created havoc when revealed. The play explores more relevant issues besides exposing the typical Indian mindset of preference of boy child to the girl from time immemorial; it is the failure of relationships in a hypocritical Indian family, comprising of a father (Patel), mother (Bharati) and two children (Chandan and Tara), and their neighbour (Roopa). It also unravels the trauma of disability which the two children are facing in the play. As Mahesh Dattani exposed in an interview to Lakshmi Subramanyam:

> I focus on cultural emphasis on masculinity and how all the characters are at conflict with that. The parents, the grandfather, and the neighbour- they are all in that sense in tension with their own sensibilities as opposed to cultural sensibilities they may have knowingly or unknowingly subscribed to. (*Muffled Voices*, 129)

Consequently, Tara is not the story of the protagonist of the play *Tara* only, but of every girl child born in the Indian family whether urban or rural. The situation is inflamed when there is some mental or physical deformity in her- a really bitter example of child abuse present in the Indian societies. Dattani takes Patels, as the members of Gujarati community, to depict the whole world's situation, not only in India. In fact, sex tests are mostly availed of by middle and upper classes; and often in highly educated families in Gujarat. Indian couples living in the USA, the UK and other western countries also come to Ahemdabad for these tests because they are banned in the west. It was recently discovered in Britain that the highest usage of ultra sound sex test was among the Patel community from Gujarat which has to face the burden of dowry even there. Anand Ben Patel, the president of the BJP's women's wing says that because of the conservative nature of Gujarat and the prevalence of dowry system, particularly in the Patel community, female foeticide has risen to an alarming rate. As Roopa comments on this community:

> ROOPA. The Patels in the old days were unhappy with getting girl babies – you know dowry and things like that – so they used to drown them in milk. ... So when people asked about how the baby died, they could say that she choked while drinking her milk. (*CP*1, 349)

We are a country with along history of female foeticide and an equally long history of material discrimination against girl children, and women in general. The birth of a son was certainly preferred to that of a daughter. In the *Rgvedic* hymn, Indra is invoked to grant ten sons to the bride. We meet in hymns with prayers for sons and grandsons, male offspring, male descendents and male issues and occasionally for wives but never for daughters. Even forgiveness is asked for sons but no blessing is ever prayed for female issues. Sridhar Kakar, makes a very fine point when he says:

> In daughterhood in Indian girl is a sojourn in her own family and with marriage she becomes less a wife than a daughter-in-law. It is only with motherhood that she comes into her own as a woman and she can make a place for herself in the family, in the community and in her life circle. (*The Inner*, 52)

Tara is a story of co-joined twins separated at birth, by a surgical procedure, intended to favor the boy (Chandan) over the girl (Tara). The play unwraps in London with Chandan, now a playwright, reminiscing about his childhood days spent with his sister Tara, told through Chandan's reflections on his childhood memories. Tara's story is also a manifestation of the feminine struggle for expression both physically and emotionally in a patriarchal Indian family. Tara and Chandan are the two sides of the same self rather than two separate entities and for Dan to write the story of his own childhood, he has to write Tara's story too. His twin sister Tara, whom he had almost erased from his memory, "She was lying deep inside, out of reach..."(*CP*1, 324) The young Chandan and Tara walk in here with Tara declaring that they have "always been inseparable. The way we started in life. Two lives and one body, in one comfortable womb. Till we were forced out... And separated."(*CP*1, 325) This opening indicates that the play can be read at different and diverse level, as one about the feminity in men: the other side of gender that we all carry within us. Chandan, who is now Dan in London, writes Tara's story to rediscover the neglected half of him, as a means of becoming whole. He says: "I have my memories... But now I want them to come back. To masticate my memories in my mind and spit out the result to the world in anger." As Dattani asserts in an interview to Sachidananda Mohanty:

> *Tara* is about a boy and a girl, Siamese twins. I have taken medical liberty over here because Siamese twins are invariably of the same sex and they are surgically separated at birth. It was important for their survival and the play deals with their emotional separation. (*The Plays*, 171)

Through a series of flashbacks, we get an insight into their early life. The play revolves around the Siamese twins, Chandan and Tara Patel; an operation to separate the twins at birth, leaves Tara crippled for life. Fighting against the prejudices the society has for the crippled Tara, the protagonist of the play. Dattani mentioned to Lakshmi Subramanyam:

> I see *Tara* as a play about the male self and the female self. The male self being preferred (if one is to subscribe to conventional categories of masculine traits and feminine traits) in all cultures. The play is about the separation of self and the resultant angst. (*Muffled*, 129)

The family of Patels is a highly conflicted one in which, like all other plays of Dattani, some dark secret is hidden behind the relationship of husband and wife, which results in hysteria in Bharati, and in making Mr.Patel abnormal.

Bharati's father, although absent, influences their actions and is an epitome of Dattani's excellence in depicting how the family rules over us and how patriarchy dominates even being invisible. He was a wealthy man in politics and was very close to becoming the chief minister. He had been a consistent upholder of values pertaining to males. He further strengthened his indulgence for male grandchild by leaving his property after his demise to Chandan and not a single penny to Tara. His will is a testament that is meted out to girls in Indian society. Mr.Patel and Chandan's exchange of words reveals this prejudice:

PATEL. He (grandfather) left you a lot of money.

CHANDAN. And Tara?

PATEL. Nothing.

CHANDAN. Why?

PATEL. It was his money. He could do what he wanted with it. (*CP*1, 360)

Patel himself seems to be an emblematic and typical father, who tries to push his male and female children into separate grooves, into the stereotyped gender roles that would help them fit into society, at the cost of hurting them both, since their own preferences seem contradictory to these expectations. He wants Chandan to grow up like a 'man' and favours him for higher education abroad and a good career as he says "Chandan is going to study further and he will go abroad for his higher studies." (*CP*1, 352) Patel tries to fetch him to office with him, but Chandan is not interested in business as he would prefer to be a writer, while it is Tara, who seems more inclined to go into a career like her father's; but there are no such offers for her. Tara observes this game of patriarchy and says:

> Men in the house were deciding on whether they were going to do hunting while the women looked after the cave. (*CP*1, 328)

Patel is furious at his wife, Bhararti when he sees Chandan helping his mother with knitting and loses his cool, accusing her of turning Chandan "into a sissy-teaching him to knit!"(Dattani, *CP*, 2000, 351) Tara is discouraged frankly and overtly even when she is more intelligent, sharp and witty and will perform well if given opportunity in life. Patel thinks of sending Tara too, to college only when Chandan refuses to go without her. Thus, together they struggle with their feminine aspects as after the physical division the father wants to separate them emotionally too. Separately they experience society's disapproval based on gender - defined roles, Chandan through his passive artsy male persona and Tara through her bold assertive female persona. Their understanding of this deep relationship is stronger in the later half of the play, when the siblings, who were surgically separated at three months, show their feelings for each other. There is an underlying sense of trust, of closeness, that goes beyond the text, and the two character's occasional ironies about themselves and others. Patel is not only prejudiced towards Tara but is also discourteous and authoritarian with Bharati too. His anger on her exhibits a streak of harshness, even heartlessness. At times though he becomes a caring husband, but is often nasty to her. Even when he denies Bharati to donate her kidney to Tara, it was not because of his concern for his wife's health, but a cruel expression of his overbearing attitude:

> Because I don't want you to have the satisfaction of doing it. (*CP*1, 344)

Such instances are numerous where his continual dismissal of Bharati's opinions as inconsequential are evident; not paying heed to her expostulations on behalf of Tara represent him as a typical over-riding patriarchal husband.

Bharati supports Tara in the matter of higher education and other things too and protects her against all odds. Her emotional stress centers on Tara and her condition: anxiety about illness, death, her future when she grows up and also worries about effects on other children and on partners. The isolation of Tara created by restrictive social and economic life is Bharati's potential source of disturbing strain. Besides subsequent problems may come to disable children, for example, problems of adapting the disabled; emotional and behavioural problems in younger children; the special problem occurring in adolescence; stigma; social isolation; poor self-image; and reduced perceptions of control over one's life and environment. Chandan is more complacent with his handicapped life while Tara craved every moment for a complete and normal life. The awareness that she has a handicap and the humiliation meted out to her by Roopa and her friends when she is forced to show her handicapped leg to them is like a dagger-jibe to her heart.

Dattani is successful in focusing the pathetic humiliation faced by a handicapped child; the condition is more pathetic if she is a girl, as being subordinated in both ways. Tara is hurt and in her moment of deep hurt and resentment caused by the 'normal' world she wants to hear only Beethoven. She identifies herself with the musician with a disability, who established his greatness in spite of being unable to hear his own creations. Though, in the company of Chandan, she feels herself to be complete and cope with the problems and adjust relatively, but still her desire to have another leg is persistent; she desires to live normally in society that humiliates her. Throughout the play we can feel in Tara that she bears some kind of grudge against the society. She seems to have some kind of aversion with the outside world and her world consisted of only her parents and her brother who she was very close to. Tara's attachment to her brother and the internal anguish is expressed in her conversation with her brother Chandan, when she says:

> May be we still are. Like we've always been. Inseperable. (*CP*1, 325)

In spite of all this, Tara lives happily with the support of her mother and her brother; but the truth which destroys her life is the revelation that her own mother, to whom she is closest, meted out this despondent plight on her by being biased on her birth. Therefore, the play gives the most frightening instance of women blindly adhering to patriarchal values and gives us a picture of the plight and helpless condition of women in our society.

Gender discrimination replicates itself from generation to generation, violates the rights of the girl child and chokes her further development. Born into indifference and reared on neglect, the girl child is caught in a web of cultural practices and prejudices that hamper her growth and progress, both physically and mentally. In India for a girl child the period from infancy to adolescence is a perilous path. The first critical social peculiar to the life of the girl is the discovery, under social and cultural conditions already portrayed, of the anatomical differences between herself and her brother on whatever boy in her life serves this purpose. Parenthetically it should be said that it is very nearly universal to our culture for a girl to have this experience, irrespective of the pattern of her own family on the supervision with which she is provided. The feeling of loss and inferiority may be further exaggerated by her mother's preference for her brother, or her lament that she is a girl in a 'man's world'. It inflicts serious and permanent damage upon her character.

This is really what happened to Tara. The co-joined twins, Tara and Chandan were born with three legs and a repeated scan showed that there was the greater chance of success if the third leg remained as part of Tara's body. But Bharati, Tara's own mother, showed the 'jaundiced eye' or partiality to the son and supported by her father and his financial and political influence, to favour the boy over the girl, went against her husband's wishes and told doctor to make the third limb part of the boy's body. But the operation as usual failed and the whole effort went in vain because the leg very soon became a lump of the dead flesh on Chandan and had to be amputated. To think that it would have been part of Tara, makes Bharati neurotic and made her live with a sense of guilt all her life. The whole process of this tragedy has been very well exposed to the children by Mr. Patel in the end:

> A scan showed that a major part of the blood supply to the third leg was provided by the girl. Your mother asked for a reconfirmation. The result was the same. The

> chances were slightly better that the leg would survive... on the girl. Your grandfather and your mother had a private meting with Dr. Thakkar. I wasn,t asked to come. That same evening, your mother told me of her decision. Everything will be done as planned. Except- I couldn't believe that she told me- that they would risk giving both legs to the boy... maybe if I had protested more strongly! I tried to reason with her that it wasn't right and that even the doctor would realize it was unethical! The doctor had agreed, I was told. It was only later I came to know of his intention of starting a large nursing home-the largest in Bangalore. He had acquired three acres of prime land- in the heart of the city- from the state. Your grandfather's political influence had been used. A few days later, the surgery was done. As planned by them, Chandan had two legs-for two days. It didn't take them very long to realize what a grave mistake they had made. The leg was amputated. A piece of dead flesh which could have-might have-been Tara. (*CP*1, 378)

Bound by guilt, Bharati tries to compensate and reimburse by over protecting Tara, with excessive concern for her, smothering her with affection and even making her feel that the father loves Chandan more; she even attempts to 'buy' friendship for her daughter. She begs Roopa, a neighbour girl of Tara's age:

> If you promise to be her best friend-what I mean is if you would like to be her friend- I will be most grateful to you and I will show it... in whatever way you want me to. (*CP*1, 341)

Bharati's sense of regret is so deep that she agrees to donate her kidney to her daughter so that she may survive for a few more years. In a conversation with her son, she tells him: "I plan to give her happiness. I mean to give her all the love and affection which I can give. It's what she... deserves. Love can make up for a lot." (*CP*1, 349)

Patel always gives hints to Tara about her mother being a hypocrite as she showers love on her just for the atonement of her guilt; he tells her, "Tara, please believe me when I say that I love you very much and I have never in all my life loved you less or more than I have loved your brother. But your mother..." (*CP*1, 354)

But Tara has always been led to believe that it is she who has been discriminated by her father, and always gained the extra bit of affection from her mother. That is why, the play generates a death-like response from Tara when she learns the truth- it was her own mother's decision that deprived her what she wanted more than anything else in the world all her life- a second leg. It is a shattering discovery for the naturally ebullient Tara: "And she called me her star!"(*CP*1, 379)

This is the crucial moment in the play that practically kills the female and tears her apart from the male; Chandan moves far away, never to return, forever incomplete. Thus we see that both Patel and Bharati connive together in the working of patriarchal norms. Though Bharati has changed because of her sense of guilt, Patel carries on merrily, almost as if to rub Bharati's nose in. He remained a mute observer of the whole affair. He too believes in gender hierarchy and subscribes to the ideology of the patriarchal world. He blames his wife and father-in-law for the damage done but his complicity in the whole operation cannot be denied.

The injustices done in the name of construction of gender identities, the hierarchization and demarcation of roles does as much harm to men as to women. The viciousness of the grandfather and his mother not only takes away the life of the girl but also ruins the life of the boy who was very much attached to his sister Tara. For no fault of his own for his sister's untimely death, he feels someway responsible for it and cannot forgive himself for the atrocity done towards his sister. For that reason, he escapes to London and transforms his name from Chandan to Dan, lives without a personal history, unable to make any progress in his writing career, alive but divorced from all his realities; he thinks that his sister's tragedy is his own. Even when his father informs him about his mother's death, he refuses to come back in India. While writing the life history of his sister Tara, Dan agrees that we are destined to live out plans that are not in our control:

> Like other objects in the cosmos, whose orbits are determined by those around. Moving in a forced harmony. Those who survive are those who do not defy the gravity of others. And those who desire even a moment of freedom find themselves hurled into space, doomed to crash with some unknown force. (*CP*1, 379).

His sense of trauma and anguish is so intense that at the end of the play, we see Chandan apologizing to Tara in the most moving of all the lines in the play: "Forgive me Tara. Forgive me for making it my tragedy."(*CP*1, 380) and the two siblings holding each other in a tight hug, together once again, and whole, complete. The play *Tara* can be read in so many different ways; Dattani's view of how the 'forced harmony' of our lives is so fraught with uncertainties and so close to angst that the surfacing of even one memory can tilt the balance completely, change our paths into that of collision and self- explosion makes *Tara* an important text for the issue of a girl child.

Chandan's attention and relation to Tara before and after her death can be seen at the Imaginary and Symbolic levels as propounded by Kristeva. Before the death of Tara, he lives in the imaginary realm is that of the young child at the pre-linguistic, pre-oedipal stage. The self is not yet distinguished from what is other than the self that is the feminine self Tara and body's sense of being separate from her is not yet established even after the separation of them by Dr. Thakkar at their birth. (in the last scene when Tara and Chandan hug each other and find themselves complete). The children live in an Eden-like realm, free of both desire and deprivation. But after the death of Tara, the semiotic or Imaginary stage is subverted politically, and always threatens the closed symbolic order embodied in such convention as governments, received cultural values and grammar of standard language and this shatter the life of Chandan completely and he lost his identity completely too. Therefore, the construction of men and women are essentially different because of biology, and also because they are socially constructed differently.

The play enlightens us that no matter how much a girl outshines a boy; she will remain in the background and can never be given an advantageous position. Some epic heroines like Savitri, Gandhari, etc. are seen as the role models for women in this country. Unfortunately these role models are the products of and fashioned by millennia of patriarchal norms, which play an important role in creating women's images of themselves and in reinforcing gender dichotomy. But how is this male domination perpetuated generation after generation? Do women also contribute to it? Are they merely passive victims of the process? Don't they accelerate the pace through their sleepy and somewhat dormant subservience? In the man's world, not only men but women too perpetuate their deformed positions, even when they are educated. It is really shocking that Bharati, being an educated mother, showed such shortsightedness regarding her children and thus worsened the conditions. If she had not shown an indulgence for the male child and had done justice to her female child then both the children would have flourished happily and would have lived as healthy human beings.

Is this the punishment for Tara for having been born as a girl? What a girl should do if she gets suppressive treatment in her own home by her own parents and not by the society alone? Does she have an identity? How can her own mother, being herself a woman, treat her daughter in this manner? A girl is as much the part of body of the mother as the son is, then why is here such kind of difference towards them? These and many more questions arise naturally in the mind of any girl living in the position of Tara, which is a general sight in society among any class and community. Sometimes this kind of suppression leads to depression and acceptance of her own plight by the women and sometimes they get ready to revolt; but in some cases the truth is so shattering that it takes the life of an innocent girl, as in the case with Tara. Through her parents, we witness the ongoing gender based power struggles, the decisions made because of these struggles and the guilt and subsequent perverse behaviour. The story draws in by examining how the lives of children and adults are affected by sociatical gender preferences. Though the spheres of men and women are symmetrical and complementary, they are not equal.

The determination of the twins to express themselves and the people they encounter in their separate but simultaneous journey through life highlights the obstacles imposed on individuals by the society and those they impose upon themselves. This demonstrates the havoc of Indian society, where the first teaching of suppression of the feelings in a girl is given by the mother who, herself is in the grip of patriarchal dominance. This is carried from one generation to another making one question, "where is the escape?"

The characters are no different from the rest of us; making choices all the time between right and wrong, standing up to or surrendering to peer pressure and social expectations, for the most part; good people who sometimes make bad choices which then haunt them for the rest of their lives. *Tara* is an interesting window into our own lives and reveals to us that we may be victims too of our own prejudices, and our choices are often influenced by far too many external considerations. As the protagonist of Dattani's another play, a radio play *Clearing the Rubble* says:

> If you can't clear the rubble you have to live with it, around it and over it, because what you lost is buried in there somewhere and until you find it, you have to keep on living with the rubble. (*CP*2, 83)

Thirty Days in September by Dattani illustrates a brutally honest portrayal of the sensitive, volatile and generally taboo issue of child sexual abuse through the medium of theatre. In almost all developed countries, law decides the acts of physical, sexual or emotional abuse, or neglect of children. But the frighteningly high prevalence of such crimes with the laws being ambiguous, most children suffer in silence for their whole lives; this is due to the emphasis placed in our society on preserving family reputation at all costs. Says Dr. Kaur:

> Disbelief, denial and cover-up to preserve family reputation made child sexual abuse an invisible crime in India. It seems there is an official denial of the existence of the problem. In fact, child abuse in India is as old as the joint family system and patriarchy. Though the problem is highly pervasive, there is pretence that it only inflicts the West. This also explains why there is no legislative framework in India to prevent such abuse and there has not been much data collection and research. (*Spectrum*, 5)

Commissioned by RAHI, Dattani attacked the common notion that abuse did not happen to urban, educated class of children. According to RAHI's survey involving middle and upper middle class women in four metros of the country, 70 per cent of them had been sexually abused as children. More than 40 per cent of these were survivors of incest- the victims, who's suffering lasted much longer, often extending for their whole lives and the healing was both slow and painful. It happens across the society, among the rich and poor, irrespective of class, caste or community. The family itself leads to child sexual abuse because it polarizes adult and child, rural and urban, male and female. Therefore, it is clear the Pedophilia and incest are not new entrants to the world of sexual variants but they have certainly acquired newer, graver dimensions that demand urgent social response.

Suicidal tendencies, low self worth, addictions, panic attacks, eating disorders, workaholisms, dysfunctional relationships, promiscuity and so on, all the abnormalities happen to the abused. This is exactly what is endured by Mala, the protagonist of the play *Thirty Days in September*, who is disturbed, discontented, complaining, unreasonably demanding, aggressive and shows it directly or indirectly. She was first raped by her maternal uncle when she was only seven and suffers repeated sexual abuse by him which affects her mind and life even after fifteen years of that incident. Mala's life of the 'silent scream' is not only her own story but can be based on real lives of victims of sexual abuse. Every now and then a crime occurs against the female community; a girl is kidnapped, sold, re-sold and raped. Her individuality is lost and she is forced to bear the torture and agony. The scene, when Deepak, her boy friend, solaces her by his agreements of love to her, Mala cannot response as she is entrapped all of a sudden in her childhood, the time when her uncle first raped her and seduced her soul completely with this shameful act. This scene is presented in the play by flashbacks where we can clearly get, how step by step in these lines, the man goes on to destroy her inner and outer self and also silence her:

MAN. Touch me here.

—

You said you loved me in front of your mummy and daddy. Come on! Show it!

—

There! You feel that? It means I love you. Your uncle loves you.

Mala begins to cry.

—

Shhh! Don't cry. You want to come here in your holidays, no? Then don't cry. This is your seventh birthday, no? You are seven now. Ready for a real birthday present. Lie down. Come on, quickly.

—

If they hear you they will say you are a bad girl. This is our secret. (Like an order but in a whisper) Don't cry!

—

Help me and I will love you more than your mummy or daddy.

—

Think of your school. Be still and put your arms up, come on. Yees! What did you learn in school today? Hmmm? What? Tell me.

—

Good, Good. Keep singing... Again, don't stop until I stop. See, I love you even though you are so ugly. Keep singing... Nobody will tell you how ugly you are. But you are good only for this... Only for this. See how much I love you. See... Now go away. Quickly. (*CP*2, 42-44)

The adult finishes the act with great satisfaction while the child is in pain and agony. Sexual abuse of children has existed within close family members in homes and especially with girls, since our culture does not allow its exposure, nor are the girls allowed to report the incidents due to cultural taboos and upbringing; thus the secret is nursed till death. The child who is victim of sexual abuse or exploitation is in the under great stress and trauma. To add to the child's problem, she is repeatedly exposed to the exploiter for the sake of identification. It is grossly unfair for the child because just the sight of the man is enough to trigger the mind back to the trauma she had passed through and to destabilize her.

Unable to forget her abuse at the hands of her uncle and reduced to an incorrigible sex-hungry seductress, Mala tolerates because of her love for her uncle in her subconscious and does not feel to be a victim. She shields him from social backlash and fails to concentrate on her anger at her uncle. Her sexual intercourse with him was an approval of his love for her which gives her the affirmation that she exists. "I see this man everywhere, I can never be free of him", Mala says, with heartrending simplicity. Even the worse thing is that she could not find solace in the lap of her mother, who continuously negates her sufferings by forbidding her to make imaginative stories like this, even if she knows inwardly that she is true.

SHANTA. Mala, my daughter. What all have you been thinking all these years? You have always been so bold and frank. But sometimes, you tell stories.

MALA. That is not a story I made up and you know it. (*CP2*, 26)

The reason why the mother apparently negates the abuse and the subsequent trauma is analyzed by Dr.Kaur:

> Stigma, secrecy and shame make the problem appear as an exception rather than a rule. Society can cope with stranger forms of danger but not with intra-familial threat as it challenges the very foundation of trust, faith and familial bonds. It is a danger ever looming in some corner of our so-called secure homes. (*Spectrum*, 5)

Therefore, here again in this play, like Tara in the play discussed earlier, the protagonist Mala feels a keen sense of betrayal by her mother as she always remains silent and avoids any conversation with Mala; she also advices Mala to do the same to preserve the conventional traditional societical beliefs and family norms. Dattani throws light on such situations in real life in an interview given to Utpal K Banerjee:

> This was commissioned by a Delhi-based NGO, RAHI (Recovering and Healing from Incest), who deals with survivors of childhood sexual abuse. After asking me whether I would be interested, they initiated me to Delhi to meet some of the victims under counseling. Seven women (covering both young and middle aged) agreed to speak to me. What struck me was the scar of the abuse and the trauma that stays with you even into your adult life. Some women had benefited from counseling and found healthy relations in life, including marriage. I also met a man whose girl-friend was the survivor of such an abuse. To deal with the issue, it needed a lot of sensitivity in the way of adult-to-adult relationship. In some cases, there was a sense of betrayal if it involved the father and there was a transferred resentment against the mother who perhaps could have intervened, but didn't. Often it was a helpless mother who had just no power in society, to speak against the father as the perpetrator. (*Indian*, 164-165)

If a little girl is rejected by her mother she immediately suffers a vital loss of security necessary for her development. In order to do so successfully, what the little girl needs primarily is the unquestioned devotion and love of her mother, to which Mala is denied in the whole play. The mother remains a mute witness to the subsequent history of abuse that continues over the years and voices no protest. Mala confesses:

> The only person who can, who could have prevented all this is my mother. Sometimes I wish she would just tell me to stop. She could have prevented a lot from happening... Here are all the names of people whom I have been with. And the outline... well I just wanted a line that would put them all altogether. But if you ask me, whose face I think it is- it must be my mother's. (*CP*2, 18)

The result is a brittle relationship between the mother and daughter, a relationship based on betrayal instead of trust. Child sexual abuse spans a range of problems, but it is this complexity of the family through silence and a lack of protest that is the ultimate betrayal for the abused. In the words of Dattani:

> Though sexual abuse is at the core of the play, the mother-daughter relationship is equally important. The main protagonist, who has suffered at the hands of her uncle, feels a deep sense of betrayal that her mother did not stop the abuse and failed in her role as protector. We see the journey of the protagonist from her mid-20's to her early 30's. the betrayal, as she sees it, is as painful as the abuse. Though the play draws from real life, the focus is on the inner world. (Subramanyam, *Muffled*, 133)

Dattani takes head on the problem of portraying the twin process of victimization: Mala, who uses sex for acceptance within her social circle and her mother who is branded as a 'frozen women'. Mala's verbal duel with her mother is an optimistic benchmark of her independent attitude. Her relationship with her mother is a roller-coaster ride. The characterization of Mala has a fall and rise. In the very beginning to the whole play, she hates her mother for not being saved her from such misshapenness':

> MALA. It is true. It did happen, but you never believed me.
>
> SHANTA (turning away). I don't know what you are talking about. I will prepare alu paratha for you tomorrow; you always like that for breakfast.
>
> MALA. That is how you always pacified me and that is how I know you believed me deep down. Oh yes, you would remember that I always like alu paratha because that's what I got whenever I came to you, hurt and crying. Instead of listening to what I had to say, you stuffed me with food. I couldn't speak because I was being fed all the time, and you know what? I began to like them. I thought that was the cure for my pain. That if I ate till I was stuffed, the pain would go away. Every time I came to you mummy, you were ready with something to feed me. You knew. Otherwise you wouldn't have been so prepared. You knew all along what was happening to me, and I won't ever let you forget that! (*CP*2, 24)

The trauma of the childhood abuse dominates her adult relationships, and it makes Mala go from one relationship to another, first seeking attention and than hating it, nothing lasting beyond thirty days. Her sordid past and misplaced sense of guilt leaves her with a very-low or total lack of self worth. Mala struggles with her twisted desire for attention and her dependency on men to give her a sense of worth, "If that man had stared at my breasts, I would have felt that I truly existed." As Mahesh Dattani puts it:

> People who are abused when young go through a range of emotions starting from betrayal, anger to guilt to feeling that their body is not their own and that's it's a

tool to attract attention. The story is told in retrospect through the eyes of the survivor. (Santhanam, maheshdattani.com)

The play merges the past and the present seamlessly, depicting scenes of abuse she recalls from her childhood and then focusing on the present with a determined boyfriend, Deepak who refuses to accept that their relationship is over. Deepak continually proposes to Mala to marry him, and after getting an instinct that Mala is suffering some psychological problem, tries to give her a counselor to make sense out of that. He loves Mala, but Mala refuses to marry Deepak as she is unable to understand his true love because of her demands of only physical needs. Thus, her constant lying about her past and her short-lived affairs sets Dattani on the path of unraveling a fascinatingly complex but painful story of psychological manipulations, forced cover-ups and multiple falsehoods born out of one's need for subsistence, security and one's own worth.

MALA. I cannot stop them! I attract them.
DEEPAK. This is all in your mind.
MALA. You don't understand! I am doing something that attracts them to me.

—

DEEPAK. No. No you don't.
MALA. It is true. If I were to let that man in to my house, I will allow him to do anything.

—

MALA. You don't understand. You just don't understand.

—

DEEPAK. Hold my hand. Forget everything and just touch me.
MALA. I-I can't. I don't want to. I can't! (*CP*2, 41-42)

The conversation clearly states Deepak's concern for Mala and Mala's continuous rejection of any relationship with him anymore than physical. Deepak's love and care for Mala and a strong will to remove all psychological problems is clear in these lines:

> DEEPAK'S VOICE. I really wish she would tell me what is on her mind. She doesn't trust me, and I find that very tiring. I am exhausted. I am ready to throw in the towel. If I tell her it's off she would simply look at me. She may not say a word but her eyes would tell me what she is thinking 'See. I told you it won't work. You are wasting your time with me. Go away and leave me alone.' But she doesn't want to be left alone. She seeks company. Desperately enough to offer sex in return. Does she really feel anything? I think she wants something else. I don't know what, she doesn't know what... it doesn't take our relationship anywhere though... I don't even exist for her. I-I am tired... (*CP*2, 45)

He tries to sort out things and by revealing the secrets about Mala's psychological problems by playing a trick and calling Mala, her uncle and her mother to a restaurant and getting their reactions meanwhile different kinds of conversations, specially her Uncle's as Deepak is doubting on him for the Mala's tragic plight.

But Mala could not get over of her problems in spite of the unconditional love of Deepak, just because she is more hurt by her mother's silence who simply refuses to acknowledge the fact that her daughter has been abused; even Shanta blames Mala of enjoying illicit sex and goes on to describe the specific details that must have given her pleasure. This is really strange of a mother accusing her daughter like this, when Mala surrenders after a lots of efforts of realizing her mother about her pain and says 'I just have to learn to live with the pain', Shanta says:

> I remember, much as I was trying to forget, what I saw. Not when you were seven but when you were thirteen (Gently). Please don't misunderstand me, Mala. I remember, seeing you with my brother during the summer holidays. You were pushing yourself on him in the bedroom.
>
> —
>
> You were forcing him to say things to you.

—

To do things to you.

—

I prayed for you Mala... To our god, so He could send his Sudarshan Chakra to defend you, to defend us from the demon inside you, not outside you. But you wouldn't let me. You don't let me.

—

Why should you stop him? You were enjoying it.

—

You were an average child but you had my brother and your cousins dancing around you. That is what you wanted. (*CP*2, 7-28)

As the mother never understands, Mala's complains never ends:

Where were you during those fifteen minutes when he was destroying my soul? ... that's how long or how little it took for you to send me to hell for the rest of my life!

—

you were never for me, because you were just too busy praying. (C*P*2, 53)

And the mother's continual addressing her to be fed shut up and forget everything:

I forget, I forget everything. Be like me. (*CP*2, 29)

Although, one wonders, at times, whether a mother values the orthodox conventional values more for the honour of the family than for her own daughter and teaches the same to her to follow as she has followed is really very strange. In bringing out the entire range of issues involved, Dattani does it without being sensational or cross. The play reaches to its high point when the truth behind this indifferent behaviour of Shanta towards her daughter is revealed that she too has been a victim of incest for over ten years in her childhood, and by the same man. Whereas, Mala at least knows how to protest, Shanta was so traumatized that she even did not know how to complain. She tries to forget the reality of her life through praying and submitting herself to Lord Krishna. She even could not continue a healthy relationship with her husband because of her haunting childhood conditioning, which in turn influences her adult relationships like that of her daughter. Though, she outwardly gets angry with Mala or rather most of the times remains silent inwardly she gets frustrated by the very thought of the destructive position of her own child. In the end, in sheer disgust, she jabs a piece of glass into her mouth trying to cut her tongue. With this shocking scene, the tragedy of the two generations is complete.

Indifference, withdrawal of attention or rejection can also seriously jeopardize a child's emotional development, and can lead to physical, educational or emotional neglect. Dr. Germaine Greer analyses it and says:

> The silence that surrounds issues of anger, pain, guilt, shame and even love and joy can become an 'everyday silence' that inevitably leads to disempowerment, disillusionment and distress. — Sally Berry, Clinical Director, Women's Therapy Centre. (*The Whole*, 171)

If Shanta had not remained silent, Mala and she herself could have overcome their tragic lives. As Dattani asserts:

> It is the silence and the betrayal of the family that affects me the most. Like in this case, the mother knew that her daughter was being sexually abused by her uncle, but still chose to keep quiet. It's this silence that makes the abused feel betrayed. (Santhanam, maheshdattani.com)

The gravity of Mala's fear of speaking and low self-worth in man made world is clear by her first confession to the counselor in September 2001, when she thought herself fully responsible for her tragedy.

> MALA. I-I don't know how to begin... today is the 30th of September...2001, and my name is... I don't think I want to say my name... I am sorry. I hope that is okay with you... I am unsure about this... and a lot of other things. But this... this is the first time you see that i...

(After a long pause, where we do hear her breathing) I know it is all my fault really... it must be. I must have asked for it... somehow I just seem to be made for it. Maybe I was born that way, maybe... this is what I am meant for. It's not anybody's fault, except my own. Sometimes I wish that my mother... (it gets to be difficult for her.) I am sorry but... I can only tell you more if you turn this thing off. (*CP*2, 9)

Is this because in India, women lead a gender-circumscribed, marriage - centric existence or do we have an absence of support systems such as counselors, legal activists, sex education or public campaigns for awareness? When the opportunities within the family will ends exploiting the ignorance and trust of children? Will social intervention occur before more children of both genders are sacrificed at the alter of family honour? All these questions arise in the mind of the reader while reading all these plays of Dattani; but they always remain unanswered even after lots of efforts by social activist and reformers in the society. The world is changing and developing at different levels but the blind adherence to tradition is shocking even in the educated class. This is what Dan tells in the play *Tara*:

Nothing changes... except the date. (*CP*1, 324)

The preoccupation with gender and gender roles, which we are dealing with, becomes apparent from Dattani's very first play itself *Where There's a Will*, a comedy with slight farcical touches *Where There the Will* is embedded within the mechanics of the middle class Gujarati family; Dattani has often referred to the subversion of patriarchy in the play as one of its major concerns. It also points out about the way patriarchal men invariably fail to exist as true individual human beings as he always exist as an epitome of these conservative values. Human relationships and the family unit are at the heart of the dramatic representation. The play takes a look at the Indian middle class morality, the ensuing parody and the commercial bent. As the self made industrialist and a rich and successful businessman Hasmukh

Mehta, a patriarch, around whose life and whose family the play resolves, finds it impossible to part with his money even when he is dead.

Hasmukh Mehta, the self-made and self-centred garment tycoon, pissed off with his family and dislikes and distrusts everyone in the family. He is a patriarch, malcontent with the typical problems of familial expectations. According to him, his son Ajit is an irresponsible spendthrift and therefore to be a wastrel; his daughter-in-law Preeti too 'nice to be trustworthy; his wife downright stupid, obsessed with cooking and feeding, thus driving him crazy. What he expects is, implicit obedience to him, as he practiced it in his father's case. The play is about traditional family values meeting with seven deadly sins. According to Dattani the theme of the play deals with gender conflicts like all other plays of him and comment on the patriarchal system. It's about hunger for power and money at the cost of values.

And one night, after a heavy squabble with the family, Hasmukh passes away. But his ghost lingers on to control his family from the other world. The play is neatly divided into two halves, pre-death Hasmukh and post death Hasmukh. Hasmukh is ever present throughout the play as his ghost lingers on to control his family from the other world, through his will which he made before his demise to won the battles that he fought when alive. The promise and hope of a will and inheritance holds together Hasmukh and his family before his death and again, after his death, it is the will, crafted with chicanery by Hasmukh to dominate and laugh at his family even from his grave that holds them together and now joined by a mistress of Hasmukh, Kiran (who is dramatically thrust into the scene), whom he appointed trustee and in effect head of the family for 21years, by which time the wealth would be of little use to all his family members. Therefore his family will lead a frugal life until Ajit turns forty-five. This move renders all the members of the family to the position of pensioners. They would have to put up with the mistress, in addition, who will live with them in the same house with rein of power in her hand.

Thus, the play is about the power which dominates Indian families. Hasmukh exercises hegemonic power over the rest of his family to perpetuate his own conception of the self, which, he has, in turn, received from his father. The will here, too becomes the iconic instrument to power (through wealth), and shapes and reshapes the destiny of the family and familial relationships, even after his death. An 'exorcism of patriarchal code' as Dattani puts it; the play skillfully works his narrative around the intrigues and maneuverings of a dysfunctional Indian family. Kiran stays and manages the family and the business. Her presence disturbs the family, much to Hasmukh's delight, who had planned to teach his family a lesson and hopes they will learn how inadequate they were as his wife, son and daughter in law.

Therefore, the patriarchal paramount, Dattani's recurrent theme again appears in this play. Women, whether a daughter, wife, daughter-in-law or mistress, all is dependent on man for financial and physical security. Women have been looked down upon by men as an object to meet their needs, as a liability and a source of enjoyment. Their prime functions in marriage are to dance attendance upon their husband and to be an exciting partner in bed. The colourless and loveless relationships between the two couples in the play, Hasmukh and Sonal, and Preeti and Ajit are examples of a typically materialistic and money-minded upper middle class milieu. Especially is the life of the former one, because of the tyrannical attitude of Hasmukh who thinks his life a complete wastrel. He says,

> I soon found out what a good-for-nothing she was. As good as mud. Ditto our sex life. Mud... (*CP*1, 473)

Though Sonal has no voice of protest in front of her husband, but she says to Preethi, her daughter-in-law:

> Proud? He thinks he is king of all he surveys! And we are his subjects... he can put on all the airs he wants to, but he doesn't fool me... (*CP*1, 472)

Hasmukh Mehta is a terror for the members of his family when alive as well as when dead. As an autocrat and cynical man who always criticizes his wife, even when she takes care of him, his house, cook their food, Hasmukh kept a mistress for his satisfaction which he is not getting with his wife.

Many women can find no solution to their dilemma and are defeated in attempts at adaptation. These constitute the array of the sick, unhappy, neurotic, wholly or partly incapable of dealing with life. Whether it be 'sick headaches' or hyper-tension or the enormous collections of disorders of the reproductive system, it is all one and all arises from an inability to master unconscious feelings constantly aroused by disappointment and frustration. This happens to Sonal when even after the death of tyrannical husband, she is not able to live independently because of her husband's trickery to her and her family. Kate Millet observes:

> If one takes patriarchal government to be the institution whereby that half of the populace which is female is controlled by that half which is male, the principles of patriarchy appear to be two fold: male shall dominate female, elder male shall dominate younger. (*Sexual*, 291)

Another aspect is about a father who is overpowering not only on his wife, but also on all the people, he comes across including his son. The action in the play starts with the Ajit's talking on phone; Hasmukh dropped in from the office, and overhears him. The father refuses to invest in new business ventures thought up by him as he distrusts Ajit completely and thinks that 'If I let him have his way, we would all be paupers.' It's about father's lots of trouble passing on his legacy to his son Ajit and a will to have everything run his way and son's struggle to define himself as an individual, separate from his successful father. His son should be like him.

> A man feels himself more of a man when he is imposing himself and making others the instruments of his will.—Bertrand de Jouvenel, *Power* (Greer, *The Whole*, 288)

He not only wants him to carry on the mantle of his achievements but also groom him his way. Hasmukh is so disappointed with his married life and son that he began to speculate the aim and reason of marriage if it has to be so futile:

> HASMUKH. Why does a man marry? So that he can have a woman all to himself? No. there's more to it than that. What? Maybe he needs a faithful companion? No. if that was it, all men would keep dogs. No. No, I think the important reason anyone should marry at all is to get a son. Why is it so important to get a son? Because the son will carry on the family name? (*CP*1, 474-475)

Then Hasmukh comes to the point of his patriarchal inheritance, a legacy, which he followed and which his son too has to follow to be a true son of a father like he has been to his father, but Ajit fails to do it in his view. He continues:

> Why did I marry? Yes, to get a son. So that when I grow old, I can live life again through my son. Why did my father marry? To get me. Why did I marry? To get Ajit… Then I should be a very happy man… (but) He doesn't behave like my son. A son should make me happy. Like I made my father… happy. I listened to him. I did what he told me to do. I worked for him. I worked hard for him. I made him… happy. That is what I wanted my son to make me. (Gets a little worked up.) But he failed! Miserably! He has not a single quality I look for in a son! He has made my entire life worthless! (*CP*1, 475)

While, Ajit fiercely resists Hasmukh and will not kowtow to his father's wishes, for wanting to be his own man. As the father wants his son to be him, the son is constantly resists by popping the question:

> AJIT. … you want to run the show, play Big Boss as long as you can. Or as long as God permits. And when all of a sudden, you are 'called to a better world'. You will still want to play Big Boss. And you can do it through me. In short, you want me to be you. (460)

And what becomes of me? The real me. I mean, if I am you, then where am I? (*CP*1, 461)

These words of Ajit reflect his desperate need to have a self identity free from conventional set ups. Dattani brings up the three successive generations of the male line in the play, and indicates the compulsions under which Hasmukh behaves in the way that he does; on him lays the anus of perpetuating patriarchy and its stereotypes. While the father thinks his shoes are too big for the tender feet of his son at 23, the youngster cannot but resent the old ways and the lack of recognition of his full potential. An argument, which is more comical, reveals the hollowness of this relationship in the materialistic age:

HASMUKH. You have the right to listen to my advice.

AJIT. Thank you. You are so generous I could kiss your feet.

HASMUKH. There's no need to do that. Just polish my shoes every morning and I'll be happy.

AJIT. You will never be happy. Not until all of us dance to your tune. And I will never do that. (*CP*1, 458)

—

Anything I do is wrong for you! Just because you are a self-made man and had a deprived childhood, you feel that I am having it too easy. Nothing I do will ever seem intelligent to you. You are prejudiced. (*CP*1, 459)

That's why Hasmukh does not want to give his inheritance to his son, at least, until he will not get the lesson to be like him and he is going to make trickery Will for this, as he says:

He is going to destroy me! It won't be long before everything I worked for and achieved will be destroyed! Finished because of him! Well, I won't let it happen! I won't let it happen! I won't let it... (*CP*1, 475)

And when the Will finally comes after the death of Hasmukh, Ajit realizes the victory of his father even after his death on him. As the Will reveals that Ajit would get control over the company only after he would turn a ripe 45 and would also has to attend office everyday from 9to6 compulsorily. He says resignedly:

> AJIT. ... He is still alive. Through his will! Through his mistress!
>
> —
>
> He is making me do things he wanted me to do. Through her! In the office. Without realizing it, she has replaced father and is replacing me with father.
>
> —
>
> Everything she tells me to do is exactly what he would have wanted me to do. We are all living out a dead man's dream! Quite a price to pay for a few crores of rupees to tide us by in our old age.
>
> —
>
> All right. I can't fight him now. He has won. He has won because he's dead. But when he was alive, I did protest. In my own way. (Laughs) Yes, I'm happy I did that. Yes. I did fight back. I did do 'peep peep' to him! That was my little victory. (*CP*1, 501)

However, Preeti, Hasmukh's daughter-in-law does not suffer from his hands directly although he succinctly describes her as "Pretty, charming, graceful and sly as a snake" and sums her up as (at least true to his prediction which we get in the end) "she is an intelligent girl, I can tell you. She has her eye on my money." (*CP*1, 456) She also suffers from denying from the will as she may get her share till her still-to-be-born child turns 21. To some extent, Hasmukh is right because later Preeti speaks frankly Ajit about his autocrat father after his death:

> He was a slave driver, your father! He almost drove me mad with his bossy nature. He succeeded with your mother. (*CP*1, 501)

Preeti pays no heed to the Indian values like 'purity' or 'goodness' associated with women and for her they do not hold any significance. She breaks all the norms set by the society only for women. She is a true product of money-minded materialistic world, as she always pretend to be nice, when Hamukh was alive. She continues to blame her husband for not getting share after his death. This also shows 'selfish' behaviour of her even to her husband, without any love or affection:

> I simply listened to him and didn't 'protest' like you! I knew he didn't have long to live... After he's gone, we can have all the freedom to do what we want, and also all the money. I almost succeeded. He would have left everything to us if you hadn't 'protested'. That was your mistake! (*CP*1, 502)

Every member pretends in the family to be 'nice' to Hasmukh for his money, when he was alive, so does Preeti, as she thought this all will end with Hasmukh but her hatred of such hypocrisy is clear when even after his death, she has to live the same as before, without any right on property and freedom as Kiran replaces the dominating Hasmukh having the controlling power in her hands. Furiously she tells Ajit:

> Every day, it's the same. Make breakfast, make the beds, cook lunch, look after your mother, listen to her complaints and then, when I am just about ready to drop, you come home! Followed by the mistress of the house, literally. And when madam is ready, we all sit down for dinner and pretend everything is fine. A picture of a perfect family. The widowed mother, the expectant mother, the son who has stepped into his late father's shoes without a peep, and of course the mistress of the house. The only one left to complete the picture is your father. (*CP*1, 500)

Preeti even changes her behaviour towards her mother-in-law Sonal and the reason behind her marring to Ajit comes out, as Sonal remarks:

> Preeti was never like this before. She was nice and caring when he was alive. Now, after the will, she has become unbearable. She frightens me. Sometimes I think she is

> capable of doing anything for money... there is something wrong in desiring money with such... passion. (*CP*1, 506)

Therefore, familial conflict and no personal attachments in any relations, only the selfish motive of power in contemporary middle class Indian family is transparent clear after the death of Hasmukh. Everyone wants to live freely with some individual identity and a personal way of living, a hope of all the family members in Mehta family, which shatters by the dominating, will even after the death of chauvinistic Hasmukh.

Dattani's *Dance Like a Man*, a powerful drama, directly hits out at torn relationships in a pseudo-sophisticated society. It examines the authority and prejudices, socially and culturally revealing the darker secrets of family lives and the conflict between generations. The play tells the tale of human hearts, trapped in conflicting situations. Running at two levels, represented by two generations, the play stands on the platform of tradition, and yet transcended the limits of time and space to expose the cracks in the contemporary socio-cultural setting. It's a battle against society that prevents us from reaching out to our roots. What we call a 'modern India' is really a negation of the real India. It doesn't work that way. The story resolves around two Bharatnatyam dancers Jairaj and Ratna and now their daughter Lata. It is a reminder of those times when dance used to be considered the profession and craft of prostitutes in India. A woman as a dancer was bad enough but a man trying to become a dancer was something unheard of.

Ratna and Jairaj, two Bharatnatyam (an Indian Classical dance form) dancers, a middle class south Indian couple, two individual entrapped in a cultural chasm, reflect the past and the present Indian culture, identities and gender roles. The play opens in the living room in an old-fashioned house, an antique mansion that once belonged to Jairaj's father, Amritlal Parekh, an autocrat who is dead but a stiff reminder of their authoritative past. On one side, he is a freedom fighter and liberal minded enough to allow the son to marry a girl from another community. He wears the liberal mask in public but is appalled that his own son, his own flesh is learning to be a dancer, a craft supposedly reserved for woman, that too Devadasis. On the other hand, he is entrenched in his own tradition, and believes that Bharatnatyam is a craft of prostitutes and therefore is not able to understand Jairaj and Ratna's devotion to dance. His role in the destruction of their lives comes to us later on in their memories, the play rather begins with the entrance of Lata (a third generation) and her lover Viswas (a rich mithaiwala), whom Lata brings to meet her parents. But the parents, Jairaj and Ratna are busy making preparations for their daughters, Lata's debut and they do not pay the desired attention to Viswas.

Though Jairaj is concerned about Lata too, but Ratna seemed much worried as there is an International concert of Lata and one of their musicians has met with an accident. Ratna wants her daughter Lata to achieve distinction as a danseuse as she herself had been thwarted in her desire to make her as a dance artist because of the repressive patriarchal dominance exercised by her father-in-law, Amritlal, who expected all the members of the family to prostrate themselves before him. She considers herself a failure and for this she blames Jairaj. She vents her frustrations on Jairaj and accuses him of being a jelly in front of his dominating father. So, now from arranging the mridangam player, to requesting the media to cover the event, Ratna is taking care of everything for her daughter. Lata is on the verge of an arangetram, and there are only a few days left when the mridangist breaks an arm. Ratna is stressed and cannot rest till an alternative is found. She visits another artist and requests her to send her mridangist.

Ratna's necessity is to find some kind of consummation for her specific femininity and for herself as a human being. The circumstances, with which she is now surrounded, as well as those of her upbringing, tend to prevent these two consummations- instinct and ego- from being fused together. Conflict and compromise are almost inevitable. In attempting to gain these, an individual identity of herself as a dancer, she carries her outside her home, away from children and childbearing. She has at least formally won but in winning, she was forced, too, into dubious battle for all the other rights auxiliary to them. Thus she finds herself squarely in the middle of the most serious kind of divided purpose.

Unable to relinquish either satisfaction, she necessarily attempts to obtain both. In making the attempt, she must divide her attention and one of her occupations must be sacrificed in some measure to the other. Certainly, the tasks of a woman in bearing and educating children as well as maintaining, as best she may, the inner integrity of her home are capable of demanding all her time and best attention. It is becoming unquestionably more and more common for the woman to attempt to combine both home and child care and an outside activity, which is either work or career. When these two spheres combine it is inevitable that one or the other will become of secondary concern and, this being the case, it is certain that the home will take that position. The same case happened with Ratna too, when she used to leave her son Shankar in the hands of ayah on the times when she was out for her dance performances without knowing that she used to give him opium to get rid of her duties.

A presentation of the familial conflict of three generations, the play addresses how the younger one's view opposed to older ones and therefore arises alteration with each generation. Amritlal carries the baggage of his own times and tries to manipulate the next generation- Jairaj and Ratna to transmit it forward. Jairaj and Ratna, ironically, do the same with their own progeny, and try to pass on their preferences to Lata. Therefore, a complex story of a one generation dancing couple feeling the insecurity of advancing years and lack of financial cushion, yet hoping that the next generation will take to the craft, and also keep the kitchen fire burning with it!

In this handling down of cultural context, a number of revelations are made and several 'hidden' stories are told that begin to reveal the fissures in these spaces. Today, Lata is constantly under pressure to 'achieve all that her parents couldn't'. Lata goes through her own angst. She loves dance. But she wants to do that on her terms. She often tells Viswas that she 'wants to dance for herself and not to please anybody'. But at the same time, she is aware of her parents, particularly her mother's aspirations for her. How can she let them down? Lata is not a failure like her parents and her success is because of her own hard work and their supports. She becomes a sensation overnight. Then, there are her own plans for the future and is quite happy to marry Viswas, whose father owns half the buildings on commercial street and makes mithai and who for his part is suave and comfortable with his complete ignorance of Bharatnatyam- the passion of the preceding generation. Though Viswas has his own quirks about the dance, when he mimics Amritlal without knowing about him very well but co-incidentally in true resemblance. Finding no one around himself, Vishwas removes the old shawl of Amritlal from the cupboard and wears it and struts around, and mimics him as his son Jairaj is in front of him and he is opposing his dancing hobby:

> So, you want to be a dancer. Hah! Hah! Hah! Son, you will never amount to anything in life. Look at me. Look at what I have achieved. Yes. Look. Look. Look. (*Points to the furniture.*) What's that you say? There's more to life than money? You ungrateful wretch!
>
> —
>
> Where will you go being a dancer? Nowhere! What will you get being a dancer? Nothing! People will point at you on the streets and laugh and ask, 'Who is he?' 'He is a dancer.' 'What does he do?' 'He is a dancer.' 'Yes, but what does he do?' 'He is a dan ...'. (*CP*1, 397)

Or when after the sensational performance of Lata, he comments of its too much eroticness:

> VISWAS. I loved the ashtapadi. ... Well, it was tenderly intense and intensely tender and all that. But ...

It was too erotic. ... I admire your courage. Look, I don't mean I object to her dancing. It is her passion and it wouldn't be fair for me to ... All I'm saying is that ... What am I saying? (*Thinks.*) Yes! That it really isn't necessary to make it so ... you know. At least I don't think so. Of course, you may think so, but I don't. And I don't know what she thinks about it so ... (*Shrugs his shoulders and laughs nervously.*) (*CP*1, 435)

But Lata and Viswas have a happy married life, opposite of that of Jairaj and Ratna, whose hypocritical life began to unravel with this new couple's getting success in their career and in their life. The calm and funny exterior, with which the play began cracks and reveals the demons that they had swept under the carpet all these years.

But, this couple of third generation is not the main point of the play, not even the life of Ratna, who may not be called and escaped as being true Indian woman, plays somewhat 'negative' character in Jairaj's life and is an example of Dattani's 'strong' woman, successful in the survival of man's world, lived her life on her own way and runs the life of Jairaj too. She paid attention to her own career rather than encouraging her husband's. She was more successful in the past times than her husband because somewhat she was accepted as a dancer for being a woman and in the present times too, she has a daughter to continue her own passion, even if she herself left her career because of familial hindrance. As a self-obsessed and fascinating woman she accepted the offer of Amritlal to ruin Jairaj's career in dance life to achieve her ambitions:

AMRITLAL. Help me make him an adult. Help me to help him grow up.

RATNA. How?

AMRITLAL. It is hard for me to explain. I leave it to you. Help me and I'll never prevent you from dancing. I know it will take time but it must be done.

RATNA. I'll try. ... And once he stops dancing – what will you do with him then?

AMRITLAL. Make him worthy of you. (*CP*1, 427-428)

And, in the present, Ratna has moved from half-heartedly pushing her marginally talented husband to dance, to shoving her daughter into the limelight, to make up for the fame she never had:

> I heard Rave reviews... And why shouldn't she get reviews like this? I deserved it... my hard work has paid off, hasn't it? (*CP*1, 439)

She was so self-obsessed that she considers Lata's hard work and success as her own and wants to paste those reviews in her own album of dance. Ratna's jealousy even with her daughter is surfaced when Jairaj realizes her that it is only and only Lata's success and achievement and she begins to weep. All these indicates that on one way or other, Ratna was able to manage her life according to her own will somewhat, if not completely and she is the victim of her own perceptions and not of others.

We realize that at the receiving end of the politics of gender is not Ratna so much as is Jairaj, a victim of familial and social conceptions: kept on a leash by his father, eclipsed by his wife, a failure as a dancer, and an alcoholic. He is the only son of a successful businessman, Amritlal, a nationalist in the pre-independent era married Ratna, a Bharatnatyam artiste and abandoned family trade to continue his passion for classical dance. The father is appalled by this challenging behaviour and his stratagems finally destroy Jairaj. After the wife's betrayal, it is liquor that keeps him going.

Amritlal, a freedom fighter, comes across as a rather conservative character when it comes to dealing with 'deviance' from gender stereotypes and as one who represents a very middle-class sense of morality. Jairaj and Ratna live within such a structure: the domain of this patriarch, whose antipathy to a great many things that concern the activities of his son and daughter-in-law draws the boundary lines for their behaviour within his sphere of influence. His horror at the knowledge of his son's choice as a professional dancer and his relentless pressure at dissuading him from embarking on an effeminate career are expressed in these words of him:

> A woman in a man's world is considered progressive, but a man in a woman's world is only pathetic. (*CP*1, 427)

He alleged like many who were less knowledgeable that Bharatnatyam is a craft of prostitutes, improper for his daughter-in-law and absolutely unimaginable for his son. He felt that no self-respecting person should perform such a dance, let alone a man, and therefore did not understand Ratna and Jairaj's devotion to dance. He forbids Ratna from visiting the old devdasi who teaches her the intricacies of Bharatnatyam and cannot tolerate the sounds of dancing bells that ring through their practice sessions. At least, he wants his son to behave like a 'man'. The underlying fear is obviously that dance would turn him 'womanly'- an effeminate man and hence, he must oppose, tooth and nail, Jairaj's passion for dance. He shudders every time his son jingle-jangle past mid-practice, all pouting lips and swaying hips, on all these 'womanly' postures in the dance movements. Because in his opinion, a man's happiness lies "in being a man." (*CP*1, 426)

He derides dancing as a feminine occupation and manages to but off Jairaj's wife Ratna to thwart Jairaj' motive of dancing. Juxtaposions worry Amritlal- Can a prostitute be a dancer? Can one be a man and still dance? What kind of guru wears his hair long and walks funny? A powerful patriarch's imprinted Amritlal, therefore, vigorously disapproves of his son's career choice and the 'disreputable' company he keeps. Forced to succumb to mounting family pressures, Jairaj lives with a sense of mediocrity and his wife's treachery.

Jairaj's wife and father have colluded to achieve their own selfish ends, to perpetuate the old stereotypes and reinforce their own sense of security at his expense. He will consent to Ratna's career in dance only if she helps him pull

Jairaj out of his obsession and make him a 'manly' man. The tragedy for Jairaj is that he has chosen to pursue a career that is considered 'right' only for women. Society versus individual is again a dominating theme in the play and again here it is the family, as the microcosm of society, lays down its unwritten rules. Jairaj follows his heart's desire and becomes a dancer but has enraged his father in the process. Amritlal Parekh is disappointed because his son's ideas of happiness do not fit in with his. He says:

> I have always allowed you to do what you have wanted to do. But there comes a time when you have to do what is expected of you. Why must you dance? (*CP*1, 415)

Dattani asserts in an interview to Ranu Uniyal about *Dance Like a Man*:

> It is about Bharatnatyam dancers. Again in their old age, when they are in their 60s and they are looking back on to their struggling days, when they had their ideals and in the 50s where there was a stigma attached to the dance form; that it is dance form of the Devdasis, it's a prostitute's dance and people from respectable families didn't perform or practice that dance form. It is doubly difficult for the man, you know, what business does a man have learning a prostitute's dance. So it brings about gender roles, what is expected of gender as well. And also the tensions between the couple and how they solve, how they felt that they used their relationship to develop their careers, dances and how they reconcile to the fact that the time wasn't right for them. (*The Plays*, 182)

Two key aspects are highlighted: one is the conflict between the artist and society in India today, and the other conflict between the relationships in modern Indian family (wife/husband and father/son). In the materialistic society of contemporary India, Dattani raises a few unlikely questions about the social construct that a man is- in terms of sexuality, as the head of the family and as an artist. The stereotype of gender roles are pitted against the idea of the artist in search of creativity with the restrictive construction of the world that he is forced to inhabit. Jairaj, who choose a line of career that is discordant with conventional expectations, is a man in a woman's world. In a society, where gender equations and change in the world is defined by tacit rules can not associate dance and man together. It is given 'female' identity, which is used to question the social structure that constructs male stereotypes too. Dattani adds:

> That's true, people do find it a bit difficult to associate classical dance with men. To be frank, I just followed what my heart said and I continue to do that. I never wanted to be a rebel in the society, instead I did what I felt was right. (Chatterjee, *The Statesman*, 5)

The play provides multiple frameworks of gender and gender roles: the prostitute as a dancer and an artist to whom Ratna used to go to learn dance in her prime age; the man Jairaj as a dancer; the guru of both in their early lives who sports long hair and has an 'effeminate' walk- and the clash as how the property and money play a deciding and manipulating role in the construction and acceptation of identities. Patriarchal operation imposes certain social standards of femininity as all biological women and men in order to prove that these standards for 'femininity' are natural. Consequently, a woman or man, who does not confirm to the chosen standards, is considered unfeminine or non-masculine and therefore unnatural. Therefore man can also be constructed as marginalized to the symbolic order.

Masculinity as a concept has evolved over centuries based on human experience, cultural patterns, religious beliefs and social psychology born of economic determination. The characteristics associated with the ideology of masculinity are supremacy, loftiness, premordiality, ascendancy and creative, generative capacity. The male attributes of values, valiance, virtue, virility, violence and power have evolved universally through the civilization process.

Cultural issues such as social roles, personal ambition, passion, and a cultural dilemma and conflict faced by exponents of a fading art form are weaved together into the story. Jairaj is abandoned for having chosen a career suitable for women, therefore it is a story, all about passion and the life of an artiste, a range of human emotions, of the fire within, of ambition, hard work, understanding, sentiments, sacrifice and the price of passion- of having a frustrated and futile life. He is ostracized for he chooses to dance like a woman though his dancing is a way of expressing his identity and is shown the door because he goes against the expressed wishes of his father in opting to dance his way through life. Rebellion surfaces in the family the very moment Amritlal breathes his last. Consequently, after his father's death, he destroys all things that are dear to his father. He does not even spare the rose garden. Too much of stringency leads to revolt which, though remains undercover, gushes forth, whenever it finds an outlet and he wonders whether it has been worth all the sacrifices. All his life he has tried to achieve perfection but has always made mistakes and found it not easy to dance to different tune. The outcome is a man, sad and disillusioned who is crushed by his wife's ambition and father's inflexibility.

Both Jairaj and Ratna paid a great price to reach at this stage- Jairaj has compromised on his manliness but could not dance like a man, a regret he felt till the end of his life, and Ratna on her motherhood, pay the price with the life of her son, Shankar for being a successful dancer. There were testing times and difficult situations and one tragedy which made them both give up their dancing career. So strong is the feeling of this guilt that the albatross hangs from Ratna's neck for the rest of her life and a mere mention of her child's name puts her off. Like in all battles, a completely innocent individual becomes the victim: the baby son of the dancing couple, a loss of both for their neglect. The story unfolds the condition of both in their past and the way past affects their present and is to affect their future.

What the couple could not achieve in their life, got after death, free from the demands of family and society, are able to "dance perfectly. In unison. Not missing a step or a beat."

(*CP*1, 447) Though the play ends merrily with a contented married life of Lata and Viswas and a unity of Jairaj and Ratna, but the story as discussed above through the complex relationship between Bharatnatyam artistes Jairaj and Ratna, whose marriage stumbles through jealousness, hostilities and failures; have grown apart and have done much harm to each other.

To Dattani, the core of the play is about gender construct and resultant tension is because of transgressions from expectations and conventions. Here there is trouble because though Jairaj and Ratna are liberal enough by making their careers in a traditional dance form, Bharatnatysm, that was considered erotic and a craft of prostitutes in their times. But they expect each other the same gender roles as Jairaj wants to dance but wants Ratna to be a mother first and Ratna wants Jairaj to be a provider and be a man, therefore, form the complicated patterns in the man-woman relationships. Both Jairaj and Ratna live with the knowledge of their sacrifices and sins which yield nothing but frustration and a continuous blaming on each other. Dynamics between the successful daughter and the frustrated ambitious mother were interesting, as her husband struggles to placate her by saying, "At least you have a daughter to be jealous of."

The fissure is the relationship between Jairaj ands Ratna begin to show and finally come to an end towards the fag end of the play. The debate introduces us to the past; a past Ratna and Jairaj are still trying to cope with, a past that had seen the two of them struggling to make a name in the profession while trying to deal with Amritlal. Thus the relationship between husband and wife who have, contrary to all public impression of being a happy and well suited couple, grown apart and have done enough harm to each other.

Dance Like a Man is a play everyone can identify with as it comes with all the emotions we all have experienced- on one way up or down. There are layers to every emotion, ambition, greed, love, loneliness, just the way it is in life. The last lines of the play reverberate:

> We were only human. We lacked the grace. We lacked the brilliance. We lacked the magic to dance like God. (*CP*1, 447)

(b) Deconstruction of gendered identity

The above illustrations of the plays of Dattani constructed and perpetuated the patriarchal ideology both by men and women, but Dattani's aim is not only depicting this domination and ascendancy, but deconstructing the gendered society by the 'strong' male and female persona of present generations. Therefore, briefly, looking above at a number of ways in which Dattani uses the 'play' to 'play' with the idea of gender, now in the following part, the subversion of the social norms which gender appears to imply. Notes John McRae:

> ... as the characters' masks fall, their emotions unravel, and their lives disintegrate. For the fault is not just the characters'- it is everyone's, in a society which not only condones but encourages hypocrisy, which demands deceit and negation, rather than allowing self-expression, responsibility and dignity. (*CP*1, 46)

Dattani's feminism is not only about the elimination of differences between the sexes; nor even simply the achievement of equal opportunity: it concerns the individual's right to find out the kind of person he or she is and to strive to become that person. Aiming to dismantle all "systems of domination", Dattani even illustrates the phrase of Simone De Beauvior, "One is not born, but rather becomes, a woman. No biological, psychological, or economic fate determines the figure that the human female presents in society; it is civilization as a whole that produces this creature..." (*The Second*, 267)

According to him, women and men both are not born but rather become women and men and it is civilization that turns them likewise. When the position of women within the social whole is altered, new conceptions of the self and society come directly into conflict with older ideas about a woman's role, her destiny, and even her 'nature'. Sandra Lee Bartky writes that feminist consciousness is the experience in a certain way of certain specific contradictions in the social order.

In Dattani's patriarchal world, both men and women dominate and are dominated in the fixed societal norms. He demolishes these typecast roles by generational gap and repositioning of the male-female stereotype within patriarchy by depicting 'strong' women and 'weak' men in his plays. Dattani's women in the end may not seem 'ideal' for Indian tradition, but they are true to themselves in revealing their true inner selves and fights back. Dattani's vision of emancipation has fired the imagination of many women. It involves an escape from male-defined femininity that turns them into domesticated, cosmetized and caged birds in order to realize their inherent creative energy. He affirms:

> We are talking about communal complex, we're talking about gender battles maybe and the male-female equation have been re-examined, at least in the cities. And I think all this has to reflect in the theatre we do, and it's absolutely vital and necessary for this to happen. (Uniyal, *The Plays*, 179)

Women in Dattani's plays are marginalized, but not victims as they fight back in the end like Dolly and Alka in *Bravely Fought the Queen.* All the women characters in this play are examples of exploitation prevalent in educated urban families and also the epitomes of retaliation if they are not heard or are crushed for a very long time. These women are of course the 'Queen' referred to in the title of the play, a title which in itself is an inter-textual derivative source from a translation of a Hindi poem of the indomitable Rani of Jhansi. According to John Mc Rae:

> The title goes back to traditional Hindi text "we learnt in school... but had to translate it in English as an exercise"- but with its refrain of 'so bravely fought the manly queen' it comes right up to date in its questioning of female and male roles in society. (*Mahesh Dattani's*, 58)

Alka and Dolly have their moments of resistance that make them survive in the oppressive atmosphere of the Trivedi house. Dolly listens to the thumri of Naina Devi and defines her sexuality through a fantasy with the cook, Kanhaiya, who gratifies her emotional and physical needs which does not exist on this quotient with her emotional and physical needs which does not exist on this quotient with her husband Jiten. Therefore, a taboo issue of extra-marital relationship in Indian families is illustrated by Dattani:

> Definitely, the right values are not anything that is confrontantial.... You can't talk about a middle-class housewife about having sex with the cook or actually having a sex life, that isn't Indian either- that's confrontantial even if it is Indian. (Mee, *Mahesh Dattani's*, 163)

Alka creates her identity through acts of defiance- such as drinking alchohol and dancing in the rain. She very boldly questions the authority of her husband and asks for an explanation for his disloyalty. She also exposes the betrayal of her brother for not revealing the existence of homosexual relations between her husband and her brother. Just like Girish Karnad's play *Hayavadana*. Dattani's play *Bravely Fought the Queen* questions the patriarchal moral code which demands the faithfulness of a woman to her husband but not the faithfulness of a man to his wife, Alka is all armed to fight back and to question the norms set by men for women and this instantly reminds the readers of Dolly's lines where she says:

> And we can all go- bravely fought! Bravely Fought the Queen! Full of manly valour. (*CP*1, 296)

Dattani pronounces the idea of writing the play and taking its title, such as:

> ...*Bravely Fought the Queen* was triggered off by the poem we learnt in school, 'khoob ladi mardani who to Jhansi Wali Raani thi" and what I had witnessed at somebody's house, was some form of battle between the woman and her husband and immediately something

> triggered off and the poem came to my mind, that she was fighting very bravely. And then I immediately got this setting of a woman fighting a losing battle and the title just came to me and is reflective of Laxmi Bai's fight against the British and it was a losing battle but she never gave up. (Uniyal, *The Plays*, 183)

This attitude of Dattani is clearly revealed, when Alka desires to dress up as the Rani ki Jhansi, to be the brave queen in the costume party. She seems to be getting ready to fight back, with an imaginary sword swinging in her hand; for all that she has undergone. By focusing on sexual fantasies and subconscious desires of Alka and Dolly, which were suppressed from a long time, Dattani gives them their identity for existence. He says:

> ... it is amazing how often I have been criticized for having the women enact their sexual fantasies... My primary focus was on giving the women some kind of release from the tedium of their existence. I still continue to see that as one of more positive aspects of the play which otherwise is quite dark. (Subramanyam, *Muffled*, 130)

The liberating dance of Alka in the rain signifies the sense of freedom from the shackles of society. when she dances freely in the rain, she finds herself in a utopian world, which envisage a world free of male privilege and male hierarchy and authority over women, a world which Julia Kristeva envisage a "society in which the sexual signifier would be free to move, where the fact of being born male or female no longer would determine the subject's position in relation to power, and where, therefore, the very nature of power itself would be transformed." (Moi, *Sexuall*, 172)

When the two worlds of men and women coverage violently in Act III, all the characters stand exposed, the sham and façade ripped apart. In a review of *Bravely Fought the Queen* in BAC, Ian Shuttleworth says:

> Much of the play's tension comes from the interaction between the enclosed, claustrophobic, female world of

> Act I and the male world of business in Act II. The fact that both sexes are living lives based on fantasy is cruelly exposed when the characters confront each other in Act III, and the realities of their lives emerge. The homosexuality of one of the brothers, the crippled daughter of the other marriage, Baa's continued presence- all of these facts are concealed in the uneasy world which the characters inhabit. The play becomes a plea for humanity and for tolerance. It is equally a cry for the acceptance of Indian values that are shifting, where tradition and contemporary clash, confuse and create a new social landscape. (*Mahesh Dattani's*, 89)

We see that women have not been presented as sinners but they endure because of the men who are part of their lives. Jiten, at last, exposed to be a pathetic escapist and is driven to guilty tears and Nitin, too, exposed his homosexual relations with Praful. Therefore, both felt ashamed of their misdeeds on their wives but could not escape as it is too late now to go back. As Mahesh Dattani says in an interview to Lakshmi Subramanyam:

> I am not sure I have portrayed the women as victims in *Bravely Fought the Queen.* I see the men as victims of their own rage and repression. This has serious consequences on the lives of the women. But they do fight their battles and win some and lose some. (*Muffled*, 130)

There is yet another character, outside the Trivedi household, Lalitha, Sridhar's wife whose entry into the play introduces a relatively different schema that is totally alien to the two sisters. She is independent, free, choosy and creative. She nurtures 'bonsai plants', does a bit of creative writing for a woman's magazine and is also well-versed with the professional affair of her husband, Sridhar- a world, which is alien to the Alka and Dolly. On the one hand, it is Lalitha's attempt at formulating an identity of her own that dissolves the class hierarchy between the women in the Trivedi house and Lalitha. On the other hand, she represents the post-feminist viewpoint regarding women's status in the post modern social and cultural environment. The evening she spends in the Trivedi household is enough to tell her of the existing cruelties of the patriarchy which a modern or postmodern woman would disavow to believe. After discovering the inner realities of Dolly and Alka and the truth behind the illusory Kanhaiya and the dark auto driver etc, she realizes that 'we have a long walk ahead of us'(314) to go even after a lots of claims of the reformation of women by modern feminists. No matter how much the world proclaims about woman enfranchisement and feminine liberation, subconsciously all women are aware of the fact that they have to go long way to break shackles. Therefore, Mahesh Dattani has always been very particular about the correct portrayal of his women characters and he has no biases against them. He says to Lakshmi Subramanyam:

> I believe I can forget my own gender... So those scenes between women didn't come from an 'outside' view point at all. In fact, I am not even sure about the politics of gender since at times I don't even think about the gender of my characters. Its only when other characters in the play react to their own gender, or the gender of those around, that the issue comes alive. In that sense, contrary to what I said earlier I am on the outside looking in. And sometimes I am on the inside looking out. (*Muffled*, 130)

The fissure between conventional and current cultures having thrown up a new social landscape, the play races towards a brave culmination, laying bare the gruesome truths that lie behind the pretence of conservative Indian morality. Questions of gender, sexuality and identity are raised and the unspoken is voiced, the unseen made visible.

In *Tara*, the context is different, the issue in question is different, but the guilt is very much the same- the ramifications are different. The play deals with the cultural constructions of gender that always gives preference to male over the female. And the more, the odds faced by the physically challenged children in society highlights in the play *Tara*, and how the sincerity and inclination of a girl like Tara to prove her mettle in the world of male supremacy. Tara herself- spirited, tough, a survivor with a sense of humour and delightful repartee- fighting against prejudices and society has against the crippled and the female. Tara is often ridiculed for his artificial leg by her peers at school and the girls of her neighborhood- Roopa, Prema and Nalini. Roopa's words about Tara are representative of the attitude of Prema and Nalini, and possibly of the society at large: "She is a real freak of nature all right." (342) But as the name Tara rightfully suggests a star, the girl was a bright and shining star who did not permit this disability to surmount on herself and always became the source of happiness to her surrounders. She has the ability to laugh at it herself, and laugh at the imbecility of those who consider it great deprivation and a subject of pity or ridicule. Tara is a girl, whose complete life could have done wonders as she has a fire in her which Chandan does not have. Therefore, she is very much capable of holding her own and making the best of her life, with all its givens. Therefore, she emerges a strong character from the beginning to the end by her capacity to revolt frankly as she lashes out at her peers calling them names. As she says to Roopa:

> Get lost! And please ask Nalini and Roopa to come here. I have something to say to them- about you! Oh, wait till they hear this! They will love it. They are going to look at your tits the same way they looked at my leg! Let me see how you can face them ogling at you! You won't be able to come out of your house,you horrible creature! You are ugly and I don't want ugly people in my house! So get lost! (*CP*1, 369)

Tara outbursts in the end against men and eventually against all the systems that thinks that a girl should always be compassionate and careful and should not be selfish like everyone else 'men' and revolts her father on his forcing only Chandan to go to the office because she is unable to mask her anger and resentment. She says to Chandan:

TARA. We are more sensitive, more intelligent, more compassionate human beings than creeps like you and... and...

CHANDAN. And?

TARA. Daddy! (*CP*1, 371)

She also goes against Chandan when he advices her to be calm and polite. She says:

> How do you expect me to feel anything for anyone if they don't give me any feeling to begin with? Why is it wrong for me to be without feeling? Why are you asking me to do something that nobody has done for me? (*CP*1, 371)

Another strong female character is Bharati, though she hides herself behind the mask of love to Tara to hide her guilt towards her. Bharati worries about Tara when she says to Chandan:

> It's all right while she is young. It's all very cute and comfortable when she makes witty remarks. But let her grow up. Yes, Chandan. The world will tolerate you. The world will accept you- but not her! Oh, the pain she is going to feel when she sees herself at eighteen or twenty. Thirty is unthinkable. And what about forty and fifty! Oh God! (*CP*1, 348-349)

Under this apparent maternal love for Tara it is clear that it was not just only an act of expiation but also her moral superiority over her husband and the maternal love becomes an instrument to carve out her space within the family. Therefore, in Dattani's family, the parental love, care and protection is also a kind of fight turf wars over their children- a conflict for control and power as there is always a power structure within families and also struggles for power. As Erin Mee puts it:

> ...Dattani focuses on the family as a microcosm of society in order to dramatize the ways we are socialized to accept certain gendered roles and to give preference to what is 'male'. (*CP*1, 320)

Though Bharati's one wrong decision give her mental trauma but eventually she wins in the fight of power struggle from her husband by deciding the activities of her children.

Dattani's deep preoccupation with gender issues leads to the emergence of the idea of the twin side of one's self-quite literally embodied in one body and the separation the follows. The 'gendered' self, as Dattani refers to it, must in some sense always partake of the 'other' in order that it is complete. The fragmented self is clear as to how the Siamese Twins are first born by fragments of male and female and separated emotionally so that they could not commingle by forcing them to grow differently. Again the double naming of Dan and Chandan is itself a further example of fragmented self. This metaphor is about the separation of the multiple identities, available to us which social constructs require. As Dattani puts in an interview to Erin B Mee:

> ... about the male denying the female, and how the cultural construct of gender favours the male. Whether it's a biological woman or biological man, the favor is to the male, so I think it has to do with coming to terms with one's own self in terms of the feminine in the self. (*Mahesh Dattani's*, 159)

That is why he would prefer to say that this play is more about the 'gendered' self, about acknowledging the female side of one. Notes Erin Mee:

> Tara and Chandan are two sides of the same self rather than two separate entities and that Dan, is trying to write the story of his own childhood, has to write Tara's story. Dan writes Tara's story to rediscover the neglected half of himself, as a means of becoming whole. (*CP*1, 320)

The tale is, after all, narrated by Chandan, the male half of the whole of which the 'other' is Tara. Erin Mee again puts it:

> Dattani sees Tara, as a play about the gendered self, about coming to terms with the feminine side of oneself in a world that always favors what is 'male'... (*CP*1, 320)

Dattani ends the play with the projection of the 'whole' identity, together again, with two legs each, in Dan's memory, beyond nature and society, without the limp or the disabilities, locked in an embrace. This moment tells a lot beyond language, beyond time- a silent song of the wholeness of hug, giving equal importance to the feminine and masculine, merging on an even footing, with a hope of a completely different abled world, a world of real abilities and possibilities and gender equalities.

The end of the play *Thirty Days in September*, like all above three plays of Dattani, enlightens all characters through the revelations of hidden truths and realization of inner selves. The death of the abuser man liberates Mala and Shanta from their oppressor and new lives to their cut off tongues. It takes the victim Mala years of anguish to digest the fact that the trust bonds her abuser built have long been crushed. The object of men's desire: this is the fate that marks Mala's lives even before she become aware of the world. As Emilce Dio Bleichmar points out:

> A girl enters into the Oedipus devalued for her gender, and step by step, through the maternal and paternal phantoms, she will receive the conflicting mandates concerning her sexuality and her possible fates as a woman. She must be formed and delivered as an object of desire and must, for her achievement, develop with greater or less sophistication the arts of grace and seduction. The body, the beauty, the perfection of what is offered to the eye cannot be avoided and will thus be incorporated into the present forms which awaken admiration and desire for a man. (*La Bella*, 109)

But she at last fought against being considered just as a 'body-to-have-sex-with', and vindicates herself human being, instead of being considered merely as a people who is valuable because of her body. She rebelled against what is imposed on women as the only way of being: to assume only the role of being desired, but never that of desiring. This point is precisely the form of protest that is expressed in being capable of assuming ourselves 'as [subjects] of desire and placing in [our] phantom a man as the object which causes it.' (*La Bella*, 110)

As the realization dawns, she admits to her sickness and is willing to be treated for it. For the first time in life, she manages to focus her anger where it belongs- on her uncle who conveniently forced her and her mother's life into darkness. Mala's confession to the counselor at February 2004, after two and half year of her first confession at September 2001, is wrapped in an indescribable, fragile strength. Whereas, in 2001, she thought herself responsible for the misdeeds happened to her, she is now in 2004, she make a clean breast that it is not her own fault at all with full confident:

> MALA: Mala Khatri. February 2004... (Listening to the counsellor) Why not? ... I donot hesitate to use my real name now. Let people know. There's nothing to hide. Not for me. After all, it is he who must hide. He should change his name, not me. It is he who must avoid being recognized. In people's homes, at parties, hopefully even on the streets. He should look the other way when someone spots him anywhere on this planet. And I can make that happen. I have the power to do that now. If I use my real name... (Sighing, thinking about it almost as if it were a pleasant memory.) I wish he were here now, so I could see his face when I tell him I have nothing to hide. Because I know it was not my fault... Now. I know now. (*CP*2, 08)

Therefore, her self-destructive flight comes to an end when her latest lover Deepak who refuses to end their relationship after 30 days. He forces Mala to seek help and confront her past in the form of her uncle and she succeeds in deconstructing her tragic past, not only of her alone, but of her mother's too. Even hanta is forced to shed her 'mute' role and finally vocalize her own story of self-abuse and guilt, which had driven her to seek solace in silence. As Dattani put it herself in an interview to Lakshmi Subramanyam:

> In this play I wished to show that the impact of child sexual abuse is long term but not permanent. This is a play about healing and is positive in its ending. (*Muffled*, 133)

Consequently, one more thing is explicit here that whereas the tragedy of both Tara and Mala is inflicted by their mothers, but in the end, while Tara and Bharati separated on the revelations of the truth, Mala and Shanta at the sense of equanimity having recognized each other's struggle to survive.

Where There's a Will is quite evidently a young man's play which shows fairly optimistically that there is a way by which both men and women find happiness on their own terms. Dattani scrutinizes the questions of identity via multiple frameworks of the individual, the family, the social milieu and nationalities and he begins to locate the self in its context from the very first play *Where There's a Will*. This happy ending play gives every character their independent space out of the governance of Hasmukh and they succeed in finding their individual identities. While the old man is having a good laugh, omnipresent as a ghost, the family sees the mistress gatecrashes and asserts her rights. A few twist and turns later, the family realizes the fine intentions of the lovable mistress Kiran and they live happily ever after.

The play has several interesting aspects; one of them is portrayed by the women. "In the traditional Indian society women, be it a daughter-in-law, a wife or a mistress, are dependent on men, and this play shows what happen when they are pushed to the edge." (Raina, Sita, *CP*, 2000, 501)

Hasmukh's mistress Kiran stands outside the family unit, invisible until the autocrat dies and his will thrashes her at the centre of the action. The patriarch, Hasmukh Mehta, a highly disgruntled person, is decidedly forlorn with the manner his life has been spent- with no one living upto his expectations, the way he had lived up to his father's. he must, therefore, get back at his family; and teach them a protracted lesson and for this, he uses the tool of his will, in which, none of his family members is given their expected shares but Kiran, the mistress has to manage the entire estate for twenty-one years until Ajit's child turns twenty-one and she has also to live with the family for these years to dominate in the place of Hasmukh. Dattani's perception of gendered strength and his repositioning of the male-female stereotypes within patriarchy are presented by the 'strong' women and 'weak' men in his plays. Here too, Kiran Jhaveri, herself marginalized, almost invisible in nobody's fool and wields authority with the sensitivity and her placement into the main action deconstructs the mindsets of all the family members of the Mehta family and clears hollowness and fears inside the hard and dominant men. Kiran, the epitome of Dattani's 'strong' women, embodies certain qualities that Dattani holds as positive and strong – a necessity for a woman- smart, shrewd, calculating and worldly wise. She informs Sonal, wife of Hasmukh, of her own tragic life and the weaknesses of men, which she learnt from her mother's experience and from her own. She is a victim too, like most women who play gendered roles, but one who refuses to be victimized.

> KIRAN. I learnt my lessons from being so close to life. I learnt my lessons from watching my mother tolerating my father when he came home everyday with bottles of rum wrapped up in newspapers. As I watched him beating her up and calling her names! I learnt what life was when my mother pretended she was happy in front of me and my brothers, so that we wouldn't hate my father. And I learnt when I kept my mother away from my father, so that in return he would remain silent for these three hours and he came home, and before he fell asleep on the dining table, too drunk to harm us anymore. I served him those drinks, waiting for that moment when he would become

unconscious and I would say a prayer... Thank God he was too drunk to impose himself on us! Yes, Mrs.Mehta. My father, your husband- they were weak men with false strength.

—

Hasmukh was intoxicated with his power, I thought he was invincible. That he could rule from his grave by making this will. (*CP*1, 508)

The difference between a man and woman has been discreetly outlined by Dattani. Hasmukh could not make any place in the hearts of his family members, being an arrogant and tactless man, whereas Kiran Jhaveri being his mistress, had impressed Sonal so much that she became her confidante, much to the horror of death Hasmukh. It is in the process of dismembering the man that the woman find themselves, and bond, and perceptions of the self are redefined with the change in the centre of authority. The bonding of the wife and mistress who tear him apart ultimately undermines his wonderfully entertaining and malicious power, subverting the hegemonic power of the will. This is crucial to the performed effect of the play. Their conversations reveal the truth that Hasmukh Mehta had wanted his son to live in his own image, just as he had lived his own life in thrall to his father's shadow and even after his father's death, wants someone to be dominated over him, which he could not find in his family members, and get from the mistress. Kiran becomes part of Hasmukh's life with her eyes wide open, and aware of the benefits that she will derive from the relationship. As the converse, Hasmukh began to be irritated and fearful for taking wrong decision of making the wrong will:

KIRAN. Hasmukh Mehta was living his life in his father's shadow.

HASMUKH. That's not true.

KIRAN. He had no life of his own.

HASMUKH. Stop! I order you to stop!

KIRAN. Where were his own dreams? His own thoughts? Whatever he did was planned for him by his father.

——

SONAL. At time he even sounded like his father. So crude and loud.

HASMUKH. (crudely and loudly). You Witch! Have some resepect for your dead husband!

SONAL. Yelling at me, calling me names. 'Do this, don't do that. Have some respect for your husband!

——

KIRAN. He depended on me for everything. He thought he was the decision maker. But I was. He wanted me to run his life. Like his father had. (Pause) Hasmukh didn't really want a mistress. He wanted a father. He saw in me a woman who would father him! (Laughts. Hasmukh cringes at her laughter.) Men never really grow up! (*CP*1, 509-510)

Dattani's 'weak' men, victims of their own perceptions and mechanisms is clear here in judgment of the character of Hasmukh by Kiran and for this, "Nothing is more empowering than towering over your boyfriend and your boss in shoes that double as an offensive weapon. Stilettos-not combat trousers and pierced tongues- are a real source of girl power. (Thomas, *The Whole*, 4)

Sonal too is enlightened by the revelation of the emptiness of her husband's dictating behaviour. They began to pity on him rather of detestation because he has no individual identity and independent wish to live a free life of his own. As Kiran asserts much to the Sonal's realization how she mistakes her husband's weakness as his dominance:

KIRAN. I should have hated him. Like I should have hated my father, my brothers and my husband. But all I felt for him was pity.

HASMUKH. Enough! I say, enough! I paid you to do my work. Not ridicule me.

KIRAN. Even his attempts at ruling over you after his death through his will, are pathetic.(Hasmukh sticks his fingers into his ears and shuts his eyes). The only reason he wanted to do that because his father had ruled over his family. All his life he was merely being a good buy to his father.

SONAL. How little I know him. If I had understood him when he was alive, I would have died laughing. (*CP*1, 510)

Ajit and Preeti also accepted her as one of them and were quite at ease with her. Hasmukh Mehta, whose spirit was a mute watcher of all the developments in his house after his death was greatly disappointed and thwarted to see his mistress take the place amongst his family members which he had desired throughout his life,. The play contrasts how people can affect change or use power, which was first in the hands of the father who demands authority out of his son and daughter-in-law which they denied and now the power turned on their heads to the female clout, gives us a contrast by the manners in which the mistress garners support from all family members by her ably assumed right. Kiran uses her position of power to nurture her new family. Sonal finds her space in her husband's death. Ajit finds the buoyancy his father denied him. Sonal smiles:

I am glad you are living with us. I hope you'll stay with us forever. (*CP*1, 511)

At last, Hasmukh's ghost itself is exorcised by the new order, defeated and runs out in search of his buffalo. While the conversations with the Kiran, Sonal too found herself victim of the same perception as her husband was, for he had lived in the shadow of his father, she had also lived under the governance of her sister Minal. She confesses:

Yes, it's true of me too. I have always lived in my sister's shadow. It was always Minal who decided what we should wear, what games we should play. She even decides which maharaj is suitable for our family. Even at my husband's funeral, she sat beside me and told me when to cry. (*CP*1, 511)

Sonal comes into her own, moving beyond the manipulating hands of her sister under whose shadow she has lived. She thereupon liberates herself from the shackles of the dominance of her sister Minal as she continues:

> ... But everything is going to be different now. I can feel it. (511)
>
> —
>
> (on the phone) Hello? Yes, Minal... No, I don't need another maharaj. Not from you at least! ... I just don't, that's all... Well, as far as I'm concerned you can go jump into a bottomless pit! (*CP*1, 516)

Even, Preeti, daughter-in-law of Hasmukh come to her own terms. A surprise twist at the end revealed that Preeti had actually hastened, if not caused, the death of her father-in-law, as she replaced Hasmukh's medicine by her own vitamin tablets and when his blood pressure was high, he could not get proper medicine and died. Kiran got the truth, but does not use against her or blackmail her, rather to bond husband with wife and herself with the whole family and Preeti ultimately learns the lesson that 'giving is more important than taking'. Meanwhile, everyone get their freedom, Kiran too liberates from her past horrified memories as a business-executive-cum-mistress to a rich man and az daughter to a drunkard and as wife to another.

Men like Ajit reiterate Dattani's position on questions of gender- and he creates the space to grow as well as hungrier for his father's money. Set against each other, father and son stereotypical roles shatters with generation gap. Hasmukh continuously orders Ajit to do the same as he has done and doing in his own life. He never satisfies with Ajit and says him an ineffectual nincompoop- an estimation which even his wife seems to share- but is then shown to have resisted and even won, in however infinitesimal a way, against his father:

> AJIT. You will never be happy. Not until all of us dance to your tune. And I will never do that. (458)

...You want to run the show, play Big Boss as long as you can. Or as long as God permits. And when all of a sudden, you are 'called to a better world', you will still want to play Big Boss. And you can do it through me. In short, you want me to be you.

HASMUKH. ...Yes, I want you to be me! What's wrong with being me?

AJIt. And what becomes of me? The real me. I mean, if I am you, then where am I? (*CP*1, 460-461)

Kiran also views Ajit as a contrasting to all men she came in contact in her whole life, whether that was her own father, husband or boss Hasmukh. She finalizes that Ajit won against his father in the battle of wills:

KIRAN. Thank God, Ajit has escaped.

SONAL. Escaped?

KIRAN. He may not be the greatest rebel on earth, but at least he is free of his father's beliefs. He resists. In a small way, but at least it's a start. That is enough to prove that Ajit has won and Hasmukh has lost. (*CP*1, 510)

The most appealing and perceptive aspect of the play is Dattani's genius of giving the play a philosophical angle in the end, where the chief patriarch Hasmukh (a domineering husband, heavy father and tyrannical Boss) himself comes to the realization that it is not only the members of his family who are too blame but it is his own fault to be victim of his own false perceptions. In his moment of recognition, he becomes aware of his own shortcomings that he was mad about money and has controlled his family not through love and affection but through his will. Living in the shadow of his father, he never really grew up and tried to understand his people, even he hardly cared to explore his true self. Kiran is right that the only reason he wanted to do this is because his father had ruled over his family and therefore become a victim of his own machinations. The man who would rule over his family even after his death is exposed to be a weakling who had constantly quested for a father-substitute.

He is rude to everyone because he was insecure himself. He didn't really want a mistress but a woman who would father him, which he could not find among his family members, Hasmukh came to this realization on hearing the true nature of himself from Kiran. His own sense of self remains undefined until the women sit together and do it for him. He began to ask questions of his own real self identity, which was lost under his father's shadow:

> HASMUKH. Is it... true? Have I merely been to my father what Ajit has been to me? Have all my achievements been my father's aspirations for me? Have I been my father's ghost? If that is true, then where was I? What became of me, the real me? (Realising) Oh, my God! I sound like Aju! No-oo-o! (*CP*1, 511)

After having this discovery of his real self, he wants to live a happy life in true sense of his own free will, but could not. As he wishes in the end:

> Oh, I wish I had been more... I wish I had lived. (*CP*1, 515).

Hasmukh escapes, finally no space for him in this happy family now, to hang himself from the tamarind tree; but there is no respite yet, and the audience is told that the tree will be chopped off the next day, as an implication of pulling out the patriarchy from its very roots. Overall, the play gives us the lesson as is clear also with the very title of the play, 'Where There's a Will, there 's the way", which is significant in finding their own spaces according to the wishes by all the characters of the play- the 'traditional' family values clash with unexpected twists in the tale that completely subvert existing stereotypes.

Dance Like a Man is a play with many layers, which can work on various levels and can be seen from different perspectives. It is a comment on the changing society in postcolonial India in comparison to pre-independent India with its taboos and tradition as the play sets itself in two time periods, 1940s and 1980s, a clash between tradition and modernity. Dattani has a reputation of being a playwright who attempts to hold a mirror to society. His plays bring to fore the absurdities and hypocrisies of the society. This play is in the same league. It questions the gender specific roles assigned to man and woman by a jacketed society. Tensions in a multi-ethnic nuclear family of contemporary India are lucidly portrayed.

The play reaches to the highest peak of deconstruction in comparison to four plays discussed above as the women characters in them are revealed as strong human being or realized their true individual self after the domination of some patriarch for a long time. Man too, like Chandan and Ajit tried to revolt against autocracy of their fathers and the rules defined for men, but could not escape as desired. But in *Dance Like a Man*, both female and male protagonist lived their lives on their own way: Jairaj chooses to be a Bharatnatyam dancer as his career, a job assigned as feminine, and Ratna, also being a dancer, could not let ruin her life and career by her father-in-law and husband (though Jairaj is supportive to her) and even runs the life of Jairaj.

The title *Dance Like a Man*, itself deconstructs both male and female stereotypes by appending dance to the man, which is generally not accepted as dance is a 'womanly' form and does not contain any 'manly' quality or attribute. Jairaj with his passion for dance is all set to demolish the stereotypes that his imperious father, Amritlal, who claims to be a social reformer, carries. No sooner did Amritlal close his eyes than Jairaj changed absolutely starting by alteration in the house. Too much of stringency leads to revolt which, though remains undercover, gushes forth whenever it finds an outlet. This is the twist that the playwright gives to the stereotypes associated with 'gender' issues that view solely women at the receiving end of the oppressive power structures of patriarchal society. The play dispels this notion and explores the nature of the tyranny that even men might be subject within such structures. But Jairaj could not fully realize his potential for being conspired by his own wife and father against his dancing career. And also he has weakness of not fully free from gender stereotypes and expects Ratna to be a woman first.

Ratna emerges as the strongest women characters surviving in the man's world of all the women characters in his other plays. Though she is blamed as 'negative' character and as flawless as a disgruntled wife and an overbearing mother with jangled nerves. Partly a devoted wife and defiant daughter-in-law, Ratna is a woman of many devices. She unravels before us as a woman who had perhaps used her husband to further her own vastly superior dancing talents. No doubt, Ratna looks like a heartless wife for her decision of deserting Jairaj, devoid of all emotional attachment to her husband, but as a woman of conscience and professional dancer she takes the right step. As the dancer, wife and mother, she is over-powered by her desire to fill her life and surroundings with aesthetic excellence even at the cost of disrupting her domestic life. On asking a question in an interview to Lakshmi Subramanyam that his woman character 'Ratna' is viewed rather critically than normal, Dattani replies:

> I am not sure whether I would use the word critically. Let me put it this way. They are humans. They want something. They face obstacles. They will do anything in their power to get it. All I am focusing on in the powerlessness of these people at the end of the play. I know it is always grossly misinterpreted as their come uppance for being 'bad' women. I really can't control how people feel about these things! And I am not going to change my sensibilities for political correctness either. My only defense is to say that I am not biased against women. (*Muffled*, 131)

Though, she does not appear as a true Indian woman and Jairaj blames her to be responsible for his son Shankar's death, but Dattani refutes to assign the culpability or the status of the 'wronged' party to any one. Jairaj equally is liable and share the onus of the blame as being presented in the house when the double dose of opium is inadvertently administered to the baby by ayah. Dattani himself asserts:

> I refuse to have protagonists in a fixed role as a victim. If you have a victim, it implies that there is a persecutor and it also implies that you will eventually have a rescuer. (Ayyar, *Gay*, 4)

Ratna is not the 'negative' presence in the play according to Dattani. He has often been taken to task for being a 'woman hater' of sorts because, he says:

> [my] women protagonists fight, scheme and get a piece of the action albeit at graet personal cost. These are seen as 'negative' qualities, sadly by some women too [...] but really we have yet to see feminism find expression in Indian society. (Ayyar, *Gay*, 4)

Consequently, Dattani poses a few questions- the pigeonholing of masculinity on the sexual construct that a man is, within an Indian family- are set against the idea of the creative artist searching for artistic fulfillment within the claustrophobic constraints of the world that he inhabits. The remedy is suggested in the third generation, where the earlier sets of categories collapse and Lata is seen as a successful dancer and a mother, happily married to Vishwas, the son of a rich Mithaiwala.

The hypocrisy of present day politicians, freedom fighters and social reformers are also surfaced by Jairaj. They pretend themselves to be liberal minded enough to protect the ordinary peoples, to eradicate unwanted and repulsive practices from the society, to endow with the needs of poor and unfortunate women by giving them ashrama to live, educating and restructuring them. Amritlal, Jairaj's own father is one of them- a freedom fighter during independence and an influential politician after independence. Jairaj deconstructs and disbelieves the present structure of politics in Indian government as nothing has changed in pre and post colonial India, and we are thrust from one dominating hands to other ruling power, and are never free to wish and live of our own will. He questions Amritlal's so called 'progressive ideas', when he denied Jairaj's dance practice as a job of prostitutes:

> Where is the spirit of revolution? You didn't fight to gain independence. You fight for power in your hands. Why, you are just as conservative and prudish as the people who were ruling over us! (*CP*1, 416)

Power again plays a dominating role in Indian families. Amritlal had the power to rule and money to subdue Jairaj's ambitions. Though Jairaj also admits his power, as he was unable to get much money from dance for the miserable stipulation of Bharatnatyam dance in his times, but he revolted against all the odds connected to this traditional art and carry on with it against his father's wishes:

> And I will not have my art run down by a handful of stubborn narrow-minded individuals with fancy pretentious ideals. (*CP*1, 416)

Therefore, this chapter illuminates the hypothesis to gender roles in Indian society dealt by Dattani in all his above plays. The following points in this concern are surfaced and deconstructed by Dattani:

1. Women are in India or elsewhere or in the city or rural areas are justified in their struggle against age-old discriminations;
2. the relegation of femininity is because of the elevation of masculinity (gender roles). Men and women must be seen as people and not as gender. Thus the oppressive structure which perceives men and women as binary opposites (including role-sets apart from myriad others) has to be dismantled;
3. We cannot exonerate men for the evils perpetuated against women, as men are a party to it to whose benefit the whole system- in all the walks of life-works. Hence not only women but also men have to be emancipated;
4. the women's problem in India is but enigmatic or paradoxical as the older generation of women (mother-in-law) to some extent- because of their

social conditioning- are the perpetrators as they tend to perpetuate evil practices, viz., dowry, female infanticide, foeticide and abuse.

The strategy which Dattani uses is the 'deconstruct and transform' approach. If traditional thought is seen as a woolen sweater, the above viewpoint might be described in the following terms: 'don't throw away the wool, but rather unravel and re-stitch the jumper, perhaps several times.' Dattani's feminism is not one about the elimination of differences between the sexes; nor even simply the achievement of equal opportunity: it concerns the individual's right to find out the kind of person he or she is and to strive to become that person. Aiming to dismantle all systems of domination, Dattani challenges not only others' blind spots but also women's own, like Ratna in *Dance Like a Man*, Bharati in *Tara* and Shanta in *Thirty Days in September* etc.

All the meanderings finally arrive at the consideration of sex in this country as a status category with political implications, broadly defined as power structured relationships designed to maintain an age-old system, whereby itself are arrangements of one group of persons is controlled by another. A view of history in which a diabolical patriarchy systematically holds women in a state of submission and dependency may be termed as a conspiracy theory or interior colonization, where women are viewed as inferior intelligence, an instinctual or sensual gratification or an emotional nature both primitive and childlike and so on. In a country where women are worshipped as Kali, Durga, Saraswati, this other face of tormenting them is dreadful. Isn't our societal worship of woman merely a stratagem to lull her into submission, an extraordinary piece of sexual politics, a game the master group plays in elevating its subject to pedestal level.

'Masculine' and 'feminine' are not the complex natural distinctions we had assumed them to be but elaborate behavioural constructs for each sex within society, obviously cultural and subject to endless cross-cultural variations. Sex is biological, gender psychological and so cultural and therefore by eliminating discrimination, we would all be the same, in a perfect world with no differences in between. This is what Dattani's plays do, when his characters travel in their marginalized journey of lives struggling to dismantle the tag of 'otherness' sticked to them. As Dattani puts it in an interview to Angelie Multani:

> It is one thing focusing on these areas in the human condition that leave the individual with a sense of displacement or being the 'other'. But it's what the character does under those circumstances that make him or her interesting. Ultimately all good writing is about character revelation and journeys. The provocations that are connected with a person's marginalized identity are what spur the character into action. (*Mahesh Dattani's*, 166-167)

Thus Dattani has turned the table in favour of women. If a woman makes a man master, she can make him aware of his weaknesses and shortcomings also. Women choosing not to adhere to traditional gender roles are thrust into the 'other' suspect category and further alienated from possible solidarity with their sisters. Dattani has tried to vindicate that women should be able to live their own sexuality, taking the initiative about what they wish. In this sense, it is absolutely natural to go after what their desire demands from them- love, sex, company- anything they may be missing from men at different moments of their lives, where women are often relegated to traditionally oppressed roles This is an important consequence of Dattani's feminism; a trace we do not always perceive in its full dimension but which is there: in our daily experiences, in our love relationships, in the most intimate corners of our sexuality. It let us think that it is not because people are afraid of what people 'out there' would say about them or about us, but we, ourselves, carry a certain bias that we don't want to confront immediately. One other aspect of Dattani's play is that we have also a heterosexual bias in terms of gender-based violence, where we think men are the ones perpetuating violence against women. This is true, but we are not thinking about men who are violent to other men.

Women and men of younger generation in Dattani's play are increasingly moving away from traditional gender roles. Ultimately, change will only come with a new generation of women and men who are able to see their place in a dynamic and newly emerging democracy- one where the rights of all women, regardless of ethnicity, caste and class, will be seen as critical to political change and a just society. Basic tenet of Dattani's feminism is to deconstruct power, and to propose alternative paradigms for power sharing and the exploration of how women and men strategically redefine power, around the world in the present times, challenging the power structures, challenging the systems, dismantling injustice, exploitation and inequality in all their forms. The structures of colonialism and the structures of capitalism are beneficial to the structures of patriarchy and Dattani's characters struggle against the structures of patriarchy, as well as against the institutions that politically, socially and economically sustain sexist structures. The personal is not political but the political is personal in making the structure of gendered society and with all the above plays of Dattani, we come to conclusion that 'nothing is right or wrong, it is just perspectives'.

REFERENCES

Altekar, A.S. *The Position of Women in Hindu Civilization.* New Delhi: Motilal Banarasidass, 1962.

Ayyar, Raj. "Mahesh Dattani: India's Gay Cinema Comes of Age". *Gay Today.* 8.48, 2004. http://gaytoday.com.

Banerjee, Utpal K. "In conversation with Mahesh Dattani". *Indian Literature.* 223, Sep-Oct, 2004.

Beauvoir, Simone De. *The Second Sex.* USA: Vintage Books, 1989.

Bell, Daine. "Good and Evil: At Home and Abroad", in *Hawthorne and Winter,* September 11, 2001.

Bleichman, E. Dis."Deshilando el enigma" [Unweaving the Enigma'], in M. Lamas and F. Saal (eds.), *La Bella (in) differencia* [The Beautiful (in) difference]. Mexico: Siglo XXI, 1991.

Chatterjee, Sumita. 'Theatre is here to Stay'. *The Statesman.* 5th July 2005.

Dattani, Mahesh. *Collected Plays.* New Delhi: Penguin Books, 2005.

Dattani, Mahesh. 'Behind the Scenes'. *The Week.* 24 July 2005. The Week.com.

Engels, Frederick. *The Origin of the Family, Private Property and the State.* Introduction by Evelyn Reed. New York: Pathfinder Press, 1984.

Fraser, N. "Introduction: Revolving French Feminism", in *Revaluing French Feminism: Critical Essays on Difference, Agency and Culture,* N. Fraser and S. Bartky (eds). Bloomington and Indianapolis: Indiana University Press, 1992.

Freud, Sigmund. "Femininity" ("Die Weiblich heit"), Se, xxii, pp. 133-134, as quoted in Gail Finney, Women in Modern Drama: Freud, Feminism and European Theatre at the Turn of the Century.

Greer, Dr. Germaine. "Our Bodies, Our Selves", in *The Whole Women.* London: Doubleday, 1999.

Greer, Dr. Germaine. "Man Made Women", in *The Whole Women.* London: Doubleday, 1999.

Greer, Dr. Germaine. "Fear", in *The Whole Women.* London: Doubleday, 1999.

Greer, Dr. Germaine, "Sorrow", in *The Whole Women.* London: Doubleday, 1999.

Joshi, Pushpa. *Gandhi on Women (Collection of Mahatma Gandhi's Writings and Speeches on Women),* Centre for Women's Development Studies, Ahmedabad: Navjivan Trust. 2000.

Jouvenel, Bertrand de, *Power,* quoted in Dr. Germaine Greer's, "Masculinity", in *The Whole Women.* London: Doubleday, 1999.

Kabeer, Naila, "Subordination and Struggle: Women in Bangladesh", in *New Leif Review* 168, March/April, 1988.

Kakar, Sudhir. *The Inner World: A Psychoanalytic Study of Childhood and Society in India.* New Delhi: OUP, 1991.

Kaur, Sukhdeep, "Wounded Innocence". *The Tribune. Sunday,* October 9, 2005.

Kimmel, Michael J. "Inequality and Difference, The Social Construction of Gender Relations". *The Gendered Society.* New Delhi: OUP, 2004.

Klatch, Rebecca. "Coalition and Conflict Among Women of the New Right". *SIFNS* 4, 1988.

Mc Rae, John, "We Live in the Flicker: Reflections in Time on the Plays of Mahesh Dattani", in *Mahesh Dattani's Plays: Critical Perspectives,* Angelie Multani (ed.). New Delhi: Pencraft International, 2007.

Mc Rae, John. "A Note on the Play", in *Collected Plays.* New Delhi: Penguin Books, 2005.

Mee, Erin B. "A Note on the Play", in *Collected Plays.* New Delhi: Penguin Books, 2000.

Mee, Erin B. "Invisible Issues: An Interview with Mahesh Dattani", in Mahesh Dattani's Plays, Angelie Multani (ed.). New Delhi: Pencraft International, 2007.

Moghadam, Valentine. "Women and Identity Politics in Theoretical and Comparative Perspective", in V. Moghadam (ed.) *Identity Politics and Women: Cultural Reassertions and Feminisms in International Perspective.* Oxford: Westview Press, 1994.

Mohanty, Sachidananda. "Theatre: Reaching out to People: An Interview with Mahesh Dattani", in *The Plays of Mahesh Dattani: A Critical Response,* R.K. Dhawan and Tanu Pant (eds.). New Delhi: Prestige Books, 2005.

Moi, Toril. *Sexual/Texual Politics: Feminist Literary Theory.* London: Methuen, 1985.

Multani, Angelie. "A Conversation with Mahesh Dattani", in Angelie Multani (ed.), *Mahesh Dattani's Plays: Critical Perspectives.* New Delhi: Pencraft International, 2007.

S. Benhabib. "Feminism and the question of postmodernism", in *The Polity Reader in Gender Studies.* Cambridge: Polity Press, 1994.

S. Correa. "Religions Fundamentalism and secular politics: different sides of a single thought", in *DAWN: Special Supplement for the World Social Forum,* 16-21 January, 2004.

Santhanam, Anitha. "It's the silence that affects me most", 2001. http://www.maheshdattani.com.

Shakespeare, William. *As you like It,* Act 2, Scene 7.

Shuttleworth, Ian. "Bravely Fought the Queen: A review BAC", quoted in *Mahesh Dattani's Plays: Critical Perspectives.* Angelie Multani (ed.). New Delhi: Pencraft International, 2007.

Subramanyam, Lakshmi. "A Dialogue with Mahesh Dattani", in *Muffled voices: Women in Modern Indian Theatre,* Ed. Lakshmi Subramanyam. New Delhi: Shakti Book, 2002.

Thomas, Lesley. *Express,* Feb. 1998. Quoted in Dr. Germaine Greer (ed.), "Warm up", in *The Whole Woman.* London: Doubleday, 1999.

Uniyal, Ranu. "Conversing with Mahesh Dattani", in R.K. Dhawan and Tanu Pant (eds.), *The Plays of Mahesh Dattani: A Critical Response.* New Delhi: Prestige Books, 2005.

Upadhyay, Neelam; Pandey, Rekha; eds. *Women in India: Part and Present.* Allahabad: Chugh Publications, 1990.

Walling, Michael. "A Note on the Play", in *Collected Plays.* New Delhi: Penguin Books, 2000.

3

Eliciting and Assessing Homosexuality

We have a tendency to constantly look for 'classics' in our literature. There are very few literary works that emerge as full-blown classics. Theatre, by its very nature, is transient. But while that does not mean that plays do not last through generations of play-doers and play-goers, it also does not mean that plays that do not, perhaps, stand the test of time are irrelevant or 'bad theatre'. Drama has to confront its own times. It has simultaneously always been a mirror of society, its trends and thought-processes, while also forcing society to look at situations and think about issues that it may not want to deal with. One of the most prominent issues prevailing in present Indian society is the identity crisis where only male and only heterosexual male is considered the major element of the social system; while the female, homosexuals etc. are considered as deviant or 'others'.

Homosexuality in India is generally considered a taboo subject by both the Indian civil society and the government. Public discussion of homosexuality in India has been inhibited by the fact that sexuality in any form is rarely discussed openly. Feminist issues are discussed world wide from the 1960s to the present time; but any talk on homosexual relationships are still a clichéd issue as homosexuals themselves are afraid of coming out from the fixed behaviourial norm inflicted on them. Their sexual proclivities are still strongly forbidden by social custom and are greatly offensive to the prevailing moral and social code. In her introduction to the collection of essays *Inside/Out*, Dianna Fuss considers that the question of homosexual identity is itself folded inside a structure:

> The homo in relation to the hetero, much like the feminine in relation to the masculine, operates as an indispensable interior exclusion- an outside which is inside interiority making the articulation of the latter possible, a transgression of the border which is necessary to constitute the border as such. (3)

As Fuss's intricate sentence shows, the opposition inside/outside represents not a choice, or even a distinction, but an epistemology of the border- a spatial notion of identity and difference which can never get outside itself, but only move a boundary line or permeate it, reproducing the interior/exterior law.

The society imposes stereotypical roles on both men and women and acknowledges and legitimizes only these roles. Male and female - these are the only sexual categories which have secured social existence and the approval of the society. People who do not fit into these two classes either keep trying to fit into the rut and suffer throughout their lives a burden of living the big lie; or if they choose to live with the truth, they have to bear social ostracism and contempt. This hypocrisy is best illustrated by Duncker:

> Sex is supposed to be the moment when we are most honestly, nakedly ourselves. This is a myth. Often we use the mask of intimacy to perpetuate the most destructive physical and emotional bullying. We use our bodies to avoid the issue. We exchange loving confidences in fraudulent currency. We fake it-again and again. We do this to hide, to deny our fears, to avoid honesty. We all live ironic lives. (*Women*, 10)

The basic element in both secular and religious arguments against non-heterosexual activities is that because sex is designed for reproduction and any behaviour detracting from that end is biologically unnatural and therefore verboten. Sex has uses other than procreation, and behaviours that are apparently non-procreative may nonetheless contribute to reproductive success. And the socialization is responsible for stereotyping gender and relationships:

> The optics of a gay relationship is always viewed from a heterosexual viewpoint. Regarding marriage there are divided views in the community. Many feel that there is no need to replicate the institution of marriage in which women have borne the brunt of violence for ages. But there are others, who feel that marriage is a must. (Chauhan, *PLURAL*, 1)

Being conscious of the limitations of blaming all of contemporary Indian social problems on a post-colonial legacy, Ruth Vanita and Saleem Kidwai have argued that a homophobia of virulent proportions came into being in India in the late nineteenth and early twentieth centuries and continues to flourish today. In his article "Critically Queer", published in *glq* Butler emphasizes that:

> there is no power, constructed as a subject, that acts, but only a reiterated acting that is power in its persistence and instability. (17)

For Butler, "lesbian", as an identity, is over determined by heterosexuality. It is actually produced by homophobia, articulates the unarticulable, in its claim to sexuality, is both 'out of control' for those reasons, and oppressive in drawing exclusionary borders of specificity.

> Part of what constitutes sexuality is precisely that which does not appear and that which, to some degree, can never appear. This is perhaps the most fundamental reason why sexuality is to some degree always closeted, especially to the one who would express it through acts of self- disclosure. (Butler, *Inside/out*, 25)

(a) Historical Construction of Alternative Sexuality

However, the terms heterosexual, bisexual, homosexual, and the concept of "sexual orientation" itself are all modern sociological constructs. In earlier times too, a particular behaviour might have been being considered homosexual, but people were not labeled using such terms. An Austraian clinical psychologist reportedly coined the word 'homosexual' to explain same-sex relations in 1887. Cary Grant used the word 'gay' for the first time in a Hollywood film, *Bringing Up baby* (1939), in a role that needed him to cross-dress and move about in a transparent negligee.

The terms are western import and the law that outlaws sex between two members of the same gender came not from religious fanatics of any kind, but surprisingly, with British, who came as traders and stayed to conquer the subcontinent (eighteenth and nineteenth centuries), and were scandalized by the sexual customs of the Indians. The educational system they established however eventually created a new Indian elite which enthusiastically absorbed British ideas, including the more prurient attitudes of the Victorians toward sex. This elite, in turn, imposed their new anti sexuality on the Indian middle class. When Britain took control of India, British sexual law was imported by the colonial administration.

The 1861 legislation which changed the British penalty for sodomy from hanging to life imprisonment became Section 377 of the Indian Penal Code after independence. This law prohibited "carnal intercourse against the order of nature" and continued to prescribe imprisonment up to life as well as whippings and fines. To put it simply, homosexuality per se was not an offence, but being caught in a homosexual act was illegal. Therefore western sexual ideologies have 'invaded' Indian discourses on sexuality and identity by professionals, laypersons, "straights" or "gays", and whereby indigenous histories and cultures become invisible. Let us always remember the indisputable truth expressed in the opening articles of the universal declaration of human rights that "All persons are born free and equal in dignity and rights..." Everyone is entitled to all the rights and freedom set forth in this declaration, without distinction of any kind. The criminalization of gay behaviour goes not only against fundamental human rights, as the open letter points out, but it also works sharply against the enhancement of human freedom in terms of which the progress of human civilization can be judged. Therefore, now the revolutionary change in this sec in 2009 by the Indian government which legitimizes the relationship of the homosexuals brings a new hope in the life of homosexuals.

A marginal homophobic trend in pre-colonial India thus became dominant in modern India. Indian nationalists, including Hindus, internalized Victorian ideals of heterosexual monogamy and disowned indigenous traditions that contravened those ideals. Unfortunately this provision has become one of the most notorious forms of legal discrimination against homosexuals, who already suffer from severe social stigma in the country. It further casts a shadow of illegality on the personal lives of thousands, making them unable to live openly and with dignity, because even their families and well wishers point to the existence of the law to justify their prejudice and concerns. Families, health professionals and others often cannot accept people's sexual preferences precisely because of the law. Dr. Dayal Nihlani, a psychiatrist asserts:

> Homosexuality is a part of human experience. Anthropologists have found that homosexuality existed among primitive tribal cultures. It is not as if modern society has created it. One has to accept it rather than look at it as normal or abnormal... Homosexuals are made to suffer because of the prejudice. There is nothing wrong with them. (Chatterji, *The Statesman*, 1)

Indian newspapers, over the last twenty five years, have reported several same-sex weddings and same-sex joint suicides, mostly by Hindu female couples in small towns, unconnected to any gay movement. Several weddings took place by Hindu rites, with some family support, while the suicides resulted from families forcibly separating the lovers.

In this world of individual dignity, the homosexuals are rarely allowed to define themselves in terms of their role, their sociopolitical location, their representation of themselves as a challenge to the patriarchy. The political slogans that describe the homosexuals in purely institutional, or counter-institutional terms ('lesbianism' is a blow against patriarchy), like the symbols of their identification with women as a group, or the emblems of their rejection of the institution of compulsory heterosexuality (inscribed upon their badges and emblazoned on their banners) all are described as mere outward regalia which conceal the real human being underneath. The very role of 'lesbian' itself, which locates the individual in terms of her group membership, is described as an artificial and dehumanizing category; people are to be seen as individuals with their own separate and distinctive selves, not pigeon-holed into labeled boxes. The real identity of the lesbian is represented not in her overtly and explicitly political activities, or in her identification of herself as a lesbian, but in the private sanctum of her inner self, her unique human identity, which transcends this one limited aspect of her total being.

Indian history, geography, and demography all exhibit a rich diversity of traits, making generalization hazardous. Indian subcontinent is a spectacular mosaic of many cultures, ethnicities, religions, languages, and traditions. Sexual attitudes and practices also show considerable variation, ranging from the classic sex affirming *Kamasutra* and the world-famous erotic sculptures of ancient temples to the extreme prudishness of ascetics who condemned all forms of seminal emission and modern educated elite which still derives its inspiration from Victorian England. Both unearth and affirm that homosexuals have always existed since time immemorial in this land. Most modern Hindus are ignorant of this rich history, and believe the popular myth that homosexuality was imported into India either from medieval West Asia or from modern Euro-America. It is symptomatic of this ignorance that the democratic and secular Indian government has retained the British law criminalizing sodomy.

To begin with, India's colourful history is rife with examples of homosexuality in different forms. Homosexuality, in fact, has along history in the subcontinent; same-sex relationships are described in ancient Indian texts like the fourth century love guide, The *KamaSutra*, *The Ramayana*, and medieval *Persian* and *Urdu* poetry. Vatsyayana, while writing the *KamaSutra* in the fifth century of our era, the world's oldest sex manual, devotes an entire chapter to homosexuality. The *KamaSutra* is revolutionary because it gave an objective description of all forms of sexual behaviour; it deals without ambiguity or hypocrisy in all aspects of sexual life—including marriage, adultery, prostitution, group sex, sadomasochism, male and female homosexuality, and transvestism. The text paints a fascinating portrait of an India whose openness to sexuality gave rise to a highly developed expression of the erotic. It categorizes men who desire the other man as a 'third nature', further subdivides term into masculine and feminine types, and describes their lives and occupations (such as flower sellers, masseurs and hairdressers). Kama Sutra states that homosexual sex "is to be engaged in and enjoyed for its own sake as one of the arts." "Homophobia, and not homosexuality, is new to Indian culture," says Vinay Chandran of Bangalore-based charitable trust, Swabhava, which works with gender and sexual minorities in the country. His argument has a sound basis considering homosexual acts have been recorded in ancient Indian writings, including the *Kama Sutra*, for hundreds of years. (Manjunath, *greatreporter.com*)

Some historical evidence suggests considerable social acceptance of sexual diversity in ancient South Asia: In parts of the subcontinent, for example, centuries-old erotic sculptures depict men and women engaged in a variety of homosexual as well as heterosexual activities; some classical Hindu myths recognize, even affirm, the fluidity of gender as well as sexual identities.

Probably the best known are the erotic sculptures adorning the celebrated temple architecture of Khajuraho, where one can find couples of the same sex entwined in ecstatic postures alongside the regular couplings of members of the opposite sex. Construction of Hindu temples in stone began around the sixth century of the Common Era and reached its culmination between the twelfth and the fourteenth century when the grand pagodas of eastern and southern India, such as Puri and Tanjore, came into being. On the walls and gateways of these magnificent structures we find a variety of images: amongst scenes from epics and legends, one invariably finds erotic images including those that modern law deems unnatural and society considers obscene.

Other erotic manuals suggested that sodomy was common in Kalinga (southern Orissa state) and Panchala lin the Panjab. In general, sex for pleasure was explicitly validated (at least for males and often, as with Vatsyayana for females as well) and not necessarily linked to procreative function. According to ancient treatises on architecture, a religious structure is incomplete unless its walls depicts something erotic, for sensual pleasures (kama) are as much an expression of life as are righteous conduct (dharma), economic endeavors (artha) and spiritual pursuits (moksha).

Hindu texts have discussed variations in gender and sexuality for over two millennia. Like the erotic sculptures on ancient Hindu temples at Khajuraho and Konarak, sacred texts in Sanskrit constitute irrefutable evidence that the whole range of sexual behaviour was known to ancient Hindus. The Vedas do mention humans as being classified into three different categories: male (pums-prakriti), female (stri-prakriti) and a third sex (tritiya prakriti). Tritiya prakriti or "third sex" is the group most homosexuals identify themselves with and nowhere does it contain a straightforward condemnation of homosexuality. The Sutras seem to support the contention that homosexuality was somewhat acceptable in ancient times. Homosexuals argue today that third-gender citizens were neither persecuted nor denied basic rights. They were allowed to keep their own societies or town quarters, live together within marriage and engage in all means of livelihood. Gay men could either blend into society as ordinary males or they could dress and behave as females, living as transvestites.

Shiva, the most popular of all Hindu gods, has from the most ancient of times been worshipped primarily in the form of a *lingam* or erect phallus; in the most common ritual milk is poured over the tip of the lingam and flows down on all sides. The lingam is worshipped by males as well as by females, suggesting the existence of a sublimated homoerotic element. The Sakibhava cult, which worships Krishna (an incarnation of Vishnu), holds that only Krishna is truly male and that all other creatures are female in relation to him. Male followers of the cult dressed like women. And male poets like Kabir and Jiyasi often envisaged themselves as women in love of God. As observed by journalist Mrinal Pande:

> The cultural scene during the time allowed Kabir and other poets to openly integrate their femaleness into their poetry. (Chatterji, *The Statesman*, 1)

In Hinduism, love is regarded as an eternal force. It is seen as devotion between two people, whether romantic or platonic. Hindus believe love and devotion are important in attaining Moksha or Liberation from the cycle of rebirths. *Mahabharata, Panchatantra, Kamasutra, Shiva Purana, Krittivasa Ramayana, The Skanda Purana, Amir Khusro,* and *Baburnama.*

Among the medieval texts two engage homosexual themes: Emperor Babur's autobiographical *Tuzuki-i-Babri* contains a sentimental recollection of his erotic love for a teenage boy; Dargah Quli Khan's personal diary *Muraqqa-e-Delhi: The Moghal Capital in Muhammad Shaw's Time* briefly documents his foray into the pedastry circles of Islamic Delhi. These stories allow women to have sex with women and men to have sex with men on heterosexual terms. One may interpret these tales as repressed homosexual fantasies of a culture. Hindu medical texts dating from the first century A.D. Provide taxonomies of gender and sexual variations, including same sex desire.

But homosexuality does not need the sanction of the *Kamasutra* or any ancient text for that matter. It needs the understanding of human beings towards fellow human beings and the respect for an individual's personal choice, which harms no one else. The more one searches the Scripture, the more convinced one is that homosexuality is not a sin. Nor has God relegated us to a life of celibacy! So this begs the question: if it's so obvious that ones sexual orientation is not in and of itself a 'sin', why do so many in the religious places condemn homosexuality? Two important factors come into play: fear and prejudice. When you fear something, you wish to get away from it. It can challenge the patriarchal notion of heterosexual society of a binary differentiation of male/ female where the first one dominates the 'Other'. To most people, this means pretend it doesn't exist, subdue it, change it, or destroy it.

Denying a person the right to choose their partner is morally wrong. However much we cloak our traditions of marriage in garbs of sanctity, the truth is marriage as an institution was established for procreation and that alone, in every culture. According to Freud, homosexuals are simply those who have either failed to renounce identification with mother in favour of father (gay men) or those who have failed to retain their ties of identification to mother (lesbians). Though, Freud postulated that homosexuality was the failure of the child to adequately identify with the same-sex parent, and was therefore a problem of gender identity, development, he did not believe in either the criminal persecution or psychiatric treatment of homosexuals. In fact, when Freud was contacted by a woman whose son was homosexual, he patiently explained why he did not think her son needed to be 'cured':

> Homosexuality is assuredly no advantage, but it is nothing to be ashamed of, no vice, no degradation; it cannot be classified as an illness; we consider it to be a variation of the sexual function. ... Many highly respectable individuals of ancient and modern times have

been homosexuals, several of the greatest men among them. ... It is a great injustice to persecute homosexuality as a crime- and a cruelty too....

What analysis can do for your son runs in a different line. If he is unhappy, neurotic, torn by conflicts, inhibited in his social life, analysis may bring him harmony, peace of mind, full efficiency, whether he remains homosexual or gets changed. (*Letters*, 419-20]

There is even greater reticence on homosexuality in contemporary Indian literature—a reticence that perhaps reflects the generally conservative sexual mores of the people, and there is hardly an imaginative text that sympathetically explores the theme of male homosexuality. Ismat Chughatai's *"Lihaf" ("The Quilt")*, written in Urdu, was first published in 1942, unfolds the account of mid-20th century Muslim Nawab family where the Nawab sought his pleasures from young boys. Narrated from the point of view of a ten-year-old girl, the story focuses on the sexual relationship between an aristocratic Indian woman and her female servant. Shortly after its publication, the author appeared in court to defend herself against charges of obscenity. Then Kamala Das, a well-known poet in South Asia, published *My Story* in 1976, she created a minor scandal. The candid autobiography not only revealed her extramarital heterosexual affairs but also her adolescent crush on a female teacher and a brief lesbian encounter with an older student. More controversial is Shobha De's *Starry Nights* and *Strange Obsession* (1993), a rambunctious novel about lesbian love published by the prestigious Penguin Books of India. Her commercial success certainly indicates widespread interest among Indian readers in works that explicitly deal with nontraditional sexualities; however, the interest, to some extent, may simply be prurient curiosity. When Deepa Mehta's 1998 movie, *Fire*, was released, two unhappily married women start an affair with each other. It caused nationwide controversy and caused the topic of homosexuality to be hotly debated within public forums, an area where it had for the most part been all but silent. "Fire", was eventually banned in India, showing quite clearly that it was extremely dangerous to try and overturn the country's traditional values.

Although self-identified gay and lesbian artists are yet to break into the South Asian literary scene, a few writers of the South Asian Diaspora have begun to explore gay, lesbian, and bisexual themes with some candor. They live in either the United States or Britain—countries that have well-established gay and lesbian communities with a tradition of organized resistance—and therefore have greater sexual and artistic freedom and wider publishing opportunities. Further, their physical separation from family and community probably gives them relative privacy and greater freedom from culturally imposed constraints. Some of them are: Prafulla Mohanti's autobiography *Through Brown Eyes* (1985); Agha Shahid Ali's poems—such as "*Leaving Your City*," "*Beyond the Ash Rains*," and "*A Rehearsal of Loss*; Vikram Seth's novel in verse *The Golden Gate* (1986); Andrew Harvey's novels, *Hidden Journey* (1991 *One Last Mirror* (1985 *Burning Houses* (1986), *The Web* (1987); Hanif Kureishi's screenplays *My Beautiful Laundrette* (1986),*The Buddha of Suburbia* (1990); Suniti Namjoshi's poetry *Feminist Fables* (1981) and novels *The Conversations of Cow* (1985), *Flesh and Paper* (1986), *The Mothers of Maya Dilip* (1989), etc.

In recent years, however, attitudes towards homosexuality have shifted slightly. Gay activism in India is growing and has begin to challenge laws which criminalize homosexuality and which were inherited from the British Raj. It remains to be seen whether these emerging identities will reflect (or perhaps imitate) western constructions and whether those who adopt these identities will attempt to love these within Indian cultures, or whether differing identities will be constructed.

In September 2006, Nobel Laureate Amartya Sen and acclaimed writer Vikram Seth came together with scores of other prominent Indians in public life to demand this change in the legal regime The open letter demands that 'In the name of humanity and of our Constitution, this cruel and discriminatory law should be struck down.'

On June 29th, 2008, Delhi held its first ever gay pride march, along with similar gatherings in Bangalore and Calcutta. On June 30, 2008, Indian labour minister Oscar Fernandes backed calls for decriminalization of consensual gay sex, and the Prime Minister Manmohan Singh called for greater tolerance towards homosexuals. On July 4, 2008, gay activists fighting for decriminalization of consensual homosexuality at the Delhi High Court got a shot in the arm when the court opined that there is nothing unusual in holding a gay rally, something which is common outside India.

The Naz Foundation (India), a New Delhi based NGO is at the forefront of the campaign to decriminalize homosexuality.In December 2002 Naz India filed a Public Interest Litigation (PIL) to challenge IPC section 377 in the Delhi High Court. Gay Indians residing outside the country have formed support groups that cater to issues specific to the lesbian, gay men, bisexual and transgender community of South Asian descent. In the United States of America, *SALGA (The South Asian Lesbian & Gay Association)* in New York City, and *Trikone* in San Francisco are two such organizations. New York City is also host to a unique, monthly Bollywood-themed gay party and mixer called Sholay.

(b) Theoretical Approaches

Now it becomes important for us to analyze these aspects through the different theories which have been formulated by various critics. Lesbian and gay literary theory in the literary field has emerged prominently as a distinct field only in the 1990s, as 'liberation movement', however in the large part because of the assimilation of the viewpoints and analytic methods of Derrida, Foucault, and other poststructuralists, the earlier assumptions about a unitary and stable gay or lesbian identity were frequently put to question, and historical and critical analysis became increasingly subtle and complex. It attacked the "essentialism", fixed gender identities subscribed by society and introduce the notion of choice and allegiance into matters of sex and gender, so that sexuality is not seen as something merely 'natural' and unchanging, but rather as a construction and as subject of change. This theory appears at the post-structuralist time or post-modernist times and therefore, in spite of adhering to fixed gender identities like feminism, it rather works on shattering those 'essentialism'. One of the main points of post-structuralism was to 'deconstruct' binary opposition (like that between speech and writing, for instance) showing, firstly that the distinction between paired opposites is not absolute, since each term in the pairing can only be understood and defined in terms of the other, and, secondly that it is possible to reverse the hierarchy within such pairs, and so 'privilege' the second term rather than the first. Hence, in lesbian/gay studies the pair heterosexual/homosexual dichotomy is deconstructed in this way. With radical implications and since all such distinctions are constructed in the same way, so that to challenge this one is to challenge all the others too. Drawing upon a post-structuralist reading of Saussure, we show that such apparently elemental categories as heterosexual and homosexual do not designate fixed essences at all- they are merely part of a structure of differences without fixed terms, like Saussurean signifiers. We construct, instead an anti-essentialist, postmodernist concept of identity as a series of masks, roles and potentialities, a kind of amalgam of everything which is provisional, contingent and improvisatory. Therefore, identity is necessarily a complex mixture of chosen allegiances, social position and professional roles, rather than due to a fixed inner urge of the particular individual.

Further, what is called into question here is that distinction between the naturally-given, normative 'self' of heterosexuality and the rejected 'other' of homosexuality. The 'Other', in these formulations, is as much something within us as beyond us, and 'self' and 'other' are always implicated in each other, in the root sense of this word, which means to be intertwined or folded into each other. As basic psychology shows, what is identified as the external 'Other' is usually part of the self which is rejected and hence projected outwards. 'In general, lesbian critical reading proposes the blurring of boundaries between self and other, subject and object, lover and beloved as the lesbian moment in any text.' [Zimmerman, 'Lesbians like this and that'] Thus lesbianism is theoretically linked with notions of 'liminal' consciousness when existing categories are in process of deconstruction.

A number of queer theorists, for example, adopted the deconstructive mode of dismantling the key binary oppositions of Western culture, such as male/female, heterosexual/homosexual, and natural/ unnatural, by which a spectrum of diverse things are forced into only two categories, and in which the first category is assigned privilege, power and centrality, while the second is derogated, subordinated and marginalized. In an important essay of 1980, "Compulsory Heterosexuality and Lesbian Existence," Adrienne Rich posited what she called the "lesbian continuum' as a way of stressing how far-ranging and diverse is the spectrum of love and bonding among women, including female friendship, the family relationship between mother and daughter and women's partnerships and social groups, as well as overtly physical same-sex relations. Later theorists such as Eve Sedgwick and Judith Butler inverted the standard hierarchal opposition by which homosexuality is marginalized and made unnatural, by stressing the extent to which the ostensible normativity of heterosexuality is based on the suppression and denial of same-sex desires and relationships.

Another prominent theoretical procedure has been to undo the earlier assumption that heterosexual and homosexual are essential, universal and transhistorical types of human subjects, or identities, by historicizing these categories- that is, by proposing that they are social and discursive "constructs" that emerged under special ideological conditions in a particular culture at a particular time. A central text is the first volume of Michel Foucault's *History of Sexuality* (1976), which claims that, while there had long been a social category of sodomy as a transgressive human act, the 'homosexual', as a special type of human subject or identity, was a construction of the medical and legal discourse of the latter nineteenth century.

In a further development of constructionist theory Judith Butler, in *Gender Trouble: Feminism and the Subversion of Identity* (1990), described the categories of gender and of sexuality as performative, in the sense that the features which a cultural discourse institutes as masculine or feminine, heterosexual or homosexual, it also makes happen, by establishing an identity that the socialized individual assimilates and the patterns of behaviour that he or she enacts. Homosexuality, by this view, is not a particular identity that affects a pattern of action, but a socially pre-established pattern of action that produces the effect of originating in a particular identity. In *Gender Trouble* (1990) and *Bodies that Matter* (1993), Butler has consistently interrogated the notion of identity. Adapting Freud, feminism, Lacan and post structuralism, Butler's work has focused on the modes of representation of gay/lesbian identity and the idea of difference. Butler questions the fixed identities of heterosexuals, homosexuals and lesbians. Further, the so-called derivative nature of homosexuality, where same sex sexuality is seen as a bad copy of the original, can itself be reworked. One can demonstrate how heterosexuality that sees itself as the original is itself composed of the otherness of homosexuality. All our identities come from differentiations from other identities. Paradoxically, identities are repetitions based on performances. It is in this sense thar heterosexuality which takes itself as the only authentic form of sexuality, is a 'string of performances'.

Queer theorists now say that like gender, sexuality is a social construct. Heterosexuality sees itself as the authentic form of sexuality by relegating lesbianism and homosexuality to the background and discarding them as inauthentic. Thus the whole equation of original/

heterosexual and copy/ homosexual can be displaced. This is the main argument of Butler. Identity is a switching of roles. Identity is not closed, stable or unitary thing which is separate from an 'Other'. The 'Self' and the 'Other' are not mutually distinct species. Butler suggests that the 'Self' emerges only with a separation. To deal with this loss, the Self retains the 'Other' through a 'melancholic incorporation'. The 'Other' is thus installed in the 'Self' to attain a self-identity. The 'Self' thus contains the 'Other' within it. Without the disruption of the 'Other' inside there would be no self. This argument that suggests the insertion of the 'Other' into the 'Self' is extended to the gay/lesbian identity. The term 'queer' which may be produced due to homophobia may itself be cited as the discursive basis of opposition. The citation/ repetition of the queer identity may be used to destabilize the very discourse of heterosexuality. Identities thus escape the terms. The repetition of the terms 'we' and 'I' cannot be either summarily rejected nor can they be followed scrupulously. Butler is here suggesting an aporetic condition where one needs to both reaffirm and reject the identity 'queer', as both acceptance of a certain subject position and as the site of prospective resistance. The use of post-structuralism by queer theorists like Butler, Edelman and Fuss enables gay/lesbian theory to problematize issues of identity, marginality, authenticity and epistemology. There is an emphasis on the social context of identity.

Identity is constituted through a series of attempts to embody normative gender and sexual identities. The 'injunction to be a given gender', the repetitions and parodies of the identity (male/female) in the form of drag thus reveal the 'imitative structure of gender itself- as well as its contingency.' There is no original or primary gender which is imitated. Gender itself is a kind of imitation for which there is no original. Here imitation creates the effect of the original. Homosexuality is always present within the construction of heterosexuality itself, and unless the notion of the homosexual is spelt out there can be no 'heterosexual' at all. Heterosexuality can no more see itself, or be seen, as either pure or original, because the term/identity is constructed out of homosexuality. Butler's deconstructive argument thus reverses the hierarchy of priority and derivativeness. Heterosexuality is always the process of imitating its own idealization, and failing in its imitation. Heterosexuality needs repetition, and repeated repetitions, to naturalize it as original. Heterosexuality needs to elaborate itself because it fears being 'undone'. Heterosexuality is always afraid of its dependence upon homosexuality to construct itself. Thus these social expectations will effect even the self- conception of the homosexual individual too.

Dianna Fuss deconstructs the inside/outside opposition, where the inside stands for the heterosexual norm and the outsized is the realm of the homosexual (who is outside the norm, is a paradoxically closeted-inside-and need to come out). The outside, suggests Fuss, is formulated as a consequence of the internal lack of the heterosexual. To protect against the recognition of the lack within itself, the self erects boundaries against on 'Other' which is made to represent this lack. The homosexual is thus the ghost that haunts the heterosexual.

The gay/lesbian studies have influenced literary and cultural studies to a great extent. The retrieval of gay texts, anthologizing and publication of the gay texts, and tracing the history of gay themes has been an important development in the area. In New Historicism and Cultural Materialism, the work of Jonathan Goldberg, Alan Sinfield, among others, has focused on homosexuality in Renaissance texts (as the title of Goldberg's book suggests: *Queering the Renaissance*, 1994), the repression of the theme and a gay resistance (especially in the life and work of Oscar Wilde and Andre Gide).

(c) Mahesh Dattani's Understanding of Homosexuality

Theatre is not a mute observation, but a mechanical representation of the social dynamics which consciously or unconsciously affect the existing dynamics of human sensibility. Dattani brings the Indian drama closer to the real life experiences and tries to articulate the voice of the oppressed sections of society whose identity have been dragged in darkness, doomed to survive in perpetual silence and occupy no space in social order. This process of Dattani within the framework of dramatic structure is referred by Erin Mee as "a way of decolonizing of theatre", without any preconceived ideal of "a politically driven search for an indigenous aesthetic and dramaturgy." (*Drama*, 14)

To break the taboos, to expose the misery of sexuality marginalized sections and to reflect man's consistent struggle with his inner self, confronting with socio-ethical restrictions constitute a specific strain in Dattani's dramatic art. In the traditional society of India, the identity of gays, lesbians and homosexuals has not yet been recognized and they are left to lead a secluded life in their claustrophobic spaces. He admits:

> I have found out that sexuality can't straitjacketed or compartmentalized. They are varying degrees of love and bonding one feels for another person irrespective of gender. (Rao, *The Gentleman*, 3)

These neglected people come in the group of 'Subaltern', a term that is applied to those of 'Inferior rank'. According to Spivak, subalterns are forced to maintain silence against oppression and injustice and the entire terrain of post-colonial literary appreciation became an unpleasant Babel of subaltern voices. Leela Gandhi attributes:

> Subaltern studies defined itself as an attempt to allow the 'people' finally to speak within the jealous pages of elitist historiography and in so doing, to speak for, or to sound the muted voice of truly oppressed. (*Post*, 2)

Dattani's works aim to enhance the life experience of gay men and lesbians, help homosexuals through the difficult developmental tasks which lead to greater adjustment, satisfaction, acceptance and happiness, improve the quality of their interpersonal relationships and maximize the growth potential of the individuals being studied. What Dattani says is that it is homosexuality which causes to social exclusion and he portrays them sympathetically in his plays hoping for their inclusion into our society. A common belief among the most conservative faction is that homosexuality is a *behaviour — something that one does.* It is a chosen *lifestyle* which is abnormal, unnatural, and changeable. It is hated by God. It is a mental disorder and/or an addiction. For Dattani, homosexuality is a *sexual orientation — something that one is.* It is an unchosen *orientation* which is normal and natural for a minority of adults. It is always or almost always fixed. It is accepted by God. It is neither a mental disorder nor an addiction. He tends to favor equal rights and protections for persons of all sexual orientations, including the right to marry, with special rights for none. The core of this argument is that there are no 'homosexual' or 'lesbian' people, only homosexual or lesbian acts that anyone can enjoy:

> Only the human mind invents categories and tries to force facts into separated pigeon holes. The living world is a continuum in each and every one of its aspects. The sooner we learn this concerning human sexual behaviour, the sooner we shall reach a sounder understandings of the realities of sex. (Kinsey, *Sexual*, 639)

Through a focus on sexual expression as the meaning of homosexuality (i.e. homosexuality as an act rather than the homosexual as a type of person), differences between the homosexual and the heterosexual are dissolved. Same-sex sexuality is not a distinctive, unitary, frozen state; sexuality is innately plastic, and every human being has the physiological capacity to respond both heterosexuality and homosexuality. The theme central to Dattani's plays on homosexuality is the notion that lesbians and gay men pose no threat to either heterosexuals or the social system, but can be integrated into society and contribute to its rich variety. He favours same-sex marriage too and discards the view that procreation is the only motive in any marriage, in an interview to Bijay Kumar Das:

> You can be nurturer and provider in a same-sex marriage just as you can in an opposite sex marriage. Procreation is a choice which some married couples do not exercise. In same sex marriage procreation is not a choice you have. (*Form*, 178)

This belief is in sharp contrast to the arguments of the 'pathologists' who present lesbianism as a threat to the nuclear family and society as we know it. Same-sex love is, in this analysis, a normal, a natural and healthy aspect of the self. Dattani asserts to Erin B.Mee that it is the most burning issue of the present times as it is always present in our society from the ancient times and that he is not talking in the air:

> ....If we look at the statistics of a gay population in any given society, even if you look at it as a conservative five percent (people put it at ten, but even if you take five percent), with a population of 850million, we're talking about almost 50million people, and I think it's a real invisible issue. Almost all gay people are married in the conventional sense, so I think there are invisible issues which need to be brought out and addressed. In this case, it wasn't such a conscious attempt to say "look, here is an invisible issue, let's talk about it", I think it's there, and since it is very much a past of our society, very much a part of my society, it happens to be there. (*Mahesh Dattani's*, 157]

Dattani's liberal approach of dissolving any specific differences between lesbian and heterosexual women and gay and normal men shows a strong tendency to deny as well as minimize the differences between lesbians or gay men and heterosexuals. He brings out homosexuals and lesbians as invisible peoples, hidden in dark closets, inhabiting a shady twilight world, shrouded in cloaks of prejudice, clouds of ignorance, and fogs of taboo and mists of obscurity. We are 'invisible women'- 'the invisible minority or 'almost invisible'. If not invisible, at least concealed: 'the hidden segment', the 'hidden minority', the 'hidden population'. Into the obscurity, Dattani brings the light of reason or dispels the darkness; light is continuously being shed, candles lit, dark cupboards opened, and blankets of cloaks of ignorance removed to reveal homosexuals as they really are and the characters themselves began to question their identity and their position in society. As Dattani asserts:

> A growing number of people, gay included, are beginning to question societal pressures on people to be in single partner relationships. (Chauhan, *PLURAL*, 1)

So, we are offered 'new light on homosexuality' and 'illuminated by a few candles of factual knowledge.' although homosexuality is 'shamefacedly clouded, and 'shrouded in mystery and taboo' Dattani dispels the 'clouds of ignorance' and 'rips away the distorting cloaks of stereotype'. Dattani describes the murky depths behind the cloaks and in the cupboards, and varies with theoretical perspective.

Mahesh Dattani is never afraid and never hesitates to present the bold and powerful issues such as homosexuality to the most conventional society without any care; he is indifferent to its acceptation by the society. His motive behind the task is to force the society to think about issues that it may not want to deal with. Dattani here can be compared to Oscar Wilde who also presented the stark reality of homosexuality to the Victorians in his novel *The Picture of Dorian Gray*, which reveals homoerotic bonds between two men, the well known artist Basil Hallward and Dorian Gray. Unlike him, Dattani's plays like *Muggy Night in Mumbai* and *Bravely Fought the Queen* deals with the issue of gays and lesbians, their inner turmoil and struggle for acceptance in a conservative society of India. In one of his interviews he asserts:

> You can talk about feminism, because in a way that is accepted. But you can't talk about gay issues because that's not Indian, it doesn't happen here. (Mee, *Mahesh Dattani's*, 163]

The plays raise questions about the social, moral, psychological, cultural and biological dimensions of the gender and the construction (and sometimes confusion) of individual identity, most poignantly illustrated. Gender concepts and models are not static and, as the plays illustrate concepts and constructions of gender must be understood in reference to their particular cultural, political, social, religious and historical contexts. As a dramatist who is aware of the complexities of the cultural baggage attached to such terms, Dattani, in these plays, explores how gender identities and relations are invented, constructed, replicated, stereotyped, manipulated and sometimes reversed through language, politics, narrative and ritual. Religious conservatives generally regard homosexual behaviour by any two persons as profoundly immoral regardless of the nature of their relationship. Homosexuality is widely discussed in terms of religion, and more recently, politics. The various analysis show us how these ideologies are reflected or played out, as well as shaped, refracted, reinforced, subverted or negotiated by the particular text of context. The plays depict a conservative India, bound by familial traditions and circumscribed by fear of change. Homosexuality and lesbianism are seen with a considerable degree of suspicion and hostility on the basis of common 'stereotypes', 'myths' and 'prejudices'. D.J. West comments:

> In order to come to a balanced judgment of the matter of the correct attitude to homosexuals, one has to try to cast personal feeling to one side, and to discount the particular prejudices of our society, which has so long unthinkingly stigmatized all such persons as 'perverse', 'heretical' or 'criminal'. The task calls for a high degree of intellectual honesty. (*Homosexuality*, 257)

As indicated above, the Indian social context is one in which repressive attitudes and social latitude towards same-sex sexuality appears to be particularly intertwined. In this climate 'gay relationships', according to the commentator, have little or no place, since they disrupt conservative mores and family values. This indicates something of an ambivalent moral position; private tolerance coupled with public reprobation an attitude arguably typical of wider contemporary social values regarding same-sex sexuality in India. Against this backcloth, this chapter aims to explore ambivalent attitudes and ambiguous moral censure towards male-to-male sexuality in contemporary India.

Hindu philosopher Jiddu Krishnamurti (1895-1986), who set up a center in Ojai, California, said that homosexuality, like heterosexuality, has been a fact for thousands of years and becomes a problem only because humans over-focus on sex. When asked about homosexuality, Sri Sri Ravi Shankar (born 1956), founder of the international movement, Art of Living, said,

> Every individual has both male and female in them. Sometimes one dominates, sometimes other, it is all fluid. (Vanita, *GALVA*, 5)

Mahesh Dattani, being an iconoclast, deals with many issues prevalent in the society, which the society is either hesitant to discuss or tries to camouflage. Thus the volatile subject of homosexuality, currently raging many hot debates and discussions in numerous social circles, media, both electronic and print, becomes the theme of *On a Muggy Night in Mumbai* and *Bravely Fought the Queen*. *On a Muggy Night in Mumbai*, like all other plays dealt in the previous chapter; here also we find the concept of the divided or fragmented self. The characters wear masks which project them not as they really are but as they want to show their persona to the world. Dattani uses it externally when two characters, one gay Ed and the other, homosexual Prakash, turns out to be one and the same person. The dramatist enhances the dual personality of the character by giving two names, Prakash and Ed. The later is used to highlight the Western concept of homosexuality in contrast with the Indian presented by the first name. This is true of all the characters in the play who try to hide their homosexuality. In the views of Dattani:

> Modern Indian society is just as narrow-minded and un-accepting of differences as traditional Christian as Islamic societies. People talk about the *Kamasutra* and

> its celebration of sexuality but how celebratory of sexual expression mainstream Hindu cultures were in the past is anybody's guess. It would be simplistic to put this denial of sexual expression down to Victorian mores. I have a feeling we, as a culture, have become too boring! (Ayyar, *GAY TODAY*, 2)

As the term homosexuality is itself the deconstruction of male/ female binary oppositions and will be free from all patriarchal conventions when freely expressed in society, the unorthodox play *On a Muggy Night in Mumbai* began with a shocking scene of a couple lying in bed. The man, however, blocks the view of his partner. But as he lifts himself from the bed, the audience realizes that his partner is not what it might expect- and the viewer comes face-to-face with a middle aged, overweight, balding male who is servant of the man, Kamlesh, the main protagonist of the play. It soon becomes apparent that this Indian man- an affluent member of Bombay's haute couture- is paying a lowly security guard for sex. Therefore, the opening reveals a sexual reality not generally accepted by the heterosexual people as they consider it an 'abnormality', which is a bold concept for the Indian theatre. The play is a tragicomedy that renders contemporary gay life in India and finds its main characters grappling both privately and publicly with issues of love, sexual identity, family honor, and societal obligations. Dattani has a strong message to convey, but instead of falling into the trap of having someone in the play preach the message, the playwright creates a believable set of characters going through real life problems and hopes that his plea for acceptance and understanding of India's 'queer culture' is made clear with the stories of these characters. Dattani states:

> I'm not looking for something sensational, which audiences have never seen before. Some subjects which are under-explored deserve their space. It's no use brushing them under the carpet. We have to understand the marginalized, including the gays. Each of us has a sense of isolation within given contexts. That's what makes us individual. (De, *The Hindu*, 1)

Therefore, referred as 'a metro-sexual love story', the play brings this taboo issue like homosexual relationships, out of its conventional closet by giving the gay characters freedom of sexual choice. Dattani enacts the play only in metros not just because it is an urban tale, but because he feels the city people will best understand the hidden spaces of sexual expression. He asserts:

> Actually, it is about people in the metro who are exploring relationships. Sex is implicit. The motivations of the characters in the film are to live their lives honestly. They are the third generation urbanities. They create their own environment. They are alienated from society, seeking emotional fulfillment.
>
> (Bajeli, *The Hindu*, 3)

On a Muggy Night in Mumbai deals with homosexuality in all its colours. Humans are, by nature, emotionally androgynous beings, with the characteristics of one gender overshadowing the other. By this we mean that most women have male responses that are not induced by the society and culture, while men have a tendency to constantly suppress their feminine urges. Now that it is fashionable for men to be 'sensitive', the lines between gender specifics are becoming more blurred. Dattani designates a group of characters from elite classes to prove that same-sex sexuality is as normal and prevalent as heterosexuality, irrespective of class and caste. Alternate sexuality in India is a rare occurrence; it is treated with a sensitivity and restrain that is even rarer in our theatre.

On a Muggy Night in Mumbai confronts the politics of sexuality. The play addresses itself to the question of self-worth and integrity and plunges us straight into the lives of people who practice alternate sexualities. Penetrating into the sexual conundrum, gradually the play unfolds the inner turmoil and conflicts and an acceptance of the 'closet' position for themselves in order to live with the forced harmony of the society to be acceptable. As John McRae puts it:

> It is not simply the first play in Indian theatre to handle openly gay themes of love, partnership, trust and betrayal. It is a play about how society creates patterns of behaviour and how easy it is for individuals to fall victim to the expectations society creates. (*CP*1, 45)

The story unfolds primarily in one place: the living room of Kamlesh, a well heeled fashion designer living in Mumbai, where he invites his friends in order to confide a heartbreaking secret that he is still in love with Prakash, one of his old flames. Prakash, however, has denounced their relationship as the work of the devil and moved on to become a straight man leaving Kamlesh lonely, distraught and confused. Kamlesh tried to forget him by finding love in Sharad but could not succeed. He still endures the mental scars of his three years terminated relationship and asks his friends for help:

> Please! I am afraid! I need your help! I need you all. I am afraid. Frightened. (Pause) After Sharad went away-I decided that I didn't really need anyone to live with me. I had my work. That should have been enough. It wasn't. I felt this void. The same feeling when three years ago, Prakash left me. I would have understood if he had left me for another man, but he left me because he was ashamed of our relationships. It won't have worked between us, but he was ashamed. I was very angry. I left my parents and my sister to come here, all because of him. I know, I know I shouldn't blame him entirely for that...
>
> —
>
> For the first time in my life, I wished I wasn't gay. (*CP*1, 68-69)

Hence, the reason behind calling his friends, seeking help to erase the memory of his ex-lover Prakash, or he will go and settle in Canada. But the play does not have tragic undertones as the characters are fighters who fight with society to have their individual identities, though they also could not free themselves from the forced harmony imposed by the society. As Dattani says:

> ...they are not tragic characters. They are survivors who celebrate the life. Of course, there is tragic undercurrent. (Bajeli, *The Hindu*, 3)

As the party progresses, new surprises turn up for all the friends of Kamlesh, who represents the many facets of homosexual culture: his ex-lover witty and sharp-tongued Sharad, who does not worry about how the world views him and is still in love with Kamlesh; a television actor Bunny who is happily married and very conscious of his public image and so does not want to come out of the closet; pompous and over confident Ranjit who left India to settle in the west with his true homosexual identity; and Deepali, an aggressive lesbian who is quite comfortable with her sexuality and considers herself more sensible than others as being a woman but on the other hand she is also worried about her friend Kamlesh's restlessness. In this diversity of characters one can notice while Deepali and Sharad are very comfortable with their sexuality, Bunny behaves like a traditional Indian gay man for the acceptance of heterosexual marriage. With this fine delineation of characters, Dattani brings out the psychological pressures and fears, the real and the imaginary, gays have to live with. All these characters have different positions in society, different mentalities and different constitution but they have deep bonds with each other and equally feel defiant of the institution called heterosexual marriage, ridiculing the wedding music in the final Act. M.K.Naik says that *On a Muggy Night in Mumbai* is the record of the "changing mutual relationship, their revelations, their self discussion and self discoveries, though they are all sailing in the same boat; each has his/her own oar to put in his/her own flag to hoist."

Thereupon, the issue becomes more complex and helps Dattani to present an exciting and vibrant Indian gay community to the audience. Sharad tries to help Kamlesh by concocting a ceremony in which Kamlesh has to perform a ritual step by step suggested by Sharad. In this sacrament, Kamlesh has to tear his photograph with Prakash, hugging each other; and he feels unable to do it. But this symbolic ceremony could not be completed as when they were preparing, Kamlesh's sister Kiran arrives, unfamiliar with the happenings and the troubles of Kamlesh. Kiran is rather happy at her impending marriage to Ed. Kiran is the only heterosexual in the play and is exposed to having great compassion for the gay people and wishes they could marry for happiness; she knew her brother to be a homosexual. The affiliation between Kiran and Kamlesh is much like the siblings Tara and Chandan in Dattani's other play *Tara*- very friendly and intimate. It is a celebration of gay life, but it also deals with the middle class virtues of family values and friendship among its characters; and so like the earlier *Tara*, this is also a play that looks into sibling relationships and bonding that is at the core of the play. It creates ambiguous spaces that Kamlesh and Kiran must negotiate to arrive at the revelations that will redefine the given structures. Kiran has been unfortunate in her arranged marriage which sends her into the spiral of depression and damaged self worth. Kiran tells all of the friends of Kamlesh about her past life and her new fiancé Ed; this gives rise to be feminist leanings and a feminist issue occurs when she begins to describe the tortures inflicted by her previous husband and also by her conservative family, who, in spite of all the pain suffered by her, want her to adjust in her married life:

> KIRAN. ... the first one. I had to get away from him. To escape from those fights at night. And the nightmare wouldn't end. The humiliation of explaining to friends or neighbours... that the black eye was from banging my head against the door. Or the broken rib was from a fall... It was the cigarette burns on my arms I couldn't explain, that finally made my brother call the police... They arrested him. Oh no, justice doesn't last for very long. He was free the next day. His parents bailed him out. And my parents wanted me to ... adjust! My brother helped me with the divorce proceedings. Oh, thank God for him! And thank God that I met Ed! (*CP*1, 77)

But they are all in for a surprise when Kiran reveals the truth that Ed is no one else but Prakash, one of the friends of Kamlesh. This shocking revelation makes Dattani's characters face even more vague situations. The irony of the whole story is that the poor girl does not know that the man to whom she is going to get married is a homosexual and an ex-lover of her brother. And all the friends of Kamlesh ponder whether to tell Kiran about Prakash's sexuality, something that could end Prakash's short lived happiness. But Kamlesh holds them to their promise of not revealing anything about his relationship to anyone.

Consequently, in Act I of the play, Dattani adds a lot of new shades into the relationships of homosexual characters by presenting an intricate web of identities not only in terms of sexuality but as complex and multi-dimensional cultural, racial, social and sexual polyphony. Kamlesh is in a fix and begins to doubt his own reality, and visits to a homophobic psychiatrist to rid himself of depression. It seems to help, until "he said I would never be happy as a gay man. It is impossible to change society he said, but it may be possible for you to reorient yourself..." (*CP*1, 69)

Bunny, in the play, constructs an acceptable identity as a cover for the true self to live with the 'forced harmony' of the society in a typical Indian manner of living as he advocates:

> What's wrong with that? Huh? Do you think I will be accepted by the millions if I screamed from the rooftops that I am gay.
>
> —
>
> Camouflage! Even animals do it. Blend with the surroundings. They can't find you. You politically correct gays deny yourself the basic animal instinct of camouflage. (*CP*1, 70)

A dissimilarity and disparity is clear in the views of Sharad, who is the most upfront and outspoken about his identity. He challenges Bunny:

> Give me maquillage! Lots of rouge and glitters! Let the world know that you exist. Honey, if you flaunt it, you've got it. (*CP*1, 70)

He emphasizes again,"If any one of us can be straight, I am Madhubala." (*CP*1, 85). Sharad is the mouthpiece of Dattani himself and acts as a mirror to show the real face to everyone in the play without any defense and apology. Dattani himself comments on Sharad:

> There are shared spaces and I think Sharad is aware of these spaces. His camp humor reflects his self awareness and intelligence. (Ayyar, *GAY, 2*)

Sharad, in his usual critical vein, reprimands Ranjit and calls him a 'coconut' because of his hypercritical and escapist behaviour as Sharad put it, "You are brown on the outside and white on the inside." (*CP*1, 71)

Ranjit, very candidly reveals his comfortable relationship with another man in a foreign land to Sharad, but there he did face another kind of problem: of racial discrimination. Deepali is yet again of a different construct. On the one side, she is comfortable with his identity as a lesbian; on the other she is biased as a woman in the gender war of the society. For a moment sexuality is kept apart, when Deepali defends herself as a woman:

> I'm all for the gay man's cause. Men deserve only men. (*CP*1, 60)
>
> —
>
> I thank God. Every time I menstruate, I thank God I am a woman. (*CP*1, 66)

Or when Sharad takes on Deepali:

> SHARAD: if I had a lover, would I be such a bitch?
>
> DEEPALI: Don't- don't use that word. (*Clenches her fist at him*). You can call yourself a dog, call yourself a pig, but never never insult a female. (*CP*1, 59)

M.K.Naik's comprehensive assessment of the play is helpful for a better understanding:

> The play presents a group of well-to-do homosexuals in Bombay, their changing mutual relationships, their revelations, their self-delusions and self-discoveries. Though they are all sailing in the same boat, each has his/her own oar to put in, his/her own flag to hoist. Kamlesh is weak and sensitive: Sharad is his exact opposite, with his jaunty non-chalance. Ed assumes a double identity, with Prakash as his second avatar. Bunny is true to the 'kindred point' of home and the Homo Den; he is a good husband at home and a very competent one in his bedroom, while he enjoys himself as a gay soul in the company of the initiated. Ranjit solves his problem by going abroad where he feels he will be more readily accepted; and Deepali is a militant lesbian, who declares, 'Every time I menstruate, I thank God I am a woman.' Totally free of guilt, she is strong and bold enough to strike Ed when he becomes violent. The wedding music heard constantly in the background in the final Act is an ironic commentary on the lives of these homosexuals for whom 'marriage' can only be a doubly dirty twice-four letter word. (*Littcritt,* 6]

But, in spite of all these differences, these people have deep bonds and do care for each other. The play's primary preoccupation is with fond attachment between people, and not with passionate sexual attachment between them. Sexual alignment is only a secondary derivative of a primary love bond and that too only selectively. For example, the affinity between Deepali and Kamlesh cannot be overlooked:

> DEEPALI. If you were a woman, we would be in love.
>
> KAMLESH. If you were a man, we would be in love.
>
> DEEPALI. If we were heterosexual, we would be married. (*CP*1, 65)

Therefore, Dattani's weaving of complex structures of the identities of these gay characters within the diverse frameworks proves an intimate bond and affinity beyond the sexual relations alone, and as he asserts:

> I have found out that sexuality can't be straight jacketed or compartmentalized. There are varying degrees of love and bonding one feels for another person irrespective of the gender. (Rao, 'Mahesh Dattani')

Act II begins with the hallucinations of Ed, sitting on a bench in a park talking to someone, not visible to the audience. He is dispirited and disheartened as at not being acceptable with his real identity as a gay in the society; in order to escape from his utter isolation; he even thinks of committing suicide. The second person is none other than Kamlesh who gets visible to the audience after sometime. He consoles Prakash by his love for him and makes him realize how nice they look together as attractive as a heterosexual couple. It makes Ed confess "You saved my life!" (*CP*1, 82)

This scene, which is depicted in the dark area to represent the past life of Kamlesh and Prakash when they met first and fell in love with each other, is really a contrast to what Prakash feels now and breaks all relationship with Kamlesh. This is the irony of the play that Kamlesh who wipes away the fear of loneliness of Prakash, gets the reward of loneliness from the same person. The reason of the escape is made clear by these words of Deepali, which she affirms later on:

> It's not shame, is it? With us? ... it's fear... Of the corners we will be pushed into where we don't want to be.
>
> (*Pause*) I too was once afraid of being a woman. (*CP*1, 89)

The scene shifts again into the flat of Kamlesh, where everybody insists upon Kamlesh to tell Kiran the truth about Prakash and himself, or it may ruin the lives of all the three. The already confusing situation becomes even more complex when Kamlesh is unable to reveal the truth to Kiran and end her temporary happiness. He tells his friends that he is not concerned about Prakash, who left him because of the crap that Prakash should love a woman and be a real man, but is worrying about his sister Kiran, who has suffered so much in all her life.

KAMLESH. I want her to be... content. Like Bunny's wife. (*Pause*) I have met her. She has a considerate husband in Bunny. He does care for her. And I have seen how contented she is. Kiran has had a troubled first marriage. I helped her fight for a divorce. Those scars haven't left her.

—

Very slowly she began to find herself again. And I would pray that she would not fall apart again. I was thankful also for Prakash for making her happy again. I don't think it ever occurred to her in her wildest dreams that we were lovers. She never even asked me whether Prakash was gay. She just assumed he wasn't. (*CP*1, 85-86)

In this small act we get only a forward movement of Act I and a preparation for ACT III. No significant action is taking place and the audience get only a glimpse of the past life of Kamlesh when Prakash suddenly turncoats, leaves him and changes into Ed, wearing the garb of a handsome man and declares his love for Kiran, who unfortunately happens to be Kamlesh's sister. This sense of shame is very well expressed by Eve Sedgwick:

For certain ('queer') people shame is simply the first, and remains a permanent, structuring fact of identity: one that has its own, powerfully productive and powerfully social metamorphic possibilities. (*GLQ*, 14]

Kamlesh resigns to the changed situation without complaining for the sake of his sister and not his lover. In the play, the gay person is conceptualized as moving from an initial stage of 'identity confusion', marked by uncertainty about his or her sexual identity, through a second stage of 'identity comparison', marked by a sense of alienation from heterosexual society, to a third stage of 'identity tolerance', in which the person admits to his or her own homosexuality and seeks out the gay community. With the support and validation of other homosexuals, the person progresses to the fourth stage of 'identity acceptance' and from there to 'identity pride', the fifth stage, marked by gay activism and 'purposeful confrontation with the establishment.' But the sixth and final developmental stage for homosexuals is 'identity synthesis', in which the 'them and us' distinction is removed and with the help of supportive heterosexuals, there lingers no clear dichotomy between the heterosexual and homosexual worlds; it is not attainable in the Indian society and this leads to the 'identity crisis', which confuses homosexuals and makes them to follow the wrong path of 'identity denunciation'. As JohnMc Rae puts it:

> ... the themes of *On a Muggy Night in Mumbai* deserve to touch the whole of society and to be touched by it. It is not simply the first play in Indian theatre to handle openly gay themes of love, partnership, trust and betrayal. It is a play about how society creates patterns of behaviour and how easy it is for individuals to fall victim to the expectations society creates. (*CP*1, 60]

These circumstances throw light on the growing trend of homosexuality and its non-acceptance in the Indian society. Central to this argument is the assumption that our 'inner selves'- the way we think and feel about and how we define ourselves- are connected in an active and reciprocal way with the larger social and political structures and processes in the context of which they are constructed. It is for this reason that as many radical and revolutionary movements of oppressed peoples have argued, "the personal is political'. (Halmos, *The Personal*)

In this analysis, neither heterosexuality nor lesbianism are 'natural': both are political constructions; the former a 'compulsory institution' (Rich,A, 1980, 631-57) into which women are coerced, and which is no more natural than high rise flats or the neutron bomb', the latter a political challenge to patriarchy. Adrienne Rich (1978) describes lesbians as 'disloyal to civilization' and adds that 'a militant and pluralistic lesbian/feminist movement is potentially the greatest force in the world for a complete transformation of society.'(Rich,A, 1978, 29-38.) 'Lesbianism' says Brown 'is the greatest threat that exists to male supremacy'. (Brown, *A Brown*, 109)

The life of homosexuals is not a life chosen, but a destiny beyond choice. Oppressed peoples are often convinced of the necessity for separation, as a means of resisting assimilation into the dominant order, organizing politically, reclaiming our heritage and valuing our cultural differences.

> Instead of union, cooperation, solace, stimulations, emotional enrichment, and a maximum opportunity for creative interpersonal maturation and realistic fulfillment, there are multiple underlying factors which constantly threaten any ongoing homosexual relationships, destruction, mutual defeat, exploitation of the partner and the self, oral-sadistic incorporation, aggressive onslaughts and attempts to alleviate anxiety-all comprising a pseudo-solution to the aggressive and libidinal conflicts that dominate and torment the individuals involved. (Socarides, *IJP*, 118-25)

Act III begins with the entrance of Ed into the flat of Kamlesh. All the characters are now brought together in such a way so as to escape the conflicts and repression, secrets and scandals. Everyone gets a chance to hide their truth then seek redemption as a last resort. Tensions and moral choices collide and all the characters begin to be ripped apart. Commenting on such a situation, John McRae says:

> ... the audience must go through the classic cathartic emotions of terror and pity as the characters' masks fall, their emotions uravel, and their lives disintegrate. For the fault is not just the characters' – it is everyone's, in the society which not only condones but encourages hypocrisy, which demands deceit and negation, rather than allowing self-expression, responsibility and dignity. (*CP*1, 61]

Bunny made up a story to give some relief to Kiran in the previous act that Kamlesh is stressed because Sharad has broken up with Kamlesh. When Ed enters on the scene in the present act, Deepali gets a trick to forward this story and mould that in a way so that Ed himself asserts his true sexuality in front of Kiran. Deepali informs Kiran that the reason of break up is that Sharad wants to become normal to which Kiran replies 'that's absurd' (99). Sharad shakes his head in disbelief and then goes with the story in a hilarious travesty of 'penis power' and heterosexual privilege and dissertation on what it takes to be a real man. Commenting on Sharad's bold statements, Raj Ayyar's reaction is interesting:

> I love Sharad's gay liberation speech, where he lashes out against 'penis power' and the pathetic 'wanna be a macho man' self-delusions of many straight males. In fact, though he's such a politically incorrect queen, Sharad unwittingly reveals some of the shared spaces between feminism and gay liberation in both locate a common oppressiveness in the straight male and his desperate patriarchal clinging to phallocentric superiority, 'normalcy' and privilege. (*GAY TODAY,* 6)

Ed begins to be afraid of being caught in a trap and tries to leave the place with Kiran as soon as possible, to escape the cynical eyes of the others who knew about his relationship with Kamlesh. By the last scene, with multiple truths having spilled out all over the screen, Bunny and Ed both realize their follies. The crisis is reached when Kiran gets the knowledge that her fiancé was her brother's lover, she expels the fumes of rage, anger and other negative conflicts on him while Ed tries to commit suicide by jumping through the window. Ed confesses to Kiran at last:

> I am... sorry. I didn't mean to harm you. I only wanted to live. (*CP*1, 110)

The friends of Kamlesh, as a result, are successful in revealing the true self of Prakash in front of Kiran by constructing a difficult situation for him. On being asked by Lakshmi Subramanyam whether it is his trick to entrap characters in unusual circumstances in order to reveal social and cultural prejudices in a dominant patriarchal society, Dattani replied:

> I like the extraordinary in the day to day. I feel that it takes unusual circumstances to really bring out true

> character. It's only in times of crisis or when one is off centre that one's true nature is likely to be revealed. So I guess I use unusual circumstances more for dramatic reasons. (*Muffled Voices*, 129)

The phobia against homosexuals prevailing in the society make homosexuals psychological orphans, suffering from a state of incompletion which marked dependency needs, jealousy and possessiveness, a sense of inferiority and depression, some suicidal thoughts and attempts, and the phenomenon known as emphasis or fear of total extinction. In *Overcoming Homosexuality,* a clinical psychologist presents a similar diagnosis of homosexuality as pathological:

> Homosexuality is a symptom of neurosis and of a grievous personality disorder. It is an outgrowth of deeply rooted emotional deprivations and disturbances that had their origins in infancy. It is manifested, all too often, by compulsive and destructive behaviour that is the very antithesis of fulfillment and happiness. Buried under the 'gay' exterior of the homosexual is the hurt and rage the crippled his or her capacity for true maturation, for healthy growth and love. (Kronemeyer, 24)

And the play is summarized rightly in these words of Sharad, which is a real question everyone asks to oneself all one's lives, being tired of the hypocrisies:

> I ask myself what I have got
> And what I am and what I'm not... (*CP*1, 111)

Dattani obviously seems to have a point to make to his audience. But rather than directly preach, the playwright dramatizes and puts in characters on the stage and one begins to identify with, facing genuine, real life problems. The play, then, in a sense, is a plea for empathy and sensitivity to India's 'queer culture'. Dattani's motive behind writing the play is recapitulated by John McRae as:

> If two men want to love one another, what's the harm?" The harm now is in their oppression, symbolized throughout by the muggy heat and the failing air con. "I really wish they would allow gay people to marry,"

> says the naïve Kiran, only to get the reply from the cynical Ranjit, "They do. Only not to the same sex." It is one of the wittiest barbs in the play, but, as ever with Mahesh, in the sharp humour lies the truth of a very clever, moving and hugely dramatic tragicomedy. (*CP*1, 61-62)

Consequently, beneath the 'queer' surface the characters in the play cope with the crisis of life as 'normal' heterosexual people, and this tragicomedy finds its characters grappling both privately and publicly with issues of love, sexual identity, family honour and societal obligations. Dattani, however, says that he had no political agenda in writing *On a Muggy Night in Mumbai*:

> I'm strongly affected by social issues, especially when it comes to power-play in class and gender. A lot of my plays deal with them and they remain the leit motifs of my plays. I am, however, not a social activist. From my long experience in theatre, I know what will work in a play, that is, what will be empowered writing. My first service is to the story and I believe that the form should serve the content. Usually, there is something like a coming to terms at the end and the audience can experience a catharsis-like situation. That's deliberate and is part of my craft! (Banerjee, *Indian Literature*, 166)

A lot of unanswerable questions arise through the play as to who is a real man? The one who lives by a strict code of behaviour? Or the one who moves to his own instinctive rhythm? Should they listen to their heart's dictates and stay with a man for a lifetime and face social opprobrium or should they hide their sexuality and take a shot at marriage to see if it works? Relationships and expectations between same sex people are as different and diverse as those between heterosexuals. Then why is the society so interested in the lives of people with alternative sexuality? Is it possible for homosexuals to turn into heterosexual? Though Dattani does not claim to have all the answers as he has no political agenda in writing the play but to explore relationships which are under suspicion in the fixed societical norms, as he says:

> ... In any case, being gay or lesbian is not right or wrong, it is reality and we have to learn to accept alternate relationships and live with them, (Menon, *The Hindu*, 3)

Gay literature seems to have been beleaguered by unhappy endings. Homosexuals invariably move towards death, isolation, or a sham heterosexual marriage of the kind Ed and Kiran are heading towards. But *On a Muggy Night in Mumbai* ends on an upbeat, significantly luminous note. In the adaptation of this play into the film, *Mango Souffle*, Dattani broke new ground in his explorations of these complex structures of identity and such related issues. This obviously required adjustments in the narrative as well, but the phenomenal international response to his film requires us to lock at how such subjects are handled in terms of audiences abroad, gay or otherwise. Raj Ayyar comments on the film:

> Till recently, gay literature has been plagued by the 'victim syndrome' and the unhappy ending. Thomas Mann's Death in Venice is a classic example of this tendency. The gay man or the lesbian fades out of the novel, play or film and out of our lives in death, loneliness, AIDS or, at best, a loveless heterosexual marriage. Hats off to you in that Souffle has an almost upbeat moment of truth ending. (*GAY*, 6)

Another play, *Bravely Fought the Queen* does not deal with homosexuality or gay relationships at great length. However, one of the main protagonists, Nitin, does have shades and overtones of being homosexual. His marriage to Alka is not a very happy and throughout the play, we find Alka's suffering, being the wife of a homosexual. However, she is not aware of this fact throughout the play and thus she cannot analyze the reason of her unhappy marriage to a man who is not a caring husband. The audience and the readers of the play also become aware of this aspect of Nitin's personality only towards the end of the play. The heterosexual practice of marriage and family ensures the longevity of the patriarchal system, and therefore social structures with the support of legal and ethical state apparatus come down heavily on such homosexual preferences. This phobia against homosexuals and penalization makes the practitioners of homosexuality feel ashamed and scared of the social stigma and encourage either lie and marry or continue to live the lives of self-denial.

Dattani makes it obvious that both men and women are forced to live according to the social dictates of a dominant heterosexual society, and calls for a relaxation in the rigidity of social taboos, beliefs and value systems established centuries ago. In *BFQ*, Dattani takes up the problem of homosexuality of a married man, Nitin, a closet homosexual, who consequently is unable to satiate his wife Alka's desire which ultimately mars and unconsummated the conjugal life of both. Alka has to suffer the reluctance of her husband who is a big failure in his business, just because he is in the trap of this dangerous sexual disease. Nitin has hidden the secret of having sexual relationship with Praful (Alka's own brother) from everyone and from Alka too and the audiences learn this in the latter half of the play from Nitin's conversation with his mother that Praful tricked him into marrying his sister, Alka. Therefore, both are trapped in the same social norms and Praful plays a significant role to represent the conventional society as both Alka and Nitin are manipulated by him. As Nitin asserts to Baa:

> ...he is to blame. Praful tricked me into marrying her! ... I hate him now! Do what you want with the property but don't let him run my life! He is out to get us! Alka can stay here, or go away, or drink herself to death, I don't care. It doesn't make a difference to me! But get him out of my life! (*CP*1, 305)

Neither had he any desirability or concern for Alka nor any sympathy for her lonely and abandoned life which becomes obvious from his commitment that he does not care if Alka stays there or leave or drink herself to death. The prominent reason for this abiding and everlasting misery of Alka is Nitin's homosexuality but another one is that his old mother Baa was not ready to give him the property because of her annoyance on his marrying Alka against her will. Nitin's apathy towards Alka is obfuscated by the sympathetic treatment meted out to him as a homosexual. As a man of weak will, Nitin neither wants to disappoint his brother Jiten by refusing to divorce his wife nor Praful by divorcing his sister. And the audiences' sympathies are for the both as being exploited by the forcing power of the societical norms. Countering Erin Mee's observation that Nitin's character in BFQ is the first homosexual character in any modern Indian play, Dattani states:

> I would say the only time a homosexual character has been treated with sympathy. There have been caricatures. (*Mahesh Dattani's*, 157]

In the 1980s when Dattani wrote this play, the position of homosexuals was ridden with confusion and was seen as a result of an abusive childhood, a violent father or any other kind of domestic strife. This view also closeted Nitin who at last sympathizes with Alka and confessed his true sexuality and seeks forgiveness from her, though she does not hear as she faints after an excess drinking:

> That was a game he played. And I-I was caught in it... he told me to get married... how could I? and to whom? ... he told me that you knew. That he had told you about me. And that it didn't matter to you. He-he told me everything would work out fine... but you didn't know! He tricked you! I-I am sorry. It wasn't my fault. (*CP*1, 314-315)

Both characters find consolation and expression of their true inner desires in different ways as Alka has to make do with alcohol as concoct a fantasy about Kanhaiya and Nitin finds refuge in the 'strong arms' of the auto-driver clandestinely. And finally, the last dialogue in the play, a kind of soliloquy or confessional monologue is delivered by Nitin where his craving for a free expression of his true sexual self is clear in an address to his sleeping wife Alka, who sleeps in a drunken stupor on the living room sofa,. And all the mystery is ultimately cleaned up as we hear that Nitin is a homosexual who had fallen in love and had been seduced by Praful, and we watch him go out to the auto-rickshaw driver who waits for him in the outhouse. Nitin covers Alka's face with blanket and confesses:

> But now, you will have to sleep. You mustn't wake up, while I... while I ... I mustn't keep him waiting... (He moves towards the kitchen.) The office is not a good idea... too many people passing by ... but here- the outhouse. Perfect. Yes. Don't wake up. Stay drunk. You mustn't watch... those powerful arms ... (*CP*1, 315)

Foucault's *The History of Sexuality* holds that the hysterization of women's bodies is seen as a strategy to regulate female sexuality and discipline femininity, and the 'psychiatrization of perverse pleasure' stresses the need to develop a system for normalizing so-called deviant behaviour. (Foucault 1990. 104-5)

Dattani's play *Bravely Fought the Queen* gave a voice to the tacit homosexuals who sent thankful letters to Dattani after watching the play as Dattani asserts to Erin B Mee:

> Most of the letters were from gay people who were extremely closeted. Some of them said "I thought I was the only person in the whole world", so it was heartening to see that it evoked such a strong response, and people felt they could identify with these characters so strongly. And I got letters from women saying I think my husband is a homosexual. [*Mahesh Dattani's*, 157]

Though the reactions of the heterosexuals was varied, Dattani asserts to Erin B Mee that some people said "...brilliant, I'm glad we're talking about this at last- the liberal section of our society..." and others responds negatively, "we come to the theatre as part of a family, we come with our children and our spouses, and we don't want issues which are very embarrassing to talk about." (*Mahesh Dattani's*, 157]

Therefore, the plays somewhat prove that the traditionalist consider homosexual relationship as something aberrant, disgusting and even blasphemous, the gays think otherwise. They would feel pride and happy to assert their true identity and sanctity on some favorable situations. On the whole, the plays tackle a theme that is bound to catch the conventional Indian audiences by surprise and may raise their eyebrows. Though Mahesh Dattani is not the first to visit this unexplored piece of land, his approach is certainly different and his honest effort to portray the complexity of relationships with utmost sensitivity without any vulgarity and cheap thrills in the form of entertainment make the plays acceptable even when dealt with taboo issue such as homosexuality. According to Mahesh Dattani, much of 'mainstream' society, lives in a state of 'forced Harmony', and a stereotype like homosexuals, simply for lack of choice, out of a sense of helplessness, or out of a lack of alternatives and therefore they suffered and marginalized. How true the words of Kiran in *On a Muggy Night in Mumbai*:

> If there any stereotypes around here, they are you and me. Because we don't know any better, do we? We just don't know what else to be! (*CP*1, 107)

Dattani elaborates and constructs the theme of both the plays *Bravely Fought the Queen* and *On a Muggy Night in Mumbai* to arouse four points:

1. a belief in the basic underlying similarity of homosexual and heterosexual people;
2. a rejection of the concept of homosexuality as a central organizing principle of the personality;
3. an assertion that homosexuality is as natural, normal and healthy as heterosexuality; and
4. denial of the notion that lesbianism or male homosexuality pose any threat to the nuclear family and society as we know it.

Everyone has the right to live life as they see fit and make their own choices. There should be no discrimination on the basis of sexual preferences. As E.Goffman says:

> The individual is advised to see himself [sic] as a fully human being like anyone else, one who at worst happens to be excluded from what is, in the last analysis, merely one area of social life. He is not a type or category, but a human being. (*Stigma, 29*)

Dattani slips the rug out from under or from within the 'thing', resting its identity claim as contingent upon volition, on the one hand and material circumstances, on the other. His aim is to retain the project of identifying in order to challenge directly the social-symbolic institution of heterosexuality. Within this critical environment, performing homosexuals would be taking what de Lauretis calls "the essentialist risk" to perform the identity of homosexual against that of heterosexual. For that, such kind of performance provides a "challenge (to) the construction of heterosexual/ homosexual binary, adulterating the first term and foregrounding the *production* of the second term." (Hart, *Acting Out*, 128)

These plays of Dattani remind us those of the lesbian and gay theatre movements emerge out of a history of a political struggle. Enabled by the post- Stonewall liberation politics of identity that galvanized lesbians and gay men to come out and demonstrate to the world that "we are everywhere", lesbians and gay men established community-based theatres where lesbian and gay playwrights, actors, technicians, and others involved in the production of performance could both develop and refine their work without fear of reproach. Moreover, lesbians and gay men interested in theatre that spoke explicitly about lesbian and gay issues now had a theatre within the public sphere where sub- cultural codes, vernaculars, and customs could be articulated and shared, negotiated and contested. In New York City, for example, this process begins as early as 1958 with the founding of the Café Cino and continued with the emergence in the 1960s and 1970s of other Off-Off Broadway theatres such as La Mama, the Judson Poets Theatre, the Glines House, and the Playhouse of the Ridiculous. In these

Off-Off Broadway houses, lesbians and gay men were able to begin offering alternative representations to the standard fare of mainstream representation, what Don Shewey identifies as "frivolous fairies, psychotic bulldykes, and suicidal queens." (*Out Front*, xi)

The founding of a new generation of lesbian and/ or gay theatres in the early 1980s- such as San Francisco's Theatre rhinoceros, New York City's WOW Café, and Seattle's Alice B.Theatre- extended the cultural work of their predecessors and were essential in developing both lesbian and gay artists and audiences locally, regionally, and nationally. Together these people forged energies to stimulate and enact a sense of queer history and queer community. At once a place for queer art and queer gathering, lesbian and gay theatre remained primarily theatre of, by, and for lesbians and gay men. (Owen, *High Performance's*, 28-32)

Though the theatre of Dattani is not only for homosexuals but of, by and for heterosexuals too for presenting them that they have same emotional lives and conflicts as they have and so there is no difference between them at all. The audiences enter into the space of performance because we know that magic and transformation sometimes happen here and our curiosity gets the better of us. Dattani make audience remember that performance puts into motion any number of emotions that circulate within the space of performance and that, occasionally, this dynamic transference of energy invigorates our lives, persuades us to return again and again to the theatre. And it is the result of the efforts of people like Dattani that the Government is now becoming aware towards these social issues and the change in the sec.377 of the law in 2009 is the proof of this which legalizes the relationships of the homosexuals.

No matter how different Dattani's people are from the standard definition of normal they never appear strange or distanced from reality. This is a play about creating spaces within restricted areas of self-expression. To that extent, *On a Muggy Night in Mumbai* needs to be looked at as a radical step forward for Indian theatre. As Dattani says in an interview:

> It's not that I have done something new, but I've done something unpredictable, and I have shattered a lot of images. (Mee, *Mahesh Dattani's*, 157)

As Mahesh Dattani, through his plays focuses on many contemporary social issues, he has recurrently used subjects that touch upon the zones of experience that the 'normal' middle class society would rather sweep under the carpet and happily imagine did not exist. The preoccupation with 'fringe' issues forms an important element in Dattani's work- issues that remain latent, suppressed and rather 'invisible', or are pushed to the periphery, come to occupy centre stage- to create at least an acknowledgement of their existence. This is exactly how Dattani would penetrate below the surface, subvert the complacent beliefs that everyday reality is constructed with, and make visible the invisible issues that haunt so many of his plays. It also points towards the postcolonial design and concept that is responsible for dichotomy evident in its continuous erosion of moral and spiritual values and discipline. This uphill and bold task requires grit and forbearance which Dattani has proved that he has. In an interview given to *The Hindu*, he says:

> I write for my milieu, for my time and place- middle-class and urban Indian... my dramatic tensions arise from people who aspire to freedom from society... I am not looking for something sensational, which audiences have never seen before... some subjects, which are under-explored, deserve their space. It's no use brushing them under the carpet. We have to understand the marginalized, including the gays. Each of us has a sense of isolation within given contexts. That's what makes us individual. (3)

The positive and hopeful point is that such a play has done exceedingly well in urban India, which implies an audience that is rapidly coming to terms with its own multiple, many hued self. The message is loud and clear: gay is beautiful and if you're drawn to same-sex love, come out for your own sake and to avoid hurting others. Judith Butler too has stressed upon the necessity of conceiving lives that are lived beyond (hetero-normative) symbolic order (or social law), she argues that such 'unorthodox' lives should not just be seen as the shadowy outer margins that represent the foreclosure of hetero-normative kin and cultural boundaries, but as lives lived within the norm. Male-to-male sexuality in India can be understood in these terms, as a sexual possibility intrinsically bound up with hetero-normative contexts, rather than as necessarily separated out as an individual and social sense of self, identity or sexuality. (Butler,J., *Antigone's Clain*)

REFERENCES

Ayyar, Raj. "Interview With Mahesh Dattani". *Gay Today.* Vol. VIII, Issue 167, August 5, 2006. www.gaytoday.com.

Banerjee, Utpal K. "In Conversation with Mahesh Dattani". *Indian Literature 223.* Sep-Oct, 2004.

Bajeli, Diwan Singh. "Going Banaras over Mango Souffle". *The Hindu.* 20 Feb, 2003.

Brown, R.M. *A Brown Paper Rapper.* Oakland, CA: Dianna Press, 1976.

Butler, Judith. "Critically Queen". *glq*: a journal of lesbian and gay studies, 1993.

Butler, Judith. "Imitation of Gender Insubordination", in *Inside/out: Lesbian Theories, Gay Theories,* ed. Diana Fuss. New York: Routledge, 1991.

Butler, Judith. *Antigone's Clain: Kinship Between Life and Death.* New York: Columbia University Press, 2000.

Chauhar, Bala. "Look now we're charging", in *PLURAL.* Jan 14, 2006.

Chatterji, Shama A. "Different Strokes", in *The Statesman,* June 27, 2004.

Das, Bijay Kumar. "Mahesh Dattani in Conversation with Bijay Kumar Das", in *Form and Meaning in Mahesh Dattani's Plays.* New Delhi: Atlantic Publishers, 2008.

Dattani, Mahesh. *Collected Plays.* New Delhi: Penguin Books, 2000.

De, Aditi, "Out of the closet on the Screen", in *The Hindu.* 9 March, 2003.

Duncker, P. "Introduction", in P.Mc Neill, B. Freeman and J. Newman (eds.), *Women Talk Sex: Autobiographical Writing on Sex, Sexuality and Sexual Identity.* London: Scarlet Press, 1992.

Eve Kosofsky Sedgwick. "Queer Performativity: Henry James's The Art of the Novel", in *GLQ: A Journal of Lesbian and Gay Studies,* 1.1 (1993).

Freud, Sigmund. *Letters of Sigmund Freud, 1873-1939.* London: Hogarth Press, 1961.

Fuss, Diana. "Inside/Out", in *Inside Out: Lesbian Theories, Gay Theories,* Diana Fuss (ed.). New York: Routledge, 1991.

Gandhi, Leela. *Post Colonial Theory: A Critical Introduction.* New Delhi: OUP, 1998.

Halmos, P. *The Personal and the Political: Social Work and Political Action.* London: Hutchinson, 1978.

Henry, George W. "Psychogenic Factors in Overt Homosexuality", *American Journal of Psychiatry 93,* 1937.

Kronemeyer, R. *Overcoming Homosexuality.* New York: Macmillan. 1980.

Kinsey, A.C., W.B. Pomeroy and C.E. Martin (eds.). *Sexual Behaviour in the Human Male.* Philadelphia: W.B. Saunders Co., 1948.

Lynda Hart. "Identity and Seduction: Lesbians in the Mainstream", in *Acting Out: Feminist Performances,* Hart and Peggy Phelan (ed.). Ann Arbor: University of Michigan, 1993.

Manjunath, Chinmayee. "Homo-sexuality in India, where tradition still rules", in http://great-reporter.com/mambo/content/view/85/8/, Oct 10, 2008.

McRae, John. "A Note on the Play: *"On a Muggy Night in Mumbai",* in *Collected Plays.* New Delhi: Penguin Books. 2000.

McRae, John. "We Live in the Flicker: Reflections on Time in the Plays of Mahesh Dattani", in Angelie Multani (ed.), *Mahesh Dattani's Plays: Critical Perspectives.* New Delhi. Pencraft International, 2007.

Mee, Erin B. Drama Contemporary India. New Delhi: OUP, 2002.

Mee, Erin B. "Invisible Issues: An Interview with Mahesh Dattani", in Angelie Multani (ed.), *Mahesh Dattani's Plays: Critical Perspectives.* New Delhi: Pencraft International, 2007.

Menan, Sudha. "A Scoop of Mango Souffle". *The Hindu.* 10 March 2003. http://www.blonnet.com.

Naik, M.K. "Cindrella Still: Recent Indian English Drama", *Littcrit,* Vol. 27, No. 1 and 2, June - December 2001.

Prasad, Amar Nath. "The Plays of Mahesh Dattani: A Fine Fusion of Feeling and Form", in R.K.Dhawan and Tanu Pant (eds.), *The Plays of Mahesh Dattani: A Critical Response.* New Delhi: Prestige Books, 2005.

Rao, Krishna. 'Mahesh Dattani'. *The Gentleman,* March 2003. http://www.bordercrossings.org.

Rich, A. "Compulsory Heterosexuality and Lesbian Existence", in *Signs: A Journal of Women in Culture and Society* 1 (Summer), 1980.

Rich, A. "Disloyal to Civilization: Feminism, Racism and Gynephobia", in *Chrysalss: A Magazine of Women's Culture* 7, 1978: Reprinted in A. Rich. *On Lies, Secrets and Silence.* London: Virago, 1980.

Rich, A. *Of Women Born: Motherhood as Experience and Institution.* New York: Norton, 1976.

Shewey, Don. "Introduction", in *Out Front: Contemporary Gay and Lerbian Plays.* New York: Grove, 1988.

Socarides, C.W. 'Homosexuality - Basic Concepts and Psychodynamics'. *International Journal of Psychiatry 10,* 1972.

Subramanyam, Lakshmi. "A Dialogue with Mahesh Dattani", in Lakshmi Subramanyam (ed.), *Muffled Voices: Women in Modern Indian Theatre.* New Delhi: Shakti Book, 2002.

Vanita, Ruth. "Homosexuality and Hinduism", in *GALVA-108* (The Gay and Lesbian Vaisnava Association), 2005. http:/www.galva108.org/ Hinduism.html.

West, D.J. *Homosexuality.* Harmondsworth: Penguin, 1968.

4

Communalism
The Enemy 'Inside'

It is not difficult to conceive how the rise of terrorism or fundamentalism can become into a grim threat to various societies in the Islamic world. Undoubtedly it is born of a burning resentment of injustice or an overpowering vision of an independent and more prosperous future. The religious and social contexts largely differ, yet the premises are more or less similar. Though the nature of such uprisings may vary from country to country, they find common ground in religion and in the infallibility of theological interpretations imposed by the religious authority at the head of any extremist movement. Paradoxically, the notion of tolerance which all religion preaches is turned into intolerance within the confines of identity politics. The objective in these cases is ultimately that of gaining power and the establishment of a religious nation-state that would not hesitate to resort to even dogmatic violence to impose orthodoxy, to control the social and political lives of the people. Any opposition to this would be considered with utmost intolerance as an act of blasphemy to be castigated and brutally punished.

There is no comprehensive and final answer to the question- what is identity? It seems that the concept was first used as 'psychological identity' by Eric Erikson, a post-Freudian, who reunified under this label the 'self' psychoanalysts had fragmented into ego, super-ego, id, object relations and so forth. He argued that a person's identity grows in the course of the life-cycle, or it may degenerate, as in negative identity or identity diffusion. According to Erikson, identity is defined as a relationship between the self and others; it 'connotes both the persistent sameness within oneself (self-sameness) and the persistent sharing of some kind of essential character with others.' (*Identity*, 6).

One of the key strategies in which power operates in societies is by setting up groups and versions of the 'other' who can be both excluded from the opportunities of support and well-being that society may offer, and made a scapegoat of as the cause of social or political trouble. Theories of identity politics are crucial in preventing the position of the 'other' being reduced to that of a victim. In studying the complexities of identity, one must understand that there is a dogmatic or orthodox strain in almost all religions, yet the Hindu constructs the idea of the orthodox or the superstitious Islam, ignoring the independent actions, the humour and the humane strengths of marginalized groups which can emerge in their own right.

The most important lesson to be learnt from analyzing issues of moral and philosophic relevance to the problem of fundamentalism is to try and avoid reproducing the effects of discriminatory power in one's thought. No one has the right to impose one's views on the other. Attention to the question of identity can alert us to a much broader range of viewing other religions which are not inflexible or as dogmatic as our own, and thus may not be held to be as formidable as they are made out to be. No one can, with any certainty, lay down one universal moral philosophy. The new communitarian thinking can be one way of accepting ethnic debates without sounding ethnocentric. In the words of Mushirul Hasan:

> The constant refrain in scholarly and popular writings is how ethnic and national identities operate in the lives

of individuals by connecting them with some people, and dividing them from others. Such identities, often highlighted by the perception of a 'threat' from a group external to it, are often deeply integral to a person's sense of self, defining an 'I' by placing it against a background of 'we'. (*Islam*, 7)

Understandably, the path of Islam, Hinduism or Christianity does not allow such criminal anarchy and there are apparently political motivations behind such a strategy. A bifurcated world is there not because of race or nation: it is there because of what Mark Twain observed about the double face of terror in France: one that brought the 'horror of swift death' and the other that emerged from 'lifelong death from hunger, cold, insult, cruelty and heartbreak.' The former 'inflicted death upon a thousand persons, the other upon a hundred million.' We often forget the latter as being probably one principle cause of violence and agitation. The confusion pf misunderstandings, crude stereotypes such as suicide bombers, terrorists and fundamentalists by which we define the 'other' and the absence of self knowledge, along with American hegemony are all causes of present discontentment and violence. Islam has certainly been at the receiving end and the West has not tried to understand that most of the Muslims around the world are tolerant and peace loving. If we were to ignore the religious fanatics and the tyrants, we can easily decipher a 'core of shared values'. The attacks of 9/11 were certainly celebrated in the Islamic world, but the mourning and sympathy that they aroused in the same world was systematically blocked out by the media.

Today the Muslim constitutes the second largest religious community in India after Hindus as well as the second largest Muslim minority in the world. Approximately, 120 million Muslims are spread out over all parts of our country, and the ratio of Muslim population over Hindu population exceeds the national average (1: 7.3) in some states like Jammu and Kashmir, Assam and West Bengal. India's Muslims are as varied in language, culture and socio-economic conditions as the Hindus. There is little in common between the Muslims in Uttar Pradesh and the Muslims in Kerala or in Jammu and Kashmir. Their unifying factor is religion but the fact is that they do not even have a common language. Why do these people feel threatened, and in the face of what kind of opposition to their identity do they take steps which are defensive and compulsorily fundamental? It is not the question of putting down the threat issuing from the minority of Muslims but to understand the attitude of the majority of the Hindu population which is indirectly responsible for the rise of terrorism in India.

The rising trend of communalism and the accompanying violence have created a feeling of insecurity among the religious minorities and ethnic groups such as Muslims and this fear and discrimination led one-sixth of the country's population to fall victim to panic, suspicion and insecurity. Religious fundamentalism is on the verge of becoming religious bigotry, intolerance and narrow mindedness. First of all it is necessary to define what 'communalism' is. If a Hindu declares with pride that he is a Hindu, is this communalism? If a Muslim says, he is proud of being a Muslim and would give his life to stay a good Muslim, would that be communalism? When a minority community feels (rightly or wrongly) that it has been suppressed by decades of injustice and is being exploited and deprived and reacts and protest sharply, sometimes even violently, can this be called communalism? Do those Hindus, who accuse Muslims of hurting their religious sentiments and sensibilities by a variety of acts of omission and commission, be permitted to feel that they are above public accountability by dint of sheer superiority in numbers when they themselves commit the same sin of hurting Muslims' sentiments and faith in a systematic fashion?

Communalism can be considered an ideology which states that society is divided into religious communities whose interests differ and are, at times, even opposed to each other. The antagonism practiced by members of one community against the people of other community and religion can be termed 'communalism'. 'Communal persons' are those persons who practice politics through religion. This antagonism goes to the extent of falsely accusing, harming and deliberately insulting a particular community and extends to looting, burning down the homes and shops of the helpless and the weak, dishonoring women, and even killing persons. These power politicians are not good Hindus nor good Muslims nor Sikhs nor Christians nor Parsis nor Buddhists. They can be viewed as dangerous political 'scum'. For them God and religion are merely instruments to be used to live luxuriously as the 'king parasites' of society and attain their political goals.

Muslim attacks on India started from 10th Century A.D., but early Muslim conquerors like Mohammad Ghazni and Mohammad Gori were more interested in looting rather than establishing religious dominance. It was when Qutubuddin became the first sultan of Delhi that Islam found a footing in India. Later, it was the Moghuls who consolidated their empire and Islam in the process. Some of the policies and destruction of Hindu temples and construction of mosques over these temples by Moghul rulers aroused communal bickering between Hindu and Muslim communities According to Noor Mohammad:

> Islam also penetrated into Indian sub-continent long back through the Arab travelers. These Arab travelers entered into India through the Arabian Sea and settled in the south-west coastal areas. They did not only preach the Islamic fundamentals but also practice these and demonstrated the others by practicing equality, social justice and tolerance which attracted the downtrodden, exploited and neglected lots of the Indian population who embraced the Islam. At a later period, some Muslims invaded India from the northern side and were able to establish their rule which started from Shahabuddin Ghouri to the last Mughal ruler Bahadur Shah Zafar. Some of the Indians might have also embraced Islam to take political benefits from the rulers of the time. (*Indian Muslims*, 17)

When the British established their dominance in India through the East India Company, they initially adopted the policy of patronizing Hindus, but after the first war of Independence in 1857 in which Hindus and Muslims fought shoulder to shoulder, the British adopted the policy of 'divide and rule' which resulted in fostering communal clashes deliberately for keeping intact their hegemony. The phrase comes from the Latin *divide et impera*, which translates to "divide and rule", keeping its people divided along lines of religion, language, caste etc. The British followed this policy in India by categorizing people according to religion in the census first by treating them as separate from each other. They had based their knowledge of the peoples of India on the basic religious texts and the intrinsic differences they found in them instead of on the way they coexisted in the present. The British were also still fearful of the potential threat from the Muslims, who were the former rulers of the subcontinent, ruling India for over 300 years under the Mughal Empire. In order to win them over to their side, the British helped establish the M.A.O. College at Aligarh and supported the all India Muslim conference, both of which were institutions from which leaders of the Muslim League and the ideology of Pakistan emerged. As soon as the League was formed, they were placed on a separate electorate. Thus the idea of the separateness of Muslims in India was built into the electoral process of India. The relations between Hindu and Muslims were further strained when during the freedom struggle, power politics came into play. There was also an ideological divide between the Muslims and the Hindus of India. While there were strong feelings of nationalism in India, by the late 19th century there were also communal conflicts and movements in the country that were based on religious communities rather than class or regional ones. Some people felt that the very nature of Islam called for Muslim communal society. Thus, though the antagonism between Hindus and Muslims is an old issue, Hindu-Muslim communalism in India can be described a legacy of British rule during the freedom struggle.

Communalism operates today in a significantly changed social and political milieu. It is now perceived as a problem that impedes and wraps the process of development of our country. It is the single largest threat to the secular ideals that our Constitution emphasizes. The sectarian interests keep on fanning the flames of communal hatred.

One cannot wish away one's past, an attitude that is highly visible in the evasion to recognize the deep influences of India's Islamic inheritance. Undeniably the very notion of India's national identity is based on the contributions made by Islam. Nationalist leaders like Vivekananda, Gandhi, Nehru, and Savarkar cannot be absolved for harboring a clear-cut bias towards Muslims, a disposition of discomfort in viewing the past with its overwhelming Islamic scaffolding. These leaders are to a great extent responsible for provoking an attitude that created the rupture between the two communities. Interestingly, no such intense animosity was directed either towards the British who too had ruled India like the Muslims or towards the Buddhists, who posed the utmost danger to Hinduism. It can be argued that this perplexing treatment of the Muslims within India arose out of 'Indian nationalist thought'. The sense of Muslim oppression was used strategically by the leaders to forge a stronger national solidarity. Many Indian nationalist leaders found it useful, specially, to accept the notion of an Indian Golden Age that ended with the presumed oppression of Muslim rule.

The partition of India left both India and Pakistan devastated. The process of partition had claimed many lives in the riots. Many others were raped and looted. Women, especially, were used as instruments of power by the Hindus and the Muslims; "ghost trains" full of the severed breasts of women would arrive in each of the newly-born countries from across the borders. Fifteen million refugees poured across the borders to regions completely foreign to them, for though they were Hindu or Muslim, their identity had been embedded in the regions completely foreign to them, for though they were Hindu or Muslim, their identity had been embedded in the regions where there ancestors were from. Not only was the country divided, but so were the provinces of Punjab and Bengal, divisions which caused catastrophic riots and claimed the lives of Hindus, Muslims and Sikhs alike.

Many years after the partition, the two nations are still trying to heal the wounds left behind by this incision to once-whole body of India. Many are still in search of identity and a history left behind beyond an impenetrable boundary. The two countries started with ruined economics and lands and without an established, experienced system of government. They lost many of their most dynamic leaders, such as Gandhi, Jinnah and Allama Iqbal, soon after the partition. Pakistan had to face the separation of Bangladesh in 1971. India and Pakistan have been to war twice since the partition and they are still deadlocked over the issue of possession of Kashmir. The same issues of boundaries and divisions, Hindu and Muslim majorities and differences, still persist in Kashmir.

Partition brought with it a baffling lunacy manifested in the worst forms of mystification, chaos, arson, turmoil, calamities of rape, eviction, dislocation and refuge. The bitter memories of this madness, whether lived or learnt through narration, continue to haunt the survivors, perpetrators and their descendent generations. The violence of partition generated deep feelings of terror, fear, hostility, hatred and other negative emotions among its victims and perpetrators. At the depths of despair and madness, on both sides of the divide, the 'Other' was seen and projected as the greatest and possibly the most dangerous enemy, one that had to be pulled down as effectively and as soon as possible. Partition violence sounded the death-knell of those high moral values that were essential components of Hinduism, Islam and the Sikh faith.

On the other hand, in the post-independence era, it became a model of violent conflict resolution invoked and emulated by ethnic and religious extremists and the hawkish establishments of India and Pakistan. This chapter argues that the Partition of India epitomizes the politics of identity in its most negative form: when trust and understanding have been undermined and instead fear and insecurity reign supreme, generating angst at various levels of state and society. The trauma incurred in the process has been profound. Consequently relations between the two states, between them and some of their people, and between some of their groups have not normalized even after more than half a century; on the contrary they have consistently worsened with each passing year. Ethnic conflict currently pervades the domestic politics of the two states and the hawks in their defense establishments have been calling the shots for quite some time.

How have the governments in different parts of the world countered such violence that has been the cause of devastation and death? The demolition of the Babri Masjid, the Kashmir problem, the massacres in Punjab, the killings by the Islamic Salvation Front, or the daily blood bath in the Middle-East and then the heartless attack on the Twin Towers give a loud indication of the serious dimensions of this ongoing threat which rides unabashedly on the ideology of the coexistence of orthodoxy and violence. In present times, the press and the media also sometimes contribute to communal tensions in their own way. Many a time the news published in papers are based on hearsay rumors or wrong interpretations. Such news adds fuel to the fire and fan communal feelings. This is what happened in Ahmedabad in the 1969 riots when 'Sevak' reported that several Hindu women were stripped and raped by Muslims. Although this report was contradicted the next day, the damage had been done. It aroused the feelings of Hindus and created a communal riot. Issues like the Ram Janam Bhoomi-Babri Masjid dispute in Ayodhya, the Krishna Janam Bhoomi and nearby Masjid alteration in Mathura, the dispute between Kashi Viswanath temple and its adjoining mosque in Varanasi, and the controversial Masjid in Sambhal claimed to be the temple of Lord Shiva from the days of Prithviraj Chauhan, and Shahbuddin's (M.P.) giving a call for non-attendance of Muslims on Republic day and the observing of January 26, 1987 as 'black day', have all aggravated the ill-feeling between the two communities. The reason behind such kind of divisions can be given in the words of A.G.Noorani:

> A community that considered itself to be a distinct nation by itself, rather than a part of the nation, demanded the Partition of the country for the establishment, ironically, of another majoritarian state. (*Islam*, 121)

The realities of Muslims as citizens of the world expose us to external forces, which compound their internal struggles. their Islamic identity is increasingly a burden that they have to endure as a result of a global assault that on the one hand defines them as the aggressor and the terrorist, while on the other, it paints them as a victim and backward. Consequently, being Muslim gives others a license to judge you based on assumptions they may have. For instance, many expect the same level of groove in their social life as they see in their advocacy but because they are profoundly spiritual and very subdued in lifestyle and character; they are labeled 'conservative'. As Pye puts it:

> In the process of political development an identity crisis occurs when a community finds that what it had once unquestionably accepted as physical and psychological definitions of its collective self are no longer acceptable under new historic conditions. In order for the political system to achieve a new level of performance... it is necessary for the participants in the system to redefine who they are and how they are different from all other political and social systems. (*Binder*, 110-11)

The partition of India has given a limited distinctive identity to both communities within their territorial location and these forceful religious divisions have now become our complete national identity. The gruesome and ghastly rioting which took place in 1947 has continued to throw up countless such incidents in independent and secular India. The confronting and negotiating responses to the post-Babri

Masjid demolition and brutal bloodshed while the post-Godhra Hindu-Muslim communal violence in Gujarat in 2002 is the most recent shameful example of this. Young people may endure great discontent and refrain from agitating. Since Independence, Muslims in India have endured corruption, inequality, exploitation, political manipulations, police brutality, bureaucratic callousness, religious fanaticism without serious social protest. Politicians charge the social atmosphere with communal passion by their inflammatory speeches, writings and propaganda. They plant the seeds of distrust in the minds of the Muslims while the Hindus are convinced that they are unjustly coerced into making extraordinary concessions to the Muslims in the economic, social and cultural fields. They also exploit the deep religious traditions of both the communities and highlight the differences in their respective practices and rituals. The leaders also try to use economic arguments to instill fear and suspicion in the minds of people and prepare their followers to start a riot at the least provocation.

In this context, the very insightful and sharp analysis of the nationalist conceptualization of India's Islamic legacy is taken up by Dattani in his well-performed play *Final Solutions*. In this play, Dattani bemoaned the takeover of the symbols of his religion, by proponents of Hindutva; many like him have expressed the resolve to reclaim them. Dattani exposes the fundamentalists and orthodox persons who use religion as a cover (or mask) to realize their selfish interest. Religion is a mere ploy in their hands to further their interest in life and cherished their desired goal. Identity politics underlying the Hindu-Muslim tension in India has to be clearly grasped to explain the causes of communal riots as well as large scale killings that have taken place in recent years. These are the some issues which Mahesh Dattani foregrounds as a serious socio-political problem plaguing our nation today- the communal disharmony between Hindu-Muslim in *Final Solutions*, dealing with the recurring rhetoric of hatred, aggression, the monetary and political exploitation of communal riots, the chauvinism and parochial mindset of the fundamentalist, in the context of the India of the 1940s interspersed with the contemporary India.

The play presents different shades of the communalist attitude prevalent among Hindus and Muslims in its attempt to underline the stereotypes and clichés influencing the collective sensibility of one community against another. While tackling with the theme of transferred resentments in the context of family relations, he also presents the main cause of riots today and that is through the paid peoples by corrupted and selfish politicians. Alyque Padamsee observes:

> The demons of communal hatred are not out on the street ... they are lurking inside ourselves. (*CP*1, 161)

The chorus used by Dattani in the play is a good device to express the broad way in which the thinking of excitable elements within the two communities goes. Besides the inner resentments, fears and anxieties of the massacre of partition, there are some other reasons which enlarge this hatred further. The feeling of second grade citizens in Muslims through the food habits or kitchen fads of the two communities as Hindus are vegetarian and think of utensils getting contaminated by even the touch of a member of other community are also brought into focus in the play. Muslims, too, are conscious of the antipodal position they assume in Hindu community and are equally averse to the Hindus. Politicians exploit most of these things; hired goons help them and therefore pent up feelings take a violent shape. And thus the false feeling of superiority among Hindus and the resultant base feeling of inferiority or 'otherness' among Muslims is perhaps the worst thing in such situations. And the ridiculous situation is when the sentiments and perspectives of violence arousers and liberal minded people matches, may be in different ways but the underlying sense of 'otherness' is imprinted into the psyche of almost every character in the play, expressed through the violence of so called secularism.

The play *Final Solutions* opens with the partition of India in 1947 and then shifts between the past and the present while presenting the changing nuances of Hindu-Muslim relationships. The plot involves three generations of people who convey complex and abstract messages about guilt, tolerance, religious bias, hypocrisies and cultural prejudices. Through their challenges, the audiences are forced to take a closer look at themselves. It is about a simple Hindu family who are suddenly faced with lot of questions when two Muslim miscreants seek refuge in their house during the communal riots. Thus begins the quest for the truth of their beliefs by their father, mother, daughter and Baa (the grandmother). The story is juxtaposed deftly between two time periods - the present and the past and finally throws light on the beliefs of even those who consider themselves very liberal. In an Interview to Utpal k Banerjee, Dattani asserts:

> The story... looks at two Muslim boys who are running away from a mob and take shelter in a Hindu house. But tension develops when the householder suspects that one Muslim boy is having an affair with his daughter and prejudices surface. Incidentally, this was a turning point in my life and suddenly I lost confidence. It became a time of soul searching for me. (*Indian Literature*, 163)

The play opens with Daksha, a girl of fifteen on the stage, reading from her diary. An oil lamp converted to an electric one suggests that the period is the late 1940s. Her dairy shows her pitiful plight as a married woman in a typical Indian family as she says:

> All my dreams have been shattered... I can never be a singer, like Noor Jehan. Hari's family is against my singing film sings. His parents heard me humming a love song to Hari last night. And this morning they told him to tell me... I am just a young girl who does not matter to anyone outside her home. (*CP*1, 166)

But, soon she comes to the main point of the play and sarcastically addresses this as 'more important thing' and continues,

> Like last year, in August, a most terrible thing happened to our country. We... gained independence.... Everyone was awake waiting for midnight- like children on the last day of school, waiting for the last bell of the class before vacation. And their rushing out and screaming and shouting and fighting. (*CP*1, 166)

Mob or Chorus is used by Dattani as a stylistic device to enhance the real presentation of the Hindu and Muslim peoples. For these five men are employed with having ten masks in their hands, five for Hindu and five for Muslims by holding the stick in front of them. After her reading is finished, the Mob/Chorus accompanies her by whispering 'Freedom! At last! Freedom!'(Dattani, *CP*, 2000, 166) Daksha continues describing the event when the massacre took place- a communal riot which took her father's life. She and her mother were alone in the house and they took refuge from the flying stones in the pooja room. Some stones hurt them; some other had broken their precious things, especially Daksha's entire collection of her gramophone records, which she 'loved most'. Daksha's diary ascertains the history of division – the sense of 'us and them', the 'one and other' by linking personal experience with the political/ social hatred:

> DAKSHA. That night in Hussainabad, in our ancestral house – when I heard them outside-I knew that they were thinking the same of us. (*CP*1, 167)

Daksha closes her diary and Hardika appears on the stage. Past and present is fused on stage through the figures of Daksha and Hardika. Hardika is the grandmother or Baa of Gandhi's family in the present time. Hardika is the name given to Daksha by her in-laws. She shutters between her two identities, namely that of a girl of fifteen and that of a mature lady who has witnessed forty years of freedom. After the Babri- Masjid event and Gujarat carnage in India, one can ask whether anything has changed from the time of freedom at all. And Hardika in the play, while clashing during the 'rath yatra' in Amargaon, replies who feels that a period of forty years is not long enough to make enough changes in the country:

After forty years... I opened my diary again. And I wrote. A dozen pages before. A dozen pages now. A young girl's childish scribble. An old women's shaky scrawl. Yes, things have not changed that much. (*CP*1, 167)

And, with this, the drumbeat grows louder on the stage and the chorus is seen wearing the Hindu masks and growing to be aggressive and blood thirsty with the comments they pass. The words spoken by Chorus show the beginning of disharmony and painful period ahead, as the inner hatred and 'outsider' feeling towards Muslims is clear in these words:

CHORUS 1. The procession has passed through these lanes
Every year,
For forty years!
CHORUS 2, 3. How dare they?
—
CHORUS 4, 5. Why did they?
Why did they today?
—
CHORUS 2, 3. They broke our rath.
They broke our chariot and felled our Gods!
CHORUS 1, 2, 3. This is our land!
How dare they?
CHORUS 1. It is in their blood.
CHORUS 2, 3. It is in their blood to destroy!
—
CHORUS 5. It could have been an accident.
CHORUS 2. The stone that hit our God was no accident!
CHORUS 3. The knife that slit the poojari's stomach was no accident!
—
CHORUS 1 (*pounding with his stick*). Send ... them ... back.
—

CHORUS 2 (*pounding with his stick*). Drive ... them ... out.

—

CHORUS 3. Kill the sons of swine! (*CP*1, 168-169)

A muddle up feeling is found in these voices as while Chorus 1, 2, 3 seem to be more cantankerous, Chorus 4 and 5 seem to be polite in the beginning, but later on turn to be antagonistic like those. These words show that the bitter feelings of partition in the heart of people are still raw. Nobody thinks it is the land of Indians, as it has become the Hindu land only. And thus at the very beginning, Dattani gives us an idea about the real cause of recurrent riots in Indian society.

The scene shifts from the street to the living room of the Gandhis; the family comprises of Ramnik Gandhi, the father of the house, his wife Aruna, his daughter Smita, and his Baa Hardika. Ramnik Gandhi seems to be a very liberal-minder person towards the Hindu-Muslim relationships and does not like Hardika's telling his daughter that "those people are all demons". (Dattani, *CP*, 2000, 173). Aruna is a typical Gujarati housewife doing 'pooja - path' everyday, praying constatntly "Our Krishna will protect us." (Dattani, *CP*, 2000, 174). She is a God-fearing woman and thinks that her Krishna will do everything smooth and peaceful one day. She got overburdened by the work daily. When she complains about her uneasiness, Ramnik asks:

RAMNIK. Nobody is asking you to pray all day.

ARUNA. Who do you think is protecting this house?

RAMNIK. Who do you think is creating all this trouble? (*CP*1, 173)

The Muslim Chorus whispers on this superstitious behaviour, 'We are neither idol-makers nor idol-breakers.' (Dattani, *CP*, 2000, 173) This chorus seems to answer the questions of Hindu mob outside but gradually get emotional and worried about their displaced identity by the Hindus.

CHORUS 1. Their chariot fell in our street!

—

CHORUS 1. Was the chariot built by us?

CHORUS 2, 3. Blame the builder of those fancy thrones.

CHORUS 4. A manufacturing defect!

—

CHORUS 5. But they blamed it on us!

CHORUS ALL. Why did they? Why did they? Why?

CHORUS 5 (*emotionally*). Why?

Pause.

CHORUS 3. They say we rage their temples yesterday.

CHORUS 2. That we broke their chariot today.

CHORUS 1. That we'll bomb their streets tomorrow.

CHORUS ALL. Why would be? Why? Why? Why would we?

CHORUS 5 (emotionally). Why would we?

Chorus 1, 2, 3 and 4 spit.

CHORUS ALL EXCEPT 5. Let them send us back.

They turn to exit.

CHORUS 5 (meekly). Where? (*CP*1, 171)

Inside the house, there is Hardika, the old Baa of Ramnik, clutched in the old misdeeds happened to her and her family while partitioning. Even after forty years, she could not forget that and does not believe Muslims at all. She is an epitome of those hateful thoughts towards them, as any fanatic Hindu would be. These lines spoken by Baa clearly show his fears of both past days and incoming days when the two Muslim boys come to take shelter to Ramnik while riots outside:

> This time it wasn't the people with the sticks and stones. It was those two boys running away who frightened me. Those two who were begging for their lives. Tomorrow they will hate us for it. They will hate us for protecting them. Asking for help makes them feel they are lower than us. I know! All those memories came back

> when I saw the pride in their eyes! I know their wretched pride! It had destroyed me before and I was afraid it would destroy my family against (Pause.) They don't want equality. They want to be superior. (*CP*1, 172)

Hardika is always worried for her family because what she has seen in her times, she does not want it to happen again. Hardika once had, for a brief period, Muslim friend named Zarine forty years ago. She admired her beauty and her interest in music, "I have never met anyone as pretty as her! What a complexion! It's true that Khoja women are the prettiest in the whole world." (*CP*1, 175). But she hates the place where she lives as it is "a place where they sell unmentionable things."(*CP*1, 175). One day, her father's dry fruits and mithai shop had caught fire and her family was in financial trouble. Daksha thought that her father-in-law would give her father a job in his own shop. But it didn't happen. To know the reason, Daksha went to Zarine's home. They were preparing for the lunch. They invited Daksha as well. But she could not tolerate the smell of non-vegetarian food and vomited; this infuriated Zarine and called her names. Daksha felt humiliated and after returning home, her father-in-law was furious with her and denied her any freedom of going anywhere alone. The incident made Daksha hate Zarine and all Muslim's false pride.

The play shifts to the present; Javed, the rioter and Bobby his friend appear on the scene and the action begins. They are caught by the mob outside and they run to save themselves. When they knocked at the door of Ramnik seeking refuge, he saves the two boys, while the chorus shouts: "Kill the sons of swine!"(*CP*1, 179) The bitter hatred intensifies. The irrational behaviour of the two communities lingers for some time showing one's prowess over the other. Chorus 1, 2 shout: "We are few! But we are strong!" (*CP*1, 179) The chorus calls Ramnik 'a traitor' for protecting the boys. Deep hatred makes the chorus devoid of any human feelings. Hardika betrays her feelings by saying that she hates Javed. Aruna too wants that the boys must go away from the house. She gives them water but put the empty glass separate from other glasses as they got contaminated by their touching. Act I end with the violent words of the chorus: "Throw them out!" (*CP*1, 187) The chorus goes to the extent of saying:

You mad man! They'll stab you in the back! They'll rape your daughter. (*CP*1, 186)

At the beginning of Act II, the characters are all in the same position as at the end of Act I. But the mob outside is restless as the chariot lies broken in the street as it is and no political decision has been taken. They began to doubt the intension of their leaders and say: "They want our blood to boil." (188) And they lament that perhaps they have succeeded in their mission. Inside the house, Smita, the daughter of Ramnik, tells that she knows them. Ramnik, in spite of having a tolerant image, gets extremely uncomfortable on hearing this:

ARUNA. You – you know them?

SMITA. I know who they are.

RAMNIK. Why didn't you tell us?

SMITA. I was too confused.

HARDIKA. Where did you meet them? In college?

SMITA. (*unsure*) Well – yes.

RAMNIK. What does that mean?

ARUNA. Stop her studies! From now on she can stay at home!

RAMNIK. Where did you meet them?

SMITA. I – told you.

HARDIKA. But they are not from here. What were they doing in your college?

BOBBY. It's alright. Let me tell you –

SMITA. (*angrily*) No!

RAMNIK (*sternly*). For God's sake! Tell us how you know these ... boys! (*CP*1, 188)

Ramnik calms down only when Smita explains that Javed is Tasneem's brother and Bobby is her fiancé; Tasneem being her classmate. And when Ramnik comes to know through Bobby that Javed is here to find a suitable job for himself, he offers him a job in his own shop; an idea which Hardika strongly disapproves as she does not believe them at all. But at this offer of Ramnik, Smita reveals the truth about Javed being a violent individual: a fact told to her by Tasneem:

> SMITA (*to Ramnik*). They hire him! They hire such people!
>
> RAMNIK. They who?
>
> SMITA. Those ... parties! They hire him! That's how he makes a living. They bring him and many more to the city to create riots. To ... throw the first stone! (*CP*1, 195)

Javed turns furious at these words and calls Smita a "Traitor!" And soon Smita realizes her fault when Bobby tells her that he had succeeded in convincing javed to change his way of life. But everything is destroyed now as she again has broken Javed's trust. This natural disillusionment of such youth like Javed because of the identity problem can be demonstrated in the words of Andre Gorz:

> When, as is currently the case (national, social, occupational, ethnic or religious) identity is invoked and extolled on all fronts, this proves that it is in doubt, that it is no longer self-evident, that it is already lost. (Quoted in Ronald Inden. *Politics*, 1)

Act III opens with a spotlight on the two men sitting on the floor, looking troubled. The accusations and counter-accusations between Ramnik and Javed go on; both accusing each other and the flames of the hatred begin to erupt in their minds. Ramnik accuses Javed as representative of those wronged by his ancestors, and proves he is as 'communal' in some ways as those on the other side of the door. Ramnik proves that he is not so much liberal minded as he thinks himself to be. The distinction between him and his wife however, is that Aruna articulates this clearly from her security of being part of the dominant group, while Ramnik tries to suppress his prejudice. His views about Muslims are the same as like any Hindu, The condition gets worse when Ramnik indicts Javed as a riot- rouser and criminal and emits a few curses by crossing the line between understanding and allotting blame:

RAMNIK. Why do you distrust us?

JAVED. Do you trust us?

RAMNIK. I don't go around throwing stones!

JAVED. But you do something more violent. You provoke! You make me throw stones! Every time I look at you, my bile rises!

RAMNIK (*angrily*). Now you are provoking me! How dare you blame your violence on other people? It is in you! You have violence in your mind. Your life is based on violence. Your faith is based... (*Stops, but it is too late*). (*CP*1, 198)

This move of Ramnik, from blaming the individual to blaming the community in this single sentence is the main and insoluble problem of the society. Ramnik thinks that Javed has done an unforgivable act but still he is ready to offer Javed a job only to give him a chance. But Javed doesn't want that job as he knows very well the hypocritical characters of Hindus like Ramnik, who will never trust him even if he changes and will doubt him forever for one of other thing. He had already refused it in the previous act by sarcastically addressing Ramnik as 'sir' that Ramnik is on the side of 'majority' of the country and so he can offer him job to show him superior:

JAVED. But, sir, it is in your every move. You must know. You can offer milk to us. You can have an angry mob outside your house. You can play the civilized host. Because you know you have peace hidden inside your armpit. (*CP*1, 192)

The atmosphere of the room begins to get dense with the conversations between Javed and Ramnik; and it seems as if a quarrel is going to erupt. Javed reveals true face of Ramnik behind his 'liberal-minded' mask:

RAMNIK (*shaken*). Why must I defend myself to you? You are the criminal ... no matter how much you attack me, you cannot justify your being a riot-rouser. (*Suddenly slaps Javed.*) You ... you scum. If I had known what you were ...

JAVED. You would have let the mob kill me. And you wouldn't have minded if (points to Bobby) he had died as well. You don't hate me for what I do or who I am. You hate me because I showed you that you are not as liberal as you think you are. (*Goes to the main door and stands outside.*) There's no danger outside now ... (*CP*1, 198)

Ramnik, therefore, proves himself to be more repulsive, provocative and a proud Hindu who always feel himself in 'majority' while neglecting Muslims as 'minority'. The subtext is clear- the home/family/society/nation are firmly Hindu, the two young men, literally and metaphorically the outsiders, the transgressors. Bobby, however, controls the situation, makes them cool down and tells Ramnik the childhood story of Javed, which is the main reason of his revolting attitude and behaviour. That time Javed was the hero among his neighbourhood boys. But one day, a minor incident changed all that. Javed and his friends, including Bobby were playing cricket on their street when a postman dropped a letter in hurry and requested Javed to hand over the letter to the owner. And "Javed took the letter ... and opened the gate. Immediately a voice boomed, 'What do you want?'... 'Leave it on the wall,' the voice ordered. Javed backed away, really frightened. ... as the man came out with a cloth in his hand. He wiped the letter before picking it up, he then wiped the spot on the wall the letter was lying on and he wiped the gate!." (*CP*1, 200)

The neighbour began his prayers with the praying bell continuously. Bobby and Javed had never been noticed that bell so intensely and individually before as that voice of bell was no other than other voices of birds and tongas which we use to hear daily unconsciously. Bobby says:

> It (ringing bell) didn't mean anything. You don't single out such things and hear them, isolated from the rest of the din. But at that moment ... we all heard only the bell. (*CP*1, 201)

And the next day, Javed took revenge by throwing pieces of meat and bones into his neighbours, at backyard, which the man got very furious, wept and screamed on the street. Seeing this Bobby and other friends were frightened, at what Javed had done and did not speak to him for many days. The impact on Javed of this incident was, in Bobby's words:

> And for Javed, he was – in his own eyes- no longer the neighbourhood hero. (*CP*1, 201)

The play, thus, shows the journey of a Muslim youth into being a rioter and back. Some politicians start taking an interest in these agitations and in some cases they incite anti-social elements to keep these agitations alive, and when these anti social elements indulge in loot and arson, it is the youth who are blamed for these destructive activities. The frustrated youth, thus, become more frustrated and the unrest among them further increases. But those angry youth who feel victimized by outrageous injustice, or those who feel even mildly annoyed with existing structures and opportunities will collectively act to pressurize the power-holders to bring some change. The Muslim mob generally gets infuriated when any objectionable statements or provocative slogans are shouted against their community and they feel threatened by the other group. These members of the 'other' group take out religious procession such as Drills, demonstrations, rath yatras, etc, showing strength and challenge. Or when they compare the standard of living of their community and low representation in government and other services, and therefore are forced either to revolt or to conceal their religious identity because of fear of exclusion.

Bobby confesses to Ramnik that not only Javed, but he too suffers in this way. Javed rebelled because he is proud of his religion, but Bobby used to feel ashamed of his religion and the fear of being the 'minority' forced him to hide his real identity and he changed his name from Babban to Bobby. Now Bobby and Javed want to leave the house as the road is clear. Ramnik could not let go Javed as he is a criminal and must be arrested. Hearing this Javed laughs and says sarcastically, which is a good example of corruption in politics today:

> JAVED. Arrest me? When they have been looking the other way all along. How do you think we got into the street? In their vans. They will arrest me. Don't worry. To please people like you. And a few innocent Muslims to please everyone. (*CP*1, 204)

Ramnik is shocked to hear such revelations and so is the audience, especially with the mouth of the rioter himself. Javed says that he was there when the procession was going from the street and he began to throw the stones for which he was hired by the political leaders. Those leaders used to hire many such rebellious youth in the name of religion to fulfill their cheap wishes to getting higher positions in politics. The provocative speeches that Javed, like his fellow recruits, is privy to, serve precisely this purpose of legitimizing the conceptual principles of the organization through its emotional impact. Javed's experience is not exceptional but a collective experience in fact, this bonding with the other youth who have undergone the same process of initiation as himself that keeps Javed attached to his group. Javed is realizing his fault now and is disillusioned. He does realize that his faith is taken advantage of by those who will profit by the riots and he goes on describing how he and others get involve blindly in these things:

> It was different when I used to attend the meetings. I was swayed by what now appears to me a cheap sentiment. They always talked about motherland and fighting to save our faith and how we should get four of theirs for every one of ours.
>
> —
>
> Anyone sitting at home, sipping tea and reading the newspapers, will say that it is obvious that a minority

> would never start a riot, we are too afraid, that it had to be politically motivated. Try telling it to a thousand devotees swayed by their own religious fervour, united by their fantasies of persecution, constantly reassuring themselves that this is their land by taking out processions. (*Looks at Bobby.*) Anyone could tell. Not when he has his delusions as well. Delusions of valour and heroism. Of finding a cause to give purpose to his existence. 'The time has come', somebody would say. 'This is jehad- the holy war! It is written!' 'Yes!' I would say. 'I am ready. I am prepared!'
>
> —
>
> And I became a hero once again. We hugged each other for being true sons of our mothers. (*CP*1, 205-206)

Though, now Javed realizes his fault and foolishness of such promises, he finds himself unable to get out of it. Like a child on a giant-wheel in a carnival, to which he goes for pleasure but after the first and second ride all the joy is replaced by fear. He says:

> To shout and scream like a child on a giant wheel in a carnival. The first screams are of pleasure. Of sensing an unusual freedom. And then ... it becomes nightmarish as your world is way below you and you are moving away from it ... and suddenly you come crashing down, down, and you want to get off. But you can't. You don't want it any more. It is the same feeling repeated over and over again. You scream with pain and horror, but there is no one listening to you. Everyone is alone in their own cycles of joy and terror. The feelings come faster and faster till they confuse you with the blur created by their speed. You get nauseous and you cry to yourself, 'Why am I here? What am I doing here? The joyride gets over and you get off. And you are never sure again. (*Pause*) It is a terrible feeling. Being disillusioned.
>
> (*Pause*) Don't we all have anger and frustration? Am I so unique? Now that I am alone ... I hate myself. (*CP*1, 204-205)

After throwing the stone on the procession, he plans to kill the pujari with a knife whose ringing of the bell irritates him like the sound of bell of his neighbour in his childhood. But he could not succeed, as his conscience began to revolt against this misdeed. His knife fell down and he finds himself in the carnival again, unable to get rid of it even though he wanted to get off. His conscience begins to ask him questions, like the Hamlet in Shakespeare's play *Hamlet*, and he backs off:

> There were screams all around, and I was screaming too, but no longer with joy as fear came faster and faster confusing me! I got nauseous and I cried. 'Why am I here? What am I doing here? Get me off! I want to get off!' I was so close to him and I could ... I could have ... I could have ... I let go of the knife. The knife fell to the ground. The joyride was over.
>
> —
>
> The carnival continued. (*CP*1, 208)

Javed gives voice to the individual participating in such riots and reveals how mechanisms of 'othering' influence the self. How does phobia, the irrational fear of the other, grip one's mind? Ramnik sympathize him after hearing all these Bobby and Javed's illustration of their lives, who observes:

> You are brave. Not everyone can get off. For some of us it is not even possible to escape. (*CP*1, 378)

For Ramnik, Javed appears to be lucky as he himself cannot escape from the sins of his forefathers whose crimes arising from communal hatred haunt and torture him. Smita and Aruna enter the scene. They are getting ready with the buckets to fill water from the tap outside the house. Smita insists Bobby to go with her for this purpose- an idea which shocks Aruna as she can never approve this. Being a typical Hindu-woman, doing pooja-path daily, Aruna believes in purity, a hypocritical sham; the meaning of which Smita could not understand. Aruna used to say always, "Always be pure. Pure in your mind, in your deeds." (*CP*1, 173)

These lines, from the Hindu text *Gita,* do not mean that the only purity is of body and home, it goes beyond this. It needs the purity of mind and soul - pure enough to look at every individual with an equal eye. But Aruna can not understand this, as what she believes is taught to her by her mother, and to her mother by her mother. This chain goes on and half knowledge in anything becomes dangerous in present time. Smita, an essentially secular character, tells her mother not to impose anymore religious prejudices on her. She accuses her mother of stifling her with her orthodox religious practices. Aruna is shocked because she had always regarded Smita as an ally in her constant battle against her rational and skeptical husband. The smug and often parsimonious Aruna is shaken out of her complacency through Smita's outburst against her rigid and restrictive practices that have for long choked her. Aruna gets infuriated on Smita's not believing on her so called religion and wants her to follow those rules which are written:

> ARUNA.I shudder to think what will become of your children. What kind of sanskar will you give them when you don't have any yourself? It's all very well to have progressive ideas. But are you progressing, or are you drifting? God knows, I don't want all this violence. How could I, when I won't even harm a goat or a chicken? But to throw everything just like that? Doesn't it mean anything to you? For so many generations we have preserved our sanskar because we believe it is the truth! It is the way shown to us by our saints. We must know no other path. And I will not have all perish to accommodate someone's else's faith. I have enough faith and pride to see that it doesn't happen. I shall uphold what I believe is the truth.
>
> SMITA. It is the truth only because you believe in it. (*CP*1, 210)

Subtle details are introduced that added complex layers to the characters even as the scene plays out what is commonly and simplistically termed "the generation gap". Aruna is deeply religious and assumes that her daughter, on account of being born a Hindu, has automatically inherited her beliefs. She is quite unprepared for the violence of her daughter's accusation, and her question shows both her bewilderment and hurt. Living with one religion or believing in some illogical tenets blindly irritates and stifles Smita; however she does not reveal her thoughts to her mother. Because if Aruna finds Smita's liberal ideas match with those of Ramnik, she may feel herself alone and isolated with her ideas as Muslims used to feel among Hindus. Smita says:

> SMITA. Please, mummy, don't try so hard! You are breaking me. Ever since I was small, you have been at me to go to the temple, make garlands, listen to your reading from the *Gita*. I love you, mummy, that's why I did that. I listened to you and I obeyed you. I tolerated your prejudices only because you are my mother. Maybe I should have told you earlier. But I'm telling you now, I can't bear it! Please don't burden me any more! I can't take it!" (*CP*1, 213)

An alliance in the play is that between Smita and Bobby who feel suffocated in following the principles of only one religion as they are liberal minded, tolerant and believe in one religion of 'humanity'. They are not conservative to divide the society into stereotyped sections and categories of only Hindus and Muslims. They are desperate to escape from its clutches, to leave behind the baggage of social, religious and communal identities that seem to trouble them in all their relationships and actions. This however, is one possible 'final solution'- to deny any context, to attempt to live on your own terms, to reject the past or any other social framework of identity and self-formation. As Professor K.N.Pannikkar pointed out in the Fourth V.P. Chintan Memorial Lectures in 1990:

> The anti-communal struggle is a negative struggle. It is a struggle which tries to evolve ways and means to oppose communal propaganda. The agenda is set by them and the secular forces are made to respond to it. At

every stage the secular forces are either trying to counter, say, a Mahant Avaidanath or an Advani. They are ahead of us. It is necessary to reverse this order. If so, we have to transform our struggle against communalism to a struggle for secularism. Such a struggle can be meaningful only if it is a part of a struggle for a humane society- a society in which human beings are recognized and respected as human beings and not as "Hindu", "Muslim" or any other religious denomination. Such a struggle is possible only if we integrate the struggle for secularism with the larger struggle for a just society. (Noorani, *Islam*, 138)

Smita is undaunted to speak up for what she thinks is right, maintaining that she had kept her silence only to remain non-partisan to both her parents. When Ramnik asks her why she didn't tell him how she felt, her reply is that she didn't want to tell him because that would have been a triumph for him over Aruna as a way of dominating her. She says:

SMITA. How easy it would have been for us to join forces and make her feel she was wrong. How easy to just push her over because you will have me telling her exactly what you wanted to tell her yourself. (*To Aruna*) What would you have done? Shut yourself from us? We wouldn't have let you off so easily. We would've hounded you. We wouldn't have let you forget that the spirit of liberalism ran in our blood and you were the oddity- you were the outsider! What would happen to you then? How weak and frustrated would you feel? You go get what I mean, don't you, Mummy? (*CP*1, 386)

So does the initially unassertive Bobby (Babban), who hides behind a name that conceals the identity into which he was born, and with which he has always been uncomfortable. Javed and Aruna is another such pair- they are both individuals who have a strong belief in their faith, in the things that shape their identities and their ideas of their selves. They have same proud, strength and same fear and weakness, which is clear through these words of Javed to Aruna:

> JAVED (to Aruna). You said the same thing. To her. What I told Babban, you told her ... you said you wouldn't listen to her criticism because she was not proud of her- what did you call it? – Inheritance. I said religion. Same thing. I suppose. (Pause) We are not very different. You and me. We both feel pride. (*CP*1, 214)

Therefore Dattani's characters have their own rationale for their actions. As Javed, the young Muslim fundamentalist, has a resentment against the world because of the 'otherness' and deionization of his community and religion, Daksha hates Muslims because her father was killed in communal riot and because she herself suffered a lot in her in-laws house because of her Muslim friend Zarine. Such religious and historical fanaticism is not only self-limiting for each of these individuals but is also the primary cause for the barriers that are constructed between them and the larger world. Although all the characters are not the same like the different peoples in the society. Contrasted with such fanaticism are the doubtful pacifism of Bobby; the shaky liberalism of Ramnik and the escapism of Smita arising from sheer avoidance. Aruna is the archetypal pious Hindu woman, but changed with times like Javed. When Smita asks her to help her with the filling of the water by Bobby and Javed's help, firstly, she denies but later on, replies that 'they' can help with the general water but "not God's vessel". With these characters, Dattani wants to show that breaking free from and prejudices whether religious or historical, depends entirely on the individual will. In the words of A.G. Noorani:

> A minority sense of identity is shaped by its understanding of its own history. Its self-image is influenced, no less, by the image the majority groups have a minority- an image shaped, in turn, by their

understanding of history. Not frequently, historical perceptions clash. History does not address itself in the same language to different peoples. (*Islam*, 121)

The climax of the play is reached when playing the role of a pacifier between Ramnik and Javed, Dattani eventually has Bobby, performing the ultimate and daring act of liberation- handling and caressing the Hindu god, Krishna subverting all the stifling structures of his given social identity. He says that Krishna smiles at our trivial pride and trivial shows:

BOBBY. Your God! My flesh is holding Him! Look, Javed! And He does not mind!

—

He does not burn me to ashes! He does not cry out from the heavens saying He has been contaminated!

—

Look how He rests in my hands! He knows I cannot harm him. He knows His strength! I don't believe in Him but He believes in me. He smiles! He smiles at our trivial pride and our trivial shame.

—

See, Javed! He doesn't humiliate you. He doesn't cringe from my touch. He welcomes the warmth of my hand. He feels me. And He welcomes it! I hold Him who is sacred to them, but I do not commit sacrilege. (*To Aruna*). You can bathe Him day and night, you can splash holy waters on Him but you cannot remove my touch from His form. You cannot remove my smell with sandal paste and attars and fragrant flowers because it belongs to a human being who believes, and tolerates, and respects what other human beings believe. That is the strongest fragrance in the world! (*CP*1, 225)

Bobby sees himself as a human being who believes, and tolerates, and respects what other human being believe. Bobby's liberalism troubles Aruna who believes in purity strongly and thus she wants to know if there is anything left sacred in the world. Bobby answers so truthfully:

> The tragedy is that there is too much that is sacred. But if we understand and believe in one another, nothing can be destroyed.... And if you are willing to forget, I am willing to tolerate. (*CP*1, 225)

This reminds us the great Shakespearean dictum, "forget and forgive". If the Hindus and Muslims forget the past and forgive each other for the wrongs done in the past, then the road to understanding and cooperation will be free of thorns. The shocking revelation of the play is reached in revealing a big secret from Ramnik to his mother Hardika of his family. The mercenary gain that one party derives from the communal riots of the past is the baggage of guilt of his father's 'black' deeds that Ramnik has carried for long. The shop of Zarine, Hardika's friend, had been burnt down by Ramnik's father and grandfather in the name of communal hatred. After which they bought it at a fraction of its cost. Ramnik clearly acts out of a personal motivation- his sense of guilt is the driving force behind his conscious and structured liberalism. That's why he was offering a job to Javed in that same shop just to amend his forefather's misdeeds. Ramnik has never revealed the guilt of the past to his mother, saving her the weight of the burden that he has had to carry all alone. It also explains the reasons for Ramnik's extreme tolerance. And when this is revealed to a crushed Hardika, who seemed secure in her hatred of the other party, shatters her sense of being in the right. She asks Ramnik:

> HARDIKA. Do you think ... do you think those boys will ever come back?
>
> RAMNIK. If you call them they will come. But then again- if it's too late – they may not. (*CP*1, 226)

There is nothing left to say after these last lines of the play; audience is left to speculate over the situation and decide what is right or wrong. The play encourages communities to open a dialogue in order to rectify the current situation of communalism. It is not limited to questions which face India but a dilemma that the entire world is currently encountering. It is a confrontation between Arabs and Jews, whites and blacks, Hindus and Muslims, traditional and modern, and above all, between the innocent general people and crafty politicians. Dattani brilliantly handles the difficult contour of the play with a subtle dramatic mechanism of using the family to mirror the community, as also using the community to reveal the hidden ugliness within the family unit. Are there any final solutions to the problem of communal riots, disputes and acts of hatred? Can we come out of this vicious circle? Alyque Padamsee asks:

> Is life a forward journey or do we travel around in a circle, returning to our starting point? Can we shake off our prejudices or are they in our psyche like our genes? Will we ever be free or ever-locked in combat ... Are they any final solutions? (*CP*1, 161)

But, Like all other plays, Dattani offers no resolution and the end is inconclusive; it leaves the viewers delving deep in search for an answer to the problem posed and find a 'final solution' itself. If the anger can be expunged from our range of emotions, only then can we live peacefully. But this is not possible at all. A Hindu has always inherited a preconceived notion of what a Muslim is like. The open-ended finale leaves us musing as to what solution there can be to the mutual hatred and intolerance that prevails between the Hindus and Muslims in India. As Vijay Tendulkar in his essay "Muslim and I" points out, "A Muslim was someone you stayed away from." (Choudhury, *Vijay Tendulkar*, 63)

Blame game is in full swing. As it is to be expected, political parties blame each other, residents blame the government and the police. Violence comes as an out pouring of anger and frustration. First of all, who is a citizen, who is an "outsider"? Everyone that lives in this land, no matter how far the generations that have lived here go back, came from somewhere. The earlier generations shaped the character of this city as it sees it. A city is a living, changing, amorphous creature that cannot be frozen in time and that image taken to be its true representation. "Whose city is it, anyway?" Well, it is the city of every single person living here, whether those who landed here yesterday at the airport, bus station or train station and are setting up homes as we speak, or those whose families have been living here for generations.

There is no reason to believe that the newcomers do not have an equal interest in having a rounded, complete, fulfilling life in the city they have chosen to make their home. Newcomers also definitely look for signs of welcome. If given half a chance, many of them would do just that, just right in. they too would like to live a life of grace and charm, I assure you. They too would like to see the infrastructure improved. They too want the crime rate down. They too want fewer accidents, better schools, better transportation, fewer power cuts and water shortages, packs for their children, safe roads, and justice and liberty for all.

Instead of looking outward for the sources of our problems, we would do well to look inward, at our own feeling toward this city we've called home for generations. What are our strengths and capabilities? What are our weaknesses? Let's asses those and act accordingly. Let's not blame our weaknesses on "outsiders." Let's not act in haste and look for scapegoats. Let us be a city worthy of our heritage, if we so care about it. While we spend our energies fighting the demons of humanity- discrimination, injustice, intolerance, human rights abuses- we forget that the demons are not just out 'there'; they may inhibit within. Likewise, our advocacy platform is shrouded in abstract terms so fickle that it can be a weapon of attack in one instance and equally come under attack in another.

Labeling any oppositional discourse as homogenous overlooks the fact that it may have within it diversity and the lack of any unitary religious framework. The leaders of many Islamic regimes get co-opted into the western view that regards various Muslim sects as belonging to one fundamentalist category and, therefore, posing a threat. Thus it becomes imperative to have knowledge of another culture so that the understanding of our own culture and political thoughts gains in a deeper awareness of human relationship. Though we are faced with a very uncertain future we must try to re-examine the concept of secularism and try to view the politics of difference with the clarity and broad-mindedness that the issue of fundamentalism demands. There is a liberal communitarian model which might be an answer to the debate. It is important to address the question of the way we should conceive of human reasoning once we accept that there is no universally comprehensive and privileged stance or point of view. We have to conceptualize on the Nietzschean idea of liberation of thinking for multiplicity through the demolition of platonic hierarchies by keeping in view the constant 'dream' of harmonization which underpins all shifts and the adventures of the dialectic.

The present economic and political tensions call for a new agenda for social reconstruction within which socialism does not need to be replaced but must put forward a programme to salvage a world from inequality, exploitation, hunger and the abuse of power. Such a move might lead the world away from disorientation and a delusional course. A dialogue between left-wing politics and the anti-essentialist theoretical basis would help to throw light on the nature of the social and political struggle, characteristics of the major crisis in contemporary world politics and capitalism. Past politics need to be reviewed in order to revitalize the institutions of democracy around the world.

While the politics of exclusion is rife in our lives, and it may indeed compel one to claim an affiliation, Dattani chooses neither to remain on the fringes nor to be fully absorbed. Rather, he wants to chart out his own destiny, create his own space, which he can share with others while still undergoing an experience that is deeply personal. To do this, he has to defy stereotypes. Defiance, though painful, remains for him an empowering option mainly because when defying, he not only goes against the dominant, but also challenges himself to reason, and to accept the consequences of thought and action. Nevertheless, one must defy on principle and not just for the sake of being exceptional. Social justice advocacy, therefore, should give expression and recognition to personal marks of resistance in challenging deep-seated prejudices that permeate human reason and action. Otherwise, it loses significance and passion. Certainly, the challenge in advocacy rests with the personal. Core values we espouse can no longer concern just 'those people' out there but must concern 'us' right there. Nor can they be externalized or dealt with in a technical, mechanical or surgical fashion. Dattani has to search his soul not only to make peace with his conscience but also to accept the consequences of his conviction. The dramatic canvass of Dattani is not a static and mechanical survey of human experience corresponding with the clash of the motives at the level of the familial relationship or at the level of individual's own aspiration in context of social order. As a creative artist, it is broad enough to interact with innumerable visible and invisible socio-cultural forces. As he himself asserts in his talk on 11th Feb.2001 at Ravindra Kalakshetra as a part of Krishi Festival Plays to celebrate the 50th anniversary of Bengali Theatre in Bangalore:

> Man has created a very complex language called theatre. A language that has the ability to redefine the natural concepts of time, space and movement. A language that goes beyond the verbal, a movement that goes beyond the physical. Through this language of theatre he has been able to see himself for who he is, what he has made of himself and what he aspires to be."
>
> (Dattani, *JIWE*, 1)

It is not difficult to conclude that the Ghost of Partition stalks South Asia, haunting the minds and souls of many of its people. It bequeathed a negative, aggressive and violent mode of thinking, behaving and realizing a political objective. It is possible that in the long run both sides may be fatigued by the high cost of such an undertaking, or one of them gives up such a path realizing that it cannot win the competition. A clear and strong message from the Security Council of the United Nations and major states outside it to

India and Pakistan to abandon the path of conflict may also help. Perhaps a process of forgiveness for the crimes committed during Partition initiated by intellectuals from both sides can miraculously lead to reconciliation and mutual acceptance. Whatever it is, Dattani's intention is clearly to bridge the gap between people, and set straight some of the events of history distorted by time so that they are no more partitions of hearts or of countries.

REFERENCES

Banerjee, Utpal K. "In Conversation with Mahesh Dattani", in *Indian Literature,* 223, Sep-Oct, 2004.

Choudhury, Shama: Gita Ranjan; eds. *Vijay Tendulkar.* New Delhi: Katha, 2001.

Dattani, Mahesh. *Collected Plays.* New Delhi: Penguin Books, 2000.

Dattani, Mahesh. "Contemporary Indian Theatre and its Relevance", in *Journal of Indian Writing in English,* Vol. 30, No. 1, January, 2002.

Erikson, Eric. "The Problem of Identity", in Maurice Stein et al. (eds.), *Identity and Anxiety.* Glence, III, 1960.

Hasan, Mushrul. "Introduction", in *Islam, Communities and the Nation: Muslim Identities in South Asia and Beyond.* New Delhi: Manohar Publications, 1998.

Inden, Ronald. "Transcending Identities in the Modern World", in Kathryn Dean (ed.), *Politics and the End of Identity.* London, 1997.

Mohammad, Noor. "Introduction", in Indian Muslims: Percepts and Practices, New Delhi: Rawat Publications, 1999.

Noorani, A.G. "Muslim Identity: Self - Image and Political Aspirations", in Hasan, Mushirul (ed.), *Islam, Communities and the Nation: Muslim Identities in South Asia and Beyond.* New Delhi: Manohar Pub, 1998.

Padamsee, Alyque. "A Note on the Play; Final Solutions", in *Collected Plays.* New Delhi: Penguin Books, 2000.

Pye, Lucian, "Identity and Political Culture", in *Binder* (ed.), op.cit.

5

Perfect Strokes
Dattani's Technical Skills

The major circumstance of all theatre is human experience, and the key principle of all drama is human action. By dramatizing human experiences, playwrights draw the attention of a community to certain characters, revealing their fear and dreams, their mistakes and successes, and their joys and deaths. Vision begins as an experience of an artist, who extends it into an artwork and ultimately projects it in such a way that it affects the experience of the viewer.

Performance is the main goal of a written play, although the modes differ with cultural variations and from time to time. What mattered in 'life' were the larger structures of society and history in which individuals and collectives choose between one action and another. The audience should be encouraged to concentrate on these structures and their own relationship to them rather than become bound up with the fate of an individual, and a proper synthesis of theme and technique in a dramatic structure helps to produce a feeling in the audience towards something more intangible than the spaces themselves. When the audience began to find similarity between the actor and themselves and began to think that if the characters were not so irretrievably located in their specific spaces they could perhaps find a way out. And this realistic presentation of the world shocks the audience into considering their own lives.

Dramatic techniques are used in multiple ways by playwrights to convey different angles of the story, whether it is lighting pattern, which is used to follow the dialogue or music to show the play's mood. These techniques are valuable tools that enable the playwright to conjure up a fake reality, but believable enough for the audience to accept it. It can also include irony, foreshadowing, imagery and contrast to name some. It will therefore be apt to analyze some of the techniques used by Mahesh Dattani in his plays performed on the stage more for the live audience than for the readers. However the readers too can appreciate and the division of the stage in different sections to project the movement in time and space and hence are able to follow the storyline in a more lucid manner. Dattani always lays emphasis on theatre and the performance of the actor – not on printed words. All his plays are experimented on the stage and some of his plays were staged first and printed afterwards. As Michael Walling puts it:

> To Mahesh, a play is never really finished. Plays only really happen in the theatre, as ephemeral events. The apparently permanent printed text is just one approximation to what might occur when the piece is performed. (*CP*1, 229)

Mahesh Dattani is a realistic playwright and bold enough to reflect his own time truly with his brilliant and innovative techniques in theatre; being the director of his own plays, he is against using mythological mode, as he says frankly to Sachidananda Mohanty in an interview:

> I think the use of myths or legends has its own problems because you already have a mindset towards that. So what invariably might happen is that if you see yourself as a radical, you would try to pass an antithesis to popular myths or legends. Hopefully not? Or sometimes you might just project the same values that are there, knowingly or unknowingly. Supposing you did a play

like *Liberation of Sita*, it amounts to sacrilege. And as for the other forms, I think it has a lot to do with the context.

As for realism, this may be true. I think realism is one of the forms that I use. Because of its popularity in the West, it continues to the relevant. It has got a new lease of life due to television. Playwrights are writing realistic scripts for the stage in order to get accepted. I see realism as one of the forms that I've made use of. I've used the chorus as a narrative device, and I've used time and space in different ways in my plays. I think all the tools of theatre are available to a playwright and you just use them the way your sensibility allows you to use them. (*The Plays*, 172-173)

But, his plays are never far from ancient and universal theories, whether it is *NatyaSastra* of Bharat Muni or the *Poetics* of Aristotle. According to Aristotle, the key elements of a complete play are plot, character, thought, diction, melody and spectacle. A dramatist controls the essential visual ingredients of a play as much as the melodic or thoughtful ones. A playwright conceives the essentials of the spectacle, and then the production team- director, designers, technicians, and actors- furnish the reality. The playwright usually conceives the place where the action happens and indicates the nature of the light, costumes, and properties required for the appropriate physical atmosphere and for the action that will occur in it. Though just the physical environment does not furnish the essential spectacle as it live through the physical details of the actors together- for instance, hand gestures, eye movements, nods of the head, walking or tears- communicate the emotions of the play.

A variety of theatrical and technical modes are effectively employed. The plays of Dattani illustrate the continuous struggle of contemporary urban Indian in familial, social and cultural spheres to create his individual identity and for depicting this conflict; he chooses expressionistic technique. Expressionism is an attempt to discover a technique and method which will express what the dramatist imagines the inner reality of his drama to be, more perfectly and impressively than any of the other dramatic styles of theatre are capable of doing. It is an artistic style in which the artist attempts to depict not objective reality but rather the subjective emotions and responses that objects and events arouse in him. He accomplishes his aim through distortion, exaggeration, primitivism, and fantasy and through the vivid, jarring, violent or dynamic application of formal elements. In a broader sense expressionism is one of the main currents of art in the later 19th and the 20th centuries, and its qualities of highly subjective, personal, spontaneous self-expression are typical of a wide range of modern artists and art movements.

Unlike Impressionism, its goals were not to reproduce the impression suggested by the surrounding world, but to strongly oppose the artist's own sensibility to the world's representation. The expressionist artist substitutes to the visual object reality his own image of this object, which he feels as an accurate representation of its real meaning. The search of harmony and form is not as important as trying to achieve the highest expression intensity, both from the aesthetic point of view and according to idea and human critics. The plays often dramatize the struggle against bourgeois values and established authority, and it often dramatizes the spiritual awakening and sufferings of their protagonists.

In this technique, the dramatist uses divided stage settings at different levels to unmask the distorted psyche of modern man and to picture the whole society and its troubles in this mechanized world. Apart from multi-level sets, various symbols and symbolic devices are used, often with the use of masks to unravel the hidden conflicts within the mind of the character. The technique of flashback and flash forward is used to move the plot backward and forward to illustrate a considerable or a highly disturbed time sequence on the stage. And the present chapter demonstrates how Dattani elaborates this technique in all of his plays with a new insight and perspective.

The sacred space of the stage is defined, redefined, and altered simultaneously by superb lighting design and by the actors who map out different territories both central and peripheral, as they slow-march on the edges of the frame whilst the parallel narrative continues on the centre stage. Stylized movements, clearly inspired by Bharatnatyam and Kucchipudi dance forms are used to convey movements, transitions, continuation within the text and the sub-texts. Fade-in and fade-out used as to indicate the passage of time; use of shadows on the faces in the night and day scenes; light used as to create hidden dark spaces as used in thrillers; use of backlight as an "invisible light" in the representation of absolute darkness. These are aptly used by Dattani in his plays that will be clear by the further explanation of his plays with the technical perspectives. The issues raised by Dattani in his plays are enhanced by his innovative techniques of the stage settings and other theatrical elements. The stage setting of the plays of Dattani is as fragmented as his middle class families. The themes of continual subversion of men by women emotionally in Dattani's plays also co-related with his plot and stage settings and therefore functions to complete each other.

Besides, his use of simple language for the conversations between the characters on stage became almost part of the audience's conversation. This device of "staging the audience" brings to the forefront not only the issues that Dattani raises in his plays, but the fact that there is, at some level, no "fourth wall" distancing possible anymore. By this way Dattani entraps the audience in his net as when they cannot easily separate themselves from the characters and actors on the stage, they also cannot separate themselves from the issues they raise. To make the inner thought in the minds of the characters, he introduced the technique of 'thought' instead of 'asides' in his plays. 'Thought' is followed by 'voice-over' in commensurate with the themes of the play.

Dattani's stage settings are again like his theme, both constructed and deconstructed one, as it is said that he chooses his location within the dynamics of pre-existing structure of the contemporary urban Indian family. On the other hand his older setting is deconstructed by the newer realities of the society entering into the same family, blasting the given stereotypes the shape the structures. These all are presented on the stage through multi level, multi dimensional spaces and situating characters on different levels according to the fragmented family inhabited it. As he addresses:

> The function of drama, in my opinion, is not merely to reflect the malfunction of society, but to act like freak mirrors in a carnival and to project grotesque images of all that passes for normal in our world. It is ugly, but funny. (Roy, *The Hindu*, 2)

In *Bravely Fought the Queen*, the opening image is one which encapsulates the idea of performance: the mask. Dolly is first seen wearing a mud mask, which is a hyper-naturalistic image, but it is also a very symbolic one. The use of white mask to hide the real skin beneath it which is darker in skin is a very skillful presentation of Dattani to present the pleasant faces with a utility potential. The image of Dolly's mask sets up the whole play's exploration of acting as being. While the other characters like Nitin, use the mask to deny his sexual truth and seem normal. Alka and Dolly constantly re-invent themselves through fiction, in which they perform their own life-plays, in which they perform the characters of contented, successful middle class Indian wives. Dolly also suppressed the reality of Daksha's disability and the violence of her birth under the fiction of the dancer-daughter, who is away at school and the biggest fiction of 'Kanhaiya' who is an invisible satisfaction of her love. In the beginning when Dolly enters in a formal sari, completing her make up to recreate herself into a society lady, she unravels performance as a way of living and a mode of being in modern Indian hypocritical society. Towards the end of the play, the masks begins to fall bit by bit, when both Alka and Dolly present themselves in their nighties, abandoning false make-ups, and all the real truths of their unsuccessful marriages, spastic Daksha, homosexual Nitin, and illusory Kanhaiya revealed.

The stage setting makes a symbolic impact on audiences, and with that in mind, Dattani considers broadly both the style and the type of setting that might best serve the play. The style of the setting has to do with the way it creates the reality of the places in the play. The multi-layered reality in this play suggested by the split stage into multiple levels, into three acts, created in the mise en scene utilization, more constantly into an internalized reality of the veiled acidity. The level occupied by the silhouetted, ever tortured/torturing presence of Baa is common to both acts. The play opens and much of the action of the play takes place in the living room of Dolly and Jiten Trivedi, as an implication of mask put forward to strangers. Reality is to be found in the inner chambers- in the kitchen which is a witness to imagined Kanhaiya as well as real scandals of Nitin and the dark auto-driver and upstage in Baa's bedroom where Baa herself is a living embodiment of dark past carrying her own burden of guilt, and much of the actions in this level come to us through flashback. But what is really innovative on the part of Dattani's theatrical setting is the time collapsed and the action of the Act II takes place as a replay of the same segment of time over which the events of Act I had unfolded, only with a different cast and different location. In the other words, the audience witnesses the action that had been playing out in the Trivedi brother's office in Act II during the same period of time their wives had been waiting for them at home. For example, while in Act I, we heard Lalitha, Alka and Dolly's side of the telephone conversations they had with their husbands in the office:

> LALITHA (dials). Hello? It's me. Ya... It looks like you've got the dates mixed up... No, she wasn't expecting me... No, it's not just that. She tells me they are going out somewhere... (*CP*1, 240)

We don't hear the voice on other side of the office this time, as the action takes place at home. But in Act II, where the scene is of the office of Trivedi brothers, we get to hear the men's words spoken during the calls:

> SRIDHAR.(on the phone). Hello? Lalitha? Just got in. ya. What? ... Mixed up what dates? ... Is she there? ... Then what's your problem? ... They? Who's they? (Looks at Nitin) Yes, but they are here... Look, I think she has got her dates missed up... (*CP*1, 270)

The outcome is a complex theatrical experience on the part of the audience, actions visually played off against each other in a sort of theatrical equivalent of the split-screen technique sometimes used in films and in television. The divided spaces on stage also connote the divided and fragmented self of all the characters- of inside and outside spaces, of mask and the real face, of inner truth and the performance as a way of living. So the stage space is also symbolically divided into 'inner' space and 'outer' or 'other' space. The 'inner' spaces are Dolly's living room, the office of Trivedi brothers, the Baa's room, whereas the 'outer' space beyond these are the ground occupied by the beggar-woman, the yard area apparently given over to Kanhaiya, the prostitutes of grand road, and the outhouse where Nitin meets the autorikshaw driver for sex. These outer spaces which are the 'other' for the hypocritical middle class, are intimately related to the emotional terms of Baa, Dolly, Alka, Nitin, because they are spaces of desire. Alka goes 'out' into the rain to dance; Dolly goes 'out' to meet Kanhaiya; Sridhar goes 'out' into the Grant road to find the prostitute and by taking benefit of the girl first, revenges to Jiten; and it is in the 'out' house where Nitin is able to meet his true transsexual self with the rickshaw driver. In this space of desire, the aspects of personality normally left hidden are given a life and a freedom and this 'coming out' is a metaphor of discarding the mask, of social and sexual honesty with regard to identity. Recapitulating it through the view of Michael Walling:

> The constantly shifting nature of Mahesh's stage space became the starting point for a kaleidoscopic approach to the text. Our set centred on a slightly abstract inner space, furnished with three white blocks, which represented the Trivedi household and the office. The

> only naturalistic element in this area was the bar: a glowing blasphemous shrine to alcohol, with the all-seeing eye of the television above it. Around this central area was another world: red and dusty full of torn newspapers, discarded whisky bottles and cigarette packets, the beggar-woman's tarpaulin, a wheelchair. This was an India at once alluring and terrifying, both for the bourgeois characters in the play and for its western audience. This was the world of Kanhaiya, the sexually alluring young cook who might or might not be Krishna; of the dark auto driver who embodies Nitin's sexual guilt; of Alka's liberating dance in the rain; and of Baa, the living embodiment of the past with its attendant guilt and shame. Baa, white-haired in a white sari, wandered constantly through this space, her presence undercutting the apparent naturalism, and upsetting the fragile fictions which the characters had created. (*CP*1, 229-230)

Exposed to an alien environment from the family, some 'person' acts as a 'catalyst' to reveal dark secrets of the family's relationships and its generational conflicts in all the plays of Dattani. Lalitha, in this play, performs as a 'catalyst', as the true revelations and deconstruction began with the entrance of her into the Trivedi's household. Her habit of nurturing Bonsais became the dominant metaphor for Dattani, to unveil the attitudes of the power-ridden society towards women and to explore the self and identity in the play. The stunted growth, the bizarre shape, the grotesque reality of the bonsai becomes resonant in the existence of all the characters that people the play. Laitha explains:

> You stunt their growth. You keep trimming the roots and bind their branches with wire and... stunt them. (*CP*1, 244)

How true this is for a woman who is a creation like a bonsai, as her desires are constantly trimmed and cut so that they spread only to a particular level and van not attain the required height. Their roots are not given ample space to stretch. Alka, Dolly and Lalitha are all bonsais of different kind, but this is especially the representation of Dolly's tortures- Daksha's mother- to whom Lalitha actually brought the tree to present as a gift. Even it's bearing fruits (that are, however, inedible, like Daksha) and turns into a dwarf, stunted in every way and yet surviving and looks pretty. Lalitha says:

> You can't call them fully grown- but when they've reached their dwarfed maturity, they really look bizarre... Anyway, you plant the sapling in a shallow trey- you've got to make sure the roots don't have enough space to spread. You still have to keep trimming them as they grow. (*CP*1, 246)

Consequently, all these trimming and cutting makes bonsai pretty and expensive object, as the women appear in this play in the eyes of Jiten: continuously trimmed in different ways to create the desired effect. Besides, all the thunder, storm, rain and flooded roads are also implied symbolically of revolting outburst of both women and liberation of Alka in rain where she enjoys the real freedom. Flooded road signifies that in spite of all liberating ideas and revolts, we have a long way to go through these flooded conventional thoughts towards a real gender equation and a bias less society. Sprinkling of rainy water on bonsais by Laltha to nurture it signifies the new liberating force of the water to let the bonsai or woman grow freely. The music of thumri definitely sets the mood of a happy and romantic household for which all the three women were carving their whole lives. Probably there is an implication that what is lacking in reality is being involved in the spirit of music. The sterility of Alka's and Dolly's life is being filled with music and harmony. Dattani employs a language in this play which uses both simplicity and serration, pressing the word to its limits, flanked by equally pungent, loaded silences.

The co-mingling of content and form is continued to another play *Tara* too. The very beginning of the play is significant, as when Dan assumes the mantle of the dramatist to narrate the story of Tara in the process of writing a play,

Dattani's autobiographical takings are relevant in his positioning of Dan and self-reflexivity in giving the hardships and difficulties of Indian English writer and especially of Indian English dramatists, as Dan says:

> In poetry, even the most turbulent emotions can be recollected when one is fast asleep. But in drama! Ah! Even tranquility has to be recalled with emotion. Like touching the bare live wire. Try distancing yourself from that experience and writing about it! A mere description will be hopelessly inadequate. (*CP*1, 323)

Dattani understands the processes by which images are constructed. With *Tara*, the playwright begins to look at his own art, and at the same time continues his negotiations with questions of gender, the family and its relationship with the self. He presents autobiographical elements of his life into his plays by distancing himself and therefore is in a privileged position in relation to them. This is not to say that he escapes the lure of the image. Dattani is inside the prevailing ideology and distanced from it. Dattani again asserts in the words of Dan that he does not write in English to the dictates of Western market and also not for Indian critics. As he is aware that English literature in India is insignificant like a toilet paper, "And back home, of course, Indo-Anglian literature isn't worth toilet paper." (*CP*1, 324)

With the main theme of the play 'freaks among freaks', the craft of Dattani's script is he never descends into sensationalism. The playwright structures his play as an intimate family drama surrounding a secret about the twins' separation that was kept from them for 15 years. The story never becomes overwrought, and equally important, the comic relief never detracts from the real emotion of the play.

> CHANDAN. We've been here before.
>
> TARA. When? Oh, you mean...
>
> CHANDAN. Yes. The surgery was done here. (Tara giggles). What's so funny?
>
> TARA. You could say that we were 'separated' when we were babies in Bombay.

CHANDAN. Separated? (Understanding). Oh- right! And we find each other in Bombay.

TARA(mock-filmi style) Bhaiya! (Hugs him)

CHANDAN. Careful, we are in Bombay. You just called me a doodhwalla.

TARA. Oh, Chandu. What would I do without you?

CHANDAN. Tara, stop saying such things. (*CP*1, 334)

With this 'repartee' of the 'wild imagination' of two children, we are amused and we also see the intimacy between both of them. Besides, Roopa's wrong pronunciations of English and Kannad words to be familiar with the Patel family, is much too amusing in the whole play like 'Ogler', 'Two peas in a pot', 'One tarah', 'Concoction' etc. the audience feels less like spectators and more as if they are part of the family, helping him to remember and to forgive. *Tara* again has a multi-level set designed to collapse with the fragmented families who occupy them. Erin Mee says:

> Mahesh Dattani frequently takes as his subject the complicated dynamics of the modern urban family. His characters struggle for some kind of freedom and happiness under the weight of tradition, cultural constructions of gender, and repressed desire. Their dramas are played out on multi-level sets where interior and exterior becomes one, and geographical locations are collapsed- in short, his settings as fragmented as the families who inhabit them. (*CP*1, 319)

The lowest level is occupied by the house of the Patels, the family that the play is about, covers the major portion of the stage. It is not existent and true and seen only in memory of Dan (the older Chandan), who occupies the next level of the set; the only realistic level is the bedsitter of the older Chandan- in a suburb of London. It is his memory that unravels the action of the play for us. So much of thought has gone into the stage-settings, every small detail is defined. On the highest level, is a chair on which Dr. Thakkar remains seated throughout the play- a person who carried out the surgical separation of the twins. He is both the moving force and the objective witness, who separates Tara and Chandan immorally. Dattani asserts his position in the play as:

> Though he doesn't watch the action of the play, his connection is asserted by his sheer God-like presence. (*CP*1, 323)

There's clever craft in the way Dattani's plays out his story and its male/female roots- a surgeon's clinical descriptor of what's extolled in the operation contrasts neatly with the emotional ramifications wrought by the medical miracle. Advances in science and technology are of no import because they are tainted by their human associates- our own prejudices and desires will dictate how we use our scientific progress and how we use our technological advances. Thus, Dattani uses corruption in medical field as a secondary theme of the play, beneath the main activities but as the real cause for the apparent tragedy. This degradation is embodied through Dr. Thakkar to us, who separated twins when they were three months old with a wrong decision of doing injustice to the girl in the favour of the boy, under the pressure of the family that haunts the entire family forever. The technique used to reveal this sub-plot is by running parallely the God-like and machine-like doctor's commentary with the memories of Dan, who became an interviewer on television with Dr. Thakkar, after the publication of Dr.'s surgical achievement in a newspaper. We get into the medical world by the procedures and events described by Dr.Thakkar in his interview used in the successful separation of the twins and by a symbolic implication of the phrase 'operation theatre' used by him:

> We had had about six rehearsals with dummies to make sure that every detail was considered. In terms of the physical movements of the surgeons during the operation as well as surgical procedure. (*CP*1, 363)

In his interviews Dattani continuously used to describe the miracle of science in giving a successful life to the twins combined from chest down, "Like two babies hugging each other."(CP1, 377) What we learn later and which reveals the hollowness of this field of human mastery when Dr.Thakkar used it selfishly as he has his own mercenary reasons to go along with the unfair decision. In the words of Mr.Patel:

> I tried to reason with her that it wasn't right and that even the doctor would realize it was unethical! The doctor had agreed, I was told. It was only later I came to know of his intention of starting a large nursing home- the largest in Bangalore... (*CP*1, 378)

His cruelty not only thwarts Tara's dreams but fills her life with dejection and depression, which could have been safe, secure and a complete life if he had take a wise decision of denouncing the decisions of Bharati and her father. The social stereotypes sweep away even scientific considerations for the doctor and make a parody of his God-like comments on his medical feats that seem to reduce human beings into guinea pigs. There are many scientific technologies that affects women in different contexts like ultrasound technology, despite the fact that it is now illegal, to abort a female fetus because of a preference of male children, is one of the reasons girl-to-boy ratios in India for children under 6years of age have declined over the last ten years.(Indian Census (2001) <www.censusindia.net>) in this case, the use of the technology indicates that politics, power relations and the social value placed on having a boy determines whether the technology itself is harmful or exploitative for women. There is clear cultural preference for male children and the technology is used to reinforce social inequalities and rendering women an 'endangered species', ensuring the continued propagation of gender inequalities.

Like Lalitha in *Bravely Fought the Queen*, Roopa, the neighbor girl, plays a catalyst to reveal the dark secrets of the family. She reveals to Tara that the Patels in the olden days would drown their baby daughters in milk. She is also an embodiment of the partial view of society against disabled children in totality. She is happy with Tara until she is bribed for that by Tara's mother, of watching as mush as movies as she can on VCR at her home. But when Tara revealed her real nature by saying her 'imbecile', she outbursts "You one-legged thing!"- a comment representative of society in totality for disabled persons as being deficient from them. She further says:

> And to think I pitied you! Oh! I think you are disgusting! I only come here because your mother asked me to. No, she didn't ask me, she bribed me to be your best friend. Yes, your loony mother used to give me things. Charlie bottles, lipsticks, magazines. Now that she's finally gone crazy, I guess she won't be giving me much. So goodbye. (*Exits*) (*CP*1, 369)

About Roopa, John Mc Rae says:

> Another element I might have done well to underline is how almost everyone of his plays is subversive in some way. One of my favourites of all of his characters, the gleefully malicious Roopa in Tara, sums up this attitude to perfection: she can be irritating and dangerous, but she is also essential to the evolution of the other characters and to the thrust of the plot. If Mahesh's plays ever perplex or disturb an audience, it is part of the effect of their taking audiences forward, to face questions, scenes and issues they might prefer not to see in the theatre. The plays are not comfortable, nor were they ever meant to be. (*The Plays,* 59)

As a comic character, normal and offensive, Roopa is a crooked and corrupt figure- a representative of the society, the ever interfering, ever watching eyes into the personal lives of families and who will voice morality and laugh at the weaknesses of others while exploiting them.

The implication of 'mask' and 'symbol' is again pertinent in this play too. In the very beginning, Chandan assumes the mask of Dan to live without a self identity after loosing his other half Tara, and again Dan wears the mask of an intellectual and immigrant in London, which he thinks he is not able, for he is incapable to write even his own life story to represent in the dramatic style. A metatheatrical device is used in dropping out all the masks by Dan, when he says:

The handicapped intellectual's mask. (Mimes removing another mask). The desperate immigrant (Mimes removing yet another). The mysterious brown with the phoney accent... (*CP*1, 324)

After removing all masks and clouds over her memories, the thoughts flood in and all other levels of the stage get highlighted and his tragic story begins to be unraveled. It is Dattani's craft to introduce some symbolic implications, comments or events parallelly to reveal truths. As when Roopa, Chandan and Tara are talking about a poem titled 'The Mirror Cracked', just after the scene of Patel and Bharati talking of the revelation of stark truths of the legs of children, this implication suggests the cracking of the hypocritical mirror and the truth will be soon revealed behind this. And again when they converse about the poem, the very resemblance of Bharati to Lady of Shallot is clear:

TARA. Imagine not being able to have children because somebody gave her German measles when she was pregnant.

ROOPA. How does the poem go?

CHANDAN. 'The curse has come upon me! Cried the Lady of Shallot.'

ROOPA. I feel sorry for the lady of Shallot. Locked up. Not being able to see the world, you know. Just sitting and weaving a tapestry or something. And having a cracked mirror.

TARA. The mirror cracks later. (*CP*1, 346)

All the future predicament of Bharati's life exists here. She is going to have mirror cracked of her dark secrets about the partiality to the girl child. This guilt pervades her in the home all her life and she does not like to be societal at all, knitting and cooking all the time. And in future, she is going to be without children as Tara is going to be dead and Chandan escapes to London and never returns even on his mother's death. A curse has been fallen on her just because she had coming in hackneyed and clichéd thoughts when there was the time for decision to separate the twins.

Again, when Chandan and Roopa talk about the movie 'Sophie's Choice', it implies directly on Bharati's choice on the assessment of giving the third leg to any one of the child, girl or boy:

ROOPA. Oh. Then why is it called *Sophie's Choice*?

CHANDAN. It sounds better than *Sophie Had No Choice.*

ROOPA. Yes, I see what you mean. But what was the choice she didn't have?

CHANDAN(thinks about it). Actually, she did have a choice. (Suddenly) What would you do if you had to choose between a boy and a girl? Who would you choose?

—

ROOPA. Mmm... I would be happy with either one.

CHANDAN. That's not the point. In the film, I mean. The Nazi's will only allow her to keep one child. The other one would be taken away to a concentration camp or something.

—

Would you send your girl child to the concentration camp?

ROOPA. Definitely not! I think it's more civilized to drown her in milk, if you ask me. (*CP*1, 364-365)

The title *Tara* itself is emblematic as it suggests that the girls like Tara can not twinkle on the Indian sky, because they are not allowed to. Making Chandan the narrator/writer of the play, one of the Siamese twins, Dattani establishes the accuracy and candor in the play as no one could know better than he does. Taking minimum stage settings for raising this somber issue, Dattani is successful in presenting the true and shocking face of society to the audience, itself being a part of it, as each individual is a social element and cannot escape the societal dictates and familial choices. And his technique of revealing the skeleton in the cupboard step by step to reveal the truth and shams of Indian families is satisfying for this aim of his.

Thirty Days in September is the most somber of all his plays, having not any dialogue of comedy or humour. The weightiness and the seriousness of the problem that it addresses are maintained throughout the play. The stark reality of the Mala's life is dramatized and at no level is taken lightly. Dattani asserts:

> It was a challenge to break away from my regular form, where I sometimes see the funny side of even the tragic events that I am concerned with. But in this, (Thirty Days), I did not have that scope. There's no way you can see the funny side... (Vardhan, www.3to6.com)

Dattani sets his milieu in the upper middle class, despite the general perception about the prevalence of child abuse predominantly in the working classes, choosing this setting because he did not want them to shrink off child abuse as something that did not happen to people like them. Dattani stresses:

> I would see the setting of *Thirty Days in September* as upper middle class. I chose this setting because I did not want to give people the easy way out. I did not want them to dismiss sexual abuse as something that does not happen to people like them. (Vardhan, www.3to6.com)

To accomplish this, Dattani uses very little subplot by dealing Mala's story and the molester in the memories of her, visualizing him, and confronting those terrifying moments that will leave the spectator feeling sickened to the core. About this, Dattani says:

> I didn't see the point of offering anything more, of diluting it. I could have offered, you know, more of her boyfriend Deepak. There was plenty of scope for developing him further, and add more scenes between them, but what's the point. (Vardhan, www.3to6.com)

The action is presented starkly and in an undiluted manner, as Dattani 'traveled' with the character without exegesis and let her narrate her own story, as naturally as possible. The depressing mode of the play is also achieved by exchanging black humour, as a healing process in the play, and in keeping with that mode, hold audience, and listen to the journeys and revelations made by Mala who has suffered at the hands of an abuser, who is himself the member of the family. The audience is quite literally dragged into facing the molester and made to confront him; it is given no choice. For this, Dattani makes extensive use of monologues in the play to intensify the empathy of the audience with Mala, the abused, who is slowly recovering from her tortured and abused past. Dattani explains:

> That is why I had the monologues... That is like an anchor. So you see her as her scars are healing. So instead of humour I used the healing process. (Vardhan, www.3to6.com)

The play prolongs the intense pressures till the very end, letting raw truth speak for itself, mercilessly delivering blow after blow to the fragile construct of the family. There is a lot of movement in the play in terms of time and space shifts. The brilliant example of this is the scene, where Deepak's soothing of Mala, continuously reminds her of the words of her uncle, when first raped at the age of seven, with the words of Deepak:

> DEEPAK. Trust me Mala and tell me what is bothering you.
>
> —
>
> Help me connect with you!
> MALA. I am scared.
> DEEPAK. Of what? Of whom?
>
> —
>
> Forget everything and just touch me. (*CP*2, 39-42)

On this, Mala's uncle struck in her memory on the same level of the stage, only visible to Mala and not to Deepak, with a sense of conspiracy and urgency in his voice. Here the true love and babily touches of Deepak to Mala, reminds her of lusty activities of her uncle. Deepak continues to console her. While Deepak tries to obliterate her fears of touching and loving, her uncle continues to horrify and sicken her for these:

DEEPAK. You see? It wasn't that difficult.

MAN. Touch me here.

Mala withdraws her hand sharply, frightened.

MAN. You don't love your uncle?

DEEPAK. What's wrong?

—

Try it one more time.

MAN. Quickly before someone sees you. Touch.

DEEPAK. Please for my sake.

MAN. You said you loved me in front of mummy and daddy. Come on! Show it!

Mala hesistantly holds Deepak's hand.

DEEPAK. Thank you.

MAN. There! You feel that? It means I love you. Your uncle loves you.

Mala begins to cry.

DEEPAK (stroking her hand gently). It's okay. It's okay. Cry if you want to.

MAN. Shhh! Don't cry.

—

DEEPAK. Relax and look into my eyes. I am not going to harm you.

MAN. I won't hurt you I promise.

DEEPAK. Talk to me. Help me to help you.

MAN. Help me and I will love you more than your mummy and daddy.

—

DEEPAK. I love you.

—

You are beautiful.

MAN. ... I love you even though you are so ugly. Keep singing... Nobody will tell you how ugly you are. But you are good only for this... Only for this. See how much I love you. (*CP*2, 42-44)

The dialogue is terser and suffused with raw emotion, barely held on leash. The plot revolves around the familial system that betrays the individual- a child- who will carry the scars into adulthood, and never trust it again and for this the action and scenes works from within the psyche of the protagonist who is in some sense already alienated from her location, and is seen bereft of moorings. The aim to show the internal fractures of the familial structures is very well achieved by moving back and forth with the memory of the Mala. Dattani asserts in an interview to Lakshmi Subramanyam:

> It moves back and forth with multiple stage sets. It has three space/time zones. The play opens with the protagonist Mala progressing in therepy, confident and articulate. In a flashback the play than moves four years back when she is first I therepy. In the third time zone she is seen, in different settings- at home, at a party, at a restaurant, picking up a man... The play finally looks forward to Mala in 2004, when she feels she has got it all. (*Muffled Voices*, 133)

Deepak is introduced as a catalyst just as like in all the above plays of Dattani, someone is obtainable, to reveal the dark secrets of Mala's life and to resolve her psychological problems. He loves Mala truly and wants to cure her, as is clear by his confession, which confirms his real concern for her:

> I really wish she would tell me what is on her mind. She doesn't trust me, and I find that very tiring. I am exhausted. I am ready to throw in the towel. If I tell her it's off she would simply look at me what she is thinking 'See, I told you it won't work. You are wasting your time with me. Go away and leave me alone.' But she doesn't want to be left alone. She seeks company. Desperately enough to offer sex in return. Does she really feel anything? I thimk she wants something else, I don't know what, she doesn't know what... it dooesn't take our relationship anywhere though... I don't even exist for her. I-I am tired... (Sighing) I will give it one last

shot. I don't know about her uncle... I have a strong hunch... Well if what I think is true, then... Well, there is only one way to find out... (*CP*2, 45)

And Deepak goes on to reveal the secret of Mala's psychological problem by inviting everyone in a restaurant, Mala, her mother, her uncle; he tries to unfold the tragedy through conversations and reactions of her uncle, who Deepak thinks is responsible for Mala's condition. The audience lives through the horror of childhood abuse and the slow, painful process of overcoming its warping effects: from distance though. After being commissioned by an NGO called RAHI, that helps survivors of child sexual abuse; Dattani spent a few days with about eight survivors of child sexual abuse and listened to their experiences. He got so much involved and exhausted in that it took a long time for him to go back to the material available, which he did after a long gap and then started working on the play after putting him at a reasonable a safe distance to be objective.

Space is always a matter of limits- even when it's described as "unlimited". It has to be bounded, modified, organized, structured, and quoted. Space in necessary to structure; it is structure's raw material. Space requires a frame, a garment, a proscenium, a limit. As a universal term, space has to be able to accommodate structures of varying shapes and sizes; it swallows up everything in an unchanging term of limitation. And so discursive "space" requires that space be differentiated as space- empty, acoustic, inner, outer- from that 'Other' space that it is not; space is never without that other space. And yet the limit of space, which represents it as space, recedes, and recedes ominously, into its universal term. In the theatre, space is often invoked as the essential element, the place in which theatre distinguishes itself from the purely "literary". Even the word "theatre" means both the performance and the structure that contains it. "Theatre" is a space for visibility, even if that space is 'empty'; etymologically, the word theatre is related to sight, manifestation, miracle, as well as to theory, which suggests the complicated relation between theory and visibility- sight and site- in theatrical language.

This notion of theatre, as the space that is continuously rebounding, where limits are always redrawn, is sometimes taken to be too limited. Realists might prefer standardized bounds of the visible, while performance theorists might prefer to blur or to exclude boundaries to performance. But this is a shell game. Boundaries can move, but they can't be removed. Perception is only virtually unbounded; at the limit of space- the infinitely large or the infinitely small- there's still a space beyond 'space'. Spatial knowledge is necessarily relative, as all theatre practitioners as well as theorists know, whatever their spatial preference; it always excludes the space you don't see, can't measure, haven't imagined yet. And that's because theatrical space already includes the offstage, the outside, and the invisible.

This obsessive and absorbing technique is brilliantly used by Mahesh Dattani in all his plays. The theatre of Dattani is certainly identifiable, typified by claustrophobia and escape. Right from the beginning of his career, Dattani was trying to get out of tight places. He has been experimenting with permeable four walls, translucent scenery, and the theatre's obsessive need to establish and to transgress borders. Themes of sexuality, madness and memory interweave in his oeuvre, questioning, over and over, about how to project the inner psychological process through the outer technical skills.

The use of theatrical space and symbolic props like the doll, the framed picture of Lord Krishna and layers of screens is enlivened by excellent sound scapes- the taped monologues/ confessions of Mala, sounds of thunder and rain and a beautiful fusion of a Meera Bhajan. Like *Bravely Fought the Queen*, here again thunder and rain are used as signs to represent the time of the revelation of some dark truths. The framed picture of Lord Krishna represents the life of Shanta nad Mala both. Though both of them veil their dark secrets behind the framed glasses of the picture, Mala always wants to crack it and even does it. But Shanta wants that framed again and hide their plights behind the hypocrisies of societal norms to survive and accepted in the society. The uncle obliterates and devastates the lives of both but still willing to clear the broken glasses wiped and buried to cover his own misdeed by arranging the marriage of both again like putting new glass on the picture or beginning new life, which looks new but the reality is always transparent behind the transparent glass. Mala broke that to shatter the hypocrisy. As the man (Mala's voice) advices Shanta to marry Mala to Deepak just to hide his own transgression as his words for the frame of the picture of Krishna symbolically implies this. After placing the picture again in its place, he says:

> MAN. There. No one can tell it's broken. But you better put the glass back soon. (*CP*2, 40)

But Shanta could not relieve herself from the haunting memory of this man even after her marriage and her husband left her, and Mala too is finding it difficult to have any relationship with Deepak more than the physical. The most enduring image of course is the last scene, when the curtain, which separated the mother and her deity, finally lifts, breaking down the last barrier that stood between the mother and daughter. These last words of Mala to her mother show that all the barriers between them ended on the realization of their true inner selves, free from shackles of fear and silence of the patriarchy and chauvinism:

> MALA. ... While I accused you of not recognizing my pain, you never felt any anger at me for not recognizing yours. We were both struggling to survive but- I never acknowledged your struggle. Ma, no matter where I am, I always think of you. I want you to know that I am listening. Waiting for you to speak. I promise you I will listen. I am waiting for a sign from you... to say that you have forgiven me.
>
> —
>
> I know you will, mother. I know you have. (*CP*2, 58)

The title of the play is taken from a nursery rhyme "Thirty days has September. April, June and November. February has twenty-eight. All the rest have thirty-one!"

the singing of this rhyme while her first seduction, Mala continues to remind in all her adult relations, whom she could not let flourish for more than 30 days.

Where There's a Will, an amalgamation of emotion and comedy, is the very first play of Dattani, but he handles the spacing out of performance admirably and provides a structure to fit in with the needs of the plot so deftly, notwithstanding the fact that this is his first play. The play is divided neatly into two halves, one prior to the death of Hasmukh, and another post death or rather the first part deals with the construction of gendered stereotypical identity and the second is going to deconstruct that. Even the patriarch who exercises his power through the entire play got the realization of his true self, even though he is present the whole time in the play, alive or as a ghost.

The stage is set simply in those spaces- two bedrooms of Hasmukh/Sonal's and Ajit/Preeti's and the fancy dining-cum-living room. With family relationship as the focus of dramatic representation, Dattani's handling of the performance space suggests to his audiences the variations in the signification allotted to different spaces. The plot of the play is apparently simple; the relationships between the four main protagonists of a joint family are painfully twisted as the play begins to come alive in performance, through the complicated design of the will.

The seriousness of the issue is hidden behind the comedy in *Where There's a Will,* which accomplishes something quite extraordinary; it explores grim issues such as loveless lives and unhappy families, using the comic medium. Dattani's wicked humour is at its best in the first half, revealing itself in the abrasive venom that Hasmukh spits at everybody in general. But the latter half of the script is problematic as Hasmukh had 'goofed his plans' and is confronted by a need to have changed. He lost out because it dawned on him too late, after he had run out of options. Instead, we were given a comic variation, which caused a break from the first act and left little room for the heavy humour.

Dattani works this out with the help of his extremely self-reflexive text, where Hasmukh speaks more to the audience, directly, than to any of the other protagonists, both alive and as a ghost, taking them into confidence. It owes its effectiveness to this employment of the peculiar craft of theatre in the process of the play text looking inwards to predict the action going to be onwards. This is because of Dattani's acknowledgement that a play is 'live' only when it is performed, and performance can derive its life only in complicity with an audience that shares the entire exercise. There are many examples of the rollicking comedy of the play which comes as a result of such shared confidences as Hasmukh says to the audience:

> (Puffs on his cigarette) At the rate I'm puffing, I should be dead in forty minutes. (*CP*1, 450)

And true enough, he really dies after some minutes. The play begins with the conflict of father and son and Hasmukh's dissatisfaction with the whole family members. The infuriated Hasmukh tries to fill the 'empty spaces' in his son's head with some sense and cries:

> Son, how do I start explaining to you? (To the audience) Yes, how? You tell me. Well I'll try. (*CP*1, 459)

There's a comical treatment to everything, even the death of Hasmukh Mehta. Dattani's excellence lies mainly in making the tragic event of Hasmukh's death, gleeful, even by himself and here the talk with the audience becomes more complacent, as Hasmukh's ghost is visible and audible only to the audience. The most humorous dialogues of Hasmukh are, when his ghost after his death finds his body lying on bed, he wonders of his self predicament previously and creates amusing situation for the audience when he waits gleefully for his wife to discover his death:

> HASMUKH. ... (To the audience) Didn't I tell you that if I carried on smoking like that I'd be dead in no time? I didn't believe it myself. I thought I was joking!

Sonal enters from the kitchen and slowly makes her way up to her bedroom.

There's my wife, coming up to our bedroom. I can see through the walls. How will she react when she finds out? She will howl, she will wail, she will tear her hair and beat her head against the wall! Let's see.

—

SONAL. Are you asleep?

HASMUKH. No, I'm dead.

SONAL. Of course, he's asleep. He just has to lie down on the bed and he is dead to the world!

HASMUKH. She has a way of saying things.

SONAL. (notices the cigarette and stubs it out). Oh, so you've been smoking, have you? Do you want a second heart attack?

HASMUKH. I just had it, thank you.

SONAL. Who am I talking to? The four walls?

HASMUKH. How right you are.

Sonal lies down on the bed beside 'him'.

Don't go to sleep, you silly woman. Do I have to wait for Diwali before you find out I'm gone? (*CP*1, 476-477)

The family members weep and whine not so much for the old man but what he has left for them. And Hasmukh's ghost descends from the clouds to watch the tragic drama that his 'will' has wrecked on the family. The play uses the 'will' as a fantastic pun.

The humour in the play, however, is a major redeeming factor and has its source largely in the interjections and asides of Hasmukh as a ghost. Also, Dattani's depiction of a visible/invisible and audible/inaudible ghost extends the scope of naturalistic drams. Even when Hasmukh does die, the tragical and sad moment is presented in a comical stage direction thus:

> The two women start sobbing. Lights fade out on them. Spotlight picks up Hasmukh, or rather, his ghost. He stands arms akimbo. And for the first time in the play, he grins from ear to ear. (*CP*1, 478)

Death ceases the pain of living as the ghost of Hasmukh says, "It feels good to be dead. No more kidney problems, no backaches, no heartbeats..." (*CP*1, 479) Dattani does explore some existential angst here:

> What's this? A sandlewood garland?... When my father died, I used to put fresh flowers everyday for a whole month... (Takes a final look at his picture) So that's it. That is how the world will remember me. Until my son locks me in a trunk... (*CP*1, 487-88)

The play also hints at pathos, in the special kind of bonding that takes place between Sonal and Kiran. It is clear from the outset that the humour of the play is sheathed in black comedy and the overtones of Ibsenesque strangulation are the main tools of Dattani to look in the play at the Indian middle class morality and then proceeds to parody it. The culturally rooted idea of ghosts hanging from a tamarind tree is used to bring in more fun, even directly poking fun at the audience:

> HASMUKH. Have you ever swung on a tamarind tree? Upside down? You should try it some time. You can see the world the way it really is. It's important to get a good grip on the branch with your legs. Then you can relax your hands and head. Like this (demonstrates by lying on his back and letting his head and hands dangle over the side of the table). How do I look? I don't know about me, but you all definitely look peculiar. (Points at someone). Your shoes need polishing. (*CP*1, 496)

The smug Hasmukh is later reduced to someone who would seek refuge in the tree, but would forfeit even that, like he has forfeited life itself and thus utterly displaced both physically and symbolically. The tamarind tree here is used symbolically too, the cutting down of which signifies the pulling down of patriarchy in Mehta's family. And also new power centers in place through Kiran replacing Hasmukh, the entire perception of the world, as it were, is turn on its head, best illustrated through the physical symbol in the play by the dead father hanging upside down after becoming a ghost. Dattani seems to be suggesting his audience different ways of seeing spaces: hanging upside down from a tamarind tree (being stereotypes), cutting down the tree (shattering stereotypes), or just reinventing other ways of looking at the world as it really is. Dattani resembles Shaw here in his perspective of looking at the world, upside down and using family as the main unit to reinforce this.

Dattani is even comical in selecting names for all of the characters of the play, which is ironical too. All the four belie their names. Hasmukh is a dour-faced man who seems unable to smile as Sonal comments:

> 'A smiling face' whoever named him that cracked a very bad joke. (*CP*1, 474)

Sonal hardly shines and tarnished at best. As Hasmukh comments:

> Do you know what Sonal means? No? 'Gold'. When we were newly married, I used to joke with her and say she was as good as gold. But that was when we were newly married. I soon found out what a good-for-nothing she was. As good as mud. (*CP*1, 473)

Ajit is not triumphant and is not successful at least in his father's eyes,

> Forty-five years old and I am a success in capital letters. Twenty-three years old and he is on the road to failure, in bold capital letters! At his age, I was a mature responsible man, not eating my father's head and nibbling at papads! (*CP*1, 464)

Hasmukh thinks it is the fault of his wife for making so slapdash son. As he has given him a powerful name 'Ajit' but Sonal turns it to 'Aju' and with that made him good for nothing like her owns self.

> HASMUKH. ... I gave him a strong forceful name, Ajit. It means 'the victorious'. A powerful name like that

should be bellowed out. (Bellows). Ajit! It didn't take her long to change 'the victorious' into (mimics Soanl) 'Aju'. (*CP*1, 497)

Preeti is as unaffectionate and loveless as Hasmukh is our. Yet they live together with no choice in the matter, and function as a unit under the patriarchal order. Witty dialogues, crisp storyline, 'money make the world go round' this proverb spring to life in the play. Dattani's delightful and quick repartee is an absolutely indispensable part of his style, and the wit is never lost on the audience that is comfortable with the language as well as with the milieu. This style is clear in Act I, when Sonal is preparing salad for Hasmukh and halawa for Ajit and both contradict each other and suggest not making these:

HASMUKH. Hasn't she finished yet?

PREETI. Yes, she's coming.

AJIT. Is she still making the salad?

(Together)

HASMUKH. Is she still making the halwa?

Ajit and Hasmukh glare each other. (*CP*1, 464)

And in the last Act, when Kiran divulges the weak bossy nature of Hasmukh, just because of having lived all his life under his father's shadow having no free self identity, Sonal agrees with her, which Hasmukh's ghost negates at the same time, giving us a right example of repartee:

KIRAN. The same bossy nature?

SONAL. Yes.

(together)

HASMUKH. No.

KIRAN. Did he ever disagree with his father?

SONAL. No.

(together)

HASMUKH. Yes.

KIRAN. Did he ever do anything at all without consulting his father first?

SONAL. No, never!

(together)

HASMUKH. Yes, always! (*CP*1, 509)

Sometimes, the interplay of human emotions is so well brought out on the stage that the viewer is led into putting fictional elements of a drama behind him and living the characters himself. The power of a dramatist to reflect life through the written word complimented with the prowess of the theatrical techniques to tell tales as extensions of reality, make a good drama. Dattani's play *Dance Like a Man* consists of these elements with a complete union with its theme which represents a postcolonial condition, of ambivalent cultural moods, forms, transitions and translations in Indian society. Commenting on his craft, Dattani once said:

> The function of drama, in my opinion, is not merely to reflect the malfunction of society, but to act like freak mirrors in a carnival and to project grotesque images of all that passes for normal in our world. It is ugly, but funny. (Roy, *The Hindu*, 2)

In *Dance Like a Man*, Mahesh Dattani works on the past, present and the future to weave a family drama, using dance as a basic metaphor of about three generations of a conservative family in post-independence India. Dance here symbolizes the union between 'purusha' and 'prakriti' in the end of the life of Jairaj and Ratna and also the cause of dissonance between husband and wife. Lillette Dubey comments:

> The play *Dance Like a Man* explores relationship with rare insight and humour and its theme is based on dance and its politics. It is about power struggle rooted in Indian ambience. (*The Tribune*, 2)

At once tragic and comical, its script, narrative and presentation bring alive a powerful human drama which examines India's prevailing socio-cultural with insight and humour. It is a tale of human bonding, family relationships, generational conflict and a morality, which governs the protagonist's lives. After an engrossing and amusing start as the blossoming love affair between Lata and Viswas bubbled through their spicy dialogues the play gathered momentum, a current of realism shined through in the subsequent situation when Jairaj and Ratna, parents of Lata, seized with a dilemma, hurriedly arrive home and encounter the waiting Viswas but did not pay much attention to him because they are more worried about their daughter's live performance. The horizons of fame achieved during their prime reflect as they dream of their daughter Lata achieving excellence in the realm of dancing. The ideological conflicts between the generations- the conflict between Jairaj and his father Amritlal, a hypocrite patriot and freedom fighter, is at a diametric variance. And the bearing of unhealthy husband-wife relationship is convincingly brought alive by a perfect blend of comedy and intrigue as well as the latent stream of pathos, tragedy and frustration.

Thoroughly comical in tenor, the story makes a serious impact on the viewer, who is at once full of laughter and pain. The melancholy undertones are furthered by deep musical tones, specific to Bharatnatyam, a dance tradition that seems to have been specifically chosen by the dramatist to show the inherent weakness in the Indian system that, at one point in time, did not have the courage to give this dance to Devadasis its due. An unmistakable parallel between Jairaj and the dance form Bharatnatyam emerges during the course of the play. The playwright beautifully blends the powerful grace of the dance form, with the overwhelming torment of human emotions. Victory of perseverance over dominance is secondary, survival of the human spirit is essential. Before the 1940s, (when the first generation of this play is set-the latter generation is set in the 1980s), the 2000 year-old dance was viewed with dismay in Indian society. It was buried in British rule. According to Dattani:

> No other dance form has had such a fascinating history of oppression and renaissance... the dance was earlier preserved by the Devadasis who were the professional dancers in temples. They were, however, exploited by

> the priests, and, eventually, out of economic necessity, turned to prostitution. Hence a stigma came to be attached to the dance form itself. Even as late as the 1930s and 1940s, the dance was ignored. The prudish Victorian values of the British could not accept Bharatnatyam's erotic elements. The 'brownsahibs' too, considered it a debased and licentious remnant of our barbaric past. The anti-nauthic movement gathered momentum in the 1930s. There were social reformers who whipped up public opinion against Bharatnatyam. In the same decade, however, a few young dancers from 'respectable' families shocked the public by learning to dance from the Devadasis. It is to the credit of these enthusiasts who fought society that we are today still linked with this grand classical art form. (*The Hindu*, 5)

Dattani's writing shines with brilliant moments of simple everyday humour; he brings to life the exact flavour of the comedy that takes place in every Indian household. At the very beginning are Vishwas's playful comments on knowing that Lata's parents are out for some emergency, "Only doctors and fireman go out on emergencies. Dancers stay at home till its show time. They also stay at home when they have invited their future son-in-law to their house."(387) Lata's Gujarati boy friend Viswas stumbles into an 'alien' world of the traditional arts. Again, the horrified reaction of a Gujarati (Viswas) who finds out that a fellow Gujarati's (Jairaj's) wife has converted him to a coffee drinker is hilarious. The prospective son-in-law laments over his future parent-in-law who seem ready for the nuthouse, "What kind of people use a dummy phone." And at a very tense point of the argument about arranging a mridangam player for Lata's dance performance, Jairaj tell Viswas placatingly, "Sit down, drink your Bournvita."(*CP*1, 403)

Dattani deals with real life situations in his plays, so the script and stage directions are always realistic. His language is very accessible as it is closer to the speaking rather than the literary language. True to the Indian tradition of writing, Dattani has created various layers in this play. The crisp dialogues are powerful though in the message. Mahesh Dattani has whipped up a piquant curry of emotions, held in check with incisive psychological insight and seasoned with effortless wit. It lent the set with somewhat sepia overtone, evoking a sense of nostalgic transitions between different worlds. There is humour, which can be understood by any viewer. But, beyond all that, there is pathos, the pathos of human predicament, which he explores in a subtle fashion. It has thrill of two types of climaxes: Dramatic climax effect on viewers to experience the play as is in all his plays and; Artistic climaxes- occur in grand performances by both the mother and the daughter.

Tickles, tears, traumas, the play has them all, as a perfect structure for theatrical effect on the audience. On the surface, there are just Haha's. Dig a little deeper and there's the pathos of everyday life- family conflict and the trauma of finding their individuality. A little deeper and such issue surfaced the fate of the temple dancers or what defines manhood; the attitudes towards classical dance, changing over generations; or the balance of power in a marriage. The play probes the surface of the characters to question their deeper motivations, but the mode is comic rather than tragic, even though the concerns are serious, and one is never sure whether to laugh or cry.

The politics of aesthetics are shown to seep into the life of Jairaj and Ratna with unsettling brutality, rendering their mutual and uncommon love for a common art into a fight for self-assertion rather than reason for collaborative creativity. Initially, we see the couple completely from the outside, first from the viewpoint of their purported son-in-law Viswas and than their daughter Lata. This deliberate exteriorization of the narrative makes us stand outside the protagonist's lives and yet be part of them. Looking at this dancing couple from this viewpoint, Jairaj and Ratna with their dance-in-life theory of existence appear ridiculously self-absorbed. The conversation among the trio is so tangential as to appear ridiculous. While Vishal wants to broach the subject of their daughter's marriage, the couple is only concerned about their daughter's endangered dance performance as the only mridangam player has broken his hand. The narrative never forgets to remind us how surprising the past can be even to those who have lived through it. Everytime the characters change their mood and attitude we sense a tangible movement at the heart of the plot, though outwardly maintains a stillness that defies the enormity of the emotions divested in the drama. The bitterness and undercurrent of rivalry between the couple surfaced, parallely to their future son-in-law's mild amusement. As the anxiety and stress of facing the big day of Lata's dance performance increases, Jairaj and Ratna's tumultuous and somewhat dark past starts surfacing. The calm and funny exterior cracks, revealing the demons that they had swept under the carpet all these years.

Therefore, exposed to an alien environment to his own, Lata's fiancé Viswas unknowingly becomes the catalyst of the revelation of many dark secrets of the family. As this problem is being dealt, the skeletons in the cupboard, like all other plays of Dattani, start falling out. During his visit, few things are going on: the girl (Lata) is preparing, or being prepared by her mother, to give a big dance performance, and we learn about her conflict about fulfilling her mother's dreams; questions are raised about the parent's history as the couple are forced to confront their troubled past now two decades later and the reasons they stopped dancing, are bubbling to the surface.

Dance Like a Man is autobiographical drama which draws its authenticity from Mahesh Dattani's own training in Bharatnatyam, with traditional gurus U.S.Krishna and Chandrabhaga Devi. He says:

> I have certain fascination for the performing arts and that finds reflection in.... *Dance Like a Man.* (Bhargava, *HT*, 4)

This early personal experience influences the play with a vibrant credibility. The strong flavour of a Bharatnatyam household, the opulent saris, the sounds in the background often accompanied by carnatic background music together build up the intense sense of space that is integral to the shaping of the characters. Dattani himself asserts in an interview to U.K.Banerjee:

> I have been learning the classical dance of Bharatnatyam for six years, when I was in my twenties, from gurus UK Krishna Rao and his wife Chandrabhaga Devi. They were already in their seventies and frequently talked about the dance-scene half a century earlier. It appeared that Chandrabhaga had secretly learnt Bhartnatyam form the Devadasi, Mylapore Gauri Amma (also the guru of Rukmini Devi Arundale) and guru Kittappa Pillai. They taught me to have a passion for dance, which coloured my theatre as well ! the idea came from there. (*Indian*, 162-163)

Taking gender issues as his principal concern, Dattani asserts it with his principle passion of dance in this play to deny it as a woman issue. He says:

> I wrote the play when I was learning Bharatnatyam in my mid twenties. [...] a play about a young man wanting to be a dancer, growing up in a world that believes dance is for women... (Ayyar, *Gay*, 4)

Through the seamless movement in time and space, Dattani weaves in the intricate web of gender relationships and the givens of societal norms by moving effortlessly between the past, the present and the future. The play travels back and forth spanning three generations using the four characters on stage in which three has to play double role- Amritlal nad old Jairaj; Vishwas and the young Jairaj; Lata and the young Ratna are to be played by the same actor. Music help in evoking the appropriate time/space shift and young Vishwas and Lata and old Jairaj in present times turns to young Jairaj and Ratna and old Amritlal in the past, by just donning a waistcoat, shawl and glasses in dramatic spot lit sequences. Says Lillete Dubey:

> ... it is an amazing script... beautifully crafted. The way it moves back and forth in time, its use of one actor to

play more than one role which really tests the actor's talent" marks it as unique, as does the "strong characterization and the 'seamless' movements in time. (Sumanaspati, *The Hindu,* 2.)

The stage, crammed with old-fashioned furniture, efficiently conveys the playwright's vision of a house that is captive to the past, just like its owners. Like the characters, the stage iconography too helps to consolidate and reinforce these strong reverberations. Amritlal's house moves through time, changes character along with its owner, the back screen moves away to reveal a lush garden in the past and the living room in the present. The old cupboard, the shawl, the rose garden and the rest of the stage set all leave their impact in the juxtaposition of the stereotypes. There is much in the play to be read between the lines- the man who takes up a 'feminine' vocation is a wimp, a woman who cares about her career in a bad wife, careless mother, and manipulative human being etc. this perfect blend of the theme and emotions of the characters with the stage settings depict Dattani's excellence in the craft of communicating through theatre. Dattani's himself asserts his personal relation to this play because of firstly it is autobiographical of his own days of dance training and stigma attached to it, secondly, it is written in a style and technique inspired by the innate qualities of Bharatnatyam dance and dancers itself:

> Well, it is one of my favourite plays. I can relate a lot to it because I have performed publicly and also because I have learnt so much from my gurus. They are the kind of people who have given so much of themselves to the art form and have faced troubles and obstacles. But that has never really deterred them from carrying on with passion and dedication. And that is how I would like to approach my work. Impassioned and completely committed. (Mahesh, *The Hindu*, 4)

The reason behind the worldwide success of Dattani's plays is his understanding of his audience's psyche very well. He used to present middle class urban life to the same audience; he scrutinizes from his audience and presents it barely to the same audience. He is neither slave of them by presenting happy and fulfilled endings of his plays, nor the master to give any teaching or solution of the crisis to them. But rather presents the social circumstances shockingly beyond their expectations such as to touch and affect the audience's mind at once and make them think over it whether the situation is right or wrong. He says in an interview to U.K.Banerjee:

> I've not been a slave of what my audience expects. But nonetheless, it helps to have an understanding of the audience psyche: where are they coming from and why are they coming. (*Indian Literature*, 166-167)

Dattani therefore, does not write for social reformation but only to present the gender and class conflicts in Indian society aided by the technique to arouse a total theatrical effect on his audience, so that they may bring the thought aroused by the play to their homes and not just end up in the auditorium. He asserts:

> I am strongly affected by social issues, especially when it comes to power-play in class and gender. A lot of my plays deal with them and they remain the leit motifs of my plays. I am, however, not a social activist. From my long experience in theatre, I know what will work in a play, that is, what will be empowered writing. My first service is to the story and I believe that the form should serve the content. Usually, there is something like a coming to terms in the end and the audience can experience a catharsis-like situation. That's deliberate and is part of my craft! (Banerjee, *Indian*, 166)

In the hopeful moment in his plays *On a Muggy Night in Mumbai* and *Bravely Fought the Queen*, Dattani looks forward to a time when 'gays' of both sexes attain a free position in society which will permit them to respect themselves— a formulation that sees this freedom as positioned, this respect as permitted- not so much by their society at large as by the gays, themselves, to themselves.

Uninhabitable, yet inhabited, separate yet inseparable, the closet is not an interior from which a lesbian or gay person emerges, a door s/he chooses on a hidden or divided identity. We carry our closet within us and regulated by the law by which identity is secured through disavowal and displacement, tight border controls. And Dattani uses the theatre to rebound those borders.

He presented this brilliance of his craftsmanship in his play *Bravely Fought the Queen* with all other plays discussed in the previous chapter. In On a *Muggy Night in Mumbai*, the composition of the play and stage settings are rather based on different footings yet in the very manner of all his plays. The story line of the play is simple: boy meets boy, love each other- one boy cannot accept the gay life- so boy goes with boy's sister- as an alternative. The action of the show moves between the present and the past, and involves Kamlesh, a successful designer in Mumbai, and his relationships with his ex-lover Prakash, his sister Kiran and her fiancé Ed. The issue is serious but Dattani softens his message with large doses of flaming humour. While the dialogue cracks like a whip with zingy one –liners (the characters are otherwise traditional in popular Indian customs- right down to the last potato pakora), the play grapples with how their desires conflict with model middle-class expectations. Dattani presents the reality of being gay in modern India, via the assemblage in the flat, to the married and closeted soap opera star, to the hunky "straight" watchman who brings party favors, to the difficulties in being gay in marriage- based culture.

The frequencies of flashbacks in the play show the course of the relationship of Kamlesh and Ed until the climatic urging by Kamlesh that Ed come out of the closet and Ed's announcement that there can be no future for a male-male couple. Dattani also experiments a lot with the lightening technique such as: fade-in and fade-out as to indicate the passage of time, flashlights to create hidden, dark spaces as used in thrillers.

The hypocritical and money-centric attitude of the medical field is again attacked in the play like his play *Tara,* dealt in the previous chapter. We hear about that firstly from Kamlesh when he goes on describing his adventurous journey of coming out of his fears and anxiety by finding a psychiatrist. He realizes very soon that the doctor is not very different from the other members of the society in his views on homosexuality as he tried to change his sexuality and wanted to root out his real self, his real identity. He admits before his friends:

> I knew I needed medication. I chose the psychiatrist out of the Yellow Pages. He pretended to understand. Until he began to tell me about aversion therapy. For a while, I believed him. Because the medication helped me cope with my depression better. Until he said I would never be happy as a gay man. It is impossible to change society, he said, but it may be possible for you to reorient yourself.
>
> —
>
> I tried explaining to him that I need his help to overcome my anxiety and fears, not to be something I am not. Could he help me cope with my loneliness and fear the same way he would help a heterosexual cope with his? (*CP*1, 69)

While Kamlesh did not believe the psychiatrist that he could be changed to being a heterosexual, Prakash, his friend and lover did believe; and thus he left Kamlesh and converted himself accordingly, externally at least by assuming the guise of a handsome man with all the habits of a real man, in Kamlesh's words:

> He goes to church every week now. They put him on to a psychiatrist. He believes his love for me was the work of the devil. Now the devil has left him. (*CP*1, 85)

In the Act III, the hypocrisy of medical field is ridiculed, when Kamlesh's friends conspire and play a game to make Prakash confess the truth to Kiran, whom he is going to marry as he hypocrite himself as a heterosexual now, Deepali sarcastically illustrates Kiran how Sharad is going to become 'Straight' by finding a psychiatrist for himself. She says about Sharad:

> ... He will find himself a psychiatrist... to find someone who will help him escape to the more... acceptable world. He will go to this psychiatrist and say, 'Doctor, I want to be heterosexual.' The doctors will say, "Okay, this is a case of ego-distonic homosexuality. If that's what you really want.' It's a bit like you going to a cosmetic surgeon and telling him you want to look like Madhuri Dixit. If that's what you really want... Then the doctor will add very casually, 'We will put you on to our behavioural modification programme. Er- by the way, it will cost you twenty-five thousand. I hope that is not a problem? (*CP*1, 100)

Kiran's furious reaction is evident as she feels it to be an absurd and foolish idea of even thinking of the conversion into a normal heterosexual man and therefore proved herself as a catalyst in the play, a character to dig out the real selves from the heart of Bunny and Prakash by showing them the shamness of that very thought. It affects not only their lives but also the lives of the girls whom they marry, as she'll never get the true love from them. Both will have utter loneliness in their whole life which may never be cured; she tells Sharad:

> He loves you, Sharad. What more do you want? You will never be happier than this. You will end up being lonelier if you tried to be anything else other than who you are. And think of the poor woman you may end up marrying just as a cover-up for your shame. I know hoe it feels to be unloved. (*CP*1, 102)

Bunny and Prakash now begin to realize how wrong they have done in their lives. Prakash reacts after sometimes as he is even not ready to leave his thought of being straight, but Bunny reacts as he did suffer a lot internally for his mistake in all his life and also let his wife tolerate, as he says:

I know. Just as the man whom my wife loves does not exist. I have denied a lot of things. The only people who know me- the real me- are resent here in this room. And you all hate me for being such a hypocrite. The people who know me are the people who hate me. That is not such a nice feeling. I have tried to survive. In both worlds. And it seems I do not exist in either. I am sorry, Kiran, I lied to you as I have lied to the rest of the world. I said to you that I am a liberal-minded person. I am not them but I accept them. Actually, it is they who are liberal-minded. They have accepted me in spite of mine letting down of them so badly. I deny them in public, but I want their love in private. I have never told anyone in so many words what I am telling you now- I am a gay man. Everyone believes me to be the model middle-class Indian man. I was chosen for the part in the serial because I fit into common perceptions of what a family man ought to look like, I believed in it myself. I lied- to myself first. (*CP*1, 102-103)

An implication of the male privileged society is also depicted when Sharad ridicules the thought of conversion into 'straight' and the conventional definition of 'manliness' or 'a real man'. He shatters the male/female dichotomy in which the first one is always dominating. His idea proves that the homosexuality itself is the process of deconstruction of this partial division of the society as it comprises itself both the characteristics of male and female. He rather sarcastically remarks over what is considered and expected in behavioural activity of a man to prove himself to be a real man and of the 'penis power':

SHARAD: ... You see, being a heterosexual man- a real man, as Ed put it- I get everything. I get to be accepted- accepted by whom?- well, that marriage lot down there for instance. I can have a wife, I can have children who will all adore me simply because I am a hetero- I beg your pardon- a real man. Now why would I want to give it all up? So what if I have to change a little? If I can be a real man, I can be king. Look at all the kings around you, look at all the male power they enjoy, thrusting themselves on to the world, all that penis power! Power with sex, power with muscle, power with size. Firing rockets, exploring nuclear bombs, if you can do it five times, I can do it six times and all that stuff. (*Thrusts his pelvis in an obscene macho fashion.*) Power, man! Power!

ED: You are mad!

SHARAD: why not? All I needs is a bit of practice. I have begun my lessos. (*Demonstrates.*) Don't sit with your legs crossed. Keep them wide apart. And make sure you occupy lots of room. It's all about occupying space, baby. The walk. Walk as if you have a crcket bat between your legs. And thrust your hand forward whn you meet people. (*Speaks in a base voice, an imitation of Ed.*) Hi! Sharad! (*Squeezes an imaginary hand*) And the speech. Watch the speech. No fluttery vowels. Not 'it's so-o-o hot in here!'- but 'it's HOT! It's fucking HOT!' (*CP*1, 101)

Sharad is most aware of the fear and anxiety of the homosexuals which force them to be hypocritical, and in this process they harm themselves more than the society from which they are saving themselves. In an interview to Lakshmi Subramanyam, Dattani asserts:

> Discrimination certainly moves within class and gender constructs, in our culture at least. Sexuality is also viewed in the masculine/feminine and working class/ middle class constructs in the play. The issue seems more of preferred masculinity and feminine role playing (between Ed and Kiran). Others are not marginalized because they challenge these mainstream constructs. It's the presence of the wedding which is a major threat to the characters in the play. The oppressive heat of mainstream life around them is suitably dealt with by the air conditioning, (striving upper class status). For

> me, the most telling live in the play is when Kiran is perhaps a bit more self aware at the end of the play when she tells Ed, 'If there are any stereotypes going around, its us.' Men and women are the biggest stereotypes in the world. (*Muffled*, 131)

When the guard in the end show the photo of Kamlesh and Prakash which fell into the compound of the marriage party to Sharad, and adds that everyone is laughing on them and will take some action against them very soon, Sharad wittingly remarks:

> They can't do us harm any more than the harm we do each other. (*CP*1, 105)

A complex and multi-level stage setting is used like his other plays to make the whole interior of the house visible to the audience. There is a very telling use of stagecraft here in terms of spaces and is divided into three acting places. The first is Kamlesh's flat, where the living room is skillfully done up in the ethnic fashion. The backdrop of this area is the Mumbai skyline with its glittering lights, visible though the window of the living room- 'a real world out there, indicated by the niggling presence of the wedding going on at the ground level.' [McRae., CP1, 45] And a partial view of "Queen's Necklace" through this window implies 'that the flat is located in the up market area of Marine Drive, though not quite Pali Hill.' (52) An innovative new technique is used here by presenting dark spaces as the mental spaces which the characters use to express their innermost thoughts and therefore it provides a psychological importance as the second area is black and expansive, comprising of three levels again and set in a non-realistic mode. 'Characters in this area are immediately suspended in a 'shoonya' where they are forced to confront their inner thoughts".(52) Like W.B.Yeats's drama of mind, the conflict among these characters is psychological as it evokes the spectator's consciousness when Ed and Kamlesh on this second level of space, which is designed as a mental space, converse about whether their relationship and company is beautiful like heterosexuals or not. Their conversation is actually the questions which demand answers from the audiences who represent the same society who ridicule homosexual relationships as indicated in the scene where kids of the marriage party outside find the photo of Kamlesh and Prakash hugging each other and laugh. As John McRae puts it:

> ...his special theatrical quality in to build tension in a social context, leading to a classic dramatic confrontation which involves not only the characters themselves, but which also confronts the audiences with its own expectations and attitudes. (*CP*1, 46)

And so, this is the very area too where Prakash tells Kamlesh that he fears not to be accepted by the society with his real identity and so he is leaving him for becoming a real heterosexual man. A brilliant composition of the three scenes is presented in this level of three areas by only three characters and the audiences get aware of all the circumstances by which Prakash left Kamlesh and join Kiran to marry and how Kamlesh also resigned for his sister's sake:

KIRAN: Ed. He says I should call him Ed. I like him.

KAMLESH: You do?

KIRAN: Not that way, I mean, well... (*Laughts nervously.*)

ED (enters): Hello, Hi, Kamlesh.

Kamlesh and Kiran move to another level of the empty area. Ed continues to address them as before.

ED: Mind if I dance with your sister? ... Would you care to have this dance with me?

Soft music: 'Begin The Beguine' *or similar. Ed mimes dancing with Kiran.*

KIRAN(to Kamlesh). I quite like your friend.

ED: No problem, just follow your feet. Relax...

KIRAN: He told me how he met you at Sushma's party.

ED: There you go. Once you relax, it's a lot easier.

KIRAN: And he told me you thought he was gay! Whatever gave you that idea?

Kamlesh moves to the third level.

ED: I love ballroom dancing. It is very difficult to find the appropriate partner...

KIRAN (*laughs*): I mean, he doesn't look gay.

KAMLESH (*on the third level, as if to Ed*). Prakash, can I tell my sister about you? (*CP*1, 90)

The third area is the bedroom of Kamlesh, hidden behind a gauze wall to give it an ambiguous look. John McRae, director at the Abelians theatre, Bari Italy, says that:

> Mahesh Dattani is always adventurous in his ways of using the theatrical space at his disposal: multiple levels, breaking the bounds of the proscenium, wondrously inventive use of lighting to give height, breadth and depth. (*CP*1, 45)

Furthermore, symbolic implications are used to foreground the idea of gay relations by Dattani in the play. As the events unfold, a traditional marriage happening next door to Kamlesh's home provides an effective counterpoint to his own family's travails. On one side, there is Kamlesh's small flat where his gay group meet openly and express themselves freely and on the other side the visible and invisible signs of the outside heterosexual world which continuously imposes and interrupts this small place- the Mumbai skyline, the wedding procession with all its loud paraphernalia, the need to conceal and the ultimate discovery of the incriminating photograph by the children in the marriage party and the beautiful bride's weeping etc. which all give suggestions of the society that expects the individuals to behave in accordance with its well defined code of conduct and also give fear and acidity to the homosexuals of the room of the outside world with suffocating and unrelenting 'muggy' atmosphere. The exteriors keep exerting pressure; intruding into the 'other' spaces occupied by the characters in the play perpetually reminding them of their isolation as Ranjit in the play puts it:

> ... Don't want all this lovely cool air contaminated by all that muck outside. (*CP*1, 65-66)

Though the play relies on the security of distance and the inside world is on the top floor from there looking down the outside world of wedding frenzy gives them a sense of safety. But the marriage outside is really used to present a contrastive world of heterosexuals that of gays unions. Sharad aptly uses those ritualistic ceremonies to obliterate the bonds between Kamlesh and Prakash as opposite to the heterosexuals who use these rituals to unite two people in an everlasting compelling bond. He promised Kamlesh that after these following steps performed as a ceremony with all the ritualistic background music and all that, he will be able to forget Prakash. He says:

> As far as we are concerned, Prakash doesn't even exist. It is the opposite of a marriage- the whole world acknowledges two people who enter a union pact, so they have to stick by that. Now all of us refuse to acknowledge the existence of your relationship with Prakash, so you have to abide by that. He does not exist for you. (*CP*1, 72)

And thereupon, Sharad goes on describing steps to Kamlesh to follow to complete the process:

> SHARAD: So far, great. Now I want you to take this photo and stand near the window.
>
> —
>
> Now let's have a little ritual.
>
> —

The whole heterosexual world is run by rituals! That wedding downstairs will go on for days! (*CP*1, 72)

Sharad employs sea breeze coming from the window as the witness rather than fire used in common marriages. Fire implies 'passion' which the heterosexual couple can freely express after the marriage. But here the passion of love is going to be suppressed by disuniting two people from which the tumultness arises in their hearts- the very nature of the sea which used to hide lots of secrets in its depth and only clamor outside. Sharad also hand over a line of vow to

Kamlesh which is exactly like the common marriages, though the meaning of those words is opposite. He says:

> Now take a look at the picture. And say it out loud- 'As my friends, this city and God are witness to my vow, I break all ties with Prakash.' Then you will tear up that picture and throw it out of the window. (*CP*1, 73)

The two contrasted worlds presented by Dattani give us a sense of not only the politics of sexuality in our country, but a kind of desire to see people thinking positively about these relationships, with both the worlds co-existing, the world outside where the conventional wedding is taking place and the world inside where a lot of personal trauma is being experienced.

The air-conditioner of the room is another symbol of cool behaviour: as when it was working everything was going on calmly and coolly inside the room, the discussions, the affinities were calm, the windows and doors were closed and it was a free world. These stage directions help to reveal the true characters and bring out the mystery of man's hidden nature. There was no tumult in the minds of Kamlesh's friends, whom he invited to solve his problem and they were calmly thinking about the procedure by which his problem could be resolved. The weather outside was also not comfortable and pleasant but was extremely "muggy" as Deepali says:

> Well, it's much cooler in here… relief inside.
>
> —
>
> I meant the air con…
>
> —
>
> It's really sticky out there. (*CP*1, 64)

But when the air conditioners failed, the windows get open widely to perform a ritual of forgetting Prakash by Kamlesh and the outside heat and air and voice of wedding going on in the compound below begin to come in, the interruption begins when the hot filthy air began to come inside. And this is the time when Kiran, Kamlesh's sister arrives with his fiancé Ed who is none other than Prakash, Kamlesh's former lover. With the arrival of Ed, the air conditioner stops working, it signifies how more and more troubles some time is going to prevail. And this is the moment when all the friends of Kamlesh acknowledge the truth of why Kamlesh wants to break relations with Prakash and this revelation brings in the problems. And in the end when the window is closed and air conditioner begins to work, everything gets settled and everybody realizes their true identical self. The very telling symbol of 'fireworks' occurs again and again like other major images, and especially in the end when Ed tries to jump through the window being totally depressed. The loud screams of delight and whistles, yells and screams from the marriage party of the ground floor is also heard, which all seems to suggest the 'exploration of one's self' as all the characters in the play are seen unmasking their hidden selves one by one like the firecrackers one by one. And when everybody comes to their terms in the end the explosion of these can be seen as:

> More firecrackers and lusty yells from the wedding below. (*CP*1, 111)

On the other hand, these enhance the intensity of background to match the intensity of the moment and to suggest the wild and savage entertainment.

The title of the play is itself symbolic as the atmosphere in a 'muggy' weather is used to be obnoxiously warm, soggy, clammy and tiresome and all the characters in the play too feel ill-at-ease in not expressing their true sexuality freely and have an isolating feeling thereupon. Outwardly, they express themselves as being content and satisfied but inwardly they are very tired and hollow. As Ed, negotiating his true identity to be acceptable for survival in the society, becomes tired in the long run in the end and wants to end his tragic life and expresses his desire to live with his true self:

> SHARAD. (*runs to the door and yells out*) Guard! Guard! For God's sake somebody help!

KIRAN: Somebody save him! He will kill my brother! No!

ED (*hits out at Kamlesh, crying with anger*). Faggot! Pansy! Gandu! Gandu!

Kamlesh offers little or no resistence.

SHARAD (*screaming*). GUAAARD!

Deeplai picks up a rum bottle and hits Ed on the head. Ed staggers away, trying to keep his balance. He finally breaks down and cries.

ED (*looks at Kiran*). I am... sorry. I didn't mean to harm you. I only wanted to live. (*CP*1, 110)

He pleads again:

Where do I begin? How do I began to live? ... Will you help me? What makes a man a man? (*CP*1, 111)

This is the climax of the play as Dattani himself put it to Raj Ayyar:

...Ed's suicide attempt offers a dramatic high point in the play that clearly leads to the resolve that Ed needs to make his choices. He can no longer wear his mask. He has to do something about his situation. (*Gay*, 6]

The play ends with the self-discovery of Sharad and his words, which questions not only the minds of homosexuals but also of heterosexuals, who are also victims of the frozen code and conducts of the conventional Indian society. This self-realization is rightly observed by John McRae:

Each act builds to a climax of revelations and self discoveries. By the end of the play, Ed is seen as the most pathetic and self-deluding of all the characters, but Kamlesh too deceives himself and exploits others (The Guard, for example). The photo of Ed and Kamlesh together becomes emblematic (again a typical Dattani's touch) of all that was good in their love, but which has now turned or been turned against that love. (*CP*1, 44)

Furthermore, Dattani's humour provides a comfortable distance from which to grapple with its unusual subject. And for that Sharad is used as a comedy character to mock at the moment when any serious situation is going on so that we have a dramatic relief just as in the plays of Shakespeare. His remarks are good examples of comedic puns, which occur ironically and yet are meaningful. When Kamlesh's friends were coming to his flat one by one, Sharad imitates as if the party is going on:

> (*Mock-cheerful, claps his hands*). Well, put on your party frock! The boys are here! (*Sings as kamlesh goes to open the door*). Life is a cabaret, old chum. Come to the cabaret... (*CP*1, 58)

Sharad is in love with Kamlesh and has spent few months with him too and got familiar with the real nature of Kamlesh. So, when Kamlesh asserts that he forgot Prakash and tore up all his photographs, Sharad did not believe and tried to find it out himself. While entering the bedroom of Kamlesh, he seeks loo, as a hiding place for someone and comments:

> Yes, hold on to that confession while I nip to the loo. (*Rises and moves towards the bedroom*) Mind if I do that? I hope there is no one hiding in the loo. (*CP*1, 64)

When all friends of Kamlesh while entering into the floor address everyone except him or rather ignore him, he mocks sarcastically:

> Don't mind me. I am just the doormat. Use me for all I care. (*CP*1, 67)

He enjoys calling the guard of the building as 'the lover boy' of Kamlesh as he used to pay him for sex and addresses Ranjit 'coconut' rightly and truthfully as he left India to be accepted as homosexual. But how much he pretend, he is Indian and so brown (Indian) outside, while white (western inside like the coconut.). And again unlike the tragic heroes of Shakespeare, they succeed in effecting tragic self-realization and thereby arouse a sense of pity and catharsis in the hearts of the readers or audience. Amar Nath Prasad compares the play also to the one by Sheridan, as he implies:

> Almost all the characters of this play are types of certain behaviour which reminds us of the Restoration plays

> and sentimental comedies specially Sheridon's *The Rivals* and *The School for Scandal.* The drama also contains some powerful symbols, images and stage directions which cannot help without arousing aestheticism and rich poetry... In Sheridon's *The Rivals*, the hero, Captain Absolute, is disguised as Beverley; similarly here Ed and Prakash is the same person. This disguise creates suspense and draws astonishment from audience. (*The Plays*, 161)

The dialogue is not almost entirely in (lilting Indian) English but also in Hindi this is very effective and familiar with the Indian audience. The very beginning of the play is Hindi, the conversation between Kamlesh and the guard is in Hindi, and goes on throughout the whole play again and again:

> KAMLESH: Suno.
>
> —
>
> (*takes out some money from his wallet*)Mere kuch dost ane wale hain. Tum unko aane dena. Tum to pahchante ho sub ko.
>
> —
>
> Do bottle RC. Ek peach schnapps- who safed bautal wala, malum hai?
>
> GUARD (wearily). Hahn, saab, sab maloom hai. (*CP*1, 50)

The narration moves on its own volition. The rhythms in the emotions and conflicts emerge out of the characters with a fair fluency. Dattani cuts his material closely. The visual juxtaposition of man-in-conflict-with-man and man-in-conflict-with-woman creates a flutter of ambivalent anxieties in the narration and triggers-off innuendos on the subject of sexuality without creating a staggering distance between the audience and characters.

Final Solutions, another play by Mahesh Dattani, is altogether different in its theme from all above plays and the technique co-operating with this is also unusual. It is not just a story, it has moments, each different shade and colours and he dramatize them to make memorable. The play is divided in three acts and deals with communalism, religious fanaticism and the Hindu-Muslim riot mostly engendered by the self-centered politicians. On the second level of meaning the play also suggests the deep rooted hatred planted by our forefathers. It is based on communal riots during partition and aftermath even after forty years of independence through intermingling of the past and the present by the character of Daksha/ Hardika. She unconsciously bring in old memories and the sense of history into the mechanisms of the play through her diary, which she has written while partition and which she is reading now after forty years of partition when a riot took place in the city Amargaon. The play opens with the scene where Daksha sits, beginning the process of recording lived history: "Dear Diary, today is the first time I have dared to put my thoughts on your pages ... 31 March 1948." (*CP*1, 166) Criss-crossing a whole gamut of memories that are to construct the character that she is to become- Hardika, who realizes nothing has changed during the time of forty years, the same violence, hatred and intolerance, which she witnessed before when her father was killed in communal riots while partition. true, the mob outside was as mindless as before. This was not so much because they were responsible for the brutal killing of her father, but more on account of the punishment meted out to her for maintaining cordial relations with the Muslims. She was "Confined. Never let out of the house. Like a dog that had gone mad!" (*CP*1, 223). Her soliloquy is followed immediately by the words of the chorus, with their drumbeats and their perceivable freneticism, establishing a connectivity between the individual (Daksha/ Hardika) and society (Mob/ Chorus). Though the play begins with a delving into the past, the main action is located in the present. The audience is introduced to the convulsions of the partition through her disturbed reaction as she realizes that the "pooja room" was as vulnerable as any other part of the house and the "idol" she had grown up seeing her mother worship was "just another painted doll" (*CP*1, 167). The symbols of religious fervour right at the onset, assume connotative implications of violence, loss of faith and insecurity. When asked whether Daksha's voice wanting to write all the time in an interview to Ranu Uniyal, Dattani replies:

Absolutely and what Daksha has is her diary and through the device of the diary, she begins a dialogue with the audience and that is offered to Daksha because she can make fun of her in-laws, she could talk very honestly about her feelings, about her friendship with the Muslim girl etc. directly to the audience and that space is denied to her with the other members of her household including her husband and these are memories that she has retained even in her old age and these memories are triggered off and feelings of prejudice that had developed over the years are brought out in the present day situation. So Daksha becomes a symbol of our historical vision, our sense of history, how prejudice is formed and how we deal with the situation today. (*The Plays*, 181-182)

As far as the title of the play is concerned, Dattani himself asserted in an interview to Sachidanand Mohanty that it is inspired from *The Third Reich and the Holocaust*. The title of the play itself calls to attention, by sticking to the plural-'solutions', which imply the apparent insolubility of this situation. When sticked to the first word 'Final', the title began to ask so many questions such as if there any final solutions possible for such a violence, which is continued from a long time. It is highly suggestive which makes us think whether the evil of communal violence can be rooted out, lock, stock and barrel. There are hints and guesses in the play which whisper results, provided we pay heed to it. The character-plot potential of *Final Solutions* moves towards an open-endedness and hints at the possibilities of the resolution. Whenever, there is any search for a solution, it turns out to be temporary as there are as many solutions as there are realities to choose from and on the other side, this very search for a final solution, in fact perpetuates the cycle of violence and hatred in many other ways. And thus, this questions always remains unanswerable and this situation, incurable.

The roles given to the characters by Dattani in his plays are always rounded, complex and ever-changing- full of challenges for an actor or actress. In *Final Solutions*, the whole existence of the every character is justified in the final scene, where they themselves realize their hypocritical lives. Like Shakespeare, Dattani too mirrors a society and characters which audiences can believe in, can see themselves in. The viewers can straightforwardly identify with the crises and consciousness of others, there on the stage, in that vast space of the universe that the dramatist creates. Dattani highlights the contrast between the intelligent and friendly young bride Daksha and the grudging and revengeful grandmother Hardika by an actual split in her portrayal. Time has transformed her into a very different person. In fact, none of the characters are static. All through the play there is a free flow of ideas with each character opening a window to newer perspectives, transforming and getting transformed in the process. Javed sheds his extremist stance to arrive at a more moderate understanding of the cultural forces at work. The apologetic Bobby learns to boldly confront the truth about himself and about God. "He knows His strength! I don't believe in Him but He believes in me. He smiles!" says Bobby, "He smiles at our trivial pride and our trivial shame" (*CP*1, 224). Smita and her mother Aruna also, come to have a more honest understanding of each other, and discontinuity of the characters becomes a sign of hope.

An artist's role to shed light on those areas of human experience that might otherwise remain unilluminated by giving the flashes of lightning, the moments, and scenes in its own personal and individual way is the main element of any art of performance and Mahesh Dattani perfects in attaining on such insight and illumination. While experimenting in time and space and relating it to the memory of Daksha/Hardika, the play involves a lot of introspection on the part of the character in the play and thus induces similar introspection in the viewers. The chorus is used as 'realistic stylization' in the psycho-physical representation of the characters and also provides the audience with the visual images of the characters' conflicts. There is no stereotyped use of the characterization of the chorus because communalism has no face, it is an attitude and thus it becomes an image of the characters.

The play is replete with various stylistic devices such as the 'mob', which doubles up as the chorus and wears/sheds masks to give it the required religious colour. Through chorus, the playwright seems to communicate to the audience the present scenario of communicable frenzy and hatred. These comprising five men and ten masks on sticks (five Hindu and five Muslim masks), which lie significantly strewn all over the ramp, to be worn when required. This is the omnipresent factor throughout the play and Dattani carefully uses the same five men in black to double for any given religious group when they assume the role of the mob, which they do in a stylized fashion. The play opens with an establishment of the riot, and the two young man sought by the mob are revealed as members of the 'other community'. Naturally, this immediately makes them a threat, as the aggression of the Mob heightens to a dangerous pitch. The space of the stage is thick with ominous cries that reverberate and the same hatred and intolerance for the other always rents the air. Dattani fling a mild satire on those fanatics who don't understand the true property of religion, boast the merit of their religion and are mostly driven like dumb cattle by the egocentric and selfish politicians. There is a 'Director's Note' from Alyque Padamsee appended to the play. In it, Padamsee says:

> The mob in the play is symbolic of our own hatred and paranoia. Each member of the mob is an individual yet they meld into one seething whole as soon as politicians play on their fears and anxieties.
>
> ...this is a play about transferred resentments. About looking for a scapegoat to hit out when we feel let down,

> humiliated. Taking out your anger on your wife, children or servants is an old Indian custom. (*CP*1, 161)

The words spoken by Chorus are the indications of the domestic violence, political mischief and the social unrest, having no personal religion at all. They are only hired hoodlums to spread terror and unrest. Its location on the crescent shaped ramp that dominates the stage is indicative of its pervasive presence providing the impetus to the action. The wearing of either Hindu or Muslim masks demonstrates the manner in which ordinary people get misled by the superimposed mask of religious fundamentalism. The uniform black attire is also a visual signifier, for the blackness of heart has nothing to do with religion. Through the masking and unmasking the same person, the author seems to say a lot of things as Religion is one; God is one; only the interpretations are different. As in the stage directions, the playwright gives hints on the Mob/ Chorus:

> The players of the Mob/ Chorus do not belong to any religion and ideally should wear black. (*CP*1, 165)

The colour black is also sarcastically used to hit the government of India as it shows justice and impartiality because no colour is written or painted on black. The uniform black attire is also a visual signifier, for the blackness of heart has nothing to do with religion. Thus, through this deft use of chorus, the dramatist wants to express the hidden thoughts of both communities. The author is neither with the Hindus nor with the Muslims. He is neutral. Rather, the characters in the play express their anger at every stage and the mob seems to be symbolic of our hatred. Ramnik, the father, voices his resentment at his own father's stealthy and unjust deeds by shouting at his mother, Hardika, who, in turn comes to hate her best friend Zarine and her community, the hatred being a mode of spouting her indignation at being subjected to the small-mindedness of her in-laws. The play mocks at the politicians who use people as their puppets and also on us who give them this advantage through our own inner detestation and bitterness. Though in the end, the playwright wishes to stop this game of abhorrence and communal tension through the character of Ramnik, but no final solution seems to be possible until we kill our inner demon of revulsion.

Though, Smita and Bobby have the same anger but they seem to have escaped from this 'inner hatred' in their own ways. They are not clutched only to one religion and believe in the human love and fraternity far from this conservatism. She criticizes and hits out at her traditionalist mother Aruna, while Bobby accuses Javed for being so crazy about his religion. They both in the end show the members of the house and the audience that sympathy, compassion, kindness and humanity is the true religion of all of us above all the conservatism. though Bobby breaks through physically created boundaries but his attempt to break mental barriers are shown to be unsuccessful and hence the implication is that while one can break up space by entering it, the boundaries of the initial space still endure. In other words, it is his characters who speak, not the author. Dattani observes:

> I also know that I have a lot to say and am probably not saying it well enough. But my characters have a lot to say too, and they seem to be doing rather well at having their say ... I am completely aware that it is my character that has done the work for me. (*CP*1, xi)

Again, home has been repeatedly depicted as a space of oppression, earlier in Daksha's confinement and later when Smita comments:

> Maybe we should all run away from home like Javed. For five minutes everyday. So we can quickly gulp in some fresh air and go back in (*CP*1, 219).

Hope lies in the movements of Smita, Javed and Bobby from the limiting inner space of the house to the outer one of different options. They are the windows that open to the future and it is within their power to build bridges that past hatred had destroyed. The play, in the end, avoids clarity of the fictional situation suggesting that the 'final solutions' are ultimately in the choices that people make. When, in the beginning, the Hindu mob curses the Muslim for the injuring of their Rath-Yatra chariot, the procession and the chariot bearing the idols of the Gods are the symbolic paraphernalia used by the activists of Hinduism to reinforce their authority, the coercive authority of the power-hungry 'majority' as Javed, who is a representative of this community, perceives it. Animal images are also used symbolically as the image of 'mouse' and 'rat', suggesting the fear or the strength. In a society, where one group dominates the 'other', the dominant one behave like cats, and the subordinate one prefer to hide in their hole like mice. Likewise, the images of 'swine' and 'dead pig' connote hatred and contempt when the Hindu mob used to say this to the Muslims. Similarly, the dropping of a lizard on a milk vessel is supposed to be very inauspicious in the Hindu tradition. The family, named 'Gandhi' is significant, as it becomes a mock representation of the justice and non-violence associated with it.

The 'bell' is used again and again in the play to irritate Javed, the first time when it was used by a neighbour for prayers in the incident narrated by Bobby to Ramnik that how it changed Javed's life and transformed him from a hero to a rebel outcaste. Again, the prayer bell used by the pujari in the rath-yatra ceremony outraged him to kill pujari and in the end of the play, Aruna's prayer bell stifles him too much to leave that house for him. Any person not from the 'faith' could defile these sacred symbols. The ringing of the pooja bell recurring is projected as a signifier of religious fanaticism. In contrast, Daksha's love for the songs of Noorjahan expresses a longing for harmony. In the combative struggle between the two lies the conflict of the play.

The sets and properties in a performance is used as a method of reflection and understanding of the play properly and through the setting of this play, Dattani is successful in accentuating the internal conflicts and the subtext of the play. The set is designed to emphasize Dattani's contention as how the society affects the family and how the family unit represents society. The shifts in time and situations have again been portrayed through a multi-level stage. The cross fading of lights plays a vital role in transferring the dramatic space from one time and place to another. Although the setting, again like all other plays, is multi-level with flashbacks, yet it is more complex because both exterior and interior are presented on the stage. A crescent- shaped ramp, with the ends sloping to the stage level, is the most overpoweringly dominant space on stage, where most of the action of the Mob/ Chorus took place. Within this ramp confines a structure of the house of the Gandhis- the living room, which is not in so much detail and is shown through a "barebone presentation, with just wooden blocks for furniture." While the kitchen and the pooja room are the detailed sets as the dividing lines that separate us from each other is largely through our food habits and taboos in religious beliefs. We generally make sharp distinctions where food and food related utensils are concerned, which perhaps serve to emphasis separation in a uniquely distinctive and defined manner. Actually, Dattani used to visualize the entire stage set-up before the actual arrangement, as he asserts in an interview to Tutun Mukharjee:

> I usually have an elaborate stage design for a play, which conveys an important visual impact. for example, there is a horse-shoe-shaped ramp spanning the backspace of the stage in Final Solutions where the chorus carrying the masks crouch through the entire play. of course other directors of my plays are free to design the stage as they wish. (*The Hindu*, 4)

Another room on upper level belongs to Daksha, who is in fact the grandmother Hardika, who is sometimes seen as a girl of fifteen, thus ensuring that the past always remains in front of us and cannot be forgotten. Here an oil lamp converted to an electric one suggests the period of 1940s. She has given the place and position in such a way that the entire action of the play is seen through her eyes. Sometimes Hardika, the grandmother and Daksha, the young bride are on the same level on the same time. Unlike Dr.Thakkar of

Tara, she is not a fixed entity. Assigned a flexibility of movement between the different levels, she is a living embodiment of the past with its attendant guilt and shame. Her presence undercuts the apparent naturalism and upsets the fragile frictions, which the characters had created. Although Daksha and Hardika are the same person and this presentation is needed to show the past how and why she has developed a feeling of hatred for the Muslim community brings in the young Daksha, continues even now in the old Hardika. This ploy efficiently shows how the past moulds the present and also how the present reinterprets the past. And the characters of Daksha and Hardika self-consciously bring in old memories and the sense of history into the mechanisms of the play.

In fact, innovations with music and natural sounds intersperse the relationship between characters, using this dramatic tool to its maximum effect and are scattered liberally through the plays. The extended metaphor of music, the music of Noor Jehan, Shamshed Begum and Suraiya, occurs in the play frequently. Music is needed in life to ease the savage blows of cruelty, conservatism and callousness; music creates a sense of equality, fraternity and creativity in all men whether rich or poor, high or low; barring caste, class and religion. All religions are different in form, but one in spirit and sing the same music of love, truth, humanity and fraternity. This is the music in the play which brought Daksha and Zarine together in spite of their dissimilar religions. The music is interrupted through breaking of the gramophone records by stones while communal riots which clearly show the breaking of all kind feelings in the heart of Daksha towards the other religion:

> DAKSHA. ... A stone hit our gramophone table, breaking it. Krishna choose to destroy what I loved most. My entire collection of records broken. Lying about like pieces of glass. Shamshed Begum, Noor Jahan, Suraiya. The songs of love that I had learnt to sing with. Those beautiful voices. Cracked ... (*CP*1, 167)

One cannot help but marvel at the effortlessness in Dattani's writing technique and the unfettered command over theatre, drama, cinema and radio. Whether the closure of the narrative is open ended as in *Final Solutions* or a closed one as in *Tara*, his plays never really conclude because of their continued relevance to the reality around.

A playwright is a seer, a storyteller with special vision. Playwrights see into human existence and turn it into stories that actors will truly experience before live audiences. To dramatize life in this manner, a writer must develop skills in both literature and theatre, and must combine craftsmanship with artistry. Somehow a playwright has to develop the uncanny ability to see into the existence of people and spot the special moments, the significant turning points in human lives. By showing human changes and how people feel about them in story form, a playwright reveals the inner quality in human existence. Because each playwright views things differently, audiences are delighted. People go to the theatre not to see the same old world through ordinary eyes but to discover something special from a fresh point of view. Everyone wants to witness unusual events, to experience life in new ways. Audiences expect playwrights and their fellow artists to offer something different, original or extreme. Therefore, artists need to foster their own special ways of responding to life, to develop personal techniques for creating. Every playwright needs to be bold enough to become truly audacious, because audacity is as necessary to originality as skill is to beauty. He seems to be a genuine artist in love with his art. His plays are meant to be performed, not just read as literature as Erin Mee says:

> Dattani puts the finishing touches on his dialogue only when it is spoken aloud by actors in rehearsal – in other words, Dattani writes plays to be seen and heard, not literature to be read. (*CP*1, 320)

This chapter explains how Mahesh Dattani masters this craft and tries to give order to the chaos of life. It also describes his typical working process and sets forth some of the most functional creative principles he employs. Finally, it defines the actual elements of a play. And therefore, Dattani does not only come to know the nuances of human existence, but also perfects his craft. He tends not to be great philosophers offering unique ideas or theoretical concepts; rather, he probes the quality of contemporary life and offer sensitive responses to the world in his time. His word depends on the sensitivity and clarity of his vision. He used to look at the world and tell what he see by composing dramas with action, perception, reality and emotion then he creates valuable pieces of art and thus his art expands the world. To provide a creative work that is powerful and tightly written, Dattani produces his plays with a craftsman's care, one that evokes feelings that are both funny and sad, but ultimately human and moving. His dramatical and theatrical art can be summarized in his own words to Angelie Multani when asked how he would like his work to be received, he replied precisely but truly:

As metaphors for life. (*Mahesh Dattani's*, 171)

REFERENCES

Ayyar, Raj. "Mahesh Dattani: India's Gay Cinema Comes of Age". *Gay Today.* 8.48, 2004. http://gaytoday.com.

Banerjee, Utpal K. "In Conversation with Mahesh Dattani". *Indian Literature 223,* Sep.-Oct., 2004.

Bhargava, Vidhi. "The World's his Stage". *The Hindustan Times,* 19 December, 2004.

Dattani, Mahesh. *Collected Plays.* New Delhi: Penguin Books, 2000.

Dattani, Mahesh. *Collected Plays.* New Delhi: Penguin Books, 2005.

Dattani, Mahesh. "Preface, in *Collected Plays.* New Delhi: Penguin Books, 2000.

Dattani, Mahesh. *The Hindu.* 28 July 1995.

Dubey, Lillette. "It takes four to tango". *The Tribune,* Friday, April 26, 2002.

Mahesh, Chitra. "Stage to Screen". *The Hindu,* Friday, Oct 1, 2004.

McRae, John. "A Note on the Play *'On a Muggy Night in*

Mumbai' ", in *Collected Plays.* New Delhi: Penguin Books, 2000.

McRae, John. "We Live in the Flicker: Reflections in Time on the Plays of Mahesh Dattani", in Angelic Multani (ed.), *The Plays of Mahesh Dattani: Critical Perspectives.* New Delhi: Pencraft International, 2007.

Mee, Erin B. "A Note on the Play '*Tara'* ", in *Collected Plays.* New Delhi: Penguin Books, 2000.

Mohanty, Sachidananda. "Theatre: Reaching Out to People: An Interview with Mahesh Dattani", in *The Plays of Mahesh Dattani: A Critical Response* (R.K. Dhawan and Tanu Pant (eds.). New Delhi: Prestige Books, 2005.

Mukharjee, Tutun. "I do not write merely to read". *The Hindu.* July 26, 2004.

Multani, Angelie. "A Conversation with Mahesh Dattani", in Angelic Multani (ed.), *Mahesh Dattani's Plays: Critical Perspectives.* New Delhi: Pencraft International, 2007.

Padamsee, Alyque. "A Note on the Play: *'Final Solutions'* ", in *Collected Plays.* New Delhi ; Penguin Books, 2000.

Prasad, Amar Nath. "The Plays of Mahesh Dattani: A Fine Fusion of Feeling and Form", in R.K. Dhawan and Tanu Pant (eds.), *The Plays of Mahesh Dattani: A Critical Response.* New Delhi: Prestige Books, 2005.

Roy, Elizabeth. "Freak Mirrors and Grostesque Images". *The Hindu.* 15 March, 2002. http://www.hindu.onnet.com.

Subramanyam, Lakshmi. "A Dialogue with Mahesh Dattani", in Lakshmi Subramanyam (ed.), *Muffled Voices: Women in Modern Indian Theatre.* New Delhi: Shakti Books, 2002.

Sumanaspati. "Leading the Charge". *The Hindu,* 12th August, 2002.

Vardhan, Manisha. "I'm No Crusader; I'm a Theatre Person: Mahesh Dattani". June 2004. http://www.3 to 6.com.

Uniyal, Ranu. "Conversing with Mahesh Dattani", in R.K. Dhawan, and Tanu Pant (eds.), *The Plays of Mahesh Dattani: A Critical Response.* New Delhi: Prestige Publications, 2005.

Walling, Michael. "A Note on the Play: *'Bravely Fought the Queen'* ", in *Collected Plays.* New Delhi: Penguin Books,

6

Conclusion

Drama is 'postcolonial' in that it records the end, in independent India, of the privileged status that particular social groups and communities had acquired under colonialism. A broader perspective also reveals that the vast majority of contemporary plays are not concerned with colonialism at all but with the intersecting structures of home, family and nation in the urban society of the present or with the configurations of gender. Much of the oppositional energy in contemporary theatre, in any case, is not directed against the colonial experience but against the oppressive structures of nation, patriarchy, caste, class and tradition. Commenting upon the nature of postcolonial writing, Tahar Ben Jallouin, a writer from Morocco, says,

> We have two cultures, it is as if we had two mothers and two fathers, perhaps we don't have total control, like writers in the West, but we have two possible inner worlds, I think we are doubly clever; firstly to use the narrative techniques of the West and secondly, to exploit the narrative tradition, of the folklore, the stories from our respective countries, and we have come up a third type of literature which is unlike Western writing, which

> is essential, provincial, egocentric and onward looking. We have created literature which is open to other cultures and situations (1).

Dattani is one of such literary persons, whose experiment with drama evolves a new type both in theme and technique; one that will be essentially Indian, bringing forth real creative talent that will base itself on both tradition and technique. He did not modify himself according to canon rather he redefines the canons to increase the expressive range of his art and ideas. His dramatic writings venture to project the real life experiences with exceptional vivacity of dialogue and performance. Commenting on his own theatrical art, Dattani admitted that theatre is a reflection of what one observes. To go beyond that would be to sermonize and cease to be theatre. However giving this assessment a more explicit twist, a slight distortion to get the point across well in order, he states:

> The function of drama in my opinion is not merely to reflect malfunctions of society, but to act like 'freak mirrors' in a carnival and to project grotesque images of all passes for normal in our world. It is ugly but funny (Roy 3).

Dattani's contribution as a revolutionary progresser of Indian English drama, as a drama teacher, as a stage director, as an actor, as a Bharatnatyam dancer and as a sociologist explaining various complexities of society is an asset to Indian writing as a whole. He successfully achieved the synthesis of a thinker, an artist, an actor, a director and the preacher. As far as Indian drama in English is concerned, when the British planted the seed of English, they had no idea that a virile, tropical beanstalk would explode in the India they left behind. The stalk would reach- if not the sky- far across the ground, and entrench itself firmly in this land of a thousand tongues. And it is through the efforts of dramatists like Dattani in India that English has not remained as an imported language rather it has now returned to the West as the expression and framework of

Indian identity with the fragrance of Indian soil, soul and sensibility. With the coming of Sahitya Akademi Award, Dattani is now considered an officially recognized part of the Indian literary establishment. When asked by Erin B.Mee in an interview whether writing in English is a part of a new trend, Dattani replied:

> I think it's more of a need than a trend. It's not that I have a political motive to promote Indian English, but it is a part of Indian culture, so it has to be given its respect in India and in the world (*Mahesh Dattani's Plays* 164).

Dattani began his career on the stage in Bangalore, the city where he had grown up, and got fascinated by Gujarati plays in his childhood. Perhaps the seeds of his brilliant dramatic writings lay in his observations of these plays in his childhood and when he grow up, he needed English plays to perform but they were unavailable. So he wrote them – not as a writer writing a self-consciously literary work like a novel or a poem – but as a performer amalgamating the extra – literary polyphony of the stage in his writing and also keeping audience reception in his mind, which is the main reason of his success in the contemporary literary world. Dattani stresses in an interview to Erin B.Mee,

> I wouldn't say the only one, but I would say that I have been the most successful for various reasons: I have my own theatre company [Playpen], and I have a theatre background. I'm not writing because I'm a writer [of literature], I'm writing because I have a theatre background (*Mahesh Dattani's Plays* 156).

So, the audiences have 'connected' wherever Dattani has been performed in India and abroad. However, Dattani is sometimes blamed that his work is hardly 'Indian' because of his medium and his use of proscenium stage, but he clarifies when he says:

> Does [Indian theatre] mean traditional theatrical forms? Yes, they are wonderful, they're sophisticated, they're impressive, but are they really India? ... Are they really

reflecting life as it is now? ... What we need to do now is look at those forms and say we're approaching the twenty first century, this is who we are and this is our legacy, so where do we take that. That's not happening, and that's a matter of serious concern (Mee, *Performing Arts,* 24-25).

Influenced by such dynamic principles, Dattani acknowledges the significance of established literary tradition and simultaneously makes a praiseworthy attempt to create a tradition of his own to promote the spirit of Indian English drama at the global level. Because he knows his responsibility as a dramatist is to use appropriate words, expressions, images and dialogues to make the experiences more lively and authentic. Dattani has his own vision of the distinction of poetic experience and dramatic experience:

> In poetry even the most turbulent emotions can be recollected when one is fast asleep. But in the drama; Ah, even tranquility has to be recalled with emotion like touching a bare live wire. Try distancing yourself from that experience and writing about it! A mere description will be hopelessly inadequate(Nair 2).

Today the picture of Indian dramatic writing in English is changing as a distinct and definite theatrical identity and an idiom evolves because of the struggling, hard and significant efforts of Mahesh Dattani and dramatists like him. Says Dattani:

> It's hard work ... Not many people have that kind of time. Theatre companies have to trust new playwrights and their plays, too ... I'm an actor, I'm a director, so I know the craft of writing a play. The craftsmanship has to be worked at .... (Das, maheshdattani.com)

Though he is the director as well as a dramatist, he does not fail to mention the significant roles played by Alyque Padamsee and Lillette Dubey in successfully producing his plays outside Bangalore. His plays involve their audience so much that they even forget that they are watching a play and they begin to identify themselves with the characters of his plays. The quest for identity within the categories of the individual, the familial, the religious, the social and the national pervades in all the plays of Dattani. These plays give voice to the female within the male and the male within the female selves. His dramatic writings bring a dynamic change and innovation and though he does not revisit his roots, his plays are 'Indian' in their realistic setting of contemporary urban realities, where he gives voice to the unseen and unheard within the public arena of the stage. In his plays, he makes experiments in stage craft with specific innovations required for the communication of ideas.

Mahesh Dattani follows the familial focus and conflictual structure of Western realist drama, but with crucial differences. First, there is usually no 'protagonist' whose selfhood can render the struggle with home in individualistic terms and relate it to the idea of a singular destiny. Rather, the condition of victimization extends to all the inhabitants of home (in either a nuclear or an extended family) who are trapped by cultural constraints and economic circumstances into an impossible co-existence. Dattani brings unusual issues pertaining to sexual identity, including the hijra community, child sexual abuse, lesbianism, homosexuality, hypocrisy about HIV positive people, religious intolerance, gender inequalities, social stereotyping, or even what constitutes the contemporary Indian middle class family such as marriage negotiations, inheritance, poverty caused by natural calamities like earthquakes and droughts etc. Within these diverse themes, when asked his favourite one by Bijay Kumar Das in an interview to Mahesh Dattani, he said:

> I guess the theme of the triumph of human spirit over societal oppression seems to be the theme that connects all the issues you mention (177).

In the theatre space is often invoked as the essential element, the place in which theatre distinguishes itself from the purely "literary". Even the word "theatre" means both the performance and the structure that contains it. "Theatre" is a space for visibility, even if that space is 'empty'; etymologically, the word theatre is related to sight, manifestation, miracle, as well as to theory, which suggests the complicated relation between theory and visibility- sight and site- in theatrical language. Dattani also points out that he is a craftsman, a theatre person before being a writer and it is this intense and primary focus on the performance rather than on the literary aspect of his work that lies behind his success. For Dattani theatre is a platform to bring life on the stage and to communicate the concern for those odds of life that make human life difficult to tolerate. He conceives a situation, contemplates its various phases and transforms them in to theatrical experiences with a view to establish a direct communication with audience.

This obsessive and absorbing technique used by Mahesh Dattani in all his plays is really apt. The theatre of Dattani is certainly identifiable, typified by claustrophobia and escape. Right from the beginning of his career, Dattani was trying to get out of tight places. He has been experimenting with permeable fourth walls, translucent scenery, and the theatre's obsessive need to establish and to transgress borders. Themes of sexuality, madness and memory interweave in his oeuvre, questioning, over and over, about how to project the inner psychological process through the outer technical skills. Dattani states:

> I am practicing theatre in an extremely imperfect world where the politics of doing theatre in English looms large over anything else one does. Where writing about the middle class is seen as unfashionable... I am certain that my plays are a true reflection of my time, place and socio-economic background... in a country that has a myriad challenges to face politically, socially, artistically and culturally (*CP1*, xiv).

With home as fictional setting and family relationships as the testing ground, all his plays move outward from private experience into the public issues of caste, class, gender, ethnicity, and material survival that are rapidly redefining the middle-class urban present in India. Pervasive discontent, continued entrapment, self-hatred creates notable variations on the thematic structures popularized by Dattani in these realist dramas. By emphasizing the gap between idealized expectations and the realities of the moment, these plays collectively question the validity of inherited codes and place the urban Indian family on a recognizably 'modern' footing. The plays stress the condition of victims but do not allow the liberation of departure, adhering instead to a pattern of continued entrapment. Though he writes about 'the other' or the 'marginalized', but he brings them onto centre stage.

Dattani beautifully enmeshed stagecraft and the structure of his plays with the thematic concerns of the plays and therefore maintains a fine balance of exclusive theatrical art and seriousness of thought. As for the stage settings of all his plays, where demolishing the traditional pattern of stage, he creates split stages into different levels to achieve particular thematic effects as the exteriors merge into the interior landscapes, thus decoding the fractions of human consciousness. These divided spaces help him to reconstruct the past and the present in quick successions of memories and thus it has also become a psychological background to expose man's affinity with one's own inner self. The shadows of the past persist in the present, the awareness of which bring realization of the 'guilt' in the present which on the other hand gives birth to emotional and mental crisis and through this self awareness they travel to self defense. He also innovates in bringing two mediums of expression in his plays, 'thought' and 'speech' which represent sub-conscious and conscious mind. Besides, his employment of short dialogues, broken sentences, telegraphic conversations, inadequate expressions to present the flux of consciousness of the working of the mind of the characters make his play accessible to the mind and soul of the audience and seek the moment of emotional identification for the desired change in audience.

A quick recapitulation of all the works of Mahesh Dattani will help to clear the brilliant composition of his plays so that his innovative techniques help to make his themes impressive and touchy for the audience. The main protagonists in the plays of Dattani might be eunuchs, gay or handicapped, or women who dare to think differently from their husbands/ fathers, or marginalized Muslims or AIDS suffering people, and his dramas contain the seeds of the clash of the 'self' of individual against the pre-determined schemes of society. In the plays like *Where There's a Will, Dance Like a Man, Tara, Bravely Fought the Queen*, and *Thirty Days in September*, Dattani expresses his concern for the gender roles, where not only the women but also men suffer terribly for the restrictions of gender specified models. He takes the ground that the helplessness of an individual against the compulsions of society, generates frustration and rebellion. In these plays, he projects female images that are not weak or nervous but are aware and confident to retaliate against the wrong doers.

It is clear from his very first play *Where There's a Will*, in which Dattani represents the quirk of parental authority that makes the survival of the individual impossible. In the play the focus is on the issues like gender discrimination and the domination of patriarchal authority as Dattani himself describes it as the exorcism of patriarchal code. The first part of the play is the assertion of patriarchy; second part is the mockery of patriarchy and second part of the second act is the collapse of patriarchy. The union of Kiran and Sonal, a collective force born out of the long annals of exploitation and suffering, is an effort to abolish sexual colonialism. Though the play is a comic caricature with the family as a locale but it is also appreciated for its 'philosophical twist' because Dattani efficiently manipulates the incidents for self enlightment to expose the illusion of false authority. The humour in the play is present through the visible and invisible presence of Hasmukh, especially after becoming a Ghost, which on the other hand exposes Dattani's brilliance in dialogue, the direct exposition of action and a better opportunity for the direct communication between the audience and the actors. Besides, Hasmukh's mute observations and the free display of the inner feelings of different characters against the authority of him, is a unique device for self assessment for the characters. Therefore, a serious thought presented in a comic mode elates the pleasure of a live theatre, liberated the text from the burden of intertextual pressures and its dramatic structure, the setting of the play, verbal repartee and incongruity in human behaviour make the play a fine entertainment.

Dance like a Man is a play where the clash of motives of Jairaj with his wife and father involve the issues of identity crisis, the stigma of gender binary existing at the centre in socio-cultural thought and the perpetual conflict of man's desires and forces of destiny. Dattani forces us to "examine our own individual and collective consciousness" (Devanesen, *CP1*, 383).

The perpetual clash of human motives and deire with the traditions of family, prejudice of society and the code of culture constitute the dramatic structure of the play. The issue of gender discrimination is seen, not only in a socio-cultural context but it is found to be an integral to human consciousness and is closely associated with individual choices, self development and self identity. The role models, professional achievements, habits dresses and morality are expressed in terms of gender bias and therefore, the panic of social stigma that 'dance' is a feminine art and man's attempt at being a dancer would be a prelude to the tragedy of man as happened with Jairaj. The conflict in the life of Jairaj with his father is a conflict of colonial sensibility and progressive ideology, social expectations and individual choices. But Jairaj, the protagonist having a passion for dance, is ready to challenge all the restrictions imposed on him by his father Amritlal, an embodiment of patriarchal authority.

Along with multiple layers of suggestions beyond the spectacle at the stage, the shift of the positions of the characters as younger Jairaj and his father Amritlal denotes the shift of action in past and present. The movement of chain of events of Jairaj's life has come close to the concept of stream of consciousness. The use of narrative and cinematographic technique render the play highly conductive for Indian theatre. In the end, Jairaj and Ratna are united once again after realizing their mistakes of their whole life. They went back in time in their memory and became younger Jairaj and Ratna. The bitterness between them disappears and once again they embrace and dance perfectly in union. In his self discovery, Jairaj discovers the divine essence of human self that is neither male nor female. The play ends in a calm stoicism and the idea of 'Dance like God' imparts a rare sublimity and consolation to the storm of passion raised in the play.

Bravely Fought the Queen is set in the background of familial relationship, and is a portrait of the emotional, financial and sexual intricacies of joint family in the modern life. It tries to expose the position of women in conventional society and presents the clash between the traditional ideology and contemporary culture that has created a new canvas of familial relationship. There are five female characters in the play, entrapped in the conventional society in different ways. Dolly survives in her domestic spaces though with 'inner' suffocation and frustration. Alka is frustrated too but she does not remain silent and becomes a boozer and drug-addict. Lalitha is an emissary from the male world. Besides, the pressure of Baa in the play is the assertion of paternal authority who does not allow freedom of choice to her daughter-in-law. Daksha, Dolly's daughter has a silent presence in the play but her presence is very essential for the painful reminder of violence, wracked by Jitin.

Bravely Fought the Queen is presented on multi level stage to expose the juxtaposition of past and present and he beautifully mingles the imaginary events and the realistic events without breaking the flow of interest. In the last act, all the characters are exposed and the false appearances are lost. Dolly, who in earlier scene appeared as a tortured character, emerges as a strong and confident woman to identify her oppressor and to fight against injustice. She supports drunken Alka, reveals the painful truth about Daksha and exposes the horrors of her brother Praful.

The play *Tara* is basically related to the issue of gender bias. It is a pathetic dramatic representation of the suffering of two Siamese Twins. Tara and Chandan, like several other plays, the plot of *Tara* is arranged around familial relationship where each individual in her own way has to bear the burden of social values and their efforts to go beyond them, bring happiness in their lives. Bharti's preferred male child Chandan to female child Tara when the surgery took place on their birth which shows how Bharti's motherhood was subordinated to the expectations of patriarchal society. This made Tara cripple and this gender discrimination spoils the whole life of Tara and Chandan. Bharti and Mr.Patel could not forgive themselves so as Chandan, who went to London after the death of Tara with a new identity 'Dan', discarding all his old identity because of the guilty feeling that he is responsible for Tara's suffering. For him Tara was an inseparable part of his own inner self. The separation and death of Tara becomes a prelude to his doom. More than social dilemma, the psychological tension of each character is more prominent.

Dattani makes use of cinematographic technique in which he allows the memories to flood in, regarding Chandan's relationship with his sister. In these recollections, he reconstructs his union with his sister, their forced separation and the relationship of parents. The extensive use of flashbacks in the past of the characters reflect in the discontent in their lives, their inner psyche and external action, extends the impression that man has ultimately to bear the pain of guilt for his own wrong doings. Through the character of Dan, Dattani's message is clear. The perception of the duality of male and female is an illusion of human consciousness. Dan's incompleteness after his separation from Tara, justifies that both of them are interdependent and not independent.

Thirty Days in September is focused on the issue of childhood sexual abuse. It is a family play based on incestuous relationship in which Dattani shows how women feel humiliated and get exploited by male members of the family. Both women characters the mother Shanta and the Daughter Mala in the play were physically exploited by the same men in their childhood who happens to be Shanta's brother and Mala's uncle. Dattani categorically points out that the negligence in familial relationship is responsible for the growing discontent in children. Mala, the protagonist, is the victim of this abuse but she maintains silence against injustice. On that, the silence of her mother works as a stimulus in her life and she gradually becomes hostile and aggressive. For her, life becomes intolerable both inside and outside the family. She behaves like a trapped animal that seems to have no possibility to escape. It was not only the humiliation of her body but also the rape of her spirit, her innocence and her privacy.

The following lines of Shanta show us her helplessness in saving her child as she requests, "please save her. I did not save her. I did not know how to save her. How could I save her when I could not save myself..." (*CP2*, 55). These touchy words ring in our ear again and again. A life sized doll of seven years old girl in the background implies a psychological representation of Mala's plight in her childhood. The extensive use of monologues and incomplete sentences helps to echo the internal conflict of Mala and the condensation of the play through no any division in the form of sub-sections enhances the intensity of the emotional crisis of the characters.

As mentioned earlier, in *Final Solutions*, Dattani depicts communal disharmony through religious distrust. As its very title is suggestive enough to show us the deep rooted hatred in the minds of two communities against each other which does not seems to be solving ever. This inner hatred is the same even today, as it was sixty years ago when the massacre took place during the partition of India and Pakistan. Though Amritlal shows some courage and may be he is representing Dattani's own voice, but Dattani hesitates to make any plain solution of the situation. The play is famous for its innovative techniques as the stage setting and technique of this play such as 'crescent shaped ramp', 'chorus' and 'mask' is contrived to project the multiple layers of context, individual as well as social but at the centre the idea of communal violence is dominant. The use of chorus with mask is suggestive of Dattani's affinity with the native tradition of drama, which symbolizes that the awareness of communal disharmony and the passion for discrimination is only an external mask that covers the essential humanity that is 'one'.

The different questions asked by chorus are the questions associated eternally with the national identity of the minority who have to take recourse to carnival to protest their interest. It is not a question of society and community but of the identity of the individual. The issue of religion is associated with national identities, cultural identities and social identities. Smita with her liberalism and Aruna with her fundamentalism frame suitable concepts to expose the roots of communal violence existing Indian society. Smita, the daughter of Amritlal, seeks the solution of the problems in Indian ethics that teaches to respect all modes of religious creeds with an uncompromising spirit of tolerance. Dattani establishes that the love for humanity eliminates the dark shadows of prejudice; the solution lies not in external world but within man's own consciousness.

Dattani knows that Indian mind does not accept same-sex love and marriages either in life or in literature yet he is audacious enough to take such taboo subject in his play *On a Muggy Night in Mumbai.* Although recently we find well-known writers like Vikram Seth and Shobha De supporting the cause of same-sex marriages. The concern for the 'gays' is a radical issue and to bring it to the stage in the value oriented society in India, especially for urban audience since it is all about urban life gay/lesbian relationships, came as a challenge both to the director and the producer. As this play was later transcripted into a screen play *Mango Souffle*, Dattani admits that he has no overt agenda or message in the movie – only an exploration of relationships that is necessarily suspected by social givens. It is celebrated as the first Indian movie to address homosexuality, addressing gay issues within the territorially distinct identity of its subject.

The subject like homosexuality is rooted in human psyche. In the play, Kamlesh, being a homosexual, faces several situations that can illustrate the emotional crisis for him. In the first place, the pain is intense when Sharad arranges the rituals to burn all photographs and associated memories but secretly, he holds one of the photographs. Similarly, when Prakash and Kiran are busy in dance, Kamlesh desperately chases Prakash. When Prakash was sitting on the park bench looking around, a shadow moved around him, Prakash identified him as Kamlesh. The plight of Homosexuals in our society is thus well depicted through the charcter of Kamlesh and the unconventional language experiment with the reactions and responses of the audience, makes the play exceptional in theme and technique.

Besides the above mentioned stage plays, Dattani also exhibits his expertise in radio plays. Crime and Corruption in our society and the resulting frustration are the focus of three of his plays which are going on as a sequence of detective dramas or triology, centering Uma Rao as the main protagonist who is the daughter of the vice-chancellor of Bangalore University, the daughter-in-law of the Deputy Commissioner of Police and the wife of the Superintendent of Police. They are *Seven Steps around the Fire* (first broadcast as *Seven Circles around the Fire* by BBC Radio 4 in 1999), *The Swami and Winston* (2000) and *Uma and the Fairy Queen* (2003). Though it is really very difficult to show the real feelings of the characters through the medium of radio plays as it depends on only voice and there cannot be any facial expression. But Dattani got success through adding brilliant techniques of 'thought' and 'voice-over' in these plays, which on the other hand used for ironical effect on the audience to expose the injustice prevalent in the society.

In *Seven Steps around the Fire*, Dattani highlights the problems of hijras in our society by exhibiting their problems in our society. He dives deep into the psyche of hijras to portray characters like Kamla, Champa and few other hijras. To treat them as untouchables and again to utilize their services at the time of marriage and childbirth, speaks volumes for the double standard in our society. For the research on transsexuals, Uma meets Anarkali in jail and Champa and other hijras in their living place and in the process she indirectly get involve in the investigation of the mystery of the murder of Kamla, a hijra. But in the end, even solving the case, Uma get silent as the murderer was a minister and she has her limitations for exposing this. So the case was hushed up and not even reported in the newspaper. While solving the murder case, Uma gets absorbed in the world of eunuchs, and simultaneously embarks on a quest for her own individuality. The position of Uma is no better than Kamala and Champa. They at least enjoy their individuality and freedom in their specific domains but Uma has no freedom of choice in her home. If Anarkali is a gendered subaltern, Uma is also a subaltern in comparison of her husband. The women like Uma in our society, who are intellectual women working both inside and outside of the house and face a threatening challenge continuously in their daily lives and is lost in the sea of identity politics.

Dattani specifies the information of the places of action is indicated by different kinds of sounds. Some other sounds are also enmeshed to enhance the symbolic meanings in the plays. The play *Seven Steps around the Fire* began with the voice of Sanskrit Mantras of Hindu wedding, the sound of fire and the scream:

> Sanskrit mantras fade in, the ones chanted during a Hindu wedding. Fire. The sound of the fire grows louder, drowning the mantras. A scream. The flames engulf the scream (*CP1*, 7).

Fire indicates the passion of love in the heart of any human whether they are heterosexual or homosexual and this passion has the power to engulf any scream of social boundation if it is not allowed for the free expression. Indication of different places is heard as the running of stick on the bars of the prison to show the central jail, a Hindi movie fight scene blaring from a TV set to indicate the bedroom of Suresh and Uma, whirring of fan to designate the office of the superintendent of the police etc. As *Seven Steps Around the Fire* is a serious story but Dattani engage in this a comic relief by using Munswamy as an excellent comic foil, who is kept with Uma Rao for any trouble appointed by her husband. In *Seven Steps Around the Fire* too, Dattani used this technique and even the play ends with this,

> Uma (Voice-over). They knew. Anarkali, Champa and all the hijra people knew who was behind the killing of Kamla. They have no voice. The case was hushed up and was not even reported in the newspapers. Champa was right the police made no arrests. Subbu's suicide was written off as an accident. The photograph was destroyed. So were the lives of two young people (*CP1*, 42).

In *The Swami and Winston,* Dattani exposes the fake Sadhus through Sitaram Trivedi, who wants to cheat person in the name of religion by building Ashrams inside and outside of the country.

Sensual nature and criminal bent of mind is shown in the character of Nila in *Uma and the Fairy Queen,* for which she killed her second husband Michael. Though Nila is a famous TV star, but she is an immoral woman who used to sleep with her actor friends just to please her inner devil of lust. In the play, Dattani's new method of handling a dramatic monologue can be seen in the phone call to reveal important information.

Do the Needful, again a radio play by Dattani is also based on gay and lesbian relationships. It is a romantic comedy set around the concept of arranged marriages in the traditional society of India. The technique of 'thought' and 'voice-over' is clearly shown in the play *Do the Needful,* different from the traditionally used techniques such as 'asides' and 'soliloquies', in which what the character thinks and tells to the audience, is kept as a secret from the character spoken to. Lata and Alpesh both do not want to marry each other as they have their criminal and gay partner. To avoid the consequences of these two unnatural relationships, both the families are anxious for the hasty marriage. When their parents talk each other to fix their marriage, they secretly thought of their partners. Some examples are:

> Lata (thought.) Salim. I really wanted to cry, whine, do anything to stop it all from happening. Mummy was quicker (*CP2*, 132).
>
> Alpesh (thought.) What could I say, Trilok? How would I tell her to reject me? (*CP2*, 149)

When Lata knows that Alpesh is a homosexual, with her desire to get her lover Salim, she marries him, for Alpesh being a homosexual will have no interest in her. They come to an understanding and get married only to facilitate their own motives of fulfilling love in their own way. Finally, the scene shifts to the road, where the newly wed couple goes in a taxi only to go in their own way. Their movement justifies the title of the play, *Do the Needful.* Therefore, in the plays based on homosexuality, Dattani has exposed the psycho-pathetic condition of those who struggle against fate and society. And through the experiences of Kamlesh and Alpesh, Dattani concludes that gays suffer because they can't face society and cannot make their relationship acceptable.

Dattani's *Clearing the Rubble* depicts the feelings of earthquake victims who have been denied justice by the government when Nature has devastated them. All their reactions against both injustices are reflected in their thoughts and so the technique of thought and voice-over well-suits Dattani. In fact the play begins with the thoughts of the three persons, Salim, Jeffrey and Fatima against the backdrop of massive earthquake that devastated the land of Kutch in Gujarat.

The play *A Tale of a Mother Feeding her Child* was written again as a radio play, first broadcast on 29th October 2000 on BBC Radio. It came as a short play included in *2000 Fables*, a large drama series to celebrate the six-hundredth anniversary of the death of Geoffrey Chaucer. The play can be interpreted as a dramatic monologue as the entire action passes through the technique of stream of consciousness of Anne Gosweb, the only dramatic persona in the play. Other characters are revealed through the reconstruction of her own past. Anne Gosweb returns to a village in India after a pause of twenty years for the financial help to the draught stricken family of Jaman, with whom she had affairs previously. The different issues like poverty, the discrimination on the basis of caste, neglect of government and the social stigma for personal relationship, have successfully been interwoven in the framework of plot. Anne Gosweb came into India for two things – her anguish for unfortunate conditions of the poor in Indian society and other is her reflections on the 'guilt' that she had committed in the company of Jaman Gopalia. She seeks this opportunity as a safer outlet to compensate for the loss and to relieve the personal pain rooted in her consciousness. These two distinctive spaces of conflict dramatized in the play, extend the impression of splitted stage and in that process the text of the play has become self reflective.

Besides, two Screen plays of Dattani made a mark in Indian cinema, *Mango Souffle*, *Ek Alag Mausam* and *Morning Raaga*. *Mango Souffle* is the screen production of his own play *On a Muggy Night in Mumbai*, and proved to a great success. As a script writer, Dattani has to face the difference of the two 'languages', the problems of adaptation, and the problematics of an altered audience perspective. Though he is primarily a theatre artist, yet he is successful in his film scripts too. The reason is his strategy of casting and drawing actors from the theatre help him to retain directorial control over his material

The dreaded disease HIV positive has shaken the fabric of the society through its horror. It is our prejudice, fear and ignorance that create hatred with the people suffering with this dreadful disease. In *Ek Alag Mausam*, Aparna, an HIV positive, which she got from her husband, meets George, a truck driver, another HIV positive who falls in love with her. Death is inevitable for HIV positives but they want to live in which shows our helplessness against that incurable disease.

And Aparna's question to Dr. Machado on how to live with George indicates the inner doubts of all of us. Dr. Machado gives hope and a positive point of view to the HIV suffering peoples in the end of the play,

> The Aids virus knows no barriers of caste, creed, religion, age, gender, race. It is not prejudice, fear or ignorance that will win the battle against Aids. But understanding, precaution and above all love. Today the world over, doctors and scientists are trying to find a cure for Aids. In the interest of mankind we hope they succeed. While waiting for that cure to be invested or discovered, let us not forget – that miracles are known to happen (*CP2*, 556-57).

In this play, Dattani emphatically articulates the inarticulate to express the 'silence' of those who are the victims par excellence of the apathy of society, indifference of fate and ignominy of born out of human attitude. It is the story of the emotional sensibility of two HIV positives. It is an innovative attempt of Dattani to unmask the truth of the fact that is valid in myths. He states:

> I think Indian audience will look forward to such a film, because it has been nearly twenty years since the virus first appeared in India and people want to know the truth (Kidwai 1).

The shadows of doom and destruction are imminent in the relationship of Aparna and George from the very beginning. But, in spite of implicit horrors, there is a new discovery of happiness through love, celebration of life through death, the triumph of smile over tears and the realization of immensity of human endurance against blind certitude of society. Here again, like *Thirty Days in September*, Dattani makes no formal division and classification of actions in the form of scenes and acts. The action moves with a flux of conscience of the protagonist.

Like the depiction of dance in the play *Dance Like a Man*, Dattani deals with finer thing of life like music in *Morning Raaga*. Like dance, music too dives deep into the heart of the human beings by transcending the baser instinct and bringing joy to their minds. But in this play Abhinay's father, like Amritlal in *Dance Like a Man*, opposes such activities like dance and music. But their children of young generation do not carry any old prejudice against dancers and musicians and even helps to motivate and cultivate dance and music against all odds. In this play, Swarnlatha, a carnatic singer had a desire to sing in a city, which could not materialize earlier because of the death of her friend who was a singer. It is the son of her friend Abhinay, who with the help of Pinkie brings Swarnlatha's desire to fruition in the end. In the ending, elaborate stage settings and flashback technique helps to bring a union between the dead and the living by the music performance of Swarnlatha. Though Swarnlatha sings an Indian Raga, Pinkie joins in on the English lyrics in the concert, which again brings a beautiful and melodious synthesis between the Indian and Western music, like the plays of Dattani, where the technique may be western but the language and soul is Indian. The duality of vision, carnatic and western, merges in a sublime union conveying a profound message for all those who are swayed by the passion of music. This, on the other hand proves that the co-mingling of some forms from the outside India enhances the Indian tradition and increase interest for this in not only Indian audience but the audience of any foreign country too.

Morning Raaga is the only play of Dattani, written against a rural background marked by simplicity and sublimity. In the play, Dattani maintains tragic intensity through the conflict in inter-personal relationship. The play is an argument in support of the assumption that man can come out of his guilt only through self realization. Swarnlatha and Abhinay both make efforts to come out of their guilts. Gradually morning raga becomes a symbol of the condition of the life of Swarnlatha, Abhinay and Pinki. It brings a new hope, a new light in the life of Swarnlatha. At the end of the play, all the three – Pinki, Abhinay and Swarnlatha come together at a spot and it was not only the music of instruments but of the strings of the soul, embracing all those who feel its vibration. Therefore, music has been used as a comprehensive symbol in which duality of past and present; East and West, Carnatic and Western become one, echoing the rhythm of life.

Though these plays of Dattani bring forth some major or some taboo issues, he resists to be typecast as a 'women's writer' or a 'gay writer' or an 'Indian English Writer', as he replies to Angelie Multani:

> The worst outcome of these kind of categories is that the creator is killed instantly. Oh this is what comes from India! Oh, this is how gay life in Sri Lanka is! Oh this is what Indian women go through! Where is the writer in these remarks? And yet this is exactly how the labeling process begins (167).

His plays have different colours as on the one place it is romantic comedy and in other it is black comedy. His dialogues consists all, the witty repartee, the acid rejoinder, the focused punning etc. the straightforward language and code-mixing in some plays where he used Hindi words without translation as in *On a Muggy Night in Mumbai* and *Do the Needful* are innovations in Indian English drama. He has dispensed with the traditional techniques like asides, soliloquies, etc. and brought in 'thought', 'voice-over' and on phone conversation to suit his new themes. He used not only flashbacks to show past and present in his plays but also as the observation of the same person in two selves – young and old as he has done in the character of Daksha and Hardika in *Final Solutions*, where the attitude of the old woman is different from the view of her young age:

> Daksha. Dear Diary today is the first time I have dared to put my thought on your pages ... 31 March 1948.
>
> Hardika. After forty years ... I opened my diary again. And I wrote. A dozen pages before. A dozen pages now. A young girl's childish scribble. An old woman's shaky scrawl (*CP2*, 167).

Judging by the stage productions, Dattani's plays appeal to us as performing art. His characters move with grace from interior space to outer space in course of the play to show the movements of the play. The interplay of 'silence' and 'sound' adds to the musicality of the plays. The action in the plays split between past and present, floats in order of flashback and flash forward in a symmetrical order corresponding with the flow of consciousness of different characters. Dattani develops the thesis that past and present are not fragmented notions but they are collectively integrated in human consciousness. Rehmat Merchant says:

> Mahesh Dattani's pathos-with-a-punch approach, picked with a dash of humour, makes him the perfect candidate for chronicling urban angst. His plays are peopled with city slickens wrestling with issues in a manner close to the modern psyche ... change-the-world brand of range and impulsiveness, threatens to upset some apple carts ... subtext of complex relationships ... eager to understand mind contrasted by informed prejudice ... character growing ... build in conflict in marriage ... collapse of certain stereotypes ... prejudice holder forced to look outside the cozy community circle (4).

Therefore, Dattani's dramatic art can be rightly appreciated for its fine fabric of philosophical undertone and social consciousness. The philosophical reflections on the predicament of human destiny against the odds of socio-cultural practices, impart an exceptional depth and richness to his plays. For Dattani, moral preaching was not a motive of his dramatic art; still often he seeks grounds to defend human frailties. Though his motive is not to provide any readymade solutions in his plays yet they are significant enough to mirror the society as it is before the audience to make them think themselves about the final solutions of these social evils. The characters of Dattani do not only encounter difficulties in their living world; instead he leads his audience to see just how caught up we all are in the complications and contradictions of our values and assumptions. As Asha Kuthari Choudhuri describes:

> Most of his plays are constructed around social issues, not on any specific message. Dattani maintains the stance of a non-judgmental observer and never intrude into the plays he writes nor attempt to sermonize (26).

Time shifts, character shifts, conscience shifts but the purpose of the play is well settled in the imagination of the dramatist. In the process, the half concealed and half revealed message emerges only out of skilled direction and accurate performance. Most of the plays of Dattani are open-ended so that the viewer can treat a play like a 'roller coaster ride', which, even at its most terrifying moment one knows will rapidly and happily end on safe grounds. Therefore, his plays make audiences to think of their own lives, as he himself asserts:

> It's only when you are left hanging in air you start to question you own personality, perceptions… the theatre is a collective experience and the audience have to finish in their own heads what the playwright began (Nair 2).

Dattani is a tireless innovator who makes experiments with new theatrical devices to sustain nobility and dynamism. Therefore, besides thematic concern, the idea to visualize the consciousness of other characters through these innovative techniques is an exceptional achievement of Dattani and it admits immense possibility in the realm of Indian drama in English.

REFERENCES

Choudhuri, Asha Kuthari. *Mahesh Dattani.* New Delhi: Foundation Books, 2005.

Dasgupta, Uma Mahadevan. "The Minute I write a Play, I want to direct it". 2001. http://www.maheshdattani.com.

Das, Bijay Kumar. "Mahesh Dattani in Conversation with Bijay Kumar Das". In Bijay Kumar Das. *Form and Meaning in Mahesh Dattani's Plays.* New Delhi: Atlantic Pub., 2008.

Dattani, Mahesh. *Collected Plays.* New Delhi: Penguin Books. 2000.

Dattani, Mahesh. *Collected Plays.* New Delhi: Penguin Books. 2005.

Devanesen, Mitharan. "Note on the Play". In Mahesh Dattani's *Collected Plays.* New Delhi: Penguin Books, 2000.

Jallotin, J.B. "Interview with V. Naravani". *The Sunday Times of India,* 28 Jan, 1996.

Kidwai, Jamal. *Arts and Entertainment/Cinema-India: Truth about HIV/AIDS Coming to Indian Cinema and Next Year.* New Delhi: Inter Press Service, 2007.

Mee, Erin B. "Invisible Issues: An Interview with Mahesh Dattani". In Angelie Multani, ed. *Mahesh Dattani's Plays: Critical Perspectives,* New Delhi: Pencraft International, 2007.

Mee, Erin B. "Mahesh Dattani: Invisible Issues". *Performing Arts Journal,* 55, 1997.

Merchant R. "On Mahesh Dattani". *India Today.* 14 Feb 2000.

Multani, Angelie. "A Conversation with Mahesh Dattani". In Angelie Multani, ed. *Mahesh Dattani's Plays: Critical Perspectives,* New Delhi: Pencraft International, 2007.

Nair, Anita. "An Unveiling of a Playwright in Three Acts". *The Gentleman.* May 2001. http://www.anitanair.net.

Roy, Elizabeth. "Freak Mirrors and Grotesque Images". *The Hindu.* 15 March 2002.

Bibliography

Primary Sources

Dattani, Mahesh. *Collected Plays.* New Delhi: Penguin Books, 2000.

Dattani, Mahesh. *Collected Plays.* New Delhi: Penguin Books, 2005.

Secondary Sources

Ahmed, Durre S., ed. *Gendering the Spirit: Women, Religion & the Post-Colonial Response* - London & New York: Zed Books, 2002.

Ahmed, Aijaz. "Indian Literature: Notes Towards the Definition of a Category". In *In Theory: Classes, Nations, Literatures.* London: Verso, 1992.

Abercrombie, N., et al. *The Penguin Dictionary of Sociology,* 2nd edn. London: Penguin, 1988.

Agrawal, Beena. *Mahesh Dattani's Plays: A New Horizen in Indian Theater.* Jaipur: Book Enclave, 2008.

Beauvoir, Simone De. *The Second Sex.* New York: Vintage Books, 1989.

Beasley, Chris. *What is Feminism? An Introduction to Feminist Theory.* New Delhi: Sage Publications, 1999.

Bartky, Sandra Lee. "Towards a Phenomenology of Feminist Consciousness". In Mary Vetterling et al., eds. *Feminism and Philosophy.* Totowa: Rowman and Littlefield, 1977.

Chawdhary, Maitrayee, ed.: *Feminism in India.* New Delhi: Kali for Women & Women Unlimited, 2006.

Chauhan, Poonam S., ed. *Lengthening Shadow: Status of Women in India.* New Delhi: Manak Publications, 1996.

Choudhuri, Asha Kuthari. *Mahesh Dattani.* New Delhi: Foundation Books, 2005.

Dhawan, R.K. and Tanu Pant, eds: *The Plays of Mahesh Dattani, A Critical Response.* New Delhi: Prestige, 2005.

Devy, G.N. ed.: *Indian Literary Criticism: Theory and Interpretation.* Hyderabad: Orient Longman, 2004.

Dharwadkar, Aparna Bhargava, ed.: *Theatre of Independence, Drama, Theory and Urban Performance in India Since 1947,* New Delhi: Oxford University Press, 2005.

Das, Ram Mohan. *Women in Manu's Philosophy.* New Delhi: ABS Publications, 1993.

Das, Bijay Kumar. *Form and Meaning in Mahesh Dattani's Plays.* New Delhi: Atlantic Pub., 2008.

Engels, Fredrick, ed. *The Origin of the Family, Private Property and the State.* New York: Pathfinder Press, 1972.

Evans, Judith. *Feminist Theory Today: An Introduction to Second - Wave Feminism.* New Delhi: Sage Publications, 1992.

Falzen, Christopher, ed.: Foucault and Social Dialogue; Beyond Fragmentation, London and New York: Routledge, 1999.

Felman, Shoshama. "Women and Madness: the critical fallacy". In Catherine Belsey and Jane Moore, eds. *The Feminist Reader: Essays in Gender and the Politics of Literary Criticism.* Cambridge: Blackwell Publications, 1989.

Ganesh, Kamala ; Thakkar, Usha, Eds.: *Culture and the Making of Identity in Contemporary India,* New Delhi: Sage Pub., 2005.

Giri, V. Mohini, ed. *KANYA: Exploitation of Little Angels.* New Delhi: Gyan Publishing House, 1999.

Ghosh, S.K. *Indian Women Through the Ages.* New Delhi: Ashist Publishing House, 1989.

Jain, Nemichandra, ed.: *Asides, Themes in Contemporary Indian Theatre,* New Delhi: Bahawalpur House, National School of Drama, 2003.

Jain, Nemichandra, ed.: *Indian Theatre, Tradition, Continuity and Change,* New Delhi: Bahawalpur House, NSD, 1992.

Julia, Leslie and Mary Megee, eds. *Invented Identities: The Interplay of Gender, Religion and Politics.* New Delhi: OUP, 2000.

Kalpana, R.J., ed.: *Feminist issues in Indian Literature; Feminism and Family,* New Delhi: Prestige Pub., 2005.

Kumar, Radha, ed. *The History of Doing, Movements for Women Rights and Feminism in India, 1800-1990,* New Delhi: Zubaan Pub., 2004.

Kar, Prafulla C., ed. *Critical Theory, Western and India.,* Delhi: Pencraft International, 2005.

Kelly, L. *Surviving Sexual Violence.* Oxford: Polity Press, 1988.

Lal, Anand, ed. *Rasa, The Indian Performing Arts: The Last Twenty Five Years, Theatre and Cinema,* Calcutta, 1995.

Lal, Anand, ed.: *The Oxford Companion to Indian Theatre,* New Delhi· Manohar Pub., 2004.

Mogham, Valentine, ed. *Modernizing Woman - Gender and Social Change in the Middle East.* London: Lynne Rienner Publications, 1993.

Mann, Michael. "A Crisis in Stratification Theory". In Rosemary Crompton and Michael Mann, eds. *Gender and Stratification.* UK: Polity Press, 1986.

Minsky, R. "Lacan". In H. Crowley and S. Himmel Weit, eds. *Knowing Women: Feminism and Knowledge.* Cambridge: Polity Press, 1992.

Millet, Kate. *Sexual Politics*: New York: Doubleday, 1970.

Multani, Angelie, ed. *The Plays of Mahesh Dattani: Critical Perspectives.* New Delhi: Pencraft International, 2007.

Naik, M.K., ed. *A History of Indian English Literature.* New Delhi: Sahitya Akademi, 2006.

Poster, Mark, ed. *Foucault, Marxism and History, Mode of Production Versus Mode of Information.* Cambridge: Polity Press, 1987.

Pandey, Ashish, ed. *Academic Dictionary of Drama.* Delhi: Isha Books, 2005.

Prabhakar, Vani, ed. *Third World Sociology, Vol. I & II.* New Delhi: Dominant Pub. & Distributors, 2001.

Reddy, K. Venkata; Dhawan, R.K., eds.: *Flowering of Indian Drama: Growth and Development.* New Delhi: Prestige Books, 2004.

Ramaswamy, S. 'Indian Drama in English: A Tentative Reflection'. *Makers of Indian English Literature.* C.D. Narasimhaiah, ed. Delhi: Pencraft International, 2000.

Rangacharya, Adya, ed. *The Natyashastra.* New Delhi: Munshiram Manoharlal, 1996.

Richmond, Farley P. ; Swann., Darius L.; Zarilli, Phillip B., eds. *Indian Theatre: Traditions of Performance, Vol. I.* New Delhi: Motilal Banarasidass Pub., 1993.

Rege, Sharmila, ed. *Sociology of Gender: The Challenge of Feminist Sociological Knowledge.* New Delhi: Sage Publications, 1998.

Rowley and Grosz. "Psychoanalysis and Feminism". In S. Gunew, ed. *Feminist Knowledge: Critique and Construct.* London: Routledge, 1990.

Robertson, D. *The Penguin Dictionary of Politics,* 2nd edn. London: Penguin, 1993.

Srampickal, Jacob, ed. *Voice to the Voiceless, The Power of People's Theatre in India.* New Delhi: Manohar Pub. 1994.

Subhedar, Dr. Sunil; Varadpande, M.L., eds. *The Critic of Indian Theatre.* Delhi: Unique Pub., 1981.

Subramanyam, Laxshmi, ed. *Muffled Voice, Women in Modern Indian Theatre.* New Delhi: Shakti Book, 2002.

Seshadri, K. ed. *Stagnancy and Change in Indian Society and Politics.* Jaipur: Aalekh Pub., 1999.

Shah, Shalini, ed. *The Making of Womanhood: Gender Relations in the Mahabharata.* New Delhi: Manohar Publications, 1995.

Singh, Sushila. *Feminism: Theory, Criticism, Analysis.* Delhi: Pencraft International, 1992.

Singh, Indu Prakash. *Women's Oppression, Men Responsible.* Delhi: Renaissance Publishing House, 1988.

Spivak, Gayatri Chakrovorty (tr.). "Translator's Preface". *In Jaques Derrida, of Grammatology.* Baltimore: John Hopkins University Press, 1976.

Talwar, Urmil, and Bandana Chakrabarty, eds. *Contemporary Indian Drama, Astride Two Traditions.* Jaipur: Rawat Pub., 2005.

Tharu, Susie, and K. Lalita, eds. *Women Writing in India: 600 BC to the Present.* New Delhi: Oxford University Press, 1991.

Upadhyay, Neelam, and Rekha Pandey, eds. *Women in India: Past and Present.* Allahabad: Chugh Publications, 1990.

Visker, Rudi, ed. *Michal Foucault, Genealogy as Critique.* London - New York: Verso, 1995.

Varadpande, M.L., ed. *Invitation to Indian Theatre.* Merseyride: Lucas Books Pub., 1989.

Varadpande, M.L., ed. *Traditions of Indian Theatre.* New Delhi: Abhinav Pub., 1979.

Vishnu, A.K. "The Man, the Mistress, The Will: The Motifs in Mahesh Dattani's *Where There's a Will*", *Contemporary Indian Writing in English, Vol. II, Critical Perspectives.* ed. N.D.R. Chandra. New Delhi: Sarup & Sons, 2005.

Varsyayan, Kapila, ed. *Traditional Indian Theatre: Multiple Streams.* New Delhi: National Book Trust, 1980.

Wilkinson, Sue, and Celia Kitzinger, eds. *Feminism and Discourse: Psychological Perspectives.* New Delhi: Sage Publications, 1999.

Yarrow, Ralph, ed. *Indian Theatre; Theatre of Origin, Theatre of Freedom.* Richmond; Curzon Press, 2001.

Journal, E-journal, and Newspapers

Ahmad, Ashwin, and Anubha Sawhney. "All the World's a Stage". *Sunday Times of India,* July 3, 2005.

Arora, Kulvinder. "The Mythology of Female Sexuality: Alternative Narratives of Belonging". *Women; a cultural review,* Vol. 17. No. 2, Summer, 2006.

Ahuja, Chaman. "Theatre Thinking at Bharangam 2005", *Theatre India,* No. 6.

Alam, Arshad. "Responding to Modern Challenges", *The Book Review,* Vol. xxx, No. 5, May 2006.

Banerjee, Utpal K. "World of Marginalised Gender", *The Pioneer,* Friday, July 9, 2004.

Bhargava, Vidhi. "The World's his stage". *The Hindustan Times,* Dec. 12, 2004.

Banerjee, Utpal K. "Interactive Theatre". *The Pioneer,* June 11, 2004.

Bhattacharya, Pradip, "Common Patterns in Differing Traditions". *The Book Review.* Vol. xxx, No. 4, April, 2006.

Boyce, Paul. "Moral ambivalence and irregular practices: contextualizing male - to - male sexualities in Calcutta/ India", *Sexual Moralities, Feminist Review,* 83, 2006.

Banerjee, Sumanta. "Towards a Multi-Cultural Indian Theatre". *Theatre India.* No. VI, Nov. 2002.

Belliappa, K.C. "Problematising Indian Writing in English". *JIWE,* Vol. 30, No. 2, July 2002.

Banerjee, Utpal K. "In Conversation with Mahesh Dattani". *Indian Literature,* 223, Sep-Oct, 2004.

Bari, Rachel and M. Ibrahim Khalilullah. "Reading Dattani: A View Point". *The Literary Criterion.* Vol. XLII, 2007.

Chatterjee, Sumita. "Theatre is Here to Stay". *The Statesman,* July 5, 2005.

Chakravarty, Radha. "Interrogating Social Biases". *The Book Review.* Vol. xxx, No. 1, Jan - Feb, 2006.

Chakravarti, Paromita. "Diet of Honour and Shame". *The Book Review,* Vol. xxx, No. 5, May, 2006.

Dattani, Mahesh. "Contemporary Indian Theatre and Its Relevance". *Journal of Indian Writing in English.* Vol. 30, No. 1, Jan. 2002.

Dattani, Mahesh. "Emerging Trends in Performing Arts". *Indian Literature.* Vol. 228, July - August, 2005.

Das, Bijay Kumar. "Putting Mahesh Dattani in the Indian English Dramatic Tradition". *Journal of Indian Writing in English.* Vol. 36, No. 1, Jan 2008.

Gahlot, Deepa. "The Marriage disturbs you". *Deccan Chronicle,* Sunday, Oct 3, 2004.

Hariharan, Gita. "New Voices, New Challenges: Concerns of the Contemporary Indian Writer". *Littcrit* 57, Vol. 30, No. 1, June 2004.

Iyengar, K.R. Srinivasa, ed. *Indian Writing in English.* New Delhi: Sterling Pub., 2004.

K. Banerjee, Utpal. "An Interview: In Conversation with Mahesh Dattani". *Indian Literature,* 223, Sep - Oct. 2004.

Kumar, Sunaina "Theatre Producers don't back original work". *Times of India,* July 25, 2005.

Kumar, Meenakshi. "Scene Stealers At Work: Dattani Plays with Murder". *The Hindustan Times,* July 6, 2004.

Kumar, Meenakshi. "All The World's A Stage for Dattani". *The Hindustan Times,* Wednesday, Dec 17, 2003.

Kulkarni, Anand B. "A Case for English as a Signifier of Indian Sensibility". *The Literary Criterion.* Vo. XLII, 2007.

Kumar, Vijay. "Dattani Transforms good Themes into good theatre". *Muse India.* Issue 14, Jul - Aug. 2007. http://www.museindia.com/showfeature3.

Kumar, Sanjay. "Mirror that". *The Hindu.* Friday, Dec. 7, 2007. http://www.hindu.com/fr/2007/12/07/stories/2007/20750590300.htm.

Lal, Anand. "The Question of Meaning". *Theatre India,* No. 5, May. 2002.

Multani, Angelie. "On Mahesh Dattani's *Dance Like A Man*: The Politics of Production and Performance". *Seagull Theatre Quaterly,* Issue 11, September, 1996.

Multani, Angelie. "Final Solutions?". *JSL,* Spring, 2004.

Multani, Angelie. "A Conversation with Mahesh Dattani", *JSL,* Autumn. 2005. (Interview).

Mee, Erin B. "Contemporary Indian Theatre". *PAJ 55,* Vol. 19, No. 1, Jan. 1997.

Mee, Erin B. "Mahesh Dattani: Invisible Issue". *PAJ 55,* Vol. 19, No. 1, Jan. 1997 (Interview).

Mee. Erin B. ed. *Drama Contemporary India.* New Delhi: Oxford University Press. 2001.

Mehta, Neha. "Dance of a Paceless Film". *The Pioneer,* Oct. 3, 2004.

Mahajan, Ginnie. "Gender-bending at play". *The Hindustan Times,* Sep. 28, 2004.

Mukherji, Parul Deve. "Indian Aesthetics Revisited". *The Book Review,* Vol. xxx, No. 4, April, 2006.

Mathur, Naharika. "Clear the Rubble in Your Life". *The Pioneer.* 3 Dec. 2004.

Noorani, A.G. "Images of Islam". *The Book Review,* Vol. xxx, No. 5, May, 2006.

Naik, M.K. "Towards the New Millennium: Indian English Literature Today". *JIWE.* Vol. 29, Jan. 2001.

Oommen, Susan. "Inventing Narratives, Arousing Audiences: The Plays of Mahesh Dattani", *NTQ, 68,* Vol. XVII, Part IV, Nov. 2001.

Prakash, H.S. Shiva. "The Regional, the National and the International in Theatre". *Theatre India,* No. 6, Nov. 2002.

Ramnarayan, Gowari. "Tickles and Traumas". *The Hindu,* Thursday, Aug 4, 2005.

Rau, Rewati. "Dattani Plays Along". *The Hindustan Times,* July 19, 2005.

Rau, Rewati. "Dark Shadows over Stage Success". *The Statesman,* Oct 1, 2004.

Ramachandran, C.N. "In a Double Bind: A Note on Regional Literatures in Decolonised India". *The Journal of Indian Writing in English,* Vol. 29, No. 2, July, 2001.

Srivastava, Pallavi. "Self Life". *The Indian Express,* July 8, 2004.

Singal, Nidhi. "Wake up call". *The Statesman,* Nov. 27, 2006.

Sharma, Sumati Mehrishi. "Dance like Dattani". *The Pioneer,* June 3, 2005.

Shankar, D.A. "Indian Writing in English and the Need for Alternative Critical Paradigms". *JWIE,* Vol. 33, No. 2, July 2005.

Salam, Ziya Us. "A Film for All: Dance Like a Man". *The Hindu.* 4 October, 2004.

Verghis, Shana Maria. "Life is like a workout". *The Pioneer,* Friday, July 15, 2005. (Interview).

Walia, Shelly. "Why Blame Islam?" *The Book Review,* Vol. XXIX, No. 12, Dec. 2005.

Index

A

B

C

D